DON'T LEAVE ME ALONE

DON'T LEAVE ME ALONE

PEETER SAUTER

Translated by Adam Cullen

A TANOOKI PRESS BOOK

Copyediting by Kris Ellingboe-Olson

Typesetting by Gessert Books

ISBN: 978-1-95-430603-5

This book was originally published in Tallinn, Estonia as Ära jäta mind rahule by Peeter Sauter in 2013 by Kirjanik. © Kirjanik, 2013

First U.S. Edition: © June 2023. Translated from the Estonian by Adam Cullen. All trademarks are the property of their respective companies.

This publication was made possible by a grant from the Traducta programme of the Cultural Endowment of Estonia.

WED

"DOWN IN THE *valley where the monkeys grow*," I howled in singsong. *"How sweet it is to lie beneath a whore tree stare at the whore fruit in its branches and plan to become a monkey myself and scurry right up to the crown if only my biiiig baaaaalls weren't in the way . . ."*

◆

"I don't have any cash. But you paid already, yeah? The state fee and whatever?"

"Yeah." Laura's gaze was absent.

"How much was it?"

"I can't remember. Not much, really."

"I can't remember how much a divorce cost, either. Not a lot. It didn't go through the first time because it was never paid for. Wonder what you get for that money you pay to marry?"

"I don't know. They said, but I can't remember. I didn't take any of the extras. Only what I had to."

"You couldn't get it without that TV star?"

"They didn't offer. Not that I knew what to ask."

"Okay. It can be both sad and funny."

"Did he officiate for you, too?"

"No. I'd just heard. But none of it really matters."

She sighed. "It is what it is."

◆

What happened then? Nothing special.

The community clubhouse shut down unexpectedly. That was a downer. And a bit of not much came afterward.

Laura moved from the Lasnamäe projects to the Kristiine district right across the tracks. (Even though we'd still been looking for an apartment for her in Lasnamäe because she worked on that side of the city.)

Somehow and for some reason, we got married.

Somehow and for some reason, I didn't have to go to work anymore. At first it was terrifying, then beautiful.

Erko moved into our building on Koidu Street, which meant that the local commune also gradually moved into the space in the basement, which we called Cabbages. Or else Cabbages turned into some kind of a new club and sanctuary. It's nice when you can't be bothered to go to God and God comes to you. Cabbages started spreading into and flourishing in the next room. People came and went. But there were also quieter times when everybody was away somewhere.

Laura and I were bosom-and-butt-buddies for a long time before we slowly learned to fight more and more. We ended up in crisis mode and didn't know what to do about it. We'd have to go to the Finnish Wise Man for advice like in the epic *Kalevipoeg*. The Wise Man said that as long as you try to change the other person, you won't have any results. Try to change yourself and avoid lashing out.

◆

We could've walked. Or taken the tram. But I rode the tram the last time. To get married, that is. Maybe I was trying to avoid the same situation repeating. Could've taken a taxi, too. But then it would've had to wait a long time in front of the building. It'd feel kind of stupid to ride a taxi to the *saks* and back again. Like you were marrying a taxi driver. We don't call it a *saks* anymore, of course. That's just a word stuck in my head from Soviet times. And I don't even know what that abbreviation even meant. They're not the only letters of which I don't know the meaning, of course. I guess it was actually *zaks. Zavedenye*, or something like that. I'm sure I'd figure it out if I thought for a while, but I don't want to.

I didn't have any money. Laura, Laur, covered all the necessary fees. But I spent my very last cash on a bouquet for her. The most expensive I could afford. It cost a good thousand kroons or so. Or was it only five hundred? I reckon they know that people aren't stingy with funerals and it's unfitting to be stingy with weddings. I'd ordered several funeral wreaths from that floral shop before. It was only when Kusti died that I didn't buy a single flower. I just sat by the stove while he was incinerated along with his teddy bear and expensive shoes, which, I suppose, were the only clothes he'd ever bought new with money that he'd earned.

◆

Peeter lent me his black car. "It's been used for a wedding once before," he said.

"I can't pay you anything, you know."

"I know."

But I at least got him a car wash at the gas station and gave it an extra scrub, too. And filled the tank as well. Holy moly—it took almost sixteen gallons. That's American cars for you. Though I'm not sure what kind of a car it was. I'm no good at telling them apart.

I was afraid I'd get in an accident somewhere and we'd be late for our own wedding. You can't run late for death—maybe marriage is so fatal that you can't miss it, either. Procrastinate however much you may, you'll still get married. It was raining. I'd noticed earlier that there was a large umbrella by the rear window. We didn't have any clothes. We were dressed, that is, but in ordinary streetwear. Clean, though.

I pulled up to the yellow post in front of the "Happiness Palace," where civil weddings are performed. You say your name into the microphone and then they raise the striped arm. I rolled down the window but was too far from the post to push the button. I suppose I could have really stretched for it, but that seemed stupid, so I decided to back up and drive closer. I fumbled with the automatic transmission. I had no idea I'd be so nervous. Why was I nervous? Getting married to Laura? Driving a strange car? Just being in the wrong situation?

Somehow, I managed to reverse back to the street and nearly backed into an approaching car. Luckily, the driver managed to swerve to avoid me, but I almost ran into them. They honked twice, loud and long. Sure—people always honk when someone's getting married.

"Let's just go back home, what do you think?" I asked. I felt like I'd had enough.

"Nooooo."

I thought a bride should melt like butter, but this one was an iron bolt.

I sighed, then drove back up to the yellow post and rolled down the window. It rolled right back up. I couldn't figure out how to work the button. The window just kept going up and down. Finally I gave up pressing the button and just watched it slide back and forth, back and forth. Every time the window went down, drizzle sprayed onto my face. It felt good.

"Nice window. Slides great," I said to Laura. "But don't go getting angry. You're marrying an idiot. You should've figured that out already, though."

Laura gripped her bouquet more tightly and stared out the window.

"Are you watching the way the windshield wipers move or looking out at the rain?" I started to feel like we were testing whether we could bear being married at all.

Laura shot a glare at the window button. It was still tirelessly sliding up and down, squeaking as it went. She took the wedding bouquet in her right hand, stretched her left arm over me, and pressed the button. The glass froze. But it stopped somewhere in the middle. She pressed it again. The glass retracted and stayed there.

"I guess there's no way out for me now," I said.

Laura stared out the windshield. "I'm about to cry."

"That's just right for a bride. But I'd like it if you didn't. And if we didn't get into a fight. If there's any way that can happen."

"Are we just staying here?"

"What's wrong with this? It's such a big car. We could sleep here. And spend the rest of our lives right here. I'd like to fuck. You never wanted to live. But I do. Can't really think of anything better to do."

"Please."

I leaned over towards the yellow post and pressed the button. A voice crackled out immediately.

"Hello?"

"One Sauter and one Feldbach."

The arm went up.

SPOUSES

BEWILDERINGLY AND SEEMINGLY out of the blue, I found myself married once again. Not that I had any problem with it. Although we bickered constantly afterward, over which of us was the one who suggested it. I think that was something of a good sign. Maybe we were just arrogantly announcing, "*I'm* not going to cling to this marriage," and perhaps waiting tentatively to hear how the other would respond.

I can imagine Laura and I someday sitting together like Vladimir and Estragon in Beckett's *Waiting for Godot* and shooting our mouths off: "That's it, I'm going."

"Well, get going then. What are you waiting for?"

"I will, in just a minute. Why aren't you?"

"I could divorce you, just like that. Tomorrow, even. I just don't have the cash."

"Neither do I."

"Hey, I could go get a bottle of wine, though. Should I?"

"Suit yourself."

So I go and bring back a bottle of wine and we drink it. And then there are two possibilities. We either get into another fight or we fuck. I suppose there's actually a third choice, too. We do both. Somehow, it all seems to suit us.

But it suited Beckett and his wife, too, because that play *was* written about their life when they were poor and hanging around Paris.

Well, I reckoned you wanted to marry before the age of thirty, no matter the cost. And I couldn't figure out why you hadn't yet. You had more than enough guys, far better than me, to choose from. I was still agonizing over my divorce and didn't want to get married. And by the time you did, I didn't think it right to say no. We were fucking.

It all seemed completely different to you, though. And how's that? How should I know. You'd bought yourself a little condo a short time earlier. For a while, you'd been looking for a place in the old Soviet district where you lived before. But then you came to Kristiine, more of a wooden-house-type neighborhood, instead. Pretty close to where I was living. I was glad you did.

Right away, we came to a quick agreement to keep on living like we were before: each in their own place, going over to the other's every once in a while.

I can't imagine a better situation than that. If that's what both people want, that is. And if both feel it can work.

And I didn't know if it was going to continue being like when you lived in Lasnamäe, that Soviet district. With me hanging out elsewhere every now and then, too. Or if we were going to be living together more often. What do I really want, anyway? And what about you? Well, I turned fifty a short time later. And you turned thirty. As far as I can recall, I never thought I should remarry before fifty. I was still adapting to the new reality. But maybe I'm lying.

What will our marriage be like? Will I be sitting downstairs in Cabbages, the bohemian library in the basement, chatting away and drinking, and you'll come around to join me every now and then? Will it be like I'm married to Cabbages and everyone who goes there, the same as I am to you? Because that vibe would sit just fine with me. We do bicker all the time. Why the hell would anyone bicker in the library, though?

◆

It might have been a year ago when Erko asked: "Peeter, aren't you going to bring down your books?"

"To Cabbages, you mean?"

"Yeah. We'll make you a shelf. The Sauter shelf."

An array of cultural figures had their own shelves set aside at Cabbages to stock with books brought from home. A library of favorite books. Though I'm not sure how many of them are actually favorites. I'd been pondering what titles could make up my own shelf. True favorites—did I even have those here anymore? They've all been left behind in various places. And forgotten. I don't really read much anymore, either. And to be honest, I don't have any books. What favorites? Even if I was able to find one or two, could I be bothered to bring them downstairs? I'm a jealous person. I won't go down there to read it. You don't go taking some favorite person to Cabbages and say: Wait here, I'll come and see you sometimes. Though I guess you could. Favorite people aren't all that different from favorite books. Sometimes you'd like to stroke them and touch them and take a closer look, but not all the time. They become just as dull. But it's nice when that favorite still exists for me somewhere and isn't lost.

So, I reckoned I could try to scrape together those books for Cabbages. I flipped through some old titles when I visited my country place and tried to pick out some more colorful and nicer-looking spines. All so that I'd have a striking shelf. But at the same time, it felt stupid. And I don't really have any books like that. The most eye-catching were a couple of picture books I'd bought at airports or a London bookstore, a book on photography, and a book about books themselves. They'd all seemed attractive when I bought them. Had I ever even cracked one open, though? What do you know—the photography book was even book-marked in several places. I suppose I did browse them, though I can't really recall.

I have, however, stealthily brought some books back upstairs with me a couple of times before. It felt better that way. Then, I even had the motivation to read them. I chewed through a couple pages of Dovlatov in the original Russian. I even made it all the way through Parnas Myrny's *The Loose Woman*. But not Leonid Leonov's *The Thief*. I marveled at how those old-school novels were written and thought I should try my hand at writing one, too. But I couldn't even be bothered to make it to the last page, much less start writing.

What was that amazing thing that reading used to do for me? I feel like there was something. And I wouldn't be surprised if I thought the same about Laura soon.

◆

Smokestack was leaning against the wall of the shop. Not overly drunk, apparently. Not that it meant you could understand him. Those who've tippled half their lives are impossible to understand anymore. They're off in their own world, intoxicated or not. Maybe even their breath is like a young virgin's. They've got the heart of one, anyway.

"What're you up to, Smokestack? Lose your wallet and can't go in?"

However, I immediately spotted some crumpled half-filled bags at his feet.

"Nah," he grunted. "Just restin'."

"Got a day off then, eh?"

"Nah. Was just restin' at my mother-in-law's, can't you see?"

He reached out a brown arm.

I could tell he would have gladly kept chatting—when didn't he need an audience?—but I hurried on. Smokestack could see I wasn't up for it and didn't waste any of his wisecracks on me.

So, I went inside and realized that once again, without a second's hesitation, I'd been a little mean. Why was that? I knew the reason. Last time I saw him, Smokestack was going on and on without end on the bus and asked if I could spare him a euro before he got off.

I did.

"You know what I'll do with this? I'm going to the store and buying dish-washing soap."

"Does that give you a good buzz?"

"Ah, come off it. Need to do the dishes."

I chuckled.

But Laura and I went to the store and from a distance, I could see that Smoke-stack already had a number of items in his basket, and not one of them was a drink. I don't know what made me so melancholy. Was it that Smokestack hadn't just come up with some ruse? That he really was buying dishwashing soap? I'd hoped, of course, that he needed a hair of the dog and figured he could get himself a beer for one euro. Or was I upset that he did have enough money for groceries and still fished another euro out of me? So what? We project our own ideals onto drunks and beggars whenever we give them money, thinking that maybe we'll be forced to live like that one day and will ask for spare change, too. Is it really an ideal, though? Maybe it's just something idealized.

Well, that and the fact that he stood next to Laura for a long time, telling her how his dick is the second-longest in Estonia. Ten and a half inches, and only Max's is longer, at eleven. It was kind of funny. But not especially. And I suppose in the end, it didn't make Laura too uncomfortable. She'd heard a lot over the course of her life. Next time, I'll bring a ruler and ask Smokestack to pull out his shlong.

Smokestack also talked about mowing down dozens of Afghans back when he was in the special services (minus the fact that he's never been there). Sixty or so, he said, but he ran out of room for notches on the butt of his gun. It was a pretty good story, too. Long and detailed. I feel like Smokestack starts to believe some of his own stories after he's told them once or twice. Or he just can't tell the difference between what's real and what's fantasy. Just like how I can't say what really happened and what didn't when I read some of my old writing. And I, myself, can make up all kinds of stories while writing about Smokestack's tall tales. If he were to ever read them, he'd never remember whether he came up with all that cock and bull or it was my own fabrication. Was it ever any different with minstrels, though? Only a few researchers try to analyze those old songs as if they were true. Perhaps the singers were just poking some light-hearted fun while tipsy. Though if they really do require mythopoetic analysis, then why not all of Smokestack's stories about war, fucking, and the Singing Revolution, too? Folklore is folklore. And if it were to be recorded, then maybe some academic will filter out all kinds of creation stories and myths a couple hundred years from now.

◆

I walked out the front door of the house to go to the shop, even though I'd just come back.

A neighbor, a newspaper editor from the same town out in the country, walked past. We exchanged hellos.

Standing on the sidewalk were a few of the guys helping lift an ancient lawnmower into Marko's old Volvo.

"Where're you going with that in the middle of winter? Got to drive pretty far to find any grass."

"We're returning it to its owner," Erko grunted. Marko went back down into the cellar, into Cabbages.

"What's he going to do with that this time of year?"

"Dunno. Didn't ask."

"Maybe he's growing a secret plot of grass somewhere. Needs to be mowed."

"Could be."

"Or he's going to turn it into distillery equipment. Or a time bomb. You think you could drop me off at the store? I forgot to buy beer."

Erko stopped and gave me a serious stare. "You forgot to buy beer?"

"Yeah. Sclerosis, Alzheimer's, and something else, too, but can't remember what it was."

"Hop in, not a problem. We'll give you a ride. Otherwise you might go and quit drinking. You shouldn't change your image so recklessly. Get in, we're going to grab a few more tools from down in Cabbages."

I started to get in the car, but searched for the brush instead. There was an inch or so of fluffy snow on the Volvo's roof and I figured I'd clear it off to pass the time, which I did so in brisk, sweeping strokes. Left and right. It scattered over the sun-melted street and onto the sidewalk, which was still snowy. Extending my arm, I sent another barrage flying. And then I froze and stared in the direction it'd gone. The familiar editor had stopped next to the car to say something and was struck in the chest by a little snow.

"Oh, sorry."

He scowled at me. "There are people walking here. Not that someone like you can understand that, of course."

I was confused—we were old acquaintances. "But you understand. And that's great!" I said.

The editor paused for a moment, but luckily didn't say anything more. He walked away, frowning.

Standing next to the car, the brush dangled from my grip. We *were* old acquaintances. So what was that all about? Extremely slowly, I continued brushing snow off the roof, though still, heroically, in every direction. I wasn't in the mood to go to the shop anymore, but I did anyway, once the boys returned.

"You want us to wait for you, Peeter?" Marko asked as he stopped to let me out.

"Nah, that's alright. I'll walk."

"Come on, Peeter!" Erko insisted, grinning. "It's no problem. We're driving straight back, anyway."

"Thanks, but no. I'd rather walk."

I bought more beer than I'd originally planned, figuring I'd give a couple bottles to the boys, too. If they wanted.

Marching back towards Koidu Street, I still couldn't shake the editor's words. Why had he talked to me that way? All kinds of retorts that I could e-mail him spun around my head: "If someone like me already can't understand that people are walking down the street—and not people like me—then what point is there in saying that to someone like me? Or does the one saying it get a kick out of the whole thing?" But I dismissed the idea, telling myself: Forget it, Peeter. Don't write anything. So, once I got back to the studio, I didn't.

Strangely, though, the episode came to mind several more times. Could I be that easily offended? Even when somebody tells me off for no good reason, so far as I can see it? I'd have died in a shootout a long time ago in the Wild West. And in medieval jousting competitions. Getting offended appears to be something people find important. Who came up with that? Must be some sense to it. Does it somehow help things progress? *Once Upon a Time in America* was a great resentment saga. Getting offended and taking revenge made up half of one's life. And that's not the only one. How did Poe's nobleman's motto go? "No one provokes me with impunity." Sure, a guy like that pretty much stalks a possible affront.

What good is that insult to me now? It sets off some chemical reaction in me, releases endorphins and stirs up motivation. But I can't apply that force to digging flowerbeds. Or can I? Seeing as how it gave me a dose of energy, maybe I should have properly insulted him in return, out of politeness, so that endorphins might be released in the initiator and he might write an article about someone like me, who isn't a person and doesn't understand them.

At the same time, what's the point of fretting over Laura? Will it make me love her more? Seems to, anyway. I concentrate on her mentally—on my problem named Laura.

◆

I decided to quit writing this story. How long can you really go on tinkering with the same thing day in, day out? So, I stopped writing for a while. But then I realized I can't write about anything else. Or I don't want to. I want to write that which flows freely. Something I don't have to come up with all on my own. For a time, I tried to write about this and that and to figure out some kind of a trick to make it fluid and not have to think (I don't know when I started this endless, dogged fight against thinking, which I'll never win and will probably never really lose, either), but I couldn't. And practicing literature *is* tedious and unpleasant. Or, well, sometimes you start to kind of appreciate it, but then you remind yourself that it's literature and it just won't do. The text could write itself with me just standing there, like how a champion racecar driver is simply there while driving their car or motorcycle.

Anyway, the fight against thinking is actually a fight *with* thinking while standing on one side of it. Proper thinking only starts once that forced and wrenched thinking ends. Still, the fight is endless. Not that you actively wage it all the time. Occasionally you slink and lurk around it.

Since I couldn't turn myself into a different man or couldn't find different egos and ways of writing at first, I found myself right back where I started. I suppose you need those periods of reconsideration. Walks and wasting time. Lurking around and chatting. Although they obviously lead nowhere, they're simply a break, like how death could be a little pause before your next life once you've started repeating the same thing over and over again. Whatever it is, no one can say. I suppose just some part of living. Progress or cleansing or becoming nicer. And it doesn't only affect me, but everything around me, too. Just like that bodhisattva view that you don't give up until everything's turned out great. Though I don't imagine that turning-out-great might ever end. I don't know what'll be left of us then—just some angelic song and bright light. I guess a soiled mind can't imagine anything else, really. Or else a pure, passionate, and grand hell of demons with its endless guitar solos and pounding drums. Can't say why those should be any worse.

HOME

HOW MANY YEARS have I been living here? Probably about a hundred. I'll be hitting one hundred soon. Or have I already? And yet, I only just found out that the neighbor's dog is named Tipa. Tipa's quite a serious breed of dog (I can't say which), the same that Deutsch called a wolf and will run up to the fence barking up a storm. Siskin thought for a long while that its name was Pipa, just like her sister.

I could keep on living here for a thousand years more and still won't know the half of things. Half's even a lot to say—I don't really know a thing. Not that one needs to know everything, anyway. Such as who it was who died in this apartment before I moved in. Some old guy. I bet there's still a ton of his things in the closet next to the kitchen, which we'll probably throw out if we decide to clean it someday. All his nice old dusty possessions. Imre dug some wrinkled papers out of it and used them for drawing. I took out an old bottle thinking it contained some kind of oil or varnish, but it turned out to be sand. The man had bottled some kind of sand and kept it in the closet.

There are also some old flour tins in the kitchen, a little rusty but nice. I used a soup spoon to transfer Kustas's ashes into them because I had misgivings about taking what was obviously a box of cremated remains to the park where I planned to spread them. I spooned the ashes from one container to another next to an open window and spilled a little on the dirty windowsill and was horrified at first. How was I going to get my son's ashes back into the box, I wondered! But a second later, I laughed at my initial reaction and just blew them into the rain gutter where he himself had once tapped cigarette ash, just like he had onto the windowsill. There were bits of white bone and even a few buttons in the ashes. They'll end up in the grass in the park, too, where dogs will probably shit and people will walk and maybe some drunkard will stretch out. Me, for example. I suppose ashes are good for the grass and the trees, though, too. There are some gigantic trees growing in the cemetery nearby, at any rate.

In Estonian, the word for fence or yard—*aed*—is part of a whole range of words. Cemetery (*surnuaed*), zoo (*loomaaed*), flowerbed (*iluaed*) ... and they are all usually fenced in. All so that no one climbs in; so that nothing gets out. Even some graves are caged in, though there's not any fencing around the coffin underground. You can go in any direction from down there. The fencing is above ground so one can go and slip in and howl or simply stare dully like a wild animal in a zoo. Eh, as soon as you start writing, it turns to drivel. Luckily you can pull yourself back from it, though. Just like you can pull yourself out of any bullshit you start saying in life. And nobody can avoid that bullshit, I reckon. There's just no need to cling to it. You've got to admit that, yes, it's bullshit. But now I'm going to try to do better.

Kustas was the first of us to die here in the house on Koidu Street. We'll see if I can manage to drag out my own life here until I die. It's very possible I will. I've certainly no intention of picking myself up and going anywhere else. Not until it's the afterlife. Off to follow Kusti.

Tarmo told me something about the old guy who died in this apartment, though I can't remember a thing. Maybe nobody else has died here apart from him and Kusti, seeing how this apartment and the whole floor was only added later, probably during Soviet times. I don't even know what year the house was built. Before the occupation, certainly. Fine, I'll go and look it up—1931, architect Joosep Lukk. But there's nowhere to look up the name of the guy who lived in this apartment, nor the name and background of the man who gave the building to the Estonian Writers' Union and put down a bottle of whiskey as he did. Living here now, I've also downed at least a whole big bottle of Tullamore, though the man who gave away the house didn't come to mind as I did.

I suppose you have to choose between what memories to keep in your head. I let Joosep Lukk stay, and no doubt the year 1931 will still be there, too. But I'm not sure how many more things I want knocking around my brain.

◆

That bird that was in Kusti's room. He'd removed the little square window because it would get steamy in that little attic space. There were no windows besides that tiny square, or diamond (is a diamond just a square standing on its corner? It isn't, or is it? My idiocy only keeps growing, and maybe my vanity, too).

Kustas went into his room and I heard a strange rustling noise. He came back out and said there was a bird in his room.

We didn't know what to do about it. I didn't dare try to catch it, but Kustas had never been afraid of any animal. At our place in Klooga, he brought in a lizard that, ultimately, either got away or croaked somewhere. Kusti was my polar opposite in that sense. He'd say that animals don't want to harm you when they scratch or nip you a little; it just means they're probably a little scared and you'll be fine. I thought he'd become a veterinarian one day, but he didn't. True, if someone gets along well with animals and wants to be around them, it doesn't necessarily mean they should become a vet.

Kustas tried to cast a sheet over the bird. I didn't watch. I made myself busy at my desk in the other room, though I was actually expectantly waiting to see what would happen. I think we finally just switched off the light in Kusti's room and waited for it to be brighter outside so the bird might find its way. And in the end, it was gone.

Kusti smashed that same window somehow when he was dying. Strangely enough, he wasn't very bloody. I've seen people try to break window panes with their fists in a way that they don't cut themselves, but it hardly ever worked. Kusti must have been in a pretty mixed-up state by that point, because it's much easier to just lift the window and its frame out than to smash through the double-paned glass. Only his side was a little bloody, probably from rolling around in the shards that fell onto the mattress. His hand was completely intact. I couldn't figure out if he'd wrapped a cloth around his fist or used something else to smash it, either. Beats me what happened. I'll never find out.

There are a lot of those things that I'll never find out. By that I don't mean great worldly details about revolution in Russia or anything like that, but things that have happened to loved ones. I don't know all that much. All you can do is live on and put up with your ignorance. Since that's a source of stress, however, you concoct a simplification of events and find some way to put them into words. Before long, you start to think that's probably the way things really were. Still, what does it matter that you don't really know? If you don't, you don't. The mind is persnickety and can't bear not knowing. Undoubtedly, it leads to digging up all kinds of information. Information about big events. But when it comes to human relationships, the mind is crummy. Unless, of course, you're Hercule Poirot solving murder mysteries. And how much fun and joy is there even in solving murders? Maybe it's a relief for some murderers who've suffered enough already and wanted to come clean. The owners of Rosslyn Chapel have refused to let anyone dig into the ground beneath it. Fine, let the bodies and treasures lie there in peace, be they the mummified head of Jesus Christ, the Holy Grail, or nothing at all. Come to think of it, if I could choose whether to have the Holy Grail, Jesus's head, or nothing lying on my desk in front of me, then nothing would probably be the best choice. Are the Grail and his head anything more than nothing, or is nothing more than something? Or is something more when we don't know what lies beneath the floor and can wonder what might be down there and what it all might mean?

The bird that Kusti let go, or got out all on its own, might still be alive. It didn't die here in our apartment. That's nice.

◆

The Uus Maailm Community House is a home. What else could it be, anyway?

But whose home, and what for? Can one even ask that about a home? Sorry—you've got a home here, but whose home is it and what for? This is our home and we live here; that's the whole point of it. Still, how has it crossed people's minds to suddenly want their home to be a community house? Probably the same stupid question. Sorry, but what's wrong with you—you're all living here in your own home? For whatever reason, odd questions like that buzz around my brain, and I don't believe they're bad. A person's allowed to think, isn't he? A little, anyway. Perhaps the center's occupants are a will for the home to be bigger and more open, and a will to share that home with more people? Maybe. Alright, I've had enough of that bout of thinking. I'm glad that the community house exists and that I can sometimes share that home. It's good to have more than one home. And in a way, those homes are even related or somehow connected. I reckon that many of the people who live in the house, be it a little or a lot, have other homes, too. It's good to have alternatives in life. Almost makes you believe there might be alternatives to life itself, too. Somewhere. In a second, or third, dimension.

I biked with Siskin to Prisma last night before they stopped selling booze at ten. I dismounted before the railroad overpass tunnel so she wouldn't be afraid. We'd crashed there before when I went down too slowly where the ramp takes a sharp turn. My front wheel went sideways and when I jerked the handlebars to right it, they went crooked. I collapsed onto my side, even though I could easily have just stuck out my leg for support, because I was sure, for some reason, that it'd be fine and I'd simply pedal onward. Siskin shot her arms out to brace herself and was left with gashed, bloody, grimy palms. But she didn't cry.

Now, she was wary about us taking that path. She sits on a bar above the front wheel, her feet resting on the pegs. It's a DIY child's seat I got from Alvar and Anne. Good thing she was there, too, because things would have been much worse if she'd crashed out of a stationary rear child's seat. Instead, she just flew off the bike and into the gravel. Without a helmet, of course.

Kaku stopped us on our way and told us soup was almost ready at the community house.

So, with my backpack heavy with beers, a bottle of 19% ABV Kopke port wine, and milk for Siss's cereal and my tea, I biked back.

"What do you think—should we have dinner at the community house, Siss?"

"Sure."

She jumped off the bike by the community house. As I was stopped, the brown Camaro that's always parked out front drove past and I noticed that the driver wasn't some foreigner, but a familiar face from the commune whose name I didn't know. Siss ran in but was back following me a few seconds later. I figured that maybe it'd been a while since she was last there and she felt shy.

As Siss was running after me, I felt something snap and immediately jerked my arm behind my back to save the wine while making sure I didn't crash. A strap had come loose and the backpack dangled from one hand while I used the other to carefully brake the 1950s bike with the wobbly front wheel that I'd swiped from Grandma's garage.

"Why didn't you stay at the commune, Siss?"

"There were so many people there in the yard."

She unlocked the front door for me, I carried my bike and backpack up to the third floor and locked the bike to the handrail.

We looked out the kitchen window together. There were indeed lots of people in the commune's yard.

"You think we should still go?"

"Okay, Daddy."

Siss took along a package of meat sticks.

There were about fifteen people sitting around the table. A couple guys from Austria—Leo, and who was the other one? Simon, a Dutchman from Hungary, gave me a high-five. Erko ran off to bring us soup bowls and filled them with goulash. He was in high spirits. The commune had just gotten a new roof installed. That wasn't the reason why he was so upbeat, though. Erko's endorphins just run up and down his spine nonstop.

I was feeling a little maladroit with a brain cramp and my tongue-tied, but it was still nice to be there. I realize that it shows, but I've started paying less attention to it after a lifetime of experience. If I stutter, then I stutter—so what? I've just got to live with stuttering and not crawl into a bush. Siss crawled into my lap, which helped. Erko pretended like I was an old pal and a long-awaited guest. Still, guys and guests like those were everything to him. "Give, and you will receive." Erko's a genuine illustration of that.

The soup was spicy and tasty, with big chunks of potato floating in it.

"We just split the last drumstick, Peeter," Erko informed me with a grin.

"Great, then I dodged a bullet."

Siss politely chewed on a potato cube she'd fished out of the soup.

"Do you not like it?" Marten asked.

"Bitter!"

"It's spicy."

Later, though, Siss repeated several times that the soup was "bitter." And she gave me a couple of sloppy kisses, too. Maybe she'd seen it at a wedding somewhere. I admit the kisses were nice.

Siss had asked me not to drink beer at the commune.

"Not even one?"

"Well, I dunno. Just one, then. Don't you want to have their tea or something?"

Siss never sets ultimatums in her requests or demands.

With her perched in my lap, I finished her soup, then mine. I was warm, but Siss soon got chilly. She alternated between bites of smoked sausage and Merci chocolate.

The Austrians were speaking halting Estonian and the others spoke Estonian back.

"Daddy, I'm cold."

"Peeter, would you like beer or white wine?"

"Hm, I'll have a beer."

Erko brought me a dark beer.

"Did you want to go home, Siskin?"

"I dunno. Get me a sweater. But finish your soup first."

"Don't get sick, now."

"I won't."

Siskin sighed, though probably not because I was drinking beer.

Erko brought her a light-colored sweater and I helped to pull it on.

"Should I roll up the sleeves?" They were baggy.

"No," Siskin said, and crawled under the table to collect pebbles from the dust.

"Daddy, can I throw a rock past Erko?"

He was sitting about fifteen feet away at the other end of the table, surrounded by people.

"I don't know, Siss. Give it a try."

She was just about to fling a pebble at Erko, with whom she got along really well, but he suddenly stood up and she realized it would have accidentally been a bullseye. Erko would've no doubt realized the stone ricocheting off his forehead had been meant as a show of appreciation.

"I'll put it in his pocket as a secret later."

We sat there for a while longer. It grew darker and Siss settled more heavily in my lap. The Dutch guy took a spin on his bike and soon returned.

"Siim, are you coming with us to Hiiumaa?"

"Can't, I've got a meeting tomorrow. It's the reason I came to Tallinn."

"A meeting..."

The Austrians talked about a club in Amsterdam where the music and lights changed according to how much people danced. If no one felt like dancing, then the music stopped and the lights went out.

"I know it," the Dutch guy said. "I haven't been there in probably fifteen years."

"Daddy, I want to go."

"Bedtime?"

"I dunno, but I want to go now."

"I'll just finish my beer and we'll leave.

It wasn't very late yet. Siss had often stayed out with us as I partied till mid-night, and had occasionally even slept in someone's bed at the commune. I don't know what was different this time. Maybe she was starting to grow up. Maybe she didn't want to be like Pippi Longstocking and Tom and Annika's kids, the likes of whom were everywhere around the yard. Erko flicked on the stage lights and put on some dance music. People danced.

"Are you going to give Erko his sweater back?"

Siss pulled off the sweater. As she was handing it back to Erko, she dropped the pebble into his pocket. She'd been holding it the whole time. Erko took no notice of it and I wondered whether he was discretely pretending not to or would later puzzle over why there was a tiny dusty stone in his pocket.

◆

It was rainy and dark all mid-December. The month was preceded by a long, warm autumn. There'd been a lot of snow the two previous winters. In some places, the snowbanks alongside the sidewalks were taller than me and it was said that this winter wouldn't bring much more snow. *Why not? It still might*, I thought to myself. Once you've hit red twice in roulette, there's no law saying the next one has to be black. The likelihood is always fifty-fifty.

That Sunday, however, the sun was shining. I walked to Koidu Street early that day so I'd have time to heat the oven and move onward. I reckoned there'd be a good draft with the high-pressure system moving through, but smoke kept coming in. It didn't matter. I opened a window and the apartment door and sat in the other room to get out of the draft, eating some leftover fish I'd brought back from who-knows-which girl's place. I contemplated whether or not it'd gone bad. I'd already warmed it up several times before but hadn't finished it and stuck the rest in the fridge. Some kind of white fish. I fried it up with some onion and spurted ketchup over it, and now it was an amorphous mass. A *pläust*.

I opened the plastic container and sniffed. It smelled like good fish and put me in the mood to have some. There was an old pan on the stove that I moved elsewhere. I'd just used it to try to warm the kitchen with the gas on, though that was a fruitless attempt because the pan started to reek. The only good way to heat the kitchen is with the old wood-fired stove. It's nice and in good shape, but I can't be bothered to keep a fire going. You'd have to stay at home all day, every day to heat the oven and the stove to boot. Who knows, maybe someday I will.

Sunlight was shining in through the window and all of a sudden, I felt a burst of happiness. Firewood crackled in the oven and life felt good. One might think it was because of the sun, but when it was scorching in the sky every single day in India, all it felt like was endless torment and zero enjoyment. No doubt this was because it was the first time I'd seen sunlight in who-knows-how-many weeks. It splotched across the old, stained, faded wallpaper. Just a little longer to wait. I had a cup of weak black tea with milk on the side. Lately, the strong kind of tea that I'd drank for the last year or so, several daily quarts of tea brewed as strong as poison, had started to make my spleen ache.

The poisons are running out. I don't want to smoke; it doesn't get me going. Only once in a blue moon do I have a cigarillo to think. My liver doesn't take strong coffee anymore. It does better with pepper vodka, but shots put a burden on the rest of the organism and when you take a break from the booze after that, your heart won't pump right. I didn't know where the spleen was before, but I do now. Now, I also know where the prostate and the trigeminal nerve can be found and how thick the spine is. They showed me a model before my back operation. It was as wide as Siskin's wrist. I wonder what else I'll still learn.

I went to bring up more firewood from the cellar, and Jaan Pehk was just pulling open his storage box, too. Side by side, we pulled logs down from our stacks like two villagers or old men in a slum apartment house, chatting about ovens and how they were drafting.

"Yours is whooshing pretty well now."

"Sure, but the guy ended up making so many holes in the oven that it doesn't retain as much heat anymore."

The stonemason had perforated the stone walls, removed pail after pail of soot and ash, and afterward capped the holes. When he was done, Jaan's oven looked like a black chest of drawers.

"At least you're not living in a gas chamber anymore. Mine depends on the weather for how well it drafts. I thought it'd work today. High-pressure system and whatnot.

"They don't do well in warm weather. Should be better once it gets colder."

I'd come into a perfect life once again. Again, my life had become a handsome film about a slum neighborhood of wooden houses in Tallinn where, in a dusty and somewhat filthy cellar, under dim light, two men go about their business, not seeing one another but talking amiably about nothing. And everything is fine.

My basket filled up first, though I noticed that I'd done so a little too generously. Would I throw my back out hauling it up the stairs? Simply carrying firewood in my arms was maybe even better for my back, because it meant standing up straight. It always gets your clothes dirty and you've got to shake them out afterward and sweep the woodchips on the floor into a dustpan and empty it in the trash bin, but that's all part of the process and can be enjoyed, too.

The brown wicker firewood basket that Laura gave me as a gift looked very nice, too. I just had to learn not to fill it so much that it strained my back.

I closed the window upstairs. First the outer pane, which was streaked with dried rivulets. There's no good tool for getting rid of them in a way that doesn't streak in turn. I scribbled a reminder for myself on a scrap of paper: window drier. I've got a ton of reminders for things I should buy. Though they never come to mind when I'm at the store. I sat there with the sun shining in through the window like it was summer, positioning myself so it didn't fall directly on my face, and I didn't feel like doing a thing. The Indian summer was over and Old Man Winter was at the door. I stared out across my desk. It'd already snowed a bit, but had since melted. Now, the vivid green drizzle-damp lawn between Koidu Street and the sidewalk glittered in the sunlight. You could let a cow or some sheep graze there. Why should they be kept on a diet of munching last summer's dried hay?

Smoke drifted up outside. A pretty decent cloud of it. Was the sun drying the soaked house and creating steam? Or was Mihkel also heating downstairs and couldn't get a draft? There wouldn't be that much coming in. I reckoned I should check. It'd be absurd if the house was on fire while I just sat there by the window, staring at the sunshine and thinking—*don't leave yet, you gorgeous moment.*

Getting onto my knees on the desk, my ass sticking up in the air, I opened the window back up and peered down the façade. There was no fire or smoke coming out of any window, just the sun drying the siding, not intending to disturb my serenity but wishing to add its own note. What do I have to offer it in return, aside from what I write here, like a prayer of gratitude? Quite the level of pietism, though why not, I guess. Hallelujah! And just as the thought crossed my mind, a train tooted along in the background: hallelujah! It was heading west towards Aegviidu, I think. A swift little passenger train.

For a moment, I felt apprehensive that my drawn-out procrastination and lazing around could make the pause become disingenuous. Just in case, I opened my laptop, knowing full well that it probably wasn't the right moment to start typing. It turned out I didn't have to.

A sizzling sound came from the ceiling. I looked up as bluish sparks flew from the ancient wires protruding out of the junction box. It was a pretty sight, and I waited a bit to see if it'd stop. It looked as though someone who'd lived in the apartment before me had yanked them free. Guess they'd had a good reason. Ah, right—I remember Jess and Siss told me ages ago that they'd seen blue sparks coming out of the ceiling cables 32and heard crackling. I'd never seen it happen and figured they were pulling my leg. Appears they weren't. I don't tend to believe others, but I occasionally do believe my own baseless delusions and paranoia. Though maybe that's the right approach. If you always believed others, then you'd be jerked from left to right. It's better to exist in your own false bubble. Subjective realism. No, I had to do something before the house burned down. I didn't think to turn off the computer. I went into the hallway and flipped the breakers, figuring I should take the wires down somehow. How were they fixed to the ceiling? Just screwed in. I climbed up onto the desk. I'd need an ordinary slot head screwdriver. Did I have one? No idea. My mess of tools was in a plastic bag above the stove. Whenever I needed anything, I'd dump the whole bag out onto the kitchen floor and rummage around. My slot head screwdriver was missing, though. It had been a good one with a durable end. Had made it through twenty years or so.

I worked on the wires until they didn't crackle anymore. That meant I'd accomplished something that day. Would writing have equated to anything more? Or less? Or were the two not comparable? That's right. You don't have to compare. And it's a good thing the house didn't burn down.

LIFE

"LIFE IS NOT a takeaway," Laur mused between sips. I have no idea what she meant by it. Maybe the thought crossed her mind and there was no real point to it; she just said it out loud. I didn't ask, either. I wasn't in the mood to get into a discussion. I suppose I felt that talking trivializes thoughts. Better to keep them to yourself. Even if Laura did mean something by it, would I even make any contact with this thought? I enjoy the ideas that she gives me. That's the positive side to books and philosophers—they can engage your mind. I don't so much enjoy the things said in those books and philosophies as I do my own thoughts and feelings. Even if you get the sense that they originate from those sources, you still have your own interpretation and another person has theirs.

Laura's remark was certainly good for getting the mind working. Who the hell knows what it meant? You can't get things quick and easy, maybe? Or achieve the meaning to life? Maybe that you're speeding through a drive-through and grabbing love and the meaning of life like a burger and Coke? In that case, you could also say that life is like a restaurant where you order, but the server never comes with your food, so you're simply left to wait for it. At the same time, you could also turn the phrase around: "Life is a takeaway." Or, "Takeaway is life." And these statements might seem interesting and meaningful and on the mark, and you can ponder them at length. Everything is connected to everything else and everything contains everything, as science has found. Just like some religions have been saying for centuries. So, what's left of that debate? Only that actual burger when you're hungry? Or a god when your body is light for it? Buddha is a butt fucker, as the writer Jaan Kaplinski enlightened me. And you've got to keep going in spite of all that. To restart the old conversation from the beginning, or maybe the end.

Ideas have an easier time tricking me into believing they're something genuine and important. Once they already exist, they should be expressed somehow, too. Though good luck expressing a dream in a way that preserves its power and force. You can't. Your tongue is tied up in knots like a schoolboy trying to talk about his crush.

HAPPINESS

W E'D REACHED A phase where we didn't speak to each other. We were together, we did things together, and we were mainly silent. Like Finns. Or Sámi. It wasn't bad. Occasionally, I even felt kind of happy to have a wife who didn't talk; with whom I could be silent.

But there were also times when I couldn't figure out what kind of silence it was. You appeared to be frowning sometimes. I can't stand it when something's wrong. Sometimes it makes me sad, other times it puts me into panic mode, as if some great global catastrophe were nearing as soon as you're in a bad mood or things between us are tense. I lose it every now and then and raise my voice, saying: "Well, *now* what is it! What's so bad this time? Everything is fine. Do you really have to be this way?" And you don't understand what I'm talking about. You were simply frowning for no real reason, without the sense that anything was wrong; lost in thought, nothing more. In fact, I, myself, walk around wearing the same kind of dour expression. Anyone who sees us walking side-by-side might think we're in a fight. In reality, we're actually pretty happy and content; we just look grumpy.

I'd been staring at you for a while and you just looked away and sniffled and seemed angry. I felt my stomach start to churn. I'd been trying to suppress the feeling for a while already, but the harder you push, the more agitated it gets. To every action there is an equal reaction. Finally, I couldn't take it any longer. "Well, what is it? What'd I do wrong or poorly this time? What's the problem?"

"It's nothing," you mumbled, looking away. "Do whatever you want."

"You just want me to leave you be so you can keep sitting here looking angry and I just feel guilty?"

"Why do you think I look angry?"

"Don't you? You're not like this all the time."

"How should I know how I look all the time? I guess I'm angry, then."

"You're frowning."

"And what do you want me to do about it? It's not on purpose."

I forced myself to shut up. A fight was looming. I didn't want a fight. We'd learned how to argue a little; how to let off some steam, all to prevent a bigger fight from breaking out and so neither of us would leave, slamming the door on the way out. I bet I could publish a textbook on fighting.

◆

Being with you is an addiction. I'd had Siskin with me on Koidu Street for several days already. No, wait—I'd seen you that same morning. I've only gone without you from yesterday morning to this evening, but I haven't gotten my hit of being together and am in withdrawal. I've been lying around and not feeling like doing anything, work or otherwise. I need to see you and be able to touch you. That gets my endorphins flowing; my dopamine or whatever it is. I get high and am myself and do everything better. I'm an addict whose drug is named Laura, and I can get you pretty cheaply without a dealer, apart from yourself.

I don't know if it's the same for you. I sit at home with Siskin and wonder if I should run over to your place, if even for a minute, just to see and touch you; to become myself once again. Just so I'm not in withdrawal and moping around, depressed.

But in fact, it helps a little just to think about you. Knowing that you're there exactly the way I've seen you on so many occasions, and being with you in thought. I'm intimately aware of just the way you are. Even from far away, you give me that hit and that high.

Being with Siskin does make me happy, too, but in a different way. Lying next to her in bed and draping an arm over her or letting her hug me. Hugs and kisses with her when I haven't seen her for a while—sure, it's a high, but no replacement for yours.

Dark beer and light beer. Both are good in different ways. I wouldn't want to give up either, so what if they make me fat. Perhaps being with you does something to my body and my soul, too. Something I would never want to give up. What is it that Kelli Uustani sings? "A daily dose of kisses." Exactly. It's obvious that she means a narcotic dose. And Siss likes her latest album just as much as I do.

◆

"I don't know," you said doubtfully. "Do you think it'd be okay, or what?"

"Huh?" I had a growing sense of unease. The question had come out of nowhere, as if you were hatching some suspicious plan. Did you want to fuck somebody else? You proposed it once, and the thought kept creeping up on me again and again. At the same time, I wondered if maybe it was anxiety or a desire to cling to something. Maybe there isn't such a thing as absolute, total certainty. Even though I was sure about you. About your honesty. And compared with the life you'd had before, one that made me go a little crazy, this was still refreshing.

"If I got myself a Michael. Would that bother you? I'll show you."

You came over to the computer.

I waited, confused. You started surfing for pictures and it slowly dawned on me.

"A Jackson tattoo?"

"Yeah. Hold on, I'll show you what kinds."

"Where would you get it?"

I figured it'd be on your breasts. Where else? You've got my initials above your ass, though Michael would probably fit in nicely next to me, too.

"I don't know yet."

There were tons of Jackson tattoos online—on people's backs, arms, and elsewhere. Some of the portrait tats didn't bear much of a resemblance.

"I don't know about his face," I said hesitantly.

"Yeah, I actually wanted one of those where he's up on his toes, you know. A silhouette. I don't get why I can't find it. There were loads of them before."

"It might make Margit jealous and she'll get an even bigger tattoo of him."

"Maybe."

"And then you'll get one even bigger like that. Like it's a competition for who loves Michael more."

"No, for who's a bigger Jackson fan. Margit's son is named Joosep. But what if I had a son and named him Mihkel Joosep? Michael Joseph. That'd sure make her jealous."

"Wouldn't I have a say in what we'd name our kid?"

"Would you have anything against that?"

"I don't know."

"Look, here," you said, pointing to the screen. "Something like that, though it's not exactly what I want."

I looked. It was Michael Jackson on his tiptoes with his knees bent. We left the topic of the tattoo there. But later, when we were in bed, you whispered: "Are you asleep?"

"No," I replied. I didn't tell her I'd been dozing for a while already. It doesn't pay to tease and say stupid things in bed, otherwise you'll ruin the good vibe of being side by side under the covers. If you make a dumb joke and put a chill on that vibe, you'll feel sorry but have no chance of getting it back that same night.

Your mind had been on the tattoo ever since we talked. "I think I don't want to get one that other people already have."

"Yeah, good idea. There are endless pictures of Jackson. Pick out one you haven't seen in the tattoo gallery. You could have them do a silhouette where he's dancing. If it makes you feel good, then definitely go for it."

"You think so?"

"Sure. You have an original body. Why should the tattoo be the kind that tons of people have? I'm fine either way. I'm just glad if it makes you feel good. Sleeping with Jackson in a dream isn't like actually sleeping with someone. It's different."

You didn't answer. I don't know what it meant to you. Maybe that was better. If you orgasmed, then it certainly could have been. That's alright.

You fell blissfully asleep while fantasizing about the tattoo. I wrapped my arm around you and was happy, too. You, me, and your tattoo of Michael Jackson.

Before drifting off, I mused about the butterfly tattoo on your shoulder. You'd made a deal with a former boyfriend to both get tattoos. His was supposed to be barbed wire, I think. You went through with it and got yours, even though he reneged. Before long, your relationship and vibe fizzled out, too. I've got to make sure that I don't renege on anything we've agreed upon. You don't put up with that. I don't really, either.

"Laur, are you sleeping?"

You were and didn't reply. I'd wanted to say that I have a name for a child, too. A girl's name. I don't have a name for a boy, but go ahead and name him yourself, if we should have one.

I gently lifted my arm from over you and rolled to my other side to sleep. Nice and blissful. Alone, and at the same time together with you. I suppose I need that. Solitude and company simultaneously. You're my pet and I am yours. A puppy and a kitty. My kitty goes meow-meow-meow and the puppy goes woof-woof-woof, ay-dee, ay-daa, and both are dear to me. Thoughts get better and better as sleep draws near. At least the emotions fade.

◆

"There was a time when I reckoned it'd be alright to be impotent."

"But now you'd rather not? Is that like punishment for an old desire? Why'd you think that, anyway?"

"Everybody was pushing sex all the time."

"And they're not now?"

"Less so."

"And I don't at all."

"Not especially, no. Maybe you'd be better off with somebody else."

I didn't have the nerve to say anything further. Maybe I'm just becoming asexual. I used to think that there'd be no point in living if you couldn't fuck. Now, I don't really mind. Simply living is fine, too.

I regret having pushed sex with people, too. That was inappropriate and unkind. And I regret not having it pushed now. I've drunk away my libido. But would I give up drinking to get it back? Probably not. Does that mean drinking is better and dearer to me than my own body? Hard to say. How can you compare the two? My drinking persists out of routine and inertia. Who can even say that libido will return if you quit drinking? Learn from the old masters like Hemingway, who drank his libido away long before you. And then his talent to boot. And then he blew his brains out. There's just no need to cling so tightly to writing. I've always thought that. And I reckon I don't. It's just that there isn't much else to do. Nothing that I could be bothered to do and would fill the hours. Still, even if my writing becomes extremely poor, I can let the graphomania carry on. Who's going to stop me? Is graphomania really so depressing that it'll be the one to pull the trigger?

COMMUNITY

I'D BEEN STANDING in line to return my bottles and cans for the deposit for ages. Two guys were pulling bottles from huge trash bags and stuffing them into the machine. One finished his and went to their car to get another. It was an old two-door, 2.8-liter Mercury Luxury and a few decades old. It had fancy wheel arch extensions and stainless-steel liners. The guy himself looked nice, too: casually dressed and easygoing. He took a big bagful of bottles behind the recycling shed and tossed it onto a pile of trash, as there was no dumpster for wine bottles. His buddy was working on a bag of plastic bottles as tall as he was. He had to pause and screw the cap off of every one so the air would reinflate it and the machine could read the barcode. Still, he didn't blow into them like bums do to make it go faster.

The spring sunlight was bright and I stood in it for a minute, but I was baking in my winter jacket so I moved into the shade. The breeze was chilly, though, so I ended up going back and forth between the two. An old woman clutching a little bag circled around several times to check if she could get in to the machine yet.

An old couple in a beat-up clunker parked in the far corner of the lot. The mustachioed man pulled two bags of recycling out of the trunk and his hefty wife called after him: "One's falling!" A bottle fell out at the same moment and the old man had to set the bags down to scoop it up. Now, the circling old woman quickly took her place in line and the couple settled in at the very end. All were peering through the window, trying to gauge when the huge bag would finally run out. I kept alternating between sunlight and chilly shade. I was in no hurry and it was nice to hang around. Strange that a positive mood or contented feeling can come at completely trivial moments, whereas other days can seem rather routine and lacking anything particularly pleasant. Even while reading or working or attending a play. Nothing special. And yet, you can suddenly feel blissful and carefree while standing in line for recycling. The weather was nice and I wasn't in urgent need of anything, of course. At the same time, most days are free of any urgent needs and you can still feel rather dull, even when the sun is shining.

Toivo, whom everybody calls Deutschland, approached carrying two bags of recycling, too.

"Hey, Deutsch—come here. This is your place in line."

"Huh? No, it's not," he protested, as modest as always and unwilling to cut.

"No, no—come on," I insisted. The others in line made no comment, so Deutschland stood next to me. "Here, Toivo. These two bags of bottles are yours now, too."

"Why don't you want to return them yourself?" he asked, spreading his upward-turned palms as a witness to something obviously unjust. His moustache was neatly trimmed and his clothes clean, as always.

"I've just got to go," I said without further explanation, and waved. He smiled in bemusement as he watched me go and I still felt great, even though I was voluntarily leaving a place I'd felt well in for a solid ten minutes and didn't know if the sensation would continue elsewhere.

Walking away, I recalled the last time I'd seen Deutschland. It had involved bottles, too. Deutsch was rummaging through the dumpsters outside of your building on Vindi Street as I left one morning. For some reason, it's always nice to spot him. He used to be in a chipper mood and crack jokes every time. Nowadays, he's dourer. I took him along to Koidu Street so he could take the beer bottles that had collected over the first half of winter. On the way, Deutsch talked about Chernobyl and how many of the goons he'd served with there were now dead. He'd sliced his finger up somehow, no doubt rooting around through dumpsters, and it was dripping blood. I bandaged the cut at home while Toivo waited patiently with the finger stuck up in the air. Then I helped him bag the empty bottles; I had plenty of both.

As Toivo was walking out the door, he turned and solemnly asked: "What do I owe you?"

I reckoned it wasn't worth fooling around, so I answered just as solemnly: "Nothing."

"How's that?" Toivo frowned. "This is capital."

He'd mentioned once that he had been a glass cutter, so I took down his phone number. After Kusti died and cold air was blowing in through the window he'd smashed, I called Toivo asking if he could come and replace it. I already had a spare pane that was left lying around the apartment decades ago. I'd wanted to toss it at one point, but Kustas said the glass was fine, so let it be. When Toivo hesitated, I told him it was just an ordinary, taped-up *fortochka*[1]. He asked if I had a glass knife and since I didn't, he promised to borrow one and come over. At the time, I didn't know he was homeless. I waited, honestly believing he'd show up to fix Kustas's window. When he failed to show up, I called again, but he didn't answer. Still, he's a good guy. I don't know if I can say he embodies some ideal like Helmi does. Neither of them has many possessions or big dreams, but they're both brimming with goodness and good intentions and are friendly and never complain. They're simply observers of life, or something along those lines.

◆

Siskin and Laura and I went out to BabyBack for dinner. Proper-sized ribs and American-style pizzas. The walls are covered in all kinds of old signs like pubs usually have. Clearly, the interior decorator was going for a classic approach. One sign proudly declared: "Good homes are built, not bought." I stared at it mournfully for a while, because it sounded right and I knew I'll never build myself a home; therefore, I'll never live in a good one. But what about the house my father built? Would that be a good home for me, too? No, I think the rules are that you have to build it yourself (even though I don't know if the sign requires this); you have to pour your own sweat and tears into it. Then, you'll find love.

I was also reminded of what Tõnu told me about building his house on the island of Hiiumaa. He said he used to believe that when you build a whole new house, it'll be fresh and great for a while. But it wasn't long before he realized that wasn't true. As soon as the house is finished, it starts to deteriorate, and you've got to start renovating from day one. Just like how a person starts breaking down from the moment they're born. Your cells do constantly renew, though. Maybe a home also renews while it ages. Renovating doesn't mean endless homebuilding. I'm working on something all the time in my apartment and maybe after several years have passed, I'll have built my own home in this place that used to be someone else's. My handprints are on the doorknobs. I've stared through the windowpanes so many times that they've transformed my face. They've reflected me so much. Occasionally I've even swept the floors, mopping less frequently. In that sense, building a home is an endless process and it doesn't really matter whether anything else stood there earlier or not. Even when you build somewhere vacant, the nature of that site was there before you, with all its power and emotion. You've got to gradually domesticate it. Some places are tamed quickly, others take more time. Some become home immediately, others never do.

It's strange that such things can be turned this way and that, and there still seems to be some truth to every angle. Yet if truth can be distorted, then that means no real truth exists anywhere. Or there are a hundred truths without much of a difference between them. Perhaps the conception of truth itself is just trivial; a hollow word. Just like love. Overuse has taken away their meaning. Still, a boy and a car can't lose their meaning so easily. Talking about them is a treat, as the concepts of love, eternity, and truth without clear meaning tend to get boring. I certainly can't say if God is more like a car or truth and love. I'd probably like it to be the former. A Mercedes-Benz, for instance. Like the one Joplin asked God to buy her.

●

As I've mentioned, Cabbages is down in our basement. Mihkel once decided to fix up the space and put in an independent library. He had the time to run it by himself at first. By that, I mean he just sat there translating *Fear and Loathing in Las Vegas*. But then Mihkel started focusing on other things—studying abroad in Italy, some girls in Tartu and elsewhere, and for a while the space was closed and in a state of suspended animation. When Erko moved into the house, he turned Cabbages into a place open from seven to ten in the morning and from seven to ten at night. He was eager to run the place, buying an Italian espresso machine and making this and that to offer. Cabbages turned into a café run on the same principle as the commune's kitchen once was. Have whatever you like for a small donation (or a larger one, though whoever had that money?). I ate and drank there for free on multiple occasions, and other times tried to compensate a little if I had anything in my pockets.

Communism had basically arrived in our building. The best kind, at that. Communion and company.

●

Tarmo was reading from his new book at Cabbages—*Boiled Souls*. There was a head in a pot of soup on the cover. Pretty well-designed. Tarmo was reading a passage when me and a few others were drinking at his place. Fiction. Karl-Martin also featured in the story, which was set around Christmas. Tarmo was slouched in an armchair and through the dim evening light behind him, I could see Karl-Martin—Karla—peering in. Someone waved him in, but he kept standing there watching. He might have been smoking. Little Kaaren was with him. Karla often strolled around the neighborhood with her. It's his home turf as well.

The book release was somewhat curious, with only me and some of Tarmo's pals in attendance. Still, it was nice to sit in modest company. Tarmo's own attitude was polite and proper, and he even gave a speech. It wasn't at all careless or sloppy. The way you present something is the way it'll be received.

Erko had made sandwiches—tomato and herring. I was hungry and chowed down one after another. They were delicious. Childhood flavors are like rock-and-roll heard in your teenage years: they stay precious your entire life. I wonder what my children will retain, now that the selection has been made so vast?

Tarmo read with spirit and gusto, which was enjoyable, though he soon realized the audience wouldn't care to listen for much longer and started leaving sections out. I was disappointed by his dwindling interest and insisted he read them all the way through.

Karl-Martin had apparently finished his smoke and came in with Kaaren. He was wearing handsome black shoes and a smart-looking suit. Karla has a refined taste for classic dress. He's the grandson of the classic poet Erni Hiir and maintains a gentleman's appearance. Rightly so. Kaaren was very quiet.

I poured myself glass after glass of wine. Going up to one of the shelves, I found a book on grouse and read a couple of sections about the species aloud. I tried to make a joke about mating and hunting, but it fell flat. I didn't mind. The crowd gradually swelled—girls and boys and everyday Cabbages revelry. I pestered Tarmo to read more from his book for the newcomers; whether it was because he didn't know them or something else, he just shrugged and declined.

Karla handed him a fancy-looking bottle and I immediately went over to see what it was. Baikal, a Russian vodka infused with pine nuts. Though I was inclined to sample it, I was afraid to switch to the hard stuff. Laura and Siss were there, too, and I wanted to head upstairs and curl up soon, not stay downstairs boozing all night long. Even though that would've been fun to do with Tarmo.

I saw a girl with thick hair that spilled down to her waist. I didn't know her name, but she'd looked after Siskin the other night when I'd gone up to my apartment and left her hanging around in Cabbages, so I told her thanks. Peeter Vihma was there for the first time in a while, too. He appeared to be cheery and doing well—it was good to see him. And he had a girl with him whom I hadn't seen before. It seemed like they were together. I looked her over from the corner of my eye like a father or an older brother, for some reason. No, she seemed a-okay. I held myself back from mentioning it to Peeter, though. I was already pretty liquored up.

A guy from Tarmo's sauna club named Kuido had come to the release. As he shook my hand, he said: "I'm your doppelganger." Weird. He did indeed have a wry smirk that resembled mine. We could no doubt pretend to be doppelgangers somewhere, though I didn't start asking who he was or what he does. Maybe another time.

There was a pleasant din in the basement. I was reminded of Kerouac's descriptions of atmospheres; of how people got along favorably, effortlessly, and empathetically, even with new acquaintances, right then and there. The atmosphere in Cabbages was identical, no matter that it was fifty or sixty years later and taking place in an entirely different society and place. Such things resurface time and again, and I'm happy that they do. Or could it be that Estonia, in the current economic crisis, was in a similar position to 1950s America as it was just beginning to come out of a downturn? Who knows? Estonia's standard of living could easily be akin to that in Kerouac's days, and that's not a bad thing. I've found myself occupying a similar environment and a similar society to the one I admired when I first read Kerouac a couple decades ago.

◆

I was watching an old film; you were on the internet in the kitchen. You'd made the futon earlier and I was stretched out over the sheets. The movie was making me drowsy. I turned off the TV but didn't turn on the radio, figuring I'd lie in bed for a bit while waiting for you. I didn't undress or get under the covers.

The room was dark, lights were on in the hallway and the kitchen. I felt tired, even though I hadn't done anything all day.

I dozed a little, then woke. The light was the same and you weren't in bed.

"Laura!"

No reply. I figured you were outside smoking. I was taking a break from alcohol but decided that one beer before bed wouldn't hurt. Or two. Otherwise, I won't be able to fall asleep.

So, I got up. The light was still on in the kitchen, so I knew you couldn't be far.

You were sitting at the kitchen table, your face illuminated by the computer screen. Your head was resting in the crook of your elbow and you were asleep. It was the same pose in which you'd been falling asleep at bars and concerts lately. We share a lot in common. Neither of us does much, but we're constantly tired.

"Laur," I said softly. You didn't stir.

I walked over and stroked your head. I didn't want you to startle awake. "Laur, wake up. Let's go to bed."

Still nothing. You didn't feel my touch. I debated what to do.

I opened a beer and took a sip, then sat down on the other chair and watched you.

There wasn't much difference between my life now and what it had been like with someone else a few years ago. And yet, the gap was miles long. Even though the content of each day was pretty much the same, things now were mostly pure bliss. There were good intentions between the two of us, for the most part, and we both treated life with kindness and acceptance. It's strange that although everyday events might not differ, the very same things can make you either happy or unhappy.

I can't say if I've ever felt like one still life is sometimes happy and other times not. I don't think I have. Well-done paintings possess neither happiness nor unhappiness, be it a Vermeer or an Olav Maran. They simply are what they are. Though I suppose there is still a scrap of soft bliss or a little song somewhere deep within the scenes. I guess that means they're happy.

Evening sunlight can certainly be the kind of light that makes one happy, though; it can be a message of divine joy. And sunlight that makes one happy can similarly be melancholy and bring tears to the eyes. Right now, deep in my heart, you're the kind that makes me quite happy. Hopefully that won't reverse, and you, just the way you are, won't make me unhappy. That's just the way it always happens, I thought. Still, I don't want to make you unhappy either, with the way I ordinarily am.

I didn't want to leave you sleeping at the kitchen table like a sculpture, even though I didn't want to disturb you.

I stroked your head and softly hugged you again: "Laur. Laura."

Yet, you were somewhere very far away. You didn't move a millimeter. I couldn't even hear you breathing; that's how sound asleep you were. I decided to leave you be. There was no point in sitting there and watching over you all night long; you wouldn't fall off the chair. I knew that.

So, I went back to the bed, undressed, and slid between the sheets you'd laid. I can't remember if I was already asleep or not when you finally came in.

We didn't talk, and you fell back to sleep.

◆

Aquarium had an album titled *Radio Africa*. What kind of radio would mine be? Radio Peeter. Is it already playing softly in my head? Raimps once told me about a guy in the looney bin who could scan the radio in his head and listen to whatever music he liked. I can't remember if he could hear the daily news or Voice of America, too. Maybe he didn't dare tune in to Voice of America in case he was being spied on.

In reality, there's not really anything playing in my head. The radio is just street noise and voices coming from the house. Creaks, footsteps, and the rumbling of the tin roof when it's windy. And Siskin's soft snoring next to me. Sometimes Laura's too. And the sound of keystrokes. And beer being poured into a glass. And the simmering of macaroni in the pot. And the sizzling of fried cabbage on the pan. And spring birdsong from outside. And the neighbor's dog.

If I were to turn on the daily news, what would it be? Not much happened today, but actually, quite a lot did—in my own news world. Lilli invited me down to Cabbages for vegetarian cutlets. They were amazing, fried with arugula and spices. "A way to use up the leftovers," as Lilli said. And then Siss and Kaisa came down and Siss came up with a guessing game. One person thought of a word, and the guesser would have to ask questions to find out what it was. Siss didn't feel like going to the shop with me, but Kaisa came along and asked if she'd owe me later if I were to buy her ice cream. I told her she didn't. Kaisa debated why ice cream tastes so much better in summer than in winter. Then, Sven called and said they had so much leftover Chinese food from Katrin's daughter's birthday party, and asked if we'd be up for coming over to help them eat it, adding that there'd be something for Siss, too. He also asked if I could bring whatever books of poetry I had, saying they needed to design one for someone. So, I gathered up all the collections I had. There were a surprising number of them, which gave me a chance to think about all the poems in each one I picked up. Books by Andra Teede and Karl-Martin Sinijärv and Wisława Szymborska and Merca and Priidu Beier and Andrus Kasemaa and others. I thought about each one's design and whether it was a success or not. So, there'd be quite a lot on today's news program for me, and all completely positive.

Lilli also brought up how she's amazed by the fact that nearly every other day, TV news anchors reassure people that spring is honestly on its way. She said she came back from a trip to Southern Europe in March one year and there was still snow on the ground; that was the news over and over again. Are the news anchors even trying? Winter will always be coming, so will summer and spring. But I can't remember the news ever having been that fall is still coming, don't worry, it's well on its way. Maybe they talk about that in Russia. Who knows where else.

◆

I forgot to buy your pack of smokes again. I was clutching the shopping list you'd dictated to me when I was standing in the check-out line and I knew I shouldn't forget to buy cigarettes, but then my turn came and the cashier said hello and they're usually pretty Russian girls and I watch the way they scan items through and I suddenly remember, ah, right, I need to buy a bag, too. I pull one out from under the counter, and since I'm trying to finish paying quickly and not hold up the line for others, I find myself already fishing through my pocket for my debit card and my customer card, stuffing groceries into the bag, forgetting where I'd stuck my shopping list in the last minute, seeing that the cashier was trying to get to the next customer as quickly as possible while still being polite, and I was trying to get out of the way just as quickly, and I don't even remember the smokes anymore and I'm bagging my groceries like a cheerful Stakhanovite[2] and tossing the receipt into a trash can and walking out the door.

I shuffled my way between the puddles and shifted the heavy bag from one hand to the other and a few Russian guys walked by, pretty boozed up, and I felt like making some witty comment to them, but they were strangers and absorbed in their own conversation. I've thrown out a *privyet*[3] every now and then when I'm buzzed. There are Russian men walking around here constantly, old unemployed railway workers. Still, they're spirited as proper *muzhiki*[4] should be, and usually toss a *privyet* back. Neighbors, all the same. It's quite the Russian neighborhood overall. Old babushkas in fuzzy gray shawls. I like it. Young women pushing strollers, too.

I haven't seen Dude around in a while. It's nice to banter with him a little on the street every now and then, casually or in a stupor.

The cigarettes come to mind the second I see you, a lightning bolt to the head.

"The first thing I think about when I see you is: cigarettes."

You don't laugh, but neither do you sigh.

"I can't go right back and get them this time, my back's a little damp from giving up drinking. It'll have to dry a little and I'll change my shirt, otherwise I might get a cold."

"I'll go myself and see if the bodega's still open."

"It is. Still early. Early, early."

"I thought the windows were dark when I went past. But I'll check."

"I did bring you sparkling wine, though."

"I saw."

"Alright. There's just those Russian drunks who hang around the bodega, and they don't have much cash, either."

"I'll go check."

"Be too bad if they're closed up already."

◆

You live in an old Soviet-era house built for railway workers. I do, too, for the most part. I'm even officially registered as living there in your apartment. Or your bank's apartment, to be exact. I was astonished when you agreed to let me register there, even though we were already married. That used to be a dangerous move. People might make it official and not want to change it later. Nowadays, I suppose it doesn't really mean anything, anyway.

Where was I registered as living before here? Nowhere. Any official document was sent to where I was registered as a kid. I hung around here and there for close to fifty years, but I guess that means I was without a proper home? And do I have a home now? I'm not sure. *Moy adres ne dom I ne ulitsa*⁵. Indeed. Estonia's a fine home, indeed. And yet, that's not enough for the Estonian Population Register. And I've never received a letter at the address "Estonia".

◆

"Come and stop by sometime," I said to Märt, whom I'd run into on the street. "Cabbages is open more often nowadays. Erko moved into the house and keeps it open from seven to ten every morning and from seven to ten every night. He serves coffee, too. And you know, I hear some people have started coming every morning before work. Mihkel got a subscription to *The Economist* and a few other papers. *Sirp*[6], too. I can't remember what else."

"So the commune's at your place now."

"Yeah, who'd have guessed. But I suppose it kind of is. It's nice, though."

But Märt hasn't shown up yet. I reckon he's not a fan of the hippy life. Was he being sarcastic? I don't know. Maybe some people like it when the church and preacher move into their house, and others don't.

◆

That Ferrari drove past again. It used to belong to Kaur's wife. Now, there's some paunchy guy sitting in the driver's seat and usually another even paunchier passenger next to him. He cruises around very slowly. I suppose there are a few too many potholes in our neighborhood for a nice car like that.

It's strange, that Ferrari. You can't help but stare, even though you've seen it a dozen times before and know exactly what there is to look at: a blue Ferrari, nothing more. But you still gape at it. It makes that 12-cylinder noise from a mile away, too, of course—look, I'm coming! As if it were a beautiful naked woman walking down a crowded street. Or an ugly one, even. Or a lion. If you let a lion loose on a main street, you could rob store after store on the side streets because everyone would be watching the lion. Perhaps you could empty my pockets when my eyes are glued to a Ferrari, too. What does it represent? Something unattainable. A reminder that you're here at the daily grind, toiling over your own affairs, even a little worried about them, and then somebody breezes right past, their gaze a hundred meters over your head, never noticing you. And why should they? They move in much loftier circles. Their thoughts are more refined and meaningful and handsome. Strange that it doesn't incite obstinance and anger. Why on earth should you get mad? What'd be the point? God doesn't hear my cries. Sometimes, it can deprive you of motivation. But then, you somehow manage to forget about that Ferrari and go about your daily business. Until it returns, that is.

◆

"Check out that graffiti," Sven said.

It was a plump blue man flexing his biceps.

"That's a gym," I said.

Katrin laughed. "Yeah, that's their sign."

"There's a salon down in the basement, too, though I haven't gone there.

Maybe they'd give me a nice Russian bowl cut. And there's a liquor store on the other side run by Venus. Arenev Venus."

"Venus?" Katrin asked, frowning.

"Yeah. The company's called Arenev Venera. It's run by a woman named Venera Arenev."

"That's a palindrome, isn't it?" Sven caught on.

"I didn't believe it for a while, but then I went back to shop there again and checked. Indrek looked the company up online, too. It's true. There used to be a boiler house in the yard, but it blew up. A census worker asked people how their apartments were heated, and some of them had no idea the boiler house was gone. Old railway workers. They haven't left their apartments in years and seen that the building isn't there."

Laura chimed in.

"When I moved here, there was a butcher shop in that little booth. They closed down, unfortunately."

"It's like a tiny Russian village here. Little Russia. I like it, even though we kind of don't fit in."

I remembered that years ago, I used to live in a little Russian village in the Mustamäe neighborhood, too. It was filled with Russian soldiers who'd been left behind, just like the former railway workers here. I'm drawn to irrational places and solitary people. To *Stalker* lands. Why? I don't know. Maybe they help me to not take mundane life too seriously.

INTROSPECTION

L AURA SENT ME an SMS: "I'm afraid we're growing apart."
It made me feel dismal. What could be the reason? My lack of money?
Poor erections? All of it mixed together?

I couldn't let it get me down. I've already gone through all of it before. I simply had to accept it. No need to argue or dig in at any cost. The more you do, the more the other person wishes to break free.

◆

You forgot to buy the pack of cigarettes again.

You overdrew from your bank account again.

What else is going to happen? Not much.

The weather is nice. I toss a *privyet* to the drunk Russian guys loitering around the neighborhood.

They eye me—a stranger. But just in case, they drawl back: "*Privyet. . .*"

As always, I only remember the smokes I was supposed to buy once I get home. Only once you search the bag for it. I wonder—do you think I didn't buy them on purpose? I can't tell, and just in case, I won't ask. It would sound like I was trying to pick a fight. You're easily offended, even though I'm usually thinking exactly what I'm saying. No ulterior motives or meanings.

◆

I don't have the internet in my little nook on Koidu Street. Nor do I want it. I'm afraid I'd just waste too much time online. I don't have a TV, either, and my CD player hasn't worked in forever. What I do have is a wood-headed stove. A few candles stuck into empty bottles on the dresser. I bought the dresser from a second-hand store when I was divorced. I can't say why. It takes up quite a lot of space. Still, it's sturdy and friendly and made of hardwood. One plywood wardrobe (it isn't Karelian birch, but something similar), too. And tons of dust. There's no end to it. I can't figure out where all the dust bunnies come from; they simply appear. Maybe many things come into existence from who-knows-where. Love. Just like how mice were born of filth during the Middle Ages. Obviously—where else could they have come from?

In any case, the internet luckily hasn't come into being here at my studio, luckily or unfortunately. There's Wi-Fi in the stairway. I think it might be Marko's, but I'm not entirely sure. He used to have it and the password was: great_and_immortal_love. Or was it no_herring_at_home? I can't remember. Anyway, it could also be Cabbages' Wi-Fi trickling up from the basement.

Sometimes, I'll sit in Jaan's bar—a.k.a. on the extremely dusty old chair between our two apartments on the upper story—and will surf the web. We call it Jaan's bar because at some point, Jaan started leaving drinks out in the stairwell so that people could sit there and pass the time. They were half-empty bottles of pepper vodka and whisky and what all else. And every now and then when I was short on change, I'd pull quite a few treasures out of Jaan's bar. Later, I'd make an effort to bring a bottle of Nemiroff or Bulbash pepper vodka and leave it on the little table up there.

I find it odd that when our building has been broken into lately, the thieves still haven't discovered Jaan's bar. I reckon it's because they haven't dared to venture up so many flights of stairs. Jaan even kept an unfinished bottle of brandy on top of the mailboxes for a while, and still no one touched it. Even though we were burgled. I suppose they overlooked it. Gita was at quite a loss when her apartment had been broken into and someone ate the leftover chicken in the fridge but left the opened bottle of vodka. Teetotaler thieves.

I was a little worried about Jaan's bar. I'm afraid of drinking hard alcohol. It takes its sweet time passing through my old body, which means I'm drunk for a while. Still, I'll drink anything if there are no alternatives. Lately, I've been doing my best not to take anything from Jaan's bar. I already know the way things usually go, of course. You take good care of yourself for a spell and abstain, but then you start drinking again. That's just reality in the animal kingdom and I'm not about to go changing the rules. Even if I had the power and authority to do so, would I? Doubtful. Time has shown that when someone takes charge and starts changing things, it often turns out worse than before. So, what remains? I can't remember who asked that. Ibsen? Someone else? The question was certainly posed, but I can't recall there having been any answer.

I was sitting on the dusty chair in the dusty stairwell, surfing the internet as I often had lately. Even though I don't want to waste time online when I'm hanging around my studio, I occasionally do anyway, just to take a break. And it's better to keep the internet at a distance. Occasionally, Lilli-Krõõt walks past and we exchange a couple of words, and sometimes Jaan goes down to get firewood or comes home from somewhere. Every now and then, I hear someone coming home to a first-floor apartment and I'll call out: "Hey, Mihkel!"

"How'd you know it was me? Were you looking out the window?"

"No, I just figured those were your footsteps."

Then, I'll go downstairs and chat with him for a while. Our conversations are enjoyable, for the most part, even though neither of us tend to drag it out. A typical chat:

"Well, how've you been?"

"Oh, just fine."

"Sitting in the library, doing your thing?"

"Lately, yep."

I feel like we're a couple of New York drug dealers or other unsavory characters who are required to make small talk and shake hands on the street, both getting their own little kick out of it.

We have other types of conversations too, of course. Just recently, Mihkel told me about how he'd been caught cycling after getting sloshed and was thrown in the drunk tank for the night.

Neither Mihkel nor Marten came in today, though. Instead, I heard someone from one of the apartments without a toilet come into the stairwell to use the communal one, and figured they must hear me typing away on my laptop one story up as they did.

Soft blues guitar began trickling up from below, too. I looked up from the screen and listened. Did I know that song? I couldn't tell. Was someone playing it or was it recorded? The chords were broken by bursts of laughter and a potpourri of improvised riffs, and I still couldn't tell. For the first time in a while, I felt simple happiness and like I hadn't a care in the world again. I really didn't.

It felt somewhat silly to sit there staring off into space with emotions welling up inside. So, I focused my attention back on the internet, even though there were no more unanswered emails, and listened to the carousal coming up from downstairs. I had no inclination to join them—they had their thing going on and I was trying to get some work done.

At some point, the music got quieter and one of them went out into the stairwell, singing to themselves: "And it's a day, a real nice day . . ." I don't think that's an actual song, just some made-up lyrics. Maybe they were going down into the basement to fetch firewood. I went back into my apartment, got the basket Laura gave me, and went to fetch some, too.

I knew that by then, whoever went into the basement must have already finished and returned. I didn't actually want to run into them; I just wanted to fetch firewood like they had. That was enough.

◆

Writers fall into two categories: slackers and graphomaniacs. The slackers are somehow more endearing—they possess less self-love. Graphomaniacs, on the other hand—who, besides themselves, can be bothered to read all the things they write? Yet, at a certain age when your intestines can't adequately handle booze anymore, you've got erectile dysfunction and not enough money for gas, and there's not actually a certain activity that you enjoy aside from writing, then there's no avoiding graphomania. You simply have to accept it. True, you might claim that none of those long-winded opuses need to be published. But after a long time of writing simply for the sake of writing, your drawers can end up overflowing with unpublished manuscripts and your mood will turn sour and you must admit to yourself that you've gone insane, even though you balk from doing so. If only you could delay that confession for just a little longer! Then, maybe I won't turn out to be so crazy after all! But another side of me is frank: "What're you writhing and wriggling for, you loser? You're deranged! And you're not the first, you know. All the others have managed to get by some-how. Well, okay, not *all* of them. Certainly not every one, unfortunately."

Okudzhava, the Russian poet, writer and musician, wrote in blood on a slate, knowing full well that there was absolutely no need for it. Still, he did learn how to pluck a guitar later. Somehow. Just for a change of pace, though he knew he was a virtuoso. I myself have no musical talent, not to mention none in all kinds of other pursuits, either.

◆

Today, I'll tell you this story: There once lived an old woman who had no sub-way. So, what did that old woman do? Not much. She mostly just hung around, sitting and daydreaming somewhere with her legs crossed. Merely existing like that was just fine whenever the weather was nice. Sometimes, she had the for-tune of daydreaming with a companion. The old woman heard of another indus-trious old woman who built a subway with trains running through it. Every now and then, she wondered: Should *I* also get my act together and build something? A skyscraper, perhaps? But then, she started to think—does anyone really need a skyscraper? There are already lots of tall buildings in the city and often, the locals themselves aren't even keen on having them there. And a subway? Does Tallinn really need one? People who are in an awful hurry would certainly get to their destination faster when gridlock takes hold at rush hour. But to be hon-est, why were they in such a hurry in the first place? What if people took it easy more often? On the whole, it'd be better if they moved to the countryside, even if just for a little while. And having a subway in the countryside would be absurd. Yet, that's the thing! Absurdity alone would justify building a tiny sub-way. One that ran between Estonia's islands, for instance—Saaremaa–Hiiumaa, Kuressaare–Kärdla. The only problem is that you couldn't enjoy any of the nat-ural beauty between the two places, and there's beauty galore on the islands. You might try it once just for the thrill of the silliness, but no more. The subway would break down, the rails would rust, the train cars would also rust and turn moldy, and the tunnel would fill with sand. Though there's no doubt a certain beauty to that, too: an abandoned subway line deteriorating between Kuressaare and Kärdla like some Soviet-era military structure; bunkers on Naissaare in the Bay of Tallinn, for instance. And if that same subway were to be built between Tallinn and Naissaare, the whole island would be packed before long. Would Tõnu Kaljuste, that famous Estonian conductor and one of its few year-round occupants, be thrilled then? He'd certainly sell out more concerts during the summer, but I doubt that would put him in favor of the rail connection.

I guess I won't build a subway, then, the old woman thinks. Nor a Tower of Babel. Maybe just a little vegetable garden in the backyard. But when Lilli-Krõõt made one behind the garage last year, she was yelled at and probably turned off of the idea. In reality, there are scores of old women who have never built a subway, and you can't blame them for it. Not that anyone does. Perhaps if I were to be a simple old woman who had never built a subway, then no one would blame me for it, either. There's a sense of relief to that idea.

It seems that's the only story I'm going to tell today, and I won't be doing much else. Is this a proper way to live? I can't say. Still, it might turn out to be an all-around pleasant day. Time will tell. As long as I don't commit any royal screw-up. Have I already? I've no idea.

I haven't drunk all that much today, in fact. Just a lager and a dark beer. Well, and the next lager and dark beer that I just opened now. I slurped down a bowl of greasy borsht earlier, though. Last night, Vahur Linnuste spent a long time down in Cabbages. The evening was dedicated to him and we drank our fair share of wine. I'd bought a slightly better bottle than I usually do, and Linnuste ultimately sang for us after my incessant pestering. Nothing by Mart Saar this time, though the elderly man's voice was wonderful. The silence between pauses was profound, especially given that the small space was packed, and spontaneous applause broke out afterward. I hope he was glad he'd come, even though I called him an anarchist and vehemently protested. In the end, I apologized. He and Sirje left together and I walked with them for a short ways. It was drizzling and, since I had two hats but Linnuste had none, I pressed the warmer of the two onto his head and he didn't object. I like the idea that Linnuste now has my hat.

Still, I was baffled when Sirje sighed at one point and said: "Oh, what do you young people know about Linnuste." I immediately took their side. *Of course* young people know much more than the older generation, and that's the way it should be. I reckon that Erko might even know where the old woman's subway is at, and no doubt knows where the bear cubs sold in Pärnu are at now. I'd forgotten my greasy jean jacket in the basement; Erko brought it up in the morning, tossing it over the handlebars of my rickety bike outside my door. I felt grateful when I saw it as I was going out to buy beer, and immediately pulled it on. The younger generation should surpass the older one, and it certainly will, though they initially don't know they'll be surpassed in turn one day. It's all an endless race.

After Laura finished off her nightly bottle of bubbly, she said she didn't feel like following it with white or red—even though she'd asked me to bring both—and left. I figured she'd just gotten tired and gone home. Yet, when I was just heading out after her, she called and I could hear a drunken, raucous din in the background. When you're alone and your wife calls and you can hear boisterous, boozed-up voices in the background, then you're bound to feel miserable. So, I turned right around, trudged up to my top-floor studio, drank the last drops from a plastic bottle of cheap beer, and flopped into bed. Bitter, dismal thoughts and words stewed in my mind. I luckily held back from telling them to Laura and fell asleep, even though I harbored no delusions that things would be better in the morning. I found myself wide awake at 4 a.m. I considered going to the casino for an early-morning beer and decided I would, though I'd be kind to my organs and digestion and make something to eat first. I cooked up a hearty meal of macaroni with onion, cheese, chopped pickles, ketchup, and Mexican salsa, and devoured it. Afterward, I flopped down again and luckily fell back to sleep. It doesn't pay to go overboard with those lonely late-night drinks in the casino with other silent, mournful sad sacks.

I woke up a little after six (the time you used to get up to go to work) and felt wide-awake again. Instead of tossing and turning in bed, I got up and lit a fire in the oven. The washing machine door was open. I took out the damp laundry—two pairs of jeans, underwear, and Siskin's socks and underwear—then went back to bed to wait until it was ten o'clock. The air filled with the muggy tang of laundry detergent; I drifted in and out of sleep in that gas chamber for a couple hours more.

AFFECTION

S CRATCHING MY MOIST belly in bed after waking up, I briefly suspected that I might be in love with Laura. Just in case, I decided to push those ominous thoughts aside and do a beer run for health's sake. That's when I came up with the old woman's subway.

But today as I was sitting online in our dim and dusty stairway, Lilli walked past and said she was going to have a coffee in Cabbages. The cuffs of her pant legs were tucked into her colorful wool socks, and she was wearing slippers. I remembered that I'd lost my black scarf. No doubt I left it down there, too. I shuffled downstairs and pushed open the door to the library, where I found Lilli sweeping the floor. That's just like her—she says she's going down for a coffee, but starts furtively cleaning up instead. My building is pretty alright.

◆

There was a new guy at Cabbages. No one had seen him before and he didn't tell anyone his name, either. Not that anyone had pressed him about it. When we told him our names—"Lilli." "Erko." "Peeter." "Kaarel."—then the guy just nodded and looked away. He almost never made eye contact. Every once in a while, when someone else came in, he'd glance up without lifting his head, as if afraid that it'd be someone he didn't want to see, or wasn't supposed to. He was drunk, of course. But many of us are drunk here on occasion. For a while, he was completely silent. I suspected there had to be some reason for why he'd showed up. He hadn't brought any drinks, and we didn't have any to offer. Nevertheless, the guy kept sitting there, maybe just seeking human company.

When the guy finally started to speak, I reckoned that was the catch. He *needed* to speak.

The guy talked in a very low voice, but everyone in the room hushed. Kaarel and the other Peeter were playing chess and listened in, too. There was something else about his soft demeanor that particularly made me prick up my ears: "You see, I make bongs. *Nu*, Russian *bulbulyatori*. Customer give materials. They not hard to make, but *bulbulyator* that work good not always turn out. You know *bulbulyator*. Proper *bulbulyator* is work of art. *Nu*, art of handcraft. Folk art. When I go from school to army base, *starshina*[7] ask what I learn in school, what

45

I know to do. *Bulbulyatori*. He not know what is. *Starshina* say me to make *bulbulyator*. I take new bucket, make big-size holes in bottom. *Starshina*'s face like cloud, but he wait to see what next. I throw bucket into pond and it sink with nice bubble noise, just like *bulbulyator* should: "*Bul-bul-bul-bul.*" Pure art and total joy. I watch, pride. "You idiot! Ten days' arrest," scream *stariy*. I salute, say: "Ten days not enough, comrade officer!" "Then double that, soldier!" "Yessir. Get fucked. Twenty days' arrest." I had to pull bucket from pond and throw on dump. But before there time to take me to slammer, some guy from region headquarters come to inspect base—*podpolkovnik*[8]. He walk round looking important and making soldiers salute. *Stariy* run all round him and ass-kiss best he can. Then *podpolkovnik* stop by pigsty behind dump and stare. "What this?" "Broken bucket, comrade *podpolkovnik*." "Idiot! Ten days' arrest in stockade!" "Yes sir, ten days' arrest in stockade." *Starshina* told to climb to top of dump and bring down *bulbulyator* and clean it. Then *podpolkovnik* throw *bulbulyator* in pond and it nicely sink: "*Bul-bul-bul.*" *Podpolkovnik* and I both watch, satisfy. *Starshina* watch, too, but he still no understand thing. We taken to stockade together, but he get out ten day before me. When I go back to base, my *bulbulyator* nowhere to be seen. Maybe *podpolkovnik* take with him. But *stariy* then leave me alone and no care anymore."

The guy continued staring at his feet after finishing the joke. No one laughed very loudly, but I saw Erko chuckling and Lilli-Krōōt shaking her head. I'd heard the same joke years ago—Svere told it once. Still, this guy's performance had been remarkable. It was as if he truly believed he'd experienced it personally. His manner of storytelling had been utterly casual—ah, something like this happened to me once, you know, but it was nothing special. I suspected that Kaarel actually believed the story. Who knows what might have actually happened in the Soviet army.

I hoped the guy would tell another story; that he'd blend some other old joke with bits from his own biography. Alas, he just stared at the floor in silence. He jerked his head a couple of times as if he were about to spit, but stopped himself. Maybe he'd served time somewhere. Who knows. We didn't press him to talk.

When I went up to use the second-floor toilet and came back, the guy was gone.

"Who was that?" I asked.

"Dunno," Erko said and grinned. "First time I've seen him."

"He told that joke pretty well."

"Yeah. If he comes back sometime, I'll ask him to do a solo performance for us."

"What other stories do you reckon he could tell?"

"I bet he was flying with a Russian and a German once, and the floor fell out from under them."

"Yeah. Definitely."

"He might have fought in the Russian Civil War and bumped into Chapayev."

"So what that he seems a bit young for that."

"Ah, youth is deceiving."

"He's the spitting image of General Ivolgin."

"Hey, what if that *was* General Ivolgin?!"

"Might have been. Or at least a distant relative. Or the grandkid of Daniil Harms."

We discussed such topics for a while longer—the guy had got us on a roll, and seemingly without doing anything exceptional. No doubt the mutt could guess what would happen after his departure.

It's been several months, but no one has seen him at Cabbages again. He must be telling his stories elsewhere. Strangely, nobody from the other communes have mentioned a guy like that passing through. Perhaps he returned to his palace or castle on the outskirts of St. Petersburg.

◆

The Wi-Fi signal I use in the stairwell comes from Marko, who lives on the ground floor. I think Jaan was the one who gave me the password, though I could also be stealing someone else's internet. Kusti would always sit by the kitchen window with his computer and could pick up somebody's signal. Probably the commune's.

Also occupying the dusty stairwell is my grandpa's old Soviet-era bicycle, for which one of Anne's friends crafted a child's seat that rests on the front pegs and has worked wonderfully with Siskin. Jaan's bar consists of an old foldable table and a rickety chair. There are some bottles of whiskey there, in addition to the wealth of pepper vodka, each with a fair three finger-widths' worth of whisky in the bottom. Although I've been trying to avoid the hard stuff, I'll sometimes be sitting in our little stairwell internet café when Jaan walks by and proposes we have a little drink. But on this occasion, all the bottles were empty. Jaan was also off the sauce, though I guess he noticed my empty glass and light buzz. When I came home the next day, Jaan had set out three new bottles: Grant's whisky, Ibis brandy, and Viru Valge pepper vodka. Each was the largest size they sold—one-liters, I think. It gave me such a warm feeling. Jaan was taking care of me like a Good Samaritan. He probably thought I was short on cash and restocked the bar, even though he himself would refrain. I suppose that at times when money was really scarce, I would indeed creep up to Jaan's bar at night and pour myself a thumb-and-a-half of booze. And then creep up for a second round an hour or so later.

Today, I was just sitting in the stairwell and trying to see if Siss had written. She hadn't.

A voice echoed up from downstairs. *Lilli-Krõõt*, I thought.

And there she was, briskly coming up the stairs. I was perched on my chair like a toad and staring at her as she reached the landing.

Lilli startled when she noticed me hunched over.

"Hey, Lilli."

"Oh! You scared me. You wouldn't believe the shock I had earlier today. I'm still jumpy."

"What happened?"

"Oh nothing, really. Olavi Ruitlane's cat Button was sitting outside his door this morning with a headless pigeon. There was blood and feathers streaked all over the stairs, and the cat just stared at me like he was ready to pounce."

"Button?!"

"Yep. I tried loudly whispering 'Olavi! Olavi!' so he wouldn't think any of us had left a headless pigeon on his doorstep. There was no response. Then, I called Erko and told him to call Olavi, because I don't have his number anymore. I don't have anybody's number; my phone was stolen. Well, I do have Erko's, but he didn't pick up."

I could tell that Lilli wanted to go and I didn't want to keep her there, but I didn't know how to say it.

"Are you on your way to work out, Lilli?"

"Yep, I'm off."

She left.

I paused and thought for a moment about how the last time Button broke into our place, just as he always does, Siskin didn't want to cosset him anymore. He wasn't the teensy kitty that Siskin remembered from winter. Button was now a big black cat. Even I was looking at him askance this year. Nevertheless, I decided that he was still our local kitty and tried to find something fit for him to eat. Tinned meat, sausage, anything. Button was no longer a kitten to everyone's liking—he'd grown to become a young bandit. But I realized that having once accepted him as if he were my own cat, I should continue to treat him that way in the future. Maybe he'd accept an old fart like me, too. Doubtless he would, so long as I scrounged up something edible. The cat was our house's grown-up Button—not a shirt- or pants-button, but more like a coat button. Ever playful and up to mischief, prepared to leap from the table to the top of the wardrobe, which he'd climb into and nap in my clean underwear for an hour or so. The very same cat I'd known, though he was now quite a sizeable panther. The little Button still existed somewhere within the big Button, not that you'd be able to recognize it if you'd never been the little Button's buddy.

◆

I heard a noise coming from outside relatively early in the morning. I heard it again. What was going on out there? I'd stayed the night on Koidu Street (Laura and I were fighting for a change) and was groggy from late-night drinks. I pushed open the kitchen window.

"Anybody there?"

Erko was down on the sidewalk, tanned and as upbeat as ever. Erko was back! I wondered where he'd gone this time. Someone told me at some point. Barcelona, I think?

"Hey, Peeter, could you let me in? I left my keys in my mailbox."

So, I went down and opened the door. It was good to see him again.

CONFLICT

YOU GOT UP to go to work. I rolled over to my other side, spread my arms and legs wide onto your side of the bed, and released a little fart. I quickly fell back asleep.

"Aren't you getting up? It's already nine."

"Mm, me?"

"You wanted to ride with me to work and then go somewhere from there. You said it was the same direction. I can just go on my own, though."

"Oh, I forgot. What time're you supposed to be there?"

"Ten."

"Wake me up in a half an hour. I'll take a quick shower and come with."

You didn't answer, just going off to do your own thing. The previous night slowly came to mind. You'd badgered me for a while about whether I still loved my last girlfriend, and I finally agreed that I did. What would be the point of arguing when you were so sure of it? Then, you asked if I'd call a taxi to take you to work, and then to see Mihkel Raud, and then to a training. You were out of cash and I was out of cash and you'd maxed out your credit card, but I still had a little left before my limit. You and your coworkers wanted to give someone an autographed copy of his book, so you'd managed to get his number somewhere and asked if he could sign one. Mihkel wasn't exactly pleased, but said he'd call when he was up in the morning and you stop by his place.

You'd told me that you and Mihkel Raud have fucked in your dreams. Just like you have with several other famous musicians. I didn't ask whether your coworkers fuck them in their dreams, too.

I suddenly wasn't tired anymore, even though I can usually manage to fall asleep for at least a couple more minutes. If you get up when you're still a little drunk, it somehow helps sobriety to return faster.

I shuffled into the kitchen, popped some leftover chicken nuggets (that you might have been saving) into the microwave without a word, and got into the shower. After rinsing off, I stood naked and wet in the kitchen, even though I knew you don't like it when water drips onto the kitchen floor. You were sitting at the kitchen table, motionless and silent. Pouting. Even this early. Usually, you pout at night when you're drunk and I say something wrong. Which is almost every night.

"I dry off in a second," I mumbled, but you still said nothing. "What's wrong? Just give me a second."

"Nothing's wrong."

"Did you want those chicken nuggets?"

"No."

Ugh, I was still feeling drunk. If only I had a beer. Even a cold bottle of Nevskoe. Or a cold Baltika #8, which they don't even sell anymore. I'd have even taken a sad, cold kid's pilsner. But I had nothing.

"We squabbled again yesterday. I don't like it when we squabble," I continued whining.

You didn't look up, but you mumbled something.

"Huh?"

You mumbled again.

"What? Talk more loudly, I can't hear you. Could you at least speak clearly?"

You annunciated every word: "I can't remember any squabble."

"Oh, you don't remember. Well, if you don't, you don't. It's better not to remember, anyway. I'm going to have to learn how that works, too. I'm fifty years old already and still don't know how to do half the things that are important. Half—who am I kidding. I barely know how to do a single important thing. I can't cheat, can't lie. I'm not talking about you, you know that. Don't go getting angry again. I'm not even going to start listing all the things I don't know how to do." I could tell how nasty I sounded. I tried to just shut up. Would it work?

I stuffed my mouth so full of chicken nuggets that my cheeks bulged and it was hard to chew, then briskly rinsed the plate.

I ordered a taxi from Tulika; they let you pay by card. You went to the mailbox to get the newspaper. You have a subscription so that you can have something to do at work. Whenever you forget to take it along, you text me that I can get it from the mailbox and read it.

At your office, I read the paper for forty-five minutes while you tried to get Mihkel on the phone. He didn't pick up.

We got into a taxi to take you to your training.

"It's not easy being a groupie, you know," I joked. I thought for a moment. The life of a groupie's spouse wasn't always a walk in the park, either. Actually, I take that back—things are at least simple.

"What'd you say?"

"Nothing. Just being mean."

"Why?"

"Take us to the Central Hospital on Liivalaia Street, please."

You were silent until we were near the Central Hospital, when you whispered: "My training isn't at the Central Hospital. It's at Magdaleena Hospital. I told you yesterday.

"Take us to Magdaleena Hospital, please."

The driver was ballsy and accelerated with glee. Another car pulled out in front of us without using their turn signal shortly before the hospital. The taxi driver jammed the brakes, the tires screeched, and then he pumped them again. His manual ABS worked flawlessly.

"Thanks, man," I snapped sarcastically. Maybe he'd also had a spat with his wife the previous night and wasn't in the very best mood.

"Which door do you need to go to?" I asked you.

"Just let me out here, please," you said.

"Well, tell us which door you need, now that we're already here."

"I want to get out. Please stop the car."

The driver stopped and you left.

"Where now?" he asked.

"If only I knew."

We'd enjoyed good times and memories together—I suppose that's why we got married in the first place. When had all gone south? Was it right when we got married? Was that the reason?

Still, I had been drinkinglast night and hadn't slept much. I was just feeling grumpy.

◆

I was pretty drunk and you weren't. I was pushing you for some intimacy, even just a hug, but you weren't in the mood.

"Laur, let's play communism."

"My name's not 'Laur'. My name is Laura."

"Fine. 'Laur' is just a diminutive. It's a term of endearment. If I'm not allowed to call you Laur, then I'll just call you my little sausage. My little grilled sausage."

You just stood there, as thin as a splinter, glowering out the window, frowning and silent. I didn't want to tease you. Maybe just a little. Tauntingly and lovingly like a schoolboy does to a schoolgirl. But your pouty silence just seemed stupid.

"Fine, then it's comrade Laura. Please fuck me like a commie fucks another commie. Please?"

"I don't want to."

"You don't want to be a comrade?"

"No."

"Now, how can that be possible? I thought you were an old commie just like me. Comrade Lenin said it's as easy as pie to fuck in the time of communism. You just ask another comrade, and you get it."

"Why do you think I'd ever fuck Lenin?" Getting better. Your expression was still stern and critical, but at least you were making quips.

"True, true," I said, scratching the back of my neck. "Maybe I wouldn't have, either. Lenin would've been deprived of all his fucks. I think he had syphilis, anyway. He took some kind of medication, but maybe that was something else. Too bad there's no drug for paranoia."

"Are you paranoid?"

"Sure I am. Every sensitive poet suffers from paranoia."

"Sensitive poet?"

"What else should I call myself?"

"You were an old communist just a minute ago."

"One doesn't rule out the other."

"Okay, if you're a sensitive poet, then you can try to have a little fuck."

"Hooray!" I lumbered over to you, but you hunched over and wrapped your arms around yourself.

"I don't want you to touch me."

I was befuddled.

"But how are we going to fuck if I'm not even allowed to touch you?"

"I don't know. I guess that means you won't."

"You're just like Melissa. Can't even touch her with the tip of your finger without getting swatted."

"I'm not a cat."

"I said you're 'like' her. Should I make the bed?"

"I don't know."

I was getting annoyed. It felt like you were the one goading me. I could feel the anger bubbling inside of me and shut up to prevent an outburst. Instead, I went into the other room, sat down on the couch, unfolded an old newspaper, and glared at it. It was hard to concentrate on reading. Just you wait—one day, you'll be drunk and want to fuck, but I'll dance around it and ultimately refuse.

Of course, I knew that would never really happen.

I'd tried before to convince myself that revenge is pointless. You just end up despising yourself later. If you're cheated, don't get back at the perpetrator. Whether it always works is a whole other question.

◆

Half a glass of warm, stale beer from yesterday stood on the dusty corner of my desk. My head was aching; the room was stuffy. Tiny drunk fruit flies swum across the surface of the beer. Maybe half of them had already drunk themselves to death. I wondered—should I gulp down the flies along with the rest of the beer? It would probably improve my condition. A little fly-snack. What harm could it really do to my intestines?

I shuffled over to the sink and poured the beer down the drain. Guess I'm not man enough for a fly-flecked drink.

Overall, I'm just a giant fly who can't bring himself to devour his own species. The devil sure could. Still, I'm not much inclined to be him. I'm not that hairy, either.

◆

Siskin came to Koidu Street carrying a big duffel bag and told me she'd be staying the whole summer. She'd been planning it for a long time.

"The whole summer, huh? That's great . . ." I drawled, scratching the back of my neck and wondering what would become of me and Laura then. Would we be separated until fall?

She and I had just had a big fight. Laura got the impression that I'd wanted to leave her apartment; I felt like she'd thrown me out. I'd been somewhat intoxicated and it appeared to get on her nerves: "If you want me to leave, then just say it. Fine. Okay. I'll stay the night and take a shower in the morning, but I'm leaving for Koidu before you go to work."

Laura was silent. The next day, she called before leaving work: "I'm going home now, and I'm tired. I think I'd like to be alone."

So, I angrily got dressed and left, feeling bitter. Even though I'd been the one who offered to leave if you wanted me to, I still felt like I'd been thrown out of your apartment; that you didn't want to be with me. No doubt it was childish, but I'm also not sure I really want to be an adult. It would somehow also entail the loss of identity; indifference. Being cool and balanced about everything. Ebullient joy and outrage are silly and unfit for adults. Yet, I still enjoy being genuinely sad and then suddenly cheerful like a child from time to time. It's just difficult to avoid childish attitudes reaching the point of ridiculousness.

As I sat there with Siskin, I had a mental conversation with Laura: "Well, I guess you got what you wanted. Now, we're going to be apart till fall. Are you happy?" Luckily, I didn't text that to her. Childishness had its limits.

Two days later, Siskin called me from school: "Daddy, there's a movie on TV tonight that I really want to watch. I've seen it before, but I want to watch it again."

"Does that mean you're going to your mom's place?"

"Mm-hmm. I'd like to."

"Okay, no problem. For how long?"

"I'll come back to your place tomorrow."

I was still down in the dumps and hadn't spoken to Laura in a while, just drinking and moping around. Now, I couldn't hold myself back from calling.

"Siss went to her mom's place for the night. Should I come over to your apartment?"

A long, long silence. I was about to hang up before Laura sighed and said softly: "I don't know."

"Fine, then I won't," I answered tersely and hung up to put an end to the conversation. I'd cut myself off from Laura again and sentenced myself to loneliness and melancholy. I suppose it was because I didn't want to come off as a miserable beggar. Pride and arrogance alternate with humility and a need for intimacy and the willingness to work together.

I brooded until midnight.

Siss was gone for several days, but reaffirmed that she was staying for the summer once she returned. We enjoyed a couple of nice days together, giving me a break from the misery of solitude. But then, we bumped into her mother somewhere in town. Saskia went to talk to her for a minute, then came back.

"Daddy . . ." she began in a drawn-out voice, staring at her sneakers.

"What is it?"

I knew what it was.

"Umm . . ."

"You want to go to your mom's."

"Ye-e-e-ah. I just haven't seen Mommy in such a long time."

"No problem. Go ahead."

"And then you and Laura can be together for a while. You wanted that. Maybe you'll work stuff out, too."

"Maybe."

"Okay, I'm going then, Daddy."

Siss kissed me on the cheek and skipped away. Just like me, her mood swings are relatively abrupt.

I've got a part-time marriage and on top of that, I'm a part-time dad. I like it, actually. It's nice to be alone from time to time, even though it can be somewhat depressing. For a while, it even felt like I'd mastered the art of being alone. But then, Laura came back into the picture and everything was forgotten. If I should have to be alone again, then it won't come back as quickly as riding a bicycle.

CUISINE

I WAS MAKING cabbage soup. I'd put a whole head in and was having trouble stuffing it into your biggest pot. I added a generous helping of salt, holding the package in one hand and a spoon in the other. I tasted the soup and suddenly became absorbed in my thoughts; I can't remember what they were. In any case, I just stood there motionless, staring at the soup and holding the salt and spoon until I noticed out of the corner of my eye that your eyes were locked on me, frowning and wondering what had happened. I smirked. "The chef hypnotizes the soup."

The water was boiling, but I still just stood there.

"It looked more like the soup hypnotizing the chef," you remarked.

I put the salt away and set the spoon on the edge of the cupboard and mused that you were right. Life does manage to hypnotize me every now and then. It makes me stop, pauses my thoughts, and allows me to be present in a state of emotion, empty mind, and enchantment for just a few seconds. *I don't hypnotize life*. It happens more often with drinking, which is probably one reason why I enjoy drinking. Perhaps it'd be more frequent if I did drugs. I seem to remember it happening with weed and mushrooms. I've never tried anything else. It used to come with falling in love, too, but that hasn't happened in a long time. Do you forget how to fall in love with age? Would I even want to anymore? It's always brought along a world of trouble. That is, so long as you're not falling in love with something inanimate like nature or an object, car, idea, or dream. A person can shove you and your unrequited love into a valley of tears. I suppose it doesn't make much of a difference whether your dream is one of mankind arriving in paradise or something else, be it tiny and trivial. Dreams of payback are saddening, though. I'd never want those, even if it meant achieving bliss. At the same time, if you only dream of taking successful revenge and never actually go about taking it, then what's so wrong with that? *I feel like there's something wrong, regardless*. That's how you end up being bitter. I'd become a poisonous old codger. Though who says I won't, anyway? Uku Masing was quite a sour, cranky man, but I doubt he was ever brooding over revenge.

◆

After a casual silence, you said, totally out of the blue: "They asked me at work if I'm a lesbian."

I looked over to see what you were feeling when you said that. You appeared to be seriously flustered and continued, asking: "Why would they do that?"

"I guess they were wondering and discussing it. Though I guess it's better they asked directly than gossip behind your back."

"Does that mean I look like a lesbian?"

"I don't know what lesbians look like. I reckon they can look all kinds of different ways."

"But I'm *not* one! Why should I have to go around proving it? And even if I do, then nobody's going to believe me."

"Being a lesbian is pretty pop right now."

"But I don't want to. And I'm not."

"Is whoever asked you a lesbian?"

"I have no idea, I didn't ask."

"Well, you could."

I thought for a minute.

"I feel like you might leave the impression that you're holding a grudge against men. Though I suppose you've got reason enough to resent the whole male race."

"Why's that? I don't feel like I do."

"I think that sometimes, we both give the impression like we're angry at the world, even though we're just deep in thought. And introverted. And depressed. Moderately crazy. Just like an ordinary person should be."

"But no one thinks that you're a homosexual because of it."

"How do you know that? Whether or not a guy is gay doesn't matter anymore. It did a decade ago. Now, no one cares. But lesbians—now that's still a little intriguing. I don't know what'll happen if the intrigue ever fades."

"The apocalypse."

"But the apocalypse isn't interesting anymore, either. It's already come and gone a hundred times. We probably won't even notice when it comes for real someday. Who's got the time? Or else you won't believe that it could be the real end. And gay men, I might add, aren't at all as gloomy as lesbians. They're cheerful little buddies. For the most part, that is. Life's a ball. Maybe they were gloomy back in the Soviet days. And maybe some Soviet gays still haven't shaken their melancholy..."

I trailed off and you didn't say anything more, either. Why is it that I often talk as if I know everything, ranting on with my worldly wisdom, and you talk as if you know nothing? Even so, if I step away and observe the two of us, you seem much wiser than me. Does the fool enjoy explaining and the wise man asking?

Oh, who knows. Maybe you don't see yourself as wise and me as foolish, either, which in and of itself is a sign of wisdom. And maybe the notion of foolishness is no more than mere bragging, even if it isn't spoken aloud. I don't have the audacity to boast to others anymore, because no one cares to hear it. At the same time, I constantly boast of my foolishness to myself. Yes, I am my own most gracious listener. Luckily, no one can deprive me of that audience—it's nailed to me. Do I really even need another audience that doesn't love me as much as I do? Ah, let them be. You can never have too many fans. It is nice when you listen to me, too. And who knows what will come when you can't be bothered to listen to me anymore. Every now and then, when your mind drifts while I'm talking and you don't hear all the clever things I say, I do feel outrageously offended. I'm quite a pro at that. Perhaps I should train myself out of it a little. You can't get rid of it for good, but just a little would be fine.

◆

We'd gone out to get sandwich-making materials but ended up hanging out in Cabbages. The door was standing open when we walked past and it felt as inviting as ever. We were in no hurry, though we were hungry and Erko probably wasn't going to start making dinner yet. It's funny that we already take Erko's dinners as naturally as if he should be providing them there every evening, regardless that it's only been a couple of months. A holy communion that unites the congregation. You get accustomed to good things quickly.

I brought down my dusty, beat-up, grease-coated sandwich grill and we made grilled sandwiches. No one was amazed by how filthy it was. I added ketchup and cheap cheese to the sandwiches and started offering them to the dozen or so people hanging around, playing Erko a little. It felt good to serve people. "You've got to serve somebody," sings Bob Dylan. True, true.

The long-haired girl refused a sandwich at first, maybe because the grill was so disgustingly unsanitary. Still, everyone else was having one, so I repeated the offer. "Okay. One, please." Otherwise, she would have been the only one who turned it down.

I made sandwiches and people ate them until the bread and cheese were used up and even the ketchup bottle was nearly empty. I felt like we'd done a good deed by finishing everything off. Who knows for whom—ourselves, maybe. But in some strange way, it was a good deed for the whole world, too. We'd made ourselves the tiniest bit better, our stomachs were full, we were content, and in that way, the world *was* better.

◆

It looked to me like you were swaying.

"Are you drunk?" I asked, smiling and trying to catch your gaze.

"No," you replied, looking away. "I'm just like always."

I suppose you were just like always, or even a little more. I was sober then for some reason. I'd gone to visit my aunt, which lasted late into the evening.

I was going through things on my laptop at the kitchen table and trying to be easy on you so you didn't get angry. I opened a beer, surfing from page to page online. Suddenly, I was startled by rattling and a bang.

"Oh, oh, sorry."

You'd accidentally stepped on Melissa's tray by the kitchen door, knocking her bowls together.

Earlier, I'd bought ground turkey from the store. It was almost past the expiration date and at a reduced price.

"You want me to make turkey cutlets from the meat that's going to go bad?"

"Cutlets?"

"Sure, or whatever you'd like."

"Would I like something?"

"Are you hungry? Have you eaten?"

"I snacked a little on that . . . that Georgian cheese."

"So you don't want anything?"

"I do."

"Should I make cutlets?"

"Why?"

"I bought ground turkey. I figured that maybe you were hungry."

"Oh."

"There's cucumber and tomato, too."

You went and rinsed the vegetables. I watched you from behind my laptop. Things felt nice. We'd been bickering for over a week and then decided there was no point to it; that we'd stop fighting. Now you were a little buzzed, but we both knew it didn't matter. We wouldn't get into a fight, because that's what we'd agreed upon and nothing could make us stray from that path. We were both doing our best to be cautious and not ruin things. Your level of intoxication was a good measure of whether we'd be able to handle it smoothly.

You chopped the cucumber slowly and methodically, pausing between every slice but bringing the knife down decisively when you did. You left the chopped vegetables on the cutting board, sprinkled bits of cheese over it without spilling any on the counter, ground salt and pepper over it just the way we like, carried the board to the table, and sat down across from me.

"I'll just throw it on a pan."

"Sure. Maybe add some of that chutney or that British Bengalese thing—Bengal pickle. Or don't, if you don't want to. I can just add it to my plate."

You stared at the vegetables.

"Cucumbers and tomatoes."

"And cheese," I had to add.

"There were better ones. Cucumbers and tomatoes, I mean. At that place we were at."

"Sure were."

I watched you, thinking you were three sheets to the wind and somewhere far away. But in truth, you're pretty much the same when sober. Always somewhere else. Off in the Land of Emptiness. I guess that's something I like about you. It's something I can't understand and reckon I'd like to try out, too. Though I'm not sure I'd like to stay off in the Land of Emptiness for good.

"You know, I've been at home all day and was lying in bed at some point and thinking I'd like to fuck."

You glared at me.

"But every night when we go to bed, we're so worn out that neither of us has the energy or feels like it."

You smirked at that, though I couldn't figure out what it meant; what was underlying the expression. Maybe nothing at all—you were just thinking about me lying on the couch on Koidu Street in the middle of the day, my dick standing up, dreaming of fucking you, and you found it a little funny. Or maybe flattering. Still, neither of us made any move to go to bed together. You have to be the one to decide and initiate any intimacy; that way, it goes better for you. Honestly, you are more of a man than I am. Or at least a leader. I'm just an old, henpecked man. Have been my whole life, pecked by different hens. Though you were livid when, out of the blue, some drunk guy in line at the store asked you if you were a man and a woman. Given that you have a shaved head and not the biggest breasts anyone's ever seen—breasts that are just the right size—it's understandable that people might not be able to tell from a distance. Still, all you did was glare at him.

I watched it all happen from another register. We were in a fight and you stayed outside when I went into the grocery store. I waited with my cart for a long time, wondering when you'd come and tell me what to buy, but then I saw you already in line, so I just took my beers to the nearest register. Curiously, I watched to see if the drunk kid would keep up his antics and considered interfering, even though I didn't want to fight or get into any kind of an exchange.

The drunk boy's equally drunk, pretty, taller girlfriend found his behavior unfair and unfounded.

"She's a *girl*. How can't you see that!"

"If you say so. What do *I* know about girls, anyway?" the drunk boy hiccupped, then kissed her. They were high-spirited and talking all kind of crap loudly, some of it pretty witty. I reckon the boy liked you and wanted to tug your ponytail a little, but you simply didn't have one.

I can't remember how we made up that time. I guess we just made our own separate ways to your apartment and gradually returned to talking politely and lovingly with each other without analyzing things or poking the hornet's nest. With that, it was over—the whole pointless fight. Maybe we just get tired of things going well every now and then, which leads to an argument.

As often happens, we took turns wanting to go to bed that night. I was the first who intended to turn in, but since you were still up, I didn't feel like making the bed or falling asleep alone, so I decided to sit with you. After a while, I no longer felt drowsy. You got tired around midnight and went to put sheets on the futon. After writing on my laptop in the kitchen for a while, I realized you were still working on the futon with long breaks.

I got up to see what you were up to. You were standing next to the pulled-out futon, holding the rug we lay over it so the gap isn't as wide and to prevent sperm from leaving any splotches on the fabric. It looked like you were deep in thought.

"Want any help? Should I make it myself?"

"No," you said, springing into action. "I've got it. I'll do it myself."

Girl power. Whenever you want to do something on your own, you do it. I lingered a little to watch you put sheets on the futon. Slowly, but surely. Then, I got bored and shuffled back to my laptop.

The next time I looked at the clock, it was a quarter to two. I went out onto the communal balcony to smoke. The next time I checked the time, it was around three a.m. I was wide awake, so I had another smoke. After a while, I started to feel, not drowsy, but somewhat worn out. Three-thirty—time to go to bed. I've seen that side of three a.m. before. Many times. In summer, that's when it starts getting light—a good time to curl up and fall asleep.

One more smoke on the balcony. Would it give me a headache in the morning, after all those drinks?

I squeezed the last drops of toothpaste out of the nearly empty tube and rinsed my mouth so I wouldn't stink too much in bed next to you. I didn't feel like brushing. What's there to brush when you haven't eaten, anyway? I swallowed a couple of pills to prevent the beer from bubbling up in my gut and snuggled up next to you. Still, I wasn't sleepy. I reached out to touch you—your body was warm; my hand was cold. I waited for my palm to warm up before sliding it over your breast, holding it over your shirt and hoping that would slow my thoughts so I could fall asleep. My hand gradually warmed and I slid it beneath your shirt, back onto your breast. I couldn't tell if you were sleeping or felt anything. Gradually, I started to feel turned on. I stroked your breast and your nipple, then lifted your shirt and started licking and sucking. You softly stroked my head, though I still wasn't sure whether you were awake or half-asleep. I worked on pulling down your red-striped Marks & Spencer men's pajama pants and your panties, but you finally ended up helping because I had such a hard time. That meant you must have woken up. I licked your labia a little to get you wet and make it easier to slide in, and asked if you wanted to get on top, as you usually enjoy it more that way.

"I'm so tired. I can't," you replied at softer than a whisper."

"So can I just put it in?"

"Mhm."

It was more of a soft sigh than a response, but I interpreted it as approval and not annoyance.

I climbed on top of you and spent a good while trying to get it in, because I was relatively drunk. In the end, you guided me. I held onto your shoulders as we made love and rested my head on your shoulder. You still stroked it softly. By the time I came, I realized you were just warming up.

"I'd like to get on top," you said.

I could feel I'd stay hard—it'd been a long time since we'd last fucked. Maybe I'd even cum a second time.

"Do it."

You did, and somehow managed to get off yourself on the second round, too.

Once you'd finished, you collapsed onto me and pulled the blanket over your back without looking. I reached out to help as well as I could.

Sleep washed over you almost immediately and you turned heavy. Even so, you're so light that I felt almost no weight at all—little more than a heavier blanket.

I felt sleepier than before as I lay beneath you, staring calmly at the weak morning light filtering in through the curtains. You needed to get up at eight a.m.—sweet dreams. After a while, my penis went fully flaccid and slipped its own way out of your vagina without either of us moving. A few drops of sperm dripped out of your vulva. You were still on top of me, your legs splayed, your head resting on my shoulder, and I found myself in a state of bliss. I had a rising need to go pee; the quantity of beer I'd drunk was formidable. Still, I didn't want to disturb you. It was nice to hold you and feel the weight of your body. The need to go to the bathroom was accompanied by thirst, and I knew there was more beer in the fridge. So, I slid you off me as gently as I could. It wasn't easy, as my limbs were pinned beneath you. Somehow, I managed roll you off of me and, strangely enough, you stayed so stiffly in position that you lay on your left side exactly as you'd been on top of me. You hadn't even pulled your legs together yet. You weren't stiff or dead. I can't say what it was. Maybe you'd just felt so good in that position that your body automatically continued holding it. I slid the blanket over you, thinking you'd no doubt fold up like a jackknife before long. I swung my legs over and onto the floor, no longer making sure to leave the room on my right foot as I have for a while, having read about that somewhere. I did, however, try to keep my weight on my right leg to prevent too much pressure from being put on my bum left knee.

I shuffled into the toilet, then to the fridge. Melissa was there waiting for me and I knew that if I didn't feed her now, then she wouldn't stop meowing for a while. And would still beg for more when you woke up in a couple of hours. Ever since I started staying at your place more often, Melissa Wells' diet has increased exponentially. Though, truth be told, 'she' isn't an old lady, but rather a corpulent gentleman. Huh, what has become of that former US ambassador to Estonia? There are so many unknown things in life.

NEIGHBORHOOD

T HE WORD *USALDA*, "trust", had been graffitied onto several walls and an electrical box in my neighborhood. A triangle stood in place of the middle vowel. Must have been a local tagger. I suspect it stood out because of that center, Masonic pyramid; I can't remember if I've seen it anywhere else in Tallinn. The word was pleasing. And confusing.

If that message featured in a commercial, be it for toothpaste or tires, then I'd be suspicious. Just trust you, and that's it? Can't argue with that. But written on a wall? The artist doesn't want anything from me; they want to *give* something. Or do they also expect to receive my trust? For whom? Or what? Since there was no answer, I could play around with the message. And that was a mighty surface for it. You're going to buy beer after ten a.m.—trust. You're going to stock up on more beer, just in case, before ten p.m.—trust. You're trudging to work or hurrying to meet someone at the pub—simply trust.

A long time later, probably several years after first seeing it (the tagger had used good paint), I concluded that the message could only mean you should believe everything. Everything that exists. Trees, bushes, the city of Tallinn, and your acquaintances. I'm not sure if it also means political parties and government coalitions; more likely the things with which you come into direct contact. You knock on wood, it's wood; you touch cold metal, it's metal; you fuck, it's just a fuck and nothing more. Believe that you won't get anything else from it, and neither should you, but what you get is enough. In one of Böll's novels, the protagonist is bothered by a neon sign that advises trusting your worries to druggists. Yet Böll didn't wish to trust his worries to a druggist—he wanted to tell them to his readers. What can one miserable druggist do in comparison with thousands of readers? Nevertheless, Böll still had the desire to entrust his worries to someone. Hopefully, he didn't come into any conflict with any familiar pharmacist because of it.

◆

I certainly feel that I place my trust in that graffiti. It has a point; it has meaning. It was worth picking up paint and a brush and declaring the message to the world.

Jaakko Hallas reminisced that a laconic message also graced the wall of Mati Unt's garage: *tibu*; "chick". Poking around to find paint and a brush just to write the word "chick" on the wall of a garage—that is a true mystery. I wonder what it might mean? Life is full of mysteries. The hackberry tree started blossoming the day before yesterday, and that's quite a stunt, too. A big tree covered in blossoms. Even so, the types of mysteries that come from within people still seem more intriguing.

Connect the dots and try to guess: what's the point of life and of time and of space? Are the chick and the trust involved in the same thing? Very possible.

◆

Ruitlane's cat Button had been hanging around my place for a while. He set his eyes on me as soon as I was making my way indoors. He'd been lying in the sunlight in front of the house, but padded in as soon as I unlocked the door. He was good at that. Button can be slinking a couple yards away from the front door as if he's paying it no regard, but then shoot in front of you the second it's open. I enjoyed it when he curled up in my apartment over the winter. He'd leap off my desk and onto the side of the cupboard, then somehow manage to skitter his way up to the top. From there, he'd get into the closet (oh, no!) and fall asleep in my or Siskin's laundry basket. Often, he'd doze for an hour or two in that den while I typed away. Afterward, he'd demand to be fed and wouldn't put up with any old slop. Neither would he eat anything too hot or cold. Siskin lost interest in him by the time he'd grown out of his cute kitten phase.

Whenever I was going into my studio alone, I'd usually be happy to let Button in, even though he'd leave little pawprints here and there and would leave hair all over the couch or my bedsheets. I didn't mind. There was at least another living being in the room who was letting me work in peace. To be fair, he did sometimes walk across my warm keyboard and type something of his own.

This time, Button was in some other kind of a mood. When I was in the main room, he sat in the kitchen, and vice-versa. Occasionally, he would stand up on his back paws and rub against me somewhat amiably. He wanted something, but I couldn't figure out what it was. At some point when I'd been sitting in the main room for a while with the door between there and the kitchen open so the cat could go in and out, I heard a strange, rapid scratching noise. I ignored it.

After rousing from my work, I peeked into the kitchen. Button was nowhere to be seen. I peeked around to see where he was sleeping, wary to not startle if he suddenly charged out of a dim corner, as that's something he enjoys doing. Coal-black Button. But I couldn't find him. The kitchen window stood open and I peeked out to see if he'd crawled onto the roof. He climbed a tree outside Lilli-Krõõt's third-floor window once and couldn't get down again. When he saw her at the window, he leapt without understanding it was shut and was left hanging from the tin roof by one paw. It took Lilli some time to figure out how to work the window open without knocking Button to the ground.

Now, I could see that Jaan and Lilli's window was standing open a couple of yards from mine. Should I ask them if Button came calling? Or would he turn up all on his own?

I had a hard time staying put at my computer. Thoughts of Button were spinning around my head. I checked the closet, but he wasn't in our hampers. I climbed up onto the desk to see if he was on top. There weren't many other places to hide.

So, I went to knock on Jaan's door. After two rounds, he opened it. It'd taken him a little time to find some clothes.

"I was nude," he told me. "I like being nude."

"Sure. Who doesn't. Has Button come to your place? He disappeared from mine and we both have our kitchen windows open."

Jaan looked over his shoulder and thought for a second.

"I don't believe he has. I haven't seen him, at least."

I planned to ask Ruitlane if Button had made his way home before I went to Laura's apartment, but ended up getting drunk and forgetting. Several days have passed since then. I still haven't seen the cat. Well, I'll go ask now—better late than never.

◆

I was taking out the trash. Olavi was tinkering with his trailer. He'd been hammering away at it for the last few days, because it's spring and he needed to go fishing. He simply had to. You may write literature, but fishing is necessary. Perhaps there'd be no literature without fishing. Maybe that's where literature is caught. I suppose I catch my own fish elsewhere. But where is that? No idea. Someone wrote that whereas every other author writes constantly about luckless love, Paul Polansky doesn't. That's one way of classifying things. I wonder why he doesn't, then? Even though when I heard Paul talk, I couldn't be sure it wasn't a description of his luckless love in some way. If you look at it that way, then it's probably *impossible* to write about anything else, no matter how you try. Even if you're writing about luckless love itself.

Olavi tried this way and that to get his big inflatable raft onto the trailer with a winch. He'd been going out onto Kopli Bay to catch bream for a while already. I hazily recalled him admitting to me once that he used to tell his wife he had to go fishing so they'd had fish, but in reality, he just wanted some time to himself and couldn't always be bothered to drop a line in the water. Waiting for a fish to bite is a beautiful time. Like pursuing a romantic interest. Once you've got the fish and the woman, though, you don't seem to know what to do with them. Moaning and misery are quick to come.

I closed the lid of the dumpster. An unfamiliar girl who'd walked in through the open gate was wandering around the yard.

"Are you looking for someone?"

"I don't speak Estonian."

I switched to English.

"Looking for somebody?"

"No, no. I was told I could come and sit in this garden."

"Sure, why not."

I was confused by what was going on. The girl looked tired and a little sad, as if she'd traveled a long way to come and sit in our yard. Olavi looked over for a minute, too, but then decided his raft and trailer were more interesting.

"Where is the post office? Not the main post office, I know where that is, but somewhere here."

"Go that direction. Under the railway, to the right, and there will be a shopping center with the post office. Just ask someone where it is."

The girl looked a little lost. Where could she have come from? She wasn't Britt. There'd been some Italian girl staying at Erko's place not long ago. She had a cool "fuck it" attitude and even used the stairway bathroom barefoot. Would I be able to do something like that? Maybe after a little bit of practice. I bet I could, out of sport. Still, I have my own toilet in my apartment.

I went upstairs and opened the kitchen window. The girl was standing aimlessly in the yard. Olavi paid her no heed. Could he have some beef with women? Ah, what business is it of mine. Maybe he just felt like his English wasn't as fluent as it could be. Or maybe he'd already completely forgotten about the girl standing about 50 feet away from him in silence.

She heard the sound of the window opening and looked up.

"I can't get into the house," she called out to me.

Why hadn't she said so before?

"And you need to?"

"Yeah. I've got the keys to Erko's but I haven't got the house key."

"Hang on, I'll throw it down to you. I'm up on the second floor, just bring it back to me. What's your name?"

"Dorothea."

"I'm Peeter."

I waited in the kitchen. I can't go wasting the whole day nature-watching. Though I suppose, why not?

There was a knock on the door a couple minutes later and Dorothea handed me the keys.

"Where do you come from, Dorothea?"

"Catalonia."

"I see."

There wasn't anything else to say, so she left. Sometimes, you can say only a couple of words but be left thinking about them for a long time. All without a desire to arrive at some idea, and successfully so, still thinking all the while. Dorothy was no beauty queen, but she was pretty. That wasn't the point, though. It was simply curious that she'd shown up here out of the blue, alone and not really knowing what she was doing or what she wanted. I forgot about her before long.

The phone rang.

"What are you doing?"

"Not much."

"Where are you?"

"Koidu Street."

"Marta and I were thinking about coming and having a picnic."

"Sure, the yard's free."

"That's what we were thinking."

"Kaarel reckoned he'd stop by, too."

"Great."

I tried to get some work done, but my eyes kept straying to check the time and see when Margus and Marta and Kaarel would arrive and the party would get started. I couldn't concentrate. I didn't really feel like doing anything, and the Catalonian girl was out of mind, too. So, I just sat and stared out the window. Finally, shortly before they were due to show up, I had some faint ideas and sat down to do something with them. Somehow, I got into the flow. The positive sense of accomplishment returned. I worked for a while longer.

Then, Margus called. They were downstairs and couldn't get in.

"Do you guys have some picnic stuff with you? Food and drinks?"

"Yeah."

"Okay, just go straight to the yard. I'll be down in a minute." That's how it goes. When you've got all the time in the world, then you're short on ideas or can't be bothered to work. But when you've suddenly got to do something, then you wish you had more time to do your own thing.

◆

"My goal is to change people," the young man said, looking off into space instead of straight at me, even though we were both in the cellar and there wasn't that much distance.

"What do you want to change them to be like?" I asked, wondering—did he want to change me, too?"

"Better. More caring."

Heh, yeah. I'm certainly not all that good or caring, though many people have tried to change me. First as a Little Octobrist, then during Soviet conscription. I bet everyone has perpetually been trying to make me better. Who'll get any worse, then? Luckily, my parents didn't want to change me significantly. They had other things to do.

Does that mean I don't actually want people to be better and more caring? I'm not sure. What is "better"? How can one be "more caring"? By stroking the head of everyone who passes? As if they'd be keen on that.

"Better and more caring, huh . . ."

"Yeah. Say by going and cleaning up someone's yard for them. Maybe they'll be glad. Maybe they'll even come and help, too."

Ah, that old question, I thought. *Whether you should go and save Africans from starvation or let them die.* Albert Schweitzer was an all-around nice guy. On planes, they tell you to put your own oxygen mask on before you help others. Seems reasonable. But it's also true that if all you do is debate, then life will slowly pass you by, the African will never be aided, and the yard will never be cleaned up. Neither yours nor your neighbor's. Data Tutashkhia gave up on helping people because he saw it usually led to some kind of trouble. But I myself have never really tried to help anyone. How should I know if it'll lead to trouble or not? And if I don't help, then will it prevent trouble from coming? I doubt it.

What do I know about good deeds? Lenin was undoubtedly good, taking children into his arms and not shooting that fox. What became of the fox later, I can't say. Things didn't turn out so well for Lenin later, in spite of his good deeds. And things probably didn't go well for the subjects of those good deeds, either. Followers of Hare Krishna said they could feed the whole world. They ran a vegetarian restaurant. Got up at four a.m. and started to pray. Mother Theresa's nuns got up at around the same time and started praying, too, albeit to a different god. And during the day, when Hare Krishnas were singing on the street, the nuns were out helping people. Did they or their gods ever run into one another? Can't say. And if all gods are one in the same, does that mean the god of devil worshippers, Satan himself, counts as well? Can't say, either. There are plenty of other tough gods—Kali and Shiva, for instance. I have no idea what the old Estonian god Taara ever did or taught. Did he just drink mead and sing some songs? Or chase the Meadow Queen's daughters around like Zeus and Lucifer and all his friends did with other women?

Wolli Morgan wrote a fairy tale about elves that lived in the woods and did good deeds: "They got up early in the morning, ate, and went to do good. Late in the evening, they came back from doing good, ate, and went to sleep." Would I rather be the one who does good deeds for others or the one for whom the good deeds are done? Or could those roles be merged and you start doing nothing but good deeds for yourself? Others wouldn't be so enthused about that, I suppose. But are there really any other roles in that play? The Big Bad Wolf? I wouldn't really like that, either. Quite the conundrum.

◆

We'd somehow ended up at the premiere of a doc film about Eino Baskin. I think we'd just been drinking in town and someone invited us. We took some drinks from the bar and got more when we got to the movie theater. No one told us we couldn't. The theater was packed. No one else appeared to have drinks. Everyone was just there to watch Baskin. I don't know how old he was, but he took the stage before the film started and cracked jokes as always. But when he said, "Let's all watch the film," and started climbing the stairs on the side of the auditorium and the lights suddenly went out, I think everybody peered through the darkness to see if he'd fall. He didn't, apparently, because he was alive and kicking at the reception afterward. We'd followed others to the party, immediately filled big glasses with free drinks, and heaped up a huge bowl of all the snacks available. We'd been doing that every time we ended up at some reception for years already. I don't deny it might be impolite. I can't say if there's an element of protest against *comme il faut* to it, or if that's long forgotten and it's merely evolved into a delinquent attitude. But today, people are so polite everywhere that it's tolerated. There was only one time, at the Estonian Writers' Union, when I was well liquored up and had ducked behind a curtain to grab some booze that had been set up for serving after the event and I was grabbed by the sleeve and pulled out. That was certainly embarrassing. I didn't stick my nose back there again. They might not actually have bothered to remove me, but there were other guys at the event who might have followed me in, and things would've gotten completely out of hand. Anarchy at the Writers' Union. That's something I suppose none of us need.

Back at the Baskin party, we tippled blithely on a couch somewhere in the back for a while, constantly refilling our glasses. We had to get our fair share of the last free bottles to be brought out. Laura was daring and even brought two unfinished bottles of wine back to our table. No one lifted a finger.

"Baskin did physiotherapy where I work," Laura said. "I'd like to get a picture with him. Would you come and take a picture of me and him?"

"Not right now. I'm pretty drunk, anyway. I'm definitely not up for it now."

Laur was silent. She went out for a smoke, then came back and asked again.

"But if I really want that picture?"

"No, not right now. He's got so many friends and fans flocked around him already. He's the hero of the day. I'll take a picture of you two together another time if we see him somewhere."

"But he doesn't go anywhere anymore. We'll never run into him."

For several more minutes, Laura sat there eyeing Baskin, who was sitting over at the next table. He was surrounded by old pals and sipping serenely from a glass of wine like old men do.

"I'm going to go now and have someone take our picture."

I held my tongue, stubborn like Laura always is. She pulled out her fancy new phone (which takes better pictures than our old camera), marched over to Baskin, and reintroduced herself. As one would expect, old Baskin shot to his feet next to 30-year-old Laura and immediately found someone to photograph them. Laura swayed against him and smiled. He did too, of course. I sipped and watched. Laura looked happy. Baskin appeared to be so, too. And the woman at the table who was 28 years Baskin's junior appeared to be happy as well. In the film, Baskin said that there's no point marrying a man as old as he was in relation to his wife. That there's no real effect. Laura is . . . how much younger than me? Sometimes 20 and sometimes 19 years. I don't really know what effect it has yet, if any. But Laura standing next to Baskin certainly did look impressive. Several people commented on that when Laura uploaded the pictures to Facebook.

Riho, who had sat down across from me and whom I was delighted to see, leaned closer, grinning as always (naturally, he'd seen me eyeballing Laura and Baskin), and said softly: "A woman sees straightway, who is gaining fame and who's doing well, and she leans towards that." I looked him in the eyes and had to agree. Back when I seemed to be in the spotlight, women leaned towards me that way, too. And told me to fuck off when I fell out of it. But Laura leans towards me, too. Are things starting to go well for me? Has she sensed that? And if they stop, then will she no longer lean towards me? Is there no other reason for support? Well, but me and Siskin—we stick to each other like bread and butter. Neither of us want or expect anything from each other. We simply share the same blood, even if she's not always buddy-buddy with me. That's enough support for me. And it's one of the most genuine opportunities for it. To get romantic, you could question whether all Estonians, or all humans, or all men share the same blood, too. But maybe that's too broad. Even if you were to swig Christ's blood, which could unite us down in this godforsaken place. I haven't. I haven't had the faith in it. Still, I reckon I do have faith in something. It's odd that it's hard to understand what that actually is.

YEARNING

N O MONEY, NO love. So much, or so little, for that. No matter. Not the first time it's happened. If new money or a drop of fame should fall from somewhere, then no doubt a woman will step out from backstage—one satisfied with that money, and perhaps even with basking in the weak glow of Estonian fame. That's how it's seemed to go.

You slipped in telling me not to text you before telling me to fuck off. That was familiar, too. It had an effect. I lay in bed on my back for four days and couldn't bring myself to text you or anyone else. The tears of self-pity started to flow. At the same time, it was so silly as to make me laugh, though I didn't. When I cried at night, I thought it was because I was drunk. But the next morning, I couldn't get myself out of bed for several hours, even though I felt wide awake. In the end, I started crying again. A real Kierkegaard. I guess we'll see where this mess all ends up.

Maybe you'll run out of cash between paydays and get the idea that I might have scrounged enough up somewhere to buy you a bottle of bubbly and a pack of smokes and shish kebabs and other goodies. Maybe I'll get one more tiny chance. I didn't give into writing to you, but I was finally able to start writing a little for myself, and that helps to slowly bring you out of the pit.

I can't remember exactly what fight it had come out of. In any case, it was preceded by a visit to Jaanus's place, where we'd binged, in no particular order, on wine, grappa, and cognac. I passed out on the couch halfway through the evening. Funny—usually, your're the one who gets so trashed that you doze off while sitting on a chair. But this time, you just had a little nap while watching Eurovision (your condition for coming was that you had to be able to watch it, though ultimately, you were the only one who nodded off during the show) and were lively the rest of the night. Sometime around midnight, Jaanus made a move on you. When you came to sit next to me, asleep on the couch, he stuck his hand beneath your shirt and into your pants and said he wanted to eat you out. It's possible he couldn't get an erection after drinking so much. He'd taken sleeping pills, too, but that had the opposite reaction (I've never heard of sleeping pills acting as an aphrodisiac and making the person who didn't take them fall asleep). You woke me up and I ordered us a cab. Jaanus came to the front door, too. He'd taken a gun out of his safe and shot it into the air. It was a scene straight out of a Mati Unt novel.

I ate you out at your apartment. I suppose I needed to prove myself—you are my wife. But we didn't have sex; you weren't interested. I soon realized that you didn't want to see me anymore and got dressed. Maybe some of your exciting past adventures came to mind and it suddenly made you disgusted with me. I couldn't figure out how I was the one to blame. For what, wanting to fuck my wife? It was when I was standing at the door that you told me not to text you.

At home, all I could think about was you. About how you'd spent two straight nights at my place recently. On the first night, you fell asleep fully clothed under two blankets, drunk. On the second night—also drunk—you took your clothes off and wanted to fuck, and we did. But in the morning, you asked: "Huh. Why am I naked?"

"You took your clothes off and wanted to fuck last night."

"Oh, how awful," you said with an ironic smirk.

"Yeah. But the night before, you didn't take them off and had absolutely no intention of fucking. Oh, how awful," I grumbled, refusing to give in.

Thinking back, we only ever had sex when you wanted it. For the most part. There were exceptions, of course. You'd also ask me for oral sex, but generally didn't want to give me blow jobs. What a sob story you have. A lament.

As I toss and turn in bed, I keep seeing images of you riding me, pressing your breasts into my mouth one by one, and sensing your anguish. Anguish.

Still, raw rage and lust are better than these tears of self-pity. How do all these things go together, though—agony and rage and lust for you, all at once? Is this what it means to be human? It must be. When Margus was down in the dumps over romance, he was also furious at and lusting for his girlfriend simultaneously. Weird little creatures, we are. Yet the fact that you can see it changes nothing; it happens time and again. Would you prefer it not? No. The torment is also sweet, in a way.

Is this how people feel when they go out and murder prostitutes? Good thing I don't have a gun.

And why am I not particularly angry at Jaanus, but am merely anguishing from missing you? He was the one who made a move on you, not the other way around. Jaanus did a foul thing, but in a way, that's understandable. You, on the other hand, told me to fuck off when I don't believe I did a single thing to deserve it. That's what I don't get. It's like some force of nature comes and commits destruction without reason or explanation, and there's nothing you can do about it. I can't talk about that exciting past, either. Even that's out of bounds. It's a good thing thinking isn't out of bounds, even though my thoughts obviously aren't much to speak of.

◆

I asked my optometrist why he hadn't gotten LASIK surgery and still wears glasses.

"I'm not an idiot," he replied. He must have had to answer that question before, and that was his go-to joke. It might also have been the truth. Why can't a joke simultaneously be true? Maybe even more so, both in terms of truth and falsehood. Is there any rule that outlaws a lie also being truth and a joke? I reckon not. More like the opposite, and that nine times out of ten. Except that if anything can be everything, then can anything be definite anymore? That idea's been thought so much that it's a little shiny and threadbare from use. It's sort of a dear little thing but already becoming a bit insipid, like a distant relative at an anniversary table.

◆

All I could think of to do in my agony was call Siss. I could've called Sanka, too. She's certainly called me in that state before. Whether or not I've been able to help is another thing. Just listening and trying to be sympathetic is something, at least.

It was already ten-thirty at night, but Siss wasn't asleep yet.

"What is it, Daddy?" she asked.

"Do you remember when you were five and I was in London, and you sent me a text that said: 'daddy im o sat'? You couldn't write very well yet, but I understood and didn't really know how to help you. What could I have written, anyway? And I didn't have money to call."

"Mhm."

"You know, Sanka is also sad that way sometimes. And I am, too. It's the same for all three of us. I think it must be genetic. It's all connected because we're related.

"Okay, Daddy. I'm going to come to your place soon. Really soon."

The fact that Siss was now nine years old and could understand my situation without me having to say it bluntly made tears well in my eyes. She realized I was searching for compassion and didn't refuse to give it. She could also tell I was genuinely sad as I sought it, just like she was four years earlier. I can mentally tie that sadness to Laura, but it can wash over me for no reason, too. Laura isn't to blame for anything. She's not to blame for failing to understand the hereditary melancholy that interferes, either. In my head, I told her that as I was tossing and turning in bed, I realized that if I'm sinking in a swamp, she won't be the one to reach out a hand and save me. Siss or Sann will first. Would I reach my own hand out to Laura? I might not, either. Not out of malice, but simply because I might not understand her sadness or how serious it might be. Laura's mom and dad understand her. She's fortunate in that sense. And I've got my girls. I might even be more fortunate than her, because my girls will last longer than her mom and dad (which was a terrible thing to say).

When Laura was drunk at Jaanus's, she said that I won't live very long, and neither will she. It was a little off-putting to hear, but I could tell it was something she'd thought through and I just let it slide. I remembered her telling me once earlier that she believes she is going to die before I will. I guess that means beliefs can change. I, on the other hand, have imagined her as a tiny old lady, hunched forward a little and chain-smoking. A little like Mercia Eliade, the old fascist and, perhaps, genius who died at the age of 97 and was so feeble that he couldn't pull his precious books off the shelves. Makes one wonder if you should become a fascist to make it to such an age. Though who can say whether or not it'd work.

I reckon that call with Siss helped me to start climbing out of the hole. I didn't make it out that same day, but by the next, my head was already over the rim. At this pace, I'll be spitting in sweeping arcs and singing dirty ditties in a few days' time. And then, this whole misery and thoughts about the weight of the world and the pointlessness of life will all be gone and forgotten. Not that they won't still be lying in wait and ready to show up again. Still, there's no point in focusing on them now. It won't change anything.

◆

These things will somehow pass. You attend someone's funeral and briefly consider death more than you'd really like to (though it is nice to think about sometimes), but when you're drinking at the reception, people can't seem to stay sad and crack jokes and the mood does improve. Or you get into a huge fight and feel like the relationship and all that crap is going down the toilet. Then—surprise, surprise—less than one week later, you regret having gotten into such a big argument and feel like getting together and making up. Which you do, for the most part. But if a relationship goes so sideways that you have to break it off—well, that's a bit more difficult. For a while, at least. You can't figure out how to keep going. Yet after a while, you somehow manage to do it and no longer feel like shit all the time. It's just like after a funeral—you just don't have it in you to feel like crap all the time. You seek almost any kind of relief, no matter how trivial. And more often than not, it'll fall right into your lap. Melancholy can wear you out. I'm not sure if elation can, too. Maybe like how kids gradually tire of screaming and running around at a birthday party, even though they'd like to keep going incessantly. Sex can tire you out, though I don't think it's so sad afterward like the Romans said. Just empty. Nice emptiness. Your duty has been fulfilled, mission accomplished, God must be satisfied, and the gene inside me, too. Wait just a little longer before you start jabbing and cranking up the tension again.

◆

Siss was reading a book she'd gotten for her birthday. It taught how to make animal shadows on the wall with your hands. There were hundreds of impressive animal shapes. When I was buying it, I wondered if they'd look so nice in reality or if Siss would quickly be disappointed. Still, she'd made a dog and a rabbit before and believed in the book. I started thinking that I'm lazy; that I can't be bothered to play kid's games with her or take her to the cinema or anywhere, so she looked for buddies and activities on her own. All we do is talk—sometimes during the day, but mostly in the evening when we go to bed under separate blankets on the same couch. I read to her, and sometimes she to me. Siss doesn't put any restrictions on the selection, so sometimes I'll read her adult books or something in English and she's fine with it. Our conversations aren't too different from the ones I have with people my age, and Siss is fine with that, too. It's been that way for four years already. But we can't keep sleeping this way when she gets close to graduating from high school. Or can we? I feel like I wouldn't want to change anything. I'd just keep ticking like a wall clock.

"Daddy, is there any place I can go that's dark right now?" Siska asked from behind her hand-shadow book.

It was a summer day and the sun was shining. I thought for a minute; it wasn't a stupid question. Where to find darkness and a little bit of light on a summer day? The basement? Cabbages? I couldn't seem to come up with a good plan. It was pitch black in the toilet, but cramped and stinky. Kusti's room is just dim.

But then, Siska got in the mood to hurry to her mom's house. That was a week ago. The book is still lying here; apparently, she forgot about it. Maybe it won't even come to mind when she's back here on Koidu Street, because by then there will be new things and new interests. Her books pile up. It's the same with me. I get an appetite for them at the bookstore, but lose interest at home. Even packaging that seems enticing at the grocery store looks faded here. Only beer is a sure buy that never fades in the fridge. I'm not even all that fond of my own books at the bookstore, even when they've just been published and turned out relatively decent. Siskin doesn't fade, either. It's always nice being with her. I suppose, though, that's because she's gone every now and then and is fresher in a way afterward. Books should be taken away somewhere to freshen up, too. Just like how Tõnu deports his books to the Siberia of the attic and brings them back down from time to time.

CULTURE

BEER MAKES ME sweat. Six to ten bottles a day, as always. With a drop of wine on the side. I think I sweat more while drinking than I used to. My metabolism is getting slower and slower. I guess we'll see how slow it can go. Alcohol enters my body and doesn't come back out. It just circulates around and around there for days. Now, I even have to take pills constantly in order to drink. Medication for stomachaches. What did my doctor say? "Drinking and constantly taking medication to be able to drink? What's the point!"

I couldn't argue with that. It certainly made sense. But I didn't change anything, either. Am I just waiting for some big fiasco in order to quit drinking, and drinking away until it comes? That'd be quite the blow, and I'd feel as if I hadn't drunk enough before it happened. It'd be as if time was wasted. I know several people who have regretted not drinking at the right time. Juhan and Manfred and others. I was recommended once to fuck diligently, for as long as I can, while I can still get erect. An actor told me that. I can't say if his own period of opportunity was coming to an end by then. I haven't been more diligent in my fucking, though. I've changed very little over life in general. I was reluctant to heed his "fuck 'em and leave 'em" advice, so I just mumbled: "I'll do my best."

"No, you won't, Peeter. You won't," the drunk actor replied. That certainly sounded sad.

◆

Joonas started screening all kinds of films at home. He had a projector and showed them once a week or so. Béla Tarr and Cronenberg and others. Laura even made the effort to come once. We were pretty drunk, as we usually are whenever we go out. I feel like we otherwise wouldn't care to leave home when that time could be spent drinking. What's the point of hanging around elsewhere? Laura brought a three-liter box of wine and I had a bag of beers. I set them outside the window to chill. Joonas has a fridge, but it doesn't work. He just uses it to store other food. I'd hoped that other guests would also be drinking, but almost no one was. I can't remember who else was there. Liisa and someone else. We all sat on the floor with our backs to the wall and watched the movie on the wall. It felt more like a hangout than a movie theater. Visiting and cinema, just like how aristocrats used to perform music and plays for each other at Russian manors. Not that I ever experienced it for myself. I've just seen it in movies and read about it in books.

Laura fell asleep halfway through the film, just like she usually does when she drinks and we're out somewhere. She can somehow sleep while sitting erect, but won't react to anyone calling her name. The naps last for an hour or a little longer and afterward, she's up and at 'em again. Occasionally, she sleeps with her mouth hanging open and saliva dripping from the corner of her lip like a little kid. She never mentions it later, so neither do I. Laura's manner of crooked sleeping is contradictory to her otherwise well-kept appearance and ladylike disposition. I suppose there are lots of contradictions to her overall. Laura seems to need that rest. People sometimes sneak glances at her when she's asleep at a concert or a pub or someone's apartment, but we're usually in good company and no one bothers her. Sometimes when she starts snoring a little loudly, I'll rest my hand over hers. Every now and then, I'll suggest that she go to bed at around midnight since she's so exhausted when she has to wake up at six-thirty a.m. and can't get out of bed. But for the most part, we just stayed up and did crossword puzzles. The two of us would be hunched over the newspaper, silent and penning in letters. I can't imagine any activity better than that. Laura was right next to me or across from me, beer was in arm's reach, and some kind of salad was on the table, too. What did that guy and his wife do in Böll's book? Play board games, I think. Leapfrog? It's like weaving with the fabric of eternity. Sometimes, I wonder if Laura didn't want to go to bed to avoid me pushing for us to have sex, though I never asked if that's true or not. It'd be depressing to read that was the case from a silent response.

We watched the film, chatted a little, I finished off my beers, we took what was left of the wine, and ordered a taxi. I think. I can't really remember how we got home. Joonas and Katharina's place isn't that far of a walk. But I usually can't be bothered to go on foot when I'm drunk.

◆

Another time, Laura didn't feel like coming, but I wanted to watch the Béla Tarr film being shown that night, so I went. All I brought with me was beer and parmesan cheese for the soup Joonas and Katharina were making. Liisa was there, too. Katharina told us that she's part Hungarian, which is why she learned the language and managed to find work and a life there twice. We all listened with envy.

"Do you want butter for your bread?" Joonas asked Liisa.

"I don't eat butter."

"Never?"

"You don't even add it to food?"

"Nope," she said with a smile. Liisa is almost constantly smiling and has a rather loud laugh, too. "Why should anyone add butter to food?"

"You've got to be joking," Joonas teased amiably. "Butter is the foundation of every good meal."

"Sure is," I chimed in. I observed that I'm thicker than Joonas but maybe not heavier, because he's tall.

"I was nice and productive today," Liisa said. "I went to a flea market and bought myself a shirt."

"Ooh, I'd like to see," Katharina immediately replied.

"Do you live around here? In this neighborhood, I mean?" I asked Liisa.

"I'm right in the building across from you. The orange one. Haven't you seen me? I see you every now and then."

"I guess I haven't paid attention. My bad. Must be old age."

As I studied her, I thought she seems somehow lonely, even though she laughs a lot. Not like there's anything strange about that. Many of us are lonely, but we laugh when we're in a social setting and are gloomy or even cry when we're alone. Another thought came to mind: I'm more or less a professional loner. Laura, too, even though we're together. And maybe it wouldn't be a good idea for me to start hanging out with Liisa there like we were some lonely-hearts club. Even if all we did was talk. I wouldn't want Laura to do anything like that.

I forgot that thought before long. Joonas brought out paints and proposed we all paint something on one of the living room walls. I made a sad moon. Liisa and I stood side-by-side as we painted; I think our arms even brushed. And suddenly, it felt like no big thing.

Still, I stopped going to Joonas's place for a while after that, even though it wasn't tied to any particular thought. Now that I think about it, I would like to go. But you can't wander around and leave life hanging for too long. I have no idea what that means. If I'm not wandering around, then I don't really do much—I just sit there. But then, it really doesn't feel like you're leaving life hanging.

◆

I wouldn't really like someone who's not a fan of writing like this—Henrik, for instance—to read it and say: Oh, again with the same old endless whining and complaining. Maybe that's all this is, to be fair. But no one has to read it. It'd be pretty awful to have to read things you're not a fan of for work.

◆

Laura usually sleeps on her back, her arms crossed over her breasts. Right hand on the left breast, left one on the right. As if she's preparing for lying in a grave. Knowing her as much as I do, I won't be surprised if she really was and got a bitter kick out of it. I can tell she does whenever I occasionally push my own blanket off and slip under hers. Or when I just reach out to hold her breast. She usually makes room for my hand if she's not deep asleep. I think she likes it when I touch her breasts. Animals don't touch another female animal's breast, I don't think. It'd be hard to do that with hoofs. I've also never seen a picture of a hog or a dog sucking on a female's breasts. I suppose it's unique to humans, like laughing or talking. Animals rarely drive cars or read newspapers, too, of course. But I bet they still sometimes read and drive and smile and suck on female breasts. That much is for certain. Homosexuality has sure been identified with animals, not to mention fidelity and infidelity and sadness and shame. Tõnu's dog Mopi even wrote poetry, though we never saw it. What's wrong with having disdain for others' poems without ever reading them? And disdainful is what we are. It's no wonder Mopi always barked at us. Lord Rochester, on the other hand, dedicated a poem to his monkey, which was remarkably smarter than the man's friends and acquaintances. Though he did dedicate poems to several women, too. That used to be in vogue. Maybe I could dedicate some verses to Anna Petrovna Kern[9]. Though that's probably off-limits since Pushkin's poem. I highly doubt he'd ever challenge me to a duel. He had some bad experiences.

It feels like I'm crawling out of my love-pit and this crisis. Once a sense of absurdity comes back, I suppose I can start living again. Even though absurdity isn't a taxi that takes you someplace. You can just ride around in it and stare out the window—like a lifebuoy or a raft you're left floating on in the middle of the ocean.

Laura sometimes snores while sleeping on her back, but so softly that you've got to really strain to hear. It'd be hard to get a good recording. Laura, on the other hand, used to record my thunderous snoring and play it back to me, not that I really wanted to listen. The sound wasn't so great. Philip Glass and Steve Reich are much better. Yet, Laura didn't care to listen to them in turn, even though the monotony and tiny variations were similar. I wonder if any minimalist has ever composed a long work based on their snoring. Gavin Bryars lying in a neat bed on the stage of the Estonia Opera House, the covers pulled up to his chin, snoring so loud it echoes throughout the auditorium. Neeme Järvi conducting a string quartet next to him, something akin to "The Sinking of the Titanic".

◆

Laura was still at work. I went to the Artists' House before five for the release of a poetry collection by Albert Trapeež. Alas, the door was still locked, white sheets of paper covered the windows, and a sign on the door read "Closed". Jaan was standing in front of the first-floor café. We small talked as we usually do, but it felt as good as ever. I don't know why chatting with him is so satisfying. Something about the way he holds himself. He's like an old Indian scout, always peering around and aware of his surroundings. Always conscious of whether there's some predator, prey, or an enemy nearby. Maybe he really is Leatherstocking and Old Surehand rolled into one.

There were several clusters of people drinking in front of the café. I could tell they'd been working on getting to the Trapeež presentation for a while and might get there sometime, too. So, I grabbed a dark beer as well. And a newspaper.

Fifteen minutes later, Lemming Nagel put his motorized wheelchair into gear and started driving towards the salon.

I still had half my beer left. So, glass in hand, I followed the hefty men shuffling along like bears. The door stood propped open. Nagel started pushing all sorts of buttons on his wheelchair, but the battery was low and it refused to crawl over the relatively low doorstep. I gave him a little push. Nagel should get a hybrid motor that works partly on booze—that way, there'd be no danger of getting stuck anywhere on the way home. I wonder if you can get a ticket for drunk-driving a wheelchair on the sidewalk? Can you get your license taken away? I wouldn't be surprised. You even can for walking.

There were no decorations, no band, and really nothing at all in the salon except for bottles on the windowsill. Still, those were also important. Leonhard Lapin was sitting at a little table with a pile of the new Trapeež books beside him. Lapin paid no attention to the crowd, just signing a couple collections for friends. Everyone was waiting for something to happen, but nothing did. No one dared to start pouring the wine yet, either. I was glad I had a beer with me—it at least gave me something to hold onto.

At some point, Lapin stood up and started reading aloud, but stopped mid-poem and shrugged, figuring—ah, what's the point. Most people there already knew what was in the book, anyway. Lapin, a long white dhoti stretched over his potbelly, walked away to clink glasses and chat with Georg.

Langemets tried to give a speech, too, but had trouble getting anyone's attention because Lapin was standing with his back to the front of the room, laughing and conversing loudly. He didn't notice that Langemets, whom he'd asked to say a word at the event, was already trying to do so. Langemets raised his voice a little and others encouraged him to talk louder, but the volume only increased slightly. It would've been odd to compete with Lapin at his own book release. Though at the same time, why not? I was almost out of beer. I observed the men around me. This wasn't my generation. It was older. All accomplished. And they were having a good time together. The more meaningless or marginally absurd the reason for gathering, the better. And they truly didn't care to do anything meaningful together, either. Simply socializing was good enough. I can't say that I'm part of any group like that.

I finished my beer and grabbed a glass of wine. It was a nice, cool Italian Canti. Laura and I usually attend events like those together, which gives me a sense of bravado. I'll blithely empty glass after glass without stepping away from the wine table, then start combining abandoned half-finished drinks to make sure I still have enough when it starts to run out. I looked around, wondering whether anyone would say anything if I filled my empty beer glass with wine, but I wouldn't have got a kick out of it this time. I lacked that extra courage. There was nothing more for me to do at the release, either. I grabbed a copy and another glass of wine and went out onto the square to sit and read. There was inanity and old-school inanity that no one writes anymore. Soviet absurd that is somewhat meaningless nowadays, because that absurd no longer exists. A souvenir from the past. So what? I'm glad that it exists. And I could be wrong, too. Like I usually am. I reckon it'd be hard to live without ever being wrong. Though those people do exist, too. I've even lived with one before. It wasn't easy. And it's not worth being wrong on purpose, either. Doing so is dishonest and doesn't fool anybody. Especially not yourself. Idiocy is a skill and can't be taught. An idiocy school would be ridiculous.

◆

We'd gotten ourselves relatively drunk at a literary event. Laura had a little bottle of screw-top wine with her.

"Oh-ho," Jürgen Rooste exclaimed, pretending to be angry. "So, are our drinks not good enough for you?"

"I brought it just in case. Needed to have some wine on the way, too."

"Okay, you're forgiven," Jürgen joked.

After the event, we went to the café next-door. We'd been given coupons for a free drink there as part of the festival.

"What can I get for these?" Laura asked the woman at the bar with drunken confidence. She's confident when sober, too, of course. Laura doesn't have to borrow confidence from anyone. It's something I like about her, so long as that confidence isn't an attack against me. It's nice to shield yourself behind a confident person's back and remain bobbing in your endless uncertainty. Let them break the ice and clear the way as you serenely chug away in the mother ship's wake.

"These are for Wednesday," the bartender said. "That was yesterday. They're not valid anymore today."

"But what could you get for them on Wednesday? What free drink was it?"

"I'm not sure. Maybe a little cheaper coffee."

I scanned the drink prices. They were a little higher than in other Old Town pubs.

"What should we do?" I asked Laura softly. "Do you want something to eat or drink here?" I knew that she did, and she knew I was pretty short on cash. I was embarrassed that we'd come to beg for a free drink and probably getting anything, which was probably why I asked.

"Let's go home," Laur said resolutely.

"You sure? Go ahead and pick something out. Let's have something here."

The less money I had, the more I wanted to pay for things and prove that I *did* have money. I just don't want it to be obvious to others. Nor to myself. I don't want to feel like a bum. I wonder—when Lord Byron was broke (which he usually was), did he try to pretend he was flush with cash, too? Perhaps he did, but such that he allowed women to treat him to things. Similar substance, slightly different methods.

"Let's go home," Laura repeated.

"Sure, if that's what you want."

Laura also knew the money I had would go much farther at a regular shop, and farther was no doubt what she wanted. Both in terms of food and drink.

We ran into Margus and Marta standing in front of the Writers' Union. Margus's hair went down to his shoulders; Marta's head was shaved like Laura's. My hair was just messy as always. Margus had just presented and slunk away from the next presentation. They were wondering where to go next.

"Let's do the old-fashioned way—get a bottle of wine and sit down on the grass somewhere in the sunlight," Margus proposed.

"I'm kind of cold," Laura said, shivering.

"I'll give you my jacket," I said, starting to pull it off. "I'm fine."

"You're not going to play the gentleman again and give me your coat."

"Fine, as you please."

"Let's go to Depeka, then," Marta offered.

"Where's that?" Laura asked. She was a Tartu girl and didn't know all the old Tallinn hangs. Tartu's pubs and clubs, however, were all on her radar.

"The Depeche Mode Bar," Margus explained. "There's only one downside: they only ever play music by the Depeche Mode."

"I like their stuff," Laura said and shrugged.

"Okay. Let's go, then."

The bar was empty except for us. We went straight into the smoking room and sat there for an hour or so. I tried not to smoke, but they went through whole packs.

Lilli was standing out on the street when we left.

"Hey, Lilli—are you going to go get drinks somewhere else with Margus and Marta, or do you want to come back to the house with us?"

"I'll get drinks, sure, but later. I'm going to get a little sleep at home first. I think I'll take a different route, though." She waved and left. Lilli almost never drinks, of course. 'Drinks' is just an expression for hanging out.

Once we got off the trolley and both peed behind the electrical substation (I held Laura's purse while she squatted), I blurted out the thought that had been spinning around my head for a while—just so the spinning would stop. Even though I knew nothing good would come of it.

"Laur, when I really run out of money, then are you going to leave me?"

"Where'd you get that idea?" she answered. Unperturbed, for the moment.

"I don't know. It's just something I've been thinking. It's happened before. And people aren't so different, you know. You like it when I have money."

Laura fell behind me as we walked and went out onto the street to be farther away. I stopped to wait for her and when she realized, then she stopped, too. So, I kept walking.

I went into the Maxima on the way to her place, as usual. Laura strode up right before I went in and stopped me. The thoughts had been spinning around her head for long enough and now, she wanted to get them off her chest. There were long lines at the registers. We stood by the front doors, airing our dirty laundry loudly and drunkenly. It wasn't accomplishing anything, of course. I tried to be a little more conciliatory to keep the performance from dragging on too long, but Laura was unrelenting. Finally, I managed to cause a break in the argument. I must have managed to say something to surprise her and make her think for a moment to search for a good response, but I seized the opportunity to stomp into the store. My pockets were bulging with poetry collections that I'd bought at festival prices. They made my jacket look ridiculously distended. Six books in total. I picked out most of the things Laura wants every night: cucumbers, tomatoes, bread, cheese, sparkling wine, and a few other little things. And beer for myself. I didn't see Laura anywhere in the aisles, but she came up to me while I was standing in line to pay.

"I see you're buying yourself something nice."

"Myself? Nice?!"

That was a kick to the shins. She could clearly see that I'd picked out all the things she usually asks me to buy. I felt the anger boiling up inside of me, but I held my tongue. Then, Laur disappeared again. I figured she went home. The heavy grocery bag digging into my palm, I trudged after her.

My key wouldn't open her apartment door. It had been locked and the key left there from within. Thanks a lot—I'd been thrown out again. Damnit. Would I have to drag that heavy bag all the way to Koidu Street? I didn't want to leave it behind the door for her. Should I just toss some of the things in a dumpster? Just her food and the sparkling wine? I couldn't decide.

Instead, I sat down on the front stoop and started composing an angry text. I don't know if I was hoping she'd still open up, or what.

But then, I saw Laura coming down the street, carrying a plastic bag. It seemed a little light. I hadn't finished the text, but I quickly did: "Nice of you not to let me in when I'd come over and bought you groceries and booze like always. Last night and this morning I ate a nice thing I'd bought myself – a potato and a couple fish bites. Today's delicacies are here and I don't know what to do with them." I sent it, even though Laura was just steps away. How can you just give up your creative writing or delete it? My timeless work. I had to send it, anyway.

"What do you want: me to come in or go away?"

"I dunno. You told me you were going to Koidu Street."

"When'd I say that?"

"In the store."

"No, I didn't. I got mixed up at first, but then I told you I was coming to your place. Why're you throwing all the things I said and later corrected in my face?"

Laura shrugged.

"Do whatever you want, for all I care."

She used her own key to open the front door and didn't wait for me to come in like usual, but let the door slam in my face. I considered what to do for a few moments before going in, all the same.

Laura started shouting at me in the kitchen. Given that she'd already started, I tried waiting for her to stop. I wasn't taking her all that seriously anymore. Instead, I started thinking about if I've ever heard Laura yelling before over the three years we'd been together. Maybe I really hadn't. She's usually awfully quiet.

Laura realized that I was thinking about something else. I'd probably smirked, though it was more because of our situation than because of Laura.

"You're mocking me, fuck!" she roared before stomping away and locking herself into the bathroom.

I'd started putting groceries into the fridge but lost the desire to continue. I left the door standing open with the bag of food and drink on the floor in front of it. I slumped onto a chair, drained of energy.

Laura was in the bathroom for a long time. When she finally came back to the kitchen, she looked dismal, her frown a tiny streak on her face.

"If you want to take back calling me a fucker, then I'll stay. Otherwise, I'm going to Koidu. I don't want to be sworn at. I feel shitty enough already."

"I didn't call you a fucker."

"You didn't?"

"I didn't mean you."

"It sure sounded like it."

"I just said fuck like people always say damn it or fuck. It wasn't directed at you. But if you want, then I can take it back."

I thought for a minute about what I was feeling and what I'd do. Laura stocked the fridge with groceries, leaving me a cold beer as always. The whole situation felt stupid, any way you looked at it. I didn't actually want to leave; that was just a threat. Even though I, myself, had taken the threat seriously. Leaving would be an ugly thing to do, but after all that'd been said, there was little point in staying, either. I'd played myself into a corner. So, I opened the beer and poured it into a glass.

We sat in the kitchen and didn't make one negative comment to each other for the rest of the evening, putting the topic to rest. We'd gotten it out of our systems and just softly chatted about this and that like an old couple. At about twelve-thirty, we scooted our chairs together and started solving the crossword puzzle.

After a while, I felt tired, so I made the bed.

"I'm going to sleep."

"I won't be long."

But you didn't come to bed for a long time. The pounding bass from the pop music station you'd turned on filtered through the wall behind the futon. You, however, had shut yourself away in the bathroom. I somehow dozed off to the bass—I didn't dare turn it off in fear of you getting angry.

Finally, you came to bed. After a brief pause, you rested your hand on mine. That was a sign I could come closer. After giving it a few seconds, I did. I slipped my hand beneath your shirt, stroking one breast and then the other.

"Is this okay?"

"Okay."

My arm became hot beneath your coarse shirt, so I slid it up beneath your chin. You lay limp, your eyes closed. Since I had no real plan for what to do next, I gradually started slicking and sucking at your breasts. You still remained motionless.

"Is it really okay?" I asked. "I don't want to if you don't want to. If you don't enjoy it."

"Okay," you murmured, your lips barely moving.

I moved my hand down to your vagina and things progressed from there.

"You can eat me out if you want. My tampon'll just have to come out, but I'm too tired to do it."

"I can."

I guided your legs open a little wider and gently tugged at the string. The swollen tampon came out. I couldn't see well through the darkness, but it didn't seem all that bloody. I set it on the table, ate you out, and placed your hand on my dick. You held it limply, but it was something. Maybe you knew that if you were to tighten your grip, then things would go too fast. Before long, I couldn't resist climbing up on top of you. We had sex for a little while, then you opened your eyes.

"You can fuck me how you want. Go ahead."

I realized you weren't enjoying it this way.

"Could you get on top?"

I rolled off to your side, you wearily collected yourself, and then got on top, though you didn't want to immediately continue. Moving slowly forward on your tired and bruised knees, you came to sit on my face so I could eat you out that way. I did. I lapped for a little while, but then didn't have to give it much effort because you got going and started pressing yourself more forcefully against my face and I felt your vagina turning softer and wetter. I stared at you above me through the darkness. You were as stiff as a bow, your body arced backwards, your breasts firm and pushed forward. I reached out and stroked and grasped them. I'd never seen you look so beautiful before. You were ablaze and forceful and sexy, your entire body sensitive and reacting to my touch. That had a positive effect on me in turn. But when you slid back downward and inserted me into you, it seemed a little more problematic. The dried menstrual blood made it hard to enter.

"Come back onto my face and I'll try to get you real wet."

You did, and I tried to work a lot of saliva into your vagina before trying again. It worked well that time.

POSSESSIONS

THINGS TEND TO disappear from my apartment. There are almost no dishes left. On the other hand, that means there are fewer dishes to wash. I rinse my one plate and eat again. It's not at all hard to pick up new ones from the second-hand shop, anyway. So long, that is, as you haven't vowed not to buy a single thing for a year—like Mihkel, who soon afterward was trying to find out how to transport a toilet from Japan to Estonia. Apparently, he'd been given one in Tokyo. How else could you explain it?

The thing about dishes is that I have a cooking obsession and end up making too much food every time, so I try to pass it off to other people, and usually am successful. Sometimes, the dishes find their way back; sometimes, they don't. I only really know how to make three different kinds of food. I often get tired of them, which is another reason why I try to get others to take it.

Mihkel brought me a cup of coffee one morning and when I tried to return the mug to him, he said: "Come on—that cup was part of the coffee!" Even though I rarely drink coffee, it's nice to take care of Mihkel's mug as if it's a little piece of him sitting on my dusty old wood-heated cooking stove covered in grease. I don't think I've even heated it once this winter. Not a single time. Kind of disappointing. I didn't have any firewood short enough to fit in it, either, but that's no reason. I should probably just demolish it. It'd be a shame, but would make more space. I wonder if Tarmo and Olavi think it's a shame when they bash a fish's head in out on the water? I reckon they do. But is killing any kind of enjoyment, too? I bet it is. It's certainly not work in the way that killing is work for an executioner, and doesn't evoke any emotion to speak of. No doubt it's hard work and mostly well-compensated due to all the stress and such. It'd be interesting to look up how much executioners are paid per execution in different countries. Such as how much those who hung Saddam were paid. It didn't go so smoothly. I reckon they didn't have much practice.

DRINKING

LAURA CALLED ON Saturday night sounding extremely drunk.
"You wanna do something? Where are you?"

"I'm at Koidu. Where are you?"

"I don't know where I am."

I didn't respond. Laura was silent for a few seconds, too, then simply hung up.

By Monday, I'd reached the point where I wanted to meet up again. I was wasted. I called you.

"I could come over to your place if you want. But I'm pretty drunk. I just looked at myself in the mirror. I look like a cabbage."

"I don't know."

You were sober.

"Probably don't really need to, then."

On Tuesday, I stopped by your place during the day and since I drank the half-finished bottle of sparkling wine in the fridge, I replaced it with a new one. Slightly more expensive, because they were out of the cheap brand. I reckon you were the one who drank them all, just like how I've emptied the shop of dark beers on several occasions. You'd probably finished it off by that evening, and called me.

"What're you up to."

I myself was relatively sober.

"Oh, I don't know. Nothing really. Just sitting here by myself."

"Okay, well, if you want to be alone, that's fine. I was just thinking that there's going to be soccer on TV and . . . But if that's what you prefer, then sure."

One time when I left Laura's apartment in a fit, I snapped: "Just give me a call when you need something from the store again. Smokes and sparkling wine and groceries."

Laura was enraged, of course.

What was that old Russian cartoon where two animals kept trying to pay each other a visit? A heron and . . . who was the other? Whenever one wanted to buddy up, the other didn't. And when the second tried in turn, then the first was pissed off, threw his head back, and told him to piss off. I guess the two of us are that stork and the other creature.

◆

I developed some kind of a nervous twitch beneath my eye. Could it be from drinking? I couldn't control it. Would it stay that way? I don't want to be twitchy all the time, though it is somehow romantic, too. Like the way a romantic man limped in an old French film. And the man was so tough that the limp made him even more romantic. If a miserable man twitches, it's just repellent. How do tough men get tough? Are they born that way? Can they be tough by caring for no one and nothing else? Or is it because they've been hurt by someone or something they deeply cared for and now can no longer care anymore? No one really sees mild and gentle Jesuses as being very tough. Though Jesus himself did sing a proper lament and partied and told his parents to screw off and made wine all the time. He wasn't so mild in the least. Maybe that means he was tough. Still, he didn't limp, and I don't suppose he had a twitch, either. At least no one talks about it.

There you go—now, I'm comparing myself to Jesus. Not that I'm the first. What else is *De Imitatione Christi* really mean? And is comparing yourself to Mick Jagger any more proper? Does anyone even exist who never compares themselves to anyone else?

◆

My head's spinning again. Low blood sugar. I should eat something. Did I eat anything yesterday? A sandwich around noon, I think. Last night, I boiled some potatoes and got herring and onion ready, but didn't even start to add the sour cream because I looked at all the ingredients and knew it wouldn't go down. Today, I've been shuffling in and out of the kitchen, trying to look at food and work up an appetite. I even sat down at the kitchen table twice to eat, but nothing. No appetite, no desire. I could still drink sweet tea. Maybe that'll help a little, though liquid carries away even more blood sugar. It'd be pretty miserable if I lost consciousness and collapsed here in my apartment. Though how is it any better to collapse at someone else's place? I just have to make sure I won't take a nasty spill whenever I start to feel dizzy. Of course, you don't really have time to think anymore once it comes so suddenly. I should probably go buy a couple of beers from the shop, even though I felt like taking a break. That always has an immediate effect. But once you start, it's hard to slow down the momentum. Just like yesterday when I hoped to limit myself to just a couple of drinks.

Alright, I'm giving eating another try!

Is the pause in drinking also to blame for angst and yearning coming and knocking at the door again? I reckon it is. If you don't want to yearn, then you've got to go buy booze. There's no helping it. Yearning can be sweet, too, but it's burdensome in excessive quantities.

There's a twinge in my belly, like my body wants to vomit but has nothing to expel.

Luckily my hands aren't shaking. Just a little. Not very much.

I don't want to complain, but I am anyway. Why is that? Whose sympathy am I trying to beg for here alone? My own sympathy for myself? Self-pity. Pathetic. What would a brave man do, then? Would he ignore it? What if pity is merely self-defense? Stroking your own head and cheek to prevent yourself from breaking too much. Acting as your own mother.

A girl I once tried to live with told me: "I'm not your mother." I certainly couldn't come up with anything good to say to that. It's too bad you didn't want to be my mother?

Laur was also bothered one morning when my stomach was churning and I was having difficulties breathing. She was putting makeup on her beautiful face and asked: "What is it?"

"It's from trying to quit drinking. Your blood is thick, your heart has trouble pumping, you gasp for air, and your stomach churns. I'd be right as rain again if I could drink half a bottle of beer."

"Okay, enough then."

"You're the one who wanted to know what was wrong! You asked!"

I got angry again, pulled on my shoes, and left.

◆

"It's like I'm being punished."

"What?"

"I used to dream of finding a man who's impotent, and now . . ."

"Why was that your dream?"

"So I'd have a nice and easy life, I guess. Every guy just wanted to fuck all the time. It gets old."

I occasionally had problems getting erect or ejaculated so quickly that you didn't have a chance to orgasm and were pissed off. Not at me directly, I suppose. But you'd release a long sigh and have a sour look on your face. I didn't know what to do. I didn't figure I was to blame for anything. It's easy to think that way, of course. I'd managed to cum and it was nice to just relax and forget all my problems.

I wonder how many couples' sexual styles are a total match? I bet there are some. You and I have different periods of hypersexuality and asexuality. How could those two overlap? Only if you fucked yourself could that be possible. Or for those who go clubbing for a purpose. If you have no qualms about constantly changing partners, then life's a dream. But when you're stuck on one partner and casual flings or cheating just seem so depressing, then it's better to just go without fucking entirely.

After some time passed, I found myself in the mood to fuck constantly. While hanging around my studio on Koidu and lying next to you, both. I gave it a try, too, but you didn't feel like it. You were tired after work or just tired from drinking all night. There'd been a time when you'd get frisky while intoxicated, but now you were just exhausted. Sometimes, you'd say: "You can do me if you want, but I don't have the energy for anything."

I would do you then, sometimes, but it lost its flavor. You'd just lie on your back, your head turned, your eyes closed, your body limp. I remembered your earlier years when you'd let certain people fuck you for certain reasons. I didn't want to have that memory and I didn't want that kind of sex, either. I wanted to be together. That's when I gave up fucking, for the most part. I'd just lie next to you, tenderly reach out my hand, and rest it on your shoulder or your neck. If your hand wasn't tucked away under the pillow, I'd gently hold on to that. Whenever I felt that it was preventing her from falling asleep, I'd pull my hand away and roll over and fall asleep myself. It wasn't so bad, all in all. The fucking of our first years had turned into a time where we simply lay next to each other and felt satisfied. As long as we weren't in a fight, at least.

◆

Laura was at Cabbages, plastered. She rarely shows up at Koidu Street otherwise. She doesn't feel like sitting around and wasting time in my dusty, cluttered studio. But when there's the opportunity to spend a long evening in Cabbages or, during the summer, out in the yard where the commune built a stage and organizes poetry readings by Mihkel Kaevats or Eda Ahi or there's an Udmurt folkrock band performing or locals simply jamming like the guy who's now living in Marten's apartment, which used to be Tarmo Teder's apartment—what was his name? Something like that Swedish king, but definitely not Charles? Karl Friedrich? No, that's a beer. Well, it wasn't Charles XII; that's for sure. And it wasn't Karl Martin, either. I guess it'll remain a mystery. I didn't catch it at first. To be fair, I don't catch a lot of things. Or else I do over a very long period of time, and even then only just a little. I don't mind, actually. I don't want to catch everything in life lickety-split. Otherwise, you just hit bullseye after bullseye and when the chamber's empty, what are you going to do then? Just laze around? Karl Aleksander? No, that wasn't it. But then, Jaan Pehk said the guy strums a mean double bass, and since I trust him as an authority in most matters, I immediately saw basses in a new light. If someone does something well, it seems to give them a pass for all other kinds of things. Like how the French President consented that Jean Genet could be a thief and simply never jailed for it. Prison was a familiar place to him and no doubt even a little dear, but it turned out to be harder to return to than expected.

When Laura does come to Cabbages, she usually brings her own drink or I'll buy her a box of wine or something else and she sits there sipping it. Occasionally, she'll doze off and drool a little, but no one really cares. I suppose she enjoys sleeping that way. You can't get such a good nap in just any pub. I'm not all that worried that she might fall off the chair, either, because she sleeps that way all the time and never does. Some part of her mind must be alert 24/7. And at the same time, she sleeps so deeply and never hears anything. When she wakes up, she never knows how long she was asleep or pays much attention to where it happened. Laura would be a good soldier. She could sleep at her post but when the enemy showed up, she'd be locked and loaded. I just don't feel like carrying her from Cabbages all the way up to the third floor. I don't dare to with my bad back, either. Sometimes I'd nudge her for a while to wake her up, but she won't get up while she's in such a groggy state. Usually, she murmurs that she's going home in just a minute.

"Are you going back to your place?"

"Mhm."

"How's that going to work? You can't even stand up straight."

Still, she's left and successfully made it home many times before. Other times, if I'm patient, she will ultimately come up to my studio. There, I stick her into bed and pull off her clothes. She doesn't lift herself to help along the process of getting off her shirt and pants, as she's usually still out of it. I got angry with her once when she kept repeating that she was going to her apartment but wanted to stay in Cabbages for a little while longer. That time, I already felt pretty beat myself and could tell they wanted to close soon, so I just shrugged and went upstairs. Maybe that wasn't a nice thing to do, leaving Laura sprawled over a chair and drunk as a skunk. But I hadn't even drifted off yet before I heard someone slowly come through the front door and take off their shoes. At a snail's pace. I didn't get up, either. I was still too pissed off. Laur can move extremely slowly when she's very drunk, but she usually commits no fouls. She doesn't fall or break things. Though it also depends where she's at. In her own apartment, she'll drunkenly clean the kitchen to such a shine that there's not a mote of dust anywhere before she goes to bed, much less any unwashed mug. It's important to her. Fair—the time when we were visiting Ardo and I turned in for the night or someone put me to bed, Laura did have a black eye the next morning and didn't know how she'd gotten it. Ardo had, of course, been sticking his hand beneath her shirt and pants and begging to eat her out half the night, but Laura herself was still responsible for the eye. I was as deep asleep as I used to be when I took heavy sleeping pills. Out for four hours before opening my eyes. Ardo's a doctor and later told me he'd taken sleeping pills, but it had the opposite effect. I recalled that he'd poured different cognacs into two different glasses, one for him and one for me, then switched them according to some system of his. Maybe the sleeping pill had been crushed into the glass of cognac? Who knows.

"Hey, did you give me some kind of drug? I never pass out like that after drinking so little."

"Nope."

Well, sure—maybe he didn't. It's possible he just made the pill available to me, sticking it under my nose when I wasn't aware and I took it all on my own. That was the Eurovision party where he kept trying to get into Laura's pants.

"Listen, I'm married and my husband is right here next to me. Do you think I'm going to let you eat me out like this?"

"He's not waking up."

"Hey, did you slip something into my drink?"

"I didn't slip anything into yours."

Sure, maybe the stuff that goes around London nightclubs and is used to get them to bed without remembering anything the next day—maybe that really isn't passed around among doctors. Maybe you've got to go to London to buy it.

In any case, I woke up somehow or to something and we called a taxi. They usually idle around that suburb, so one pulled up minutes after the early-morning call. And then Ardo suddenly came out onto the stoop, carrying the gun he'd shown us earlier that night. He loaded it and shot a bullet into the treetops. I was stunned; it wasn't even funny. What good will laughing at a drunk man with a gun do?

I was glad that drunken Laura still does the exact same things that sober Laura does, and that all her morals and desires and beliefs are still the same. I reckon that I'm the same way. I've never drunkenly gone to fuck someone and then later apologize to my girlfriend for it. Though I do know the kind of woman who tells you: oh, you know, we were so drunk and it kind of just happened.

"Hey. Ardo told me you sat on his lap and that's when it all started. That he had a room for us but we didn't go in and just kept loafing around in the cold and he couldn't leave the house unattended so he had to entertain you all night and then all that happened and he said is a little Saint Peter like me really so sure he wouldn't do the same? And he said I could go ahead and give it a try with his wife and get a pretty rough result. So, did you really sit on his lap? I bet that would've seemed seductive, indeed."

Laura thought for a minute.

"I can't remember. I can't remember what all happened, exactly. But I also can't remember sitting on his lap."

Now, it was my turn to think.

"Maybe you were stumbling around and he pulled you onto his lap, then. Ardo can be a real dog who can't resist his own manipulative ideas or gets a kick out of them. But for some reason, I don't believe he'd just outright lie, either. That wouldn't fit with any intricate game of his. You'd see straight through it and then never believe a word he said ever again. He's more likely to dance right on the edge of things in a way that no one can say anything for sure."

"I don't know. I can't totally rule that out. But I also can't say for certain that I'd have sat down on his lap."

When we got home, I tried pushing for oral and regular sex, but Laura wasn't in the mood.

"You know, I just feel so nasty. Ardo kept going on about eating me out and now you come and do the same."

I felt like she was remembering some other things from the past, but I didn't want to force it and I left her alone. Her eye hadn't gone black yet by then. We started bickering again for some reason, and I left. After that, she didn't want to see me for several days. Still, I kept on about it and she finally let me come to her apartment. That's when I saw that the skin around Laura's right eye had already turned a yellowish purple.

"What happened?"

"Nothing."

"Is that from when we were at Ardo's place?"

"Yeah."

"How could you give yourself a black eye? Did someone else do it?"

"I don't remember. I guess I just bumped into something."

"Huh."

"You don't believe me? Fine, believe whomever you like. If you want to believe Ardo more than me, then go right ahead."

"I believe you. I've always believed you. There's no reason not to."

And I thought to myself that yes, I really do. I will for as long as it doesn't turn out anything's really rotten. Maybe that'll never happen. I think that's something Brits believe—so long as nothing bad has happened or you've been stiffed, then you should have absolute trust in your partner and or companion. There's no other way to do business. Or cohabitate. And I reckon Laura has the same obsession with honesty as I do. Honesty, sincerity, politeness, diligence—that's just the easiest way to live. Well, sure—we're big alcoholics as we live that life. No one's snow-white pure. Even the Pope wears red shoes. And the last pope played rock-star on stage in Krakow and waved to his groupies from the balcony. It's not good form to try to be more popish than the Pope.

Ardo wanted me to forgive him. That threw me for a loop. I hadn't even accused him of anything. How can someone who hasn't made any accusations forgive another person? In some way, I can understand that many people's motto is: if you can screw, then screw. Anyone will do. Even the neighbor's dog, if you're in the mood for it. It's your choice. And if I don't want that kind of a life for myself, then I keep my distance from it. But talk of forgiveness is almost like asking for approval. And consequently, that means you'll be allowed to do it again. If not with me, then someone else. That doesn't mean I have anything against the person or am trying to cast judgement upon them. You don't have to dislike someone, but if their behavior is shit, then you also don't have to approve of it. That goes for your own shitty behavior as well, or trying to nullify it. Saint Peter really is on the scene. Be careful.

I didn't bring the whole thing up with Laura. It just made me laugh.

I was restless while staying the night at Laura's and tried to write something instead. The next day I slept in, then took a bath and went back to bed. Laura came home in the afternoon and found me stretched out under a blanket on the couch. She flew into a rage over coming home and finding it a mess, meaning finding me asleep in bed. I jumped to my feet and fixed it up. I was pissed off in turn, because I'd done nothing wrong and hadn't been drunk and sloppy or anything of the sort. I hightailed it back to Koidu. That fight lasted for several days until I couldn't stand it anymore and pleaded for you to let me come back to your apartment, as being alone was really weighing on me.

I can't say if we'll just keep oscillating back and forth this way. Or if we'll learn to live another way and not to fight. Is fighting in some way crucial to us biological beings? The way it gives you a kind of high and then a chance to be alone and then have more passionate sex once you make up? I don't know. At the same time, Laura is the one to complain that if we take a long break from fucking and then start up again, she can't orgasm. Which means we should fuck more regularly. For some reason, that regularity doesn't work out for us. I, myself, can't seem to want it, either. We're brimming with contradictions. Still, I suppose it's not so bad as long as we know it.

ANGUISH

FYODOR D. REMARKED that life is richer than fantasy. Sure, but what else can fantasy derive from if not life? Though life can also derive from fantasy, like in Breivik's case. The egg did come before the chicken, anyway.

A mother and daughter were on the bus, the mother's hair dyed red. The girl's potato-toned hair was let down and her face wasn't made up. She might have been 14 or 15 and was in the last stage of pregnancy. Her clothes were loose, but clean. The mother's arm was in a cast (which was it, the left or the right?). The two chatted calmly about everyday things in Russian, though they didn't speak much on the whole. Of course, there needn't have been any connection between the underage girl's pregnancy and her mother's cast.

I believe it was a mother and daughter, though; that much was for sure. Not a lesbian older woman whose lover, a minor, had an unexpected pregnancy. And this is where that weakness for imagination breaks through—in that fictitious lesbian woman. But the reality could be even more complex.

I suspect that when you're about to die, it feels pretty much like everything was much simpler than I believed, and also much more complicated. There's no drug against it. And if there were, then would I even want to take it?

◆

Dima was holding Laura's hand, stroking it, and telling her something in his soft Russian. Laura was staring back at him, looking quizzical and enjoying it. Laura was as drunk as she ever was in Cabbages. I realized that, somehow. I never feel like going out anywhere without drinking, either. What's the point of me sitting there sober? What a bore. It seems like a waste of time. If you're going out, then drink your fill and who gives a fuck about what they think.

But this time, I was relatively sober. I didn't know if I should look in their direction or direct my gaze elsewhere. It was uncomfortable. I didn't want to make a big deal about the situation, but I wasn't in the mood to just sit there. I kept scanning the room with my eyes repeatedly resting on them. Dima got drunk, too, and never went home. He came upstairs and fell asleep at my place; in Kustas's nook. Laura went to work in the morning and I left for a while before coming back.

Dima, still just a little drunk, was sitting on a metal patio chair on the sidewalk in front of Cabbages. The sun was shining, Kristo was also there, and Erko brought them glasses of wine. I sat down with them for a spell and had a sip of wine, too. Dima had brought it with him the previous night, but hadn't produced the bottle. He seemed particularly entranced by the atmosphere at Cabbages.

"Hey, Laur, I don't want to complain, but when Dima was holding your hand and stroking it, then I didn't know where else to look. I really don't feel like I need to make a big thing out of it or anything, but it just made me feel uncomfortable. And you looked so happy, too. That's just how things are. For most people, I bet."

"Okay, I'll take that into account in the future."

It was spring and Laura was having all kinds of parties and gathering with her coworkers. Last time, she'd invited me along. Not anymore. But she stayed out late and was sloshed when she made it back home. I tried to instill in myself a sense of carefree kindness for when she finally returned so that no tiff would ensue as if often does when she's sloshed. It tends to happen when I make any comment that's in the least way critical or sarcastic. They come to me so easily and without even managing to think. But Laura doesn't tolerate it to the slightest degree.

"Dima doesn't have it so easy, you know," she began one morning.

"How so?" I asked hesitantly.

"He can't travel around like he'd like to."

"You mean because he's been in jail? You told me he was put away for murder, but he's served his time. If you've served your time, then you shouldn't be punished for the same thing anymore."

I couldn't wrap my mind around how that wispy, smiling and mild bisexual Dima had been put away for murder. I involuntarily wondered whether his bisexuality was connected to his time in prison. He sat there for, what, seven years? But no, it seemed to be his nature. I also involuntarily wondered if that thought was romantic to Laura. Or to all women in general. Laura had been involved with criminals before. I suppose she was attracted to them in some way. Maybe the greatest love of her life was serving time at that moment.

"No. He's got a gray passport. He's totally stateless. But you can only renew once it expires. You can't do anything before that date."

"Okay, but you can still travel abroad for six months before a passport expires. And there are no borders within the EU—travel as you may."

"He just wanted to go to Hungary. He got some job offer. But he couldn't."

"Well, that makes sense. If he wanted to fly, then they check at the airport. He could easily have taken a bus or a train."

"Yeah, well, I don't know."

I couldn't help but think that the two had discussed these things a fair amount earlier. But if Laura could talk about all of it to me so carelessly, then I guess nothing could have happened between them. It couldn't. Even though you could spot the attraction from a mile away.

"Dima's bosses told him that if he got married, then he could get an Estonian passport and travel."

"Yeah, I guess that's right."

"So, Dima started looking around for somebody to marry. He hadn't even dreamed of it before."

"Okay."

♦

I thought I heard a knock at the door. I had no idea who could be. I was lazing around at Laura's; it might have been noon. I opened the door. It was her. Laura peered around the apartment nervously.

"I called you over and over. You didn't pick up."

One time, we'd had a big debacle where I'd fallen asleep at Laura's place while she was at work. She lost her shit—it violated her home rules. That wasn't allowed. I took it personally and left. There've been lots of debacles where I've done something at Laura's home that's not allowed. So, I was nervous. What had I done now?

"Did I do something wrong again?"

"I called you and you didn't pick up and I couldn't get into my own home."

I pulled my phone out of my jacket pocket, which was hanging in the entry-way.

"I've had it on silent since we went to that play yesterday. I didn't hear it vibrate."

Still, Laura was angry because she'd lost her keys. That gave me a sense of relief. I wasn't the one to blame.

"I probably just left them in the mailbox this morning. I've done that before, but some guy always returned them."

"Is it possible you left them at work?"

"I never pull my keys out of my pocket there. Why should I?"

"But maybe they were attached to the keychain with your work keys?"

"We don't *have* any keys to get into work. We've just got buttons. And I would've heard it if my keys had fallen out of my pocket somewhere outside. I probably just left them in the mailbox. I'll go back down to check if they're there sometime. Or maybe I should ask the stylist downstairs. Damn it!"

Laura left and was back in a tick.

"Hey, what's this about leaving your keys in your mailbox? How does that work? Do you not pull them out once you lock it?"

"I never lock my mailbox."

"So why do you put the key in if you never lock it?"

"Sure, fine, maybe I do lock it, but then I sort through what I can just throw away and what not and my hands are full."

We both thought for a moment. I had my laptop open in front of me on the kitchen table. Laura was just standing there, her purse strung over her shoulder.

"Fuck this. I just can't anymore."

I wanted to tell her not to swear; that we'd figure it out somehow. But I faltered. These were currently our only ways forward.

"If you really did forget them in the mailbox, then we should have the lock changed."

"You mean calling a locksmith?"

"That'll take a while. He won't know what kind of lock it is. The call alone costs money. I'll go and see if I can get ahold of the lock."

Laura didn't really believe I could change a lock on my own. I couldn't even change the entryway lightbulb. I managed to screw in the new bulb, but it didn't light up and I didn't know how to fix it.

I studied the lock. It was attached by four screws. Phillips.

"I'm calling a locksmith."

"Go ahead and try if you want."

I unscrewed the screws. Laura didn't call. She scrolled through the internet for a while before she came and stuck her head through the doorway, telling me she'd hold onto the screws for me. Maybe she just couldn't find the right locksmith's number at first.

After working at the screw for a while, I managed to get the lock out of the metal door.

"I'll go have a look around one of those big hardware stores."

"There's a K-Rauta over there in the Tondi neighborhood."

"Where's that at?"

"You know—there's that grocery store and a hardware store somewhere across the street from it.

Alas, they didn't have one. And neither did the store a few streets down. I poked around for a while before I showed the guys my lock.

"You must have bought it at some market. It's Turkish. We don't sell those."

"You might be right." I looked, and what do you know: there were Turkish words imprinted on the side.

"Could you give me any advice?"

"The Lock Experts might have something that size, but I think they're closed today. Maybe."

I didn't know what else to do but to go and check. They were closed. I sat down on the curb with the old lock in my hand, feeling at a total loss. Had Laura been right again? Was I unable to even change a silly lock? I guess so. I called information and got the number for some locksmiths. Russian guys. They agreed to come. It was going just as Laura had expected.

"I've got the lock with me right now. Could you maybe sell me some other lock like the one I have?"

"Well, come here to the office and we'll see."

It was a real adventure tracking them down. The building in the seedy Kopli neighborhood had a large iron door and a black Mercedes parked out front. Two burly Russian guys answered my knocking and inspected the lock.

"No, we don't have anything like this. We can come and change the lock, but not today. Can it wait till Monday?"

"We're supposed to go out. It was actually going to be tonight, but we don't have a single key to lock the door with."

The Russian guys thought for a moment.

"Okay. Twenty-five euros and we'll make new keys for the lock. You'll get them tonight. But not from here. You'll have to come to the Lasnamäe neighborhood."

"Sure. What time?"

"Somewhere around eight. I'll call."

"Sounds good. We lost the keys somewhere in front of the building. Or, well, they might have been in the mailbox."

The guy immediately understood what I meant.

"We'll make the new key so that the old one won't work anymore."

I finally got the lock installed back in the door. Laura was pretty satisfied and I was, too. Who knows what it would have cost to install a whole new lock. They would probably have had to drill through the metal and saw and cut and the old holes would have remained. Now, we could go to the Reps's place for a birthday party.

We were short on cash, so we took the trolley.

There was a big crowd of great people at the party, and also a flock of younger women—all extended family. I was glad to see the hosts, too, and we chatted for a while. We ended up standing with the smokers at the kitchen window for a long time. I didn't notice that Laura was starting to look miserable as she smoked cigarette after cigarette. She asked if I'd bring her some candy and more vodka. I did, even though I wasn't drinking much that evening. I'd been hitting the bottle hard over the last few days and my intestines weren't in the best state already. Laura quickly got drunk; the ash from her cigarette fell straight onto the floor. That made me angry. At her apartment, everything has to be excruciatingly clean, but when she's a guest somewhere and her ash doesn't make it to the ashtray, then she doesn't give a shit.

"You're dropping ash on the floor."

I waited a couple of seconds before getting a rag and wiping it up. Laura didn't even glance in my direction.

"Could you please check what the last trolley time is?"

Laura didn't answer or lift a finger. She had a smart phone and data; I didn't. After a while, I saw she was chatting with someone on her phone.

"Could you please check and see what the last trolley time is?"

She didn't look up, but at least mumbled: "Okay."

I was chatting with those girls a lot. I've known them for years but now, they've changed. They're young women. And they took the time to talk to me. I don't know why they cared to. Tiuks came, too, and it was touching to see her. She'd been in an accident recently and was therefore in a particularly soft or emotional mood—she'd survived. I hugged her delicately.

I saw that Laura had taken a seat at the opposite end of the table. She was smoking and staring absently and had pretty much forgotten she was even smoking. The ash fell onto the floor again.

"Laur, you're dropping ash on the floor again."

She ignored me and didn't even move her head. I didn't know if she was plastered or simply not responding. That happens relatively frequently. I've experienced that behavior in past relationships and it really makes me angry when someone simply ignores me. It's as if I were empty space. I don't think I ever do that to anyone. True—once in an earlier life when it had been done to me for a very long time, I learned to do it myself as well. It's absolutely learned behavior and before long, you honestly don't even hear what the other person is saying. I've also seen others mistreated in that way. When I acted that way, then the person talking certainly got ticked off. They couldn't handle it. With Laura, however, I haven't wished or had the heart to give her a taste of her own medicine. Should I? It might make her understand how awful it feels, but there's hardly a chance it would improve anything between us. You truly don't have to act the way people act towards you. But what if that's the only way to make the person realize what they're doing? Otherwise, they'll just keep on behaving that way. Sure, I probably do all kinds of unkind things all the time, too. I'm sarcastic, but Laura has never been sarcastic back to me.

Still, I couldn't just let Laura keep carelessly dropping ash on the floor and act like it wasn't happening. I wordlessly got a rag and wiped it up again. By now,

I was so pissed off that I didn't even glance at her. I turned my back to her and started chatting with others.

"Bring me one more cocktail," Laura said behind me.

There was an open bottle of tequila on the table, but Laura doesn't drink that. Back in her great romantic days, men would buy shot after shot of it for her at clubs to go home with her. She'd vomited rivers of it from the doors of cabs and couldn't handle it anymore.

Would I really have wanted not to react? I automatically spun around and took Laura's glass.

"What juice do you want with it?"

"Doesn't matter. Mixed."

So, I mixed her a strong cocktail in the other room. Maybe a little too strong. Vodka filled half the glass. I wanted to make her a proper strong cocktail, but that might have been a mistake. Laura was already pretty wasted and we often fight when she gets that way. Full of herself, nose in the air, pride and arrogance and manipulation and telling me to fuck off. Such were my spiteful thoughts.

It was getting close to midnight.

"Laura, please—would you check the last trolley time?"

This time, Laura pulled out her phone and tried to look it up. Inebriation didn't make it very easy, and she lost her temper when she failed to find the time. She tried over and over again.

"Hey, you know, the last trolley will probably leave while we're standing here checking. I think it was sometime around midnight. Let's just get going."

I brought Laura her jacket and stood there, ready to help her put it on. Laura ignored my presence.

"What, so you don't want me to check what time it leaves?"

"Let's just go, otherwise it'll leave without us. Please put on your jacket."

Laura ignored me again. I stood there holding her jacket, not saying a word, for at least a good thirty seconds before I'd had enough. I don't know if anyone noticed what was happening. Finally, I hung her jacket on the edge of the chair, but it slipped off and fell to the floor where her ash had been earlier. I picked it up and hung it back on the chair, but it fell off again. So, I picked up the jacket again and folded it over the back of the chair. It stayed.

I grabbed the three beers I had left in the fridge and stuck them into a plastic bag.

Tiuks noticed me leaving.

"What are you doing?"

Even though I'd just been grumpy with Laura, I felt full of humor talking to Tiuks.

"Caught red-handed."

"Don't go yet."

"You know, that's just the way it is today. Sorry."

Tiuks didn't press me any further, though I was glad she didn't want us to leave yet. Maybe she needed a little bit of company because of the car accident, which had been very hard on her. She hadn't been wearing a seat belt, somebody t-boned her, and Tiuks was slammed against the opposite door. Maybe it was lucky she did, because it would've been much worse if she'd stayed where the car hit her.

I waited by the door to see if Laura was coming. One time—I can't remember if it was under the same circumstances—I was so furious with Laura that I left her drinking there and went home, angry. What'll become of us if that keeps happening? Laura will drink herself determinedly to death as she always says, but that could take a very long time and we might just bicker and bicker until then, just as we have so far. How is this the case? We bickered before we got married but for some reason, we still wanted to. Both of us did. What's wrong with the two of us? Are we idiots or just inherently rude? Yet, we're neither. We can be very civil towards each other, and neither of us are that downright stupid. Come to think of it, though, a lot of people seem to have that problem. Scott and Zelda, for instance. But usually, people also drink heavily in those cases. Just like us.

Tiuks brought me a little bag of strudel to go, as we hadn't had any. We'd only glared at one another and I'd chatted cheerfully with other guests.

"What a nice little bag of strudel, Tiuks!"

Laura finally came to the door. She was swaying a little, but not noticeably, and we made it down the stairs alright.

She walked at a snail's pace, no doubt aware that I was impatient and afraid we'd miss the last trolley. She had no problem moving in slow-motion.

I couldn't make myself keep her pace, so I strode about 50 feet ahead before turning around and waiting for her. This continued until we reached the trolley stop. I tried to read the timetable, but it was dark and I couldn't make out any of the numbers. I stood on my tiptoes and strained to see, but it was hopeless. Another girl standing there illuminated the timetable with her phone—one last trolley was coming in about ten minutes.

Laura finally made it to the bus stop, where she immediately stretched out on the bench and fell asleep. I stood next to her, my head empty of thoughts. The empty minutes dragged out until the trolley arrived. Not to say they were bad empty minutes. I'd stopped being angry with Laura after the walk and the fresh air. Now, the whole situation just seemed a little absurd and funny. I might have chuckled to myself. The girl standing at the trolley stop eyed Laura as she slept, but only out of the very corner of her eye.

All kinds of trolleys approached through the darkness (I guess the streetlight was out of order), but no #4. The lack of light must have been good for Laura's sleep, albeit on a hard bench. A ten-minute nap can be very refreshing for a tired mind. I strained my eyes to read the numbers as the trolleys approached, knowing that it might be difficult to get her up and the driver might not bother to wait while I struggled to lift someone sleeping on the bench. Laura herself probably wouldn't like me trying to lift her, either. Not that she's all that heavy.

The #4 was approaching!

"It's the #4, Laura. Time to get up; we're getting on."

Laura made no sign of recognition or movement. I shook her, trying not to be too rough.

"Laura, get up, please. We're getting on the trolley."

Nothing. Her eyes were still closed. Was it stubbornness, or was she really that deep asleep? Was she irritated, wondering what I was trying to do with her? Wishing I'd just go and leave her there if I really wanted to go? Thinking that she wanted to stay and it was none of my business? How's that song go? *Ain't nobody's business if I do.* That's right. If *I should take a notion to jump into the ocean, it ain't nobody's business if I do. If I go to church on Sunday, and I shimmy down on Monday . . .* That was absolutely written about Laura. Who sang it? I think a lot of artists have. Billie Holiday? Softly and tragically and with swagger. I feel like Laura is Billie's reincarnation. *So I'm gonna do just what I want to anyway, and don't care if you all despise me.*

The trolley pulled up to the stop. Damn it! What a high-maintenance young woman. I resolutely gripped Laura under the arm, tugged her to a sitting position, and then lifted her to her feet. I knew she hates when I do that, using any kind of physical force with her. Even though that song thinks differently: *I would rather my gal would hit me, than to haul right up and quit me.* Ah-ha—this is where you diverge from the song. There was no more time for pampering. Laura was wobbling but standing on her own. I tried leading her to the trolley doors. She shook free of me, stepped onto the trolley herself, and I boarded behind her like a prison guard, carrying my clinking bag of beers.

Laura lurched when the trolley pulled out of the stop. I was afraid she'd fall, so I grabbed her under the arm again. The other passengers watched us, but she didn't care. I didn't care much, either. Even though Laura looks more like she could be my daughter. The scene might have looked like a father angrily pulling his daughter out of some drunken party. A father carrying a bag of beers, that is. I pressed Laura down into a seat, knowing she didn't want me to sit next to her. I plopped down a few seats away, but not so far away that I couldn't react if she were to start falling off the seat. My mood had improved a little, probably because we were creating a comical scene for people. It wasn't all so tragic anymore. Laura fell back to sleep again in seconds.

I heard the word Tedre come over the speakers, so I grabbed Laura under the arm again and carried her out, where I immediately realized we were at the wrong stop.

"I thought they said 'Tedre', but I guess it was 'Next stop: Tedre.' We're going to have to walk one more stop. Sorry."

I took Laura's hand and we walked that way for a few minutes before she pulled free of me again and started pulling antics. She'd stop in her tracks every few steps, staring at the ground in front of her. Just in case, she pushed her fingers into her ears. I had no idea why. To not hear what I was saying? I was silent! Then, she started crying or pretending like she was. The pauses grew longer and longer. Two cyclists went past and I hoped they wouldn't run into Laura, because her slender form was barely visible in the darkness. Whenever we crossed a street, I was worried that she wouldn't care if cars were coming or not and would just stride into the crosswalk without looking in either direction. In fact, however, Laura wound her way through the cars quite carefully. She didn't want to be run over at all; at least not for now.

After waiting for a good couple of minutes while Laura simply stood about 50 feet behind me, I lost it.

"Jesus!" I yelled.

I'd had it with the whole performance. When Laura had come a little closer, I hissed: "Oh, so *I'm* domineering, huh? Which one of us here is domineering, bitching, and taking shit out on the other? Is it me?"

Laura didn't respond.

After walking a few hundred feet and waiting a few yards ahead, as usual, Laura dug the sole keys I'd had made for her earlier that day and flung them at me.

"Go and domineer, then! And leave me alone!"

The keys clinked against the asphalt. I wondered if the magnetic building key, a honking-big chunk of plastic, might break. I didn't check. Instead, I turned around and stomped a fair distance away. But I had nowhere to go—I'd left the keys to my studio at Laura's apartment. My phone was in Laura's purse. She'd flung my telephone to the ground before, too. Even if I had wanted to be temperamental, there weren't too many options. We weren't temperamental together too often—no need for both of us to be stubborn simultaneously. And it's hard to tell who feels they're superior: is it the one who's being temperamental, or the one sneering at the other's petulance? Still, there is usually some reason for sulkiness. Laura must have had one, though I still couldn't figure out what it was. What had gotten her into such a foul mood? Was it me tugging at her sleeve? She'd been acting petulant earlier already. Was it because I pulled her away from the party? Possibly. It'd set her off the last time she wanted to stay boozing with the Repses, too.

I walked maybe another hundred feet and then stopped to wait again. A group of drunk young men was approaching. Three staggering walleyes. I got the impression they might start hitting on Laura and wondered what I might do if they did. Trying to interfere might only make matters worse. No doubt Laura would be able to tell them to fuck off much better than I ever could. There was probably no point in stepping between them too soon. There would be if they really did start trying to drag her off somewhere. At the same time, it'd be even harder to get them to try to release their prey if they'd already made the decision.

Fortunately, the guys didn't see her and turned off onto another street.

By the time we'd passed the grocery store and were somewhere among the tall apartment blocks, Laura quit her ruse and started walking normally, not even swaying. The role had been acted out or she'd gotten tired of it. I've seen it played before. Several times. No doubt I'll see several more.

We crawled into bed, and I felt no emotions. My emotions arrived the following day, upon which I became grumpy. Not that I expressed it all that much. I simply didn't feel like talking. Still, I made sure not to ignore Laura the same way she had ignored me. That wasn't hard to accomplish as, to this day, I've failed to figure out how to not respond to someone addressing you directly. Or, wait—have I learned that trick? I suppose I'd remember if I really tried. But was I all that happy when I mastered the skill and returned the favor? I suppose there was some kind of bitter satisfaction. Not so much happiness.

INTERPRETATION

W E HADN'T SPOKEN much for several days. We'd exchanged only necessary monosyllabic phrases composed of monosyllabic words and
responded to each other mostly with grunts or noes. Even though we didn't
appear to be fighting. It was some kind of a watershed, difficult to describe.
Maybe Knut Hamsun or August Gailit would have been capable of putting it
into words. It was like a period of considering how and in what way to proceed.
You'd think such things would happen in marriages that had lasted for decades.
We hadn't even been married for a year yet.

A hint of amicability crept into that gloomy, quiet state on about the fourth
day. I asked if I could have some of your Coke (to mix into my white wine
so it wouldn't be so sour) and you nodded in a rather friendly way. As if we
were friends. And maybe we really are. As you were leaving, you mentioned that
you actually did have an extra apartment key and showed me where it was so I
wouldn't be stuck there. Even so, I was glad to be stuck in your apartment and
had no intention of going anywhere. I simply wanted to sit and be a gloomy man.
Just like the northern archetype of ancient days.

I don't really believe that either of us are especially northern, though. Guys
with versions of my name are found more in the south somewhere, and you're a
quarter Russian, my Nordic maiden. But I suppose the bleak few centuries our
ancestors have spent in these northern reaches have made us quiet and melancholy.

Whose book was it where someone entered a room where someone else was
already sitting, they sat together for a long time without exchanging a single
word, and then when one stood to leave, they thanked the other person, saying:
"Thanks. It was so nice to be silent in your company."

Maybe that wasn't a book, but from my own life. I can't tell anymore. I
get these things all mixed up. I don't confuse Guatama Siddhārta with Jesus of
Nazareth just yet (remind me of his last name again?), but that time can't be far
off.

◆

Listening to two men talk, I realized they seemed to be waiting for when their wives will finally cheat on them, or have at least played through the scenario in their minds. When one heard that the other's wife had been adulterous, but he was still living with her, he said: "That sure wouldn't fly with me." And when I asked the other if he knew whether or not his wife had slept with someone else—a wife he supports to stay at home while he himself sleeps around—he said: "I've got no idea, but if I were to find out, then it'd at least be a good reason."

"To kick her out?"

"Yeah."

I thought to myself that if I were that woman, then there was no chance I'd dare to sleep with someone else. I'd have no career, no income, and be kicked out onto the street. I certainly wouldn't have the guts to cheat, even if I wanted to. I simply don't dare to sleep with anyone else. I'm afraid of losing my spot in paradise. And more than that, I'm afraid I'm just a loser. I'm not that dashing cowboy who flips over tables and fucks left and right. I've also kind of had it with women who go for those bold Clint Eastwood-types.

So, what leads to those damn morals? Exhaustion? Cowardice? Comfort and laziness? A conscience and a starry sky above? Pure human congeniality? Although people are alike in the majority of things, they differ in terms of that, for some reason.

"The more I know, the more I realize I *don't* know."

That general philosophy of Aristotles stuck with me for some reason. I repeated it to another smart man over beers.

"Yes, that's just how it is," he said.

I was almost disappointed. I'd hoped he would disprove it. The idea sounded a little haughty. What does 'the more I know, the less I know' really mean? It means pride in knowing so much that there are even more things I don't know. And you don't know so much—there's much less that you don't know.

What's the point of wisdom if it's not accompanied by niceness? No one wants to hear that wisdom. And then, the wise man is left alone and sad with all his knowledge. Doesn't he know that being too proud just won't do? Being too submissive won't do, either, I suppose.

Therefore, I can certainly find out more things, but that knowledge might no longer be valid tomorrow. And will our mind's capacity be greater than yesterday, or do we just switch out knowledge like romance in our hearts? And then—oh, yes—we love the whole world and know a little something about everything, albeit not all of it. Does a person who loves and understands everyone and all things not get angry at a biting mosquito? Or at annoying music coming through the wall from the neighboring apartment? Where do they even live? And would I want to be like them in the first place? I don't even know that.

A claim might be true if it can be flipped around. The less I know, the wiser I am, the more things I know, and the less things I don't know. It sure sounds good. Maybe that means it really is true.

◆

"Nina was likely reminded of this thing or of that." Artsybashev[10] wrote that. And who was the French writer who said he had no idea what his character was thinking, but was sure that they opened the door with their left hand? Maybe they're just singing their own praises—why would they write if they didn't know what their character was thinking? Though maybe that is a nice little trick. I don't really know what I'm thinking, either. There are just emotions and semi-inexpressible semi-formed thoughts flickering in my mind. How can you describe those with words? You can only hint at them. Literature excites you and afflicts you all at once. Just like love. Dealing with your feelings. I suppose music, too. Can literature and music replace love when you don't have enough of it at any moment? And when love happens to arrive, then there's not much time for writing. I suppose the most talented poets didn't write very much, anyway. The Byrons and the Pushkins didn't write a single yard of titles altogether—they spent their time on simply loving. Not that they lived to a very old age. Maybe there'd have been more time for writing alongside romance in their later years, like Goethe. And who the hell knows which is better. One thing's for certain, though: they weren't building any buildings or doing any social work in addition to their writing and romance. They could fight in wars, drink vodka with officers, and play cards. But any sort of practical, reasonable activities? Give me a break.

◆

What does Dylan mean when he sings, *You've got to serve somebody*? I bet he doesn't really mean anything; he doesn't know what the point is. He himself once said that the words just come to him. Is he lying? Who knows. There's not much more sense to Cohen's words, either, even though one writes songs in five minutes and the other takes five years. And as for songs that are well-known, I don't know who has more. Maybe Dylan, though Cohen's hits are more overplayed. When Cohen spends five years writing a song, does he still not mean why the lyrics mean? *First we take Manhattan, then Berlin*. And what then? The Jews? Why? Do they themselves even get each other's lyrics? Two old Jews. Maybe they do. And you don't always have to understand everything. And whom of us isn't a Jew? How do I know I'm not? Maybe I am.

You've got to serve somebody. Well, it may be the Devil or it may be the Lord.

But what if you don't want to serve? Maybe that's the trick. Dylan may not be all that inclined to serve anybody, but he knows it'd end badly. In order to be saved, you've got to try to save somebody else. That already sounds Christian. Though Dylan does start ranting about Old Testament stuff when he gets going, saying that he'd rather be hanging around with King David in some cave than live in modern-day America. Nevertheless, *you've got to serve somebody*. Is that an obligation, or is it more like: "Hey, buddy—you've got no other choice."

I am indeed a slave to something—to the illusions I've been fed and adopted as my own. Vonnegut, another Jew, wrote: "Live by the foma" (i.e. harmless untruths). If you don't want to be a slave to money, then just choose some other opossum or a woman or a god or a car. Or even yourself. Still, it's a little ridiculous and pitiful to be your own slave. And man isn't exactly the very best slavedriver of himself, because then he can't be bothered to take proper care of himself. But as Peeter Volkonski remarked while constructing his "slave democracy" concept: "A slave master must always take care of his slave."

Dylan's lyric seems to imply that the slave himself chooses his master (and knows no other way). Whom do I want for my master? Laura is already, to some extent. But whom else? Kids? The Republic of Estonia? I haven't a clue. Great masters seem to be scarce. There isn't even faith that they might be found in the West, and much less in Russia. Do we have to create and raise our very own slave master?

If you're given a choice of what prison to serve time in next, is there really any point in rushing off to try a new one? I'd rather keep sitting here and make do with you. A revolt occasionally arises, but they've become weaker and weaker. The lower and upper strata are sitting together with beers and can't even remember which one didn't want it and which didn't have it in them.

NATURE

YOU BROUGHT A little basket along when we were out of town visiting some friends. It was empty. You didn't mention it and I didn't ask. I figured you were going to give it to someone as a gift. Why, though? We were staying for two days. We don't fuck when we're staying at anyone else's place anymore. I guess that means that we don't have much of an appetite for it at any cost. That we don't want to draw attention to ourselves. Those things didn't use to bother us, way back when.

While we were sleeping on mats on the floor of the open-plan living room/kitchen of our friends' house, I felt that you were more sympathetic towards me, laying your arm over my body repeatedly throughout the night. That hasn't happened in a very long time, and it made me feel good. Like we were intimate. Like we cared for each other. There have sometimes been long gaps between such indications. Maybe people just get tired of intimacy and tenderness can then seem fake. But it's saddening when it cycles between one wanting intimacy and the other not, then vice-versa. When the search for intimacy doesn't pan out, you give up. There's no point in pushing. But then, you're heartbroken. You sit alone with your need for intimacy, knowing that you won't go looking for it anywhere else, either.

I could tell that you were just being friendly because whenever you used to be turned on, you'd lay your arm over mine and then stroke me softly, no matter if it was my shoulder, my hand, or my chest. That was certainly nice and sublime. Then, we could spend a long time delaying sex while relishing simply being close and cuddling. But that hasn't happened in ages. It was nice to fall asleep with your arm draped across me now. It felt like you were showing warmth, and I was full of warmth myself. There wasn't much to talk about in general. I felt like asking why you had brought the basket, but the longer I didn't, the stranger it felt to bring it up.

Maire apparently noticed the empty basket, too, because she stuffed it with a jar of black currants and a chunk of Norwegian cheese and a little zucchini. They all fit snugly.

"Oh, thank you," you said awkwardly.

Sweltering, summery Haapsalu was dusty and devoid of people. Everyone was inside watching the Olympics. Maybe in London, where they were being held, people were also sitting indoors and watching the games on TV. The streets of London are always full of people, anyway, and maybe some Haapsalu residents were also there in the choked thoroughfares.

The bus back to Tallinn was empty. I pulled money out of my pocket as we boarded.

"Don't buy me a ticket to Tallinn," you said softly and quickly.

"Where, then?"

"I want to go mushroom-picking."

"Alone?"

"I don't care."

The driver waited patiently.

"Where do you want to go to pick mushrooms, then?"

"Doesn't matter. I don't know any good spots."

You gave the driver a pleading look.

"Could I please just buy a ticket when I get off somewhere? I don't know where I'm going yet. Somewhere wooded."

"There's woods everywhere," the driver said, furrowing his brow.

"Somewhere with pines."

"Pines?"

"Yeah. And mushrooms. A good place to forage for mushrooms."

"Mushrooms?"

"Yeah."

"I don't know where there's good woods for mushroom-picking. I never go."

All three of us were silent and unsure of what to do.

"I just don't know the right places," you repeated. "Give me a ticket to the stop at the crossroads by the big highway. I'll just get off somewhere before then."

You handed over the money.

The driver wordlessly issued you the ticket and gave back change, then waited to hear my request. I didn't know what to say, so I just sighed.

"Give me the same ticket then, too."

We took our seats and didn't talk. I couldn't tell if you wanted me to get off with you or not. I remembered you telling me about how you and your parents would go foraging for mushrooms when you were a kid. I guess you needed it now. I'd confessed that I'd never gone mushroom picking; maybe that's why you hadn't told me you wanted to go. What was I going to do now, when I got off the bus and you went into the woods? Sit down on a stump? Stretch out on the moss and try to nap? We'd slept in late that morning. The most miserable option would be to just walk around with you, though I wanted to cling to the train of your dress. And more miserable than that would be if I tried to strike up a conversation. Any topic would be pointless. I was at a loss for what to do. Your past life had broken into ours. Nothing was bad about that; I was just confused. And you weren't speaking.

It started raining. I hoped that maybe you'd cancel your plans and we'd just get new tickets from the crossroads stop to Tallinn. But you were staring at the streaks running down the window with a look of hope on your face. Would the downpour make the mushrooms sprout? I started to suspect that you anticipated I wouldn't get off in the rain, even if you still did. And then, you could be alone. I'd just be an annoyance. So, why couldn't I just let you go alone? You won't disappear in the woods like a werewolf. Nothing would go wrong. Still, I knew I would be in dire straits alone. All I'd do was go to a pub and drink so as not to be drinking alone at home, waiting for you to come back all happy from mushroom-picking. And if I were to get hammered, I'd feel guilty when you returned, elated. And just to escape the guilt, I might start picking on you to rile you up. I knew how it'd go and could imagine it already. But given that I already knew and could imagine the course of events, wasn't there any way to get around it? Not really. It's one thing to think everything through, but another to behave differently once the moment has arrived. It just slips right back into the pattern of behavior you've foreseen. I felt like rebelling; like demanding to know why you had to go and stir up this whole fiasco and make things go south with us. But that would've been a shitty thing to do. Nothing had gone south with us yet. So, I just sighed noticeably, hoping you'd realize the danger this was creating. But you didn't hear it. You continued staring intently at the forest alongside the room, which was obscured by the driving rain.

"Let's go another day, Laura. When it's' not raining . . . and I'll bring a knife and a basket," I proposed cautiously.

Again, you didn't hear me or simply didn't reply, which of course got me worked up in turn. Why did you have to ignore me?

Finally, you spoke.

"You don't *go* mushroom picking. You don't like to. Even berry picking put you in a terrible mood when you were a kid. You've told me that before."

"Yeah," I sighed. "Yeah, it did."

The rain had lightened up a little. You appeared to have lost your patience waiting for the right kinds of woods. Maybe the right kind can't be found along the highway to Haapsalu. You got up and went to the front of the bus. I didn't know what to do. You spoke to the driver but the bus didn't stop. Then, you sat in an empty seat in the front row and stared out the windshield. We weren't in any kind of a fight. Nothing was wrong at all. I couldn't understand why it felt like that, anyway, or what to do about it.

As the bus pulled into the next stop, I watched to see what you'd do. You remained seated. Two people boarded and bought tickets. From where I was sitting, it seemed like maybe you were crying. I waited a few moments before edging down the aisle to the front. There were no tears in your eyes. You were just holding your hands around them and studying the roadside. I stood next to you.

"You can come if you want to," you said without looking at me.

That suddenly lifted my spirits. I didn't care that it meant pointlessly getting off in a random place; at least we'd be together. And not fighting.

"I'd be happy to."

I seemed to have robbed you of your mushroom-nostalgia and a chance to be alone, but you'd come to terms with it.

◆

It was my first time being in the woods in years, I think. There were tall pines and thick, soft moss beneath our feet. Blackberries. Only a few mosquitos and horseflies, just like being back in someone's childhood. Something familiar. Pleasant. Still, I immediately discovered that I didn't know what to do. Not as familiar as it seemed. I munched on some wild blackberries. The sound of some boys riding a dirt bike down a path buzzed in the distance. *That* was familiar. The berries were good, but I didn't feel like eating many. I walked along a straight clearing that ran through the woods, but where was I going? It led nowhere. I'd just end up coming back from nowhere. I felt like sitting down. But where? Stumps were a little too slimy. The moss was filled with pine needles and probably somewhat damp. It was pleasant and nostalgic and boring. I wondered if I could leave already. I wish I could sigh in bliss and gush about how wonderful it is in the woods—it is, of course, but I still have no idea what to do there.

◆

Summer flew by and I hadn't done a thing. Or, well, I hadn't gone to the countryside or spent time by the sea. I haven't in several summers, actually. Now, the mornings are cool and fall-like, even though it's only August. The chill air gusts through the window when I go into the kitchen to rinse my mouth of the nasty taste left by last night's drinking, then curl back up to sleep next to Siskin. I repeat the process several times over the course of the morning, starting at around five or six and until I get up at eleven. I don't do anything after that, and neither do I want to.

But now, Ülo invited me to go kayaking with him in the evening, and I felt like it was a shame. It was a shame to give up my doing of nothing. Already regretting it, I went anyway. It was rather nice, though I occasionally felt like it was the act of doing nothing. How could that be possible? Me doing nothing is like an activity in and of itself, but this enjoyable activity was like a break from nothing with nothing. I was grateful.

Kaarel came over the next evening with the bizarre idea of blowing bubbles. Siskin and I blew bubbles at the windowsill while Kaarel took pictures. When the sun started to set and the light changed, the color of the bubbles changed as well. Their kaleidoscopes became more unique and they floated farther over the yard. Still, I was bothered the whole time by the feeling that I was wasting time. Instead of doing what, though? Instead of the nothing I'd done all morning. All I'd done was sit at my desk and write a few lines. That itself has become a delusion, but one that's somehow nice to hold onto—sitting at a desk all day long and only writing a few lines of text.

All the same, those two afternoons were some of the nicest that summer—kayaking and bubble-blowing. The fact that I wasn't able to fully enjoy them is my own problem. I suppose I've lost the habit or the ability or the desire itself.

MEDICATION

"Daddy, I've got that dermatitis thing again, I think."

"Is that right?"

"Yeah, it hurts. And I've got a blister on my tongue."

Siss stuck a forkful of macaroni into her mouth and to show me just how painful it was, she immediately squeezed out a tear.

"I can't eat anymore."

"But you said you wanted macaroni."

"Yeah. I'm hungry."

"Then chew on the other side of your mouth."

"I'm trying, but it hurts in the middle."

"Show me."

Siss swallowed her food and stuck her tongue out. I checked but couldn't see anything.

"I'll take a picture of my tongue and show it to you. Then you'll see where I've got the dermatitis."

Siss aimed her phone's camera at her tongue. I wondered if the macaroni hadn't turned out right. She didn't take a picture, but just used the phone to scrutinize her tongue,

"I can just use this as a mirror to see my tongue, too. I can see the blister."

"Show me again. Turn a little more towards the window so there's more light."

Upon closer inspection, I spotted the tiny gray blister on her tongue.

"I can see it now. I'm not sure if dermatitis can come back a year later. Maybe it can. Just like someone who used to live in this apartment coming back."

"Someone who lived here and died?"

"Died or moved away."

"Someone who moved to another apartment or the afterlife."

"It looks like it's not really hurting too much."

"Sometimes it doesn't, but other times it does. Like when I think about it."

"Then don't think about it. Though I reckon you can't not think, huh?"

"Nope."

"Well, try to eat a little more. I'll go look and see if we still have some of that cream left. The one we used the last time. Do you remember me rubbing a little bit of that cream in your mouth?"

"I think so."

"I can't have you starving. What did you eat when you had dermatitis?"

"Macaroni."

"But this is macaroni."

"It was a different kind of macaroni," Siskin sighed.

"I'll check if we've got that cream. Did you leave it here or at your mom's place?"

"I can't remember."

"Okay. Eat a little more if you can, please."

The medicine drawer was full of all different kinds of drugs that I'd collected over the years for hangovers and who knows what else. Heart medication, stomach medication, liver medication, pancreas medication. The old hypochondriac I am. None for any deathly illness. There were, however, some of Kusti's medications that I hadn't thrown away after his death. I had no idea what they were for. High blood pressure? I could check. Maybe someone else could use them. Or I could take them myself from time to time as a preventative measure, like Pippi Longstocking. Medicine is expensive stuff. How can you throw any away? I'd written the use for some of it on the packaging. I had a box of something called HerzASS for thrombosis. Margus saw it one time and asked: "So, are things really that bad with your heart?" It turned out to just be aspirin. Still, aspirin certainly comes in handy when you're hungover, short of breath, and your heart is overworked and your blood coursing slowly.

I couldn't find any dermatitis cream. None of the tubes looked anything like it.

I did, however, find Exoderil—athlete's foot cream. What real difference could there be? I bet the ingredients were the same. Some skin thing.

"Honey, I didn't find any dermatitis cream, but here's one for athlete's foot. I think it can go on your tongue, too. Should I put some on?

"Okay," Siskin said, and stuck out her tongue.

I squeezed at the tube for a few moments, but it was mostly dried up. A big splurt finally came out of the very end of the tube, and I spread it over her tongue with my fingertip. There was a lot of it, but I didn't want to waste any so I spread it all the way over the edges of her tongue.

"How's it taste?"

"I dunno. A little sweet, maybe."

"I should probably finish your milk for you now."

"Yeah. I didn't really want any more."

There were dark cookie crumbs floating on the surface. She'd dunked the cookies and eaten them, but then lost her appetite for the milk.

I gulped down the dermatitis-cookie-crumb milk.

"Daddy, I want to have the candy Kaarel gave me now."

"Can't you wait a little while? Otherwise, you'll just eat the cream off of your tongue."

Siss waited a little with a pouty look on her face, spinning the pineapple-flavored candy in and out of its wrapper.

"Alright. If you can't wait any longer, then go ahead and eat it, I suppose."

She did.

That night when Siskin was going to bed, I asked her if I should rub some more athlete's foot cream on her tongue.

"Okay," she said.

So, I did.

◆

It goes around and around and always at the same pace, and you can never seem to get out. For a long time, you manage to drink moderately, not much at all. Six to ten beers a day, but spread out over that whole day. You don't even feel a buzz as you sip them, but they still give a pleasant feeling. It's nice to just listen to the silence, read, and write. Whole weeks can tick away like that, and maybe it really is for the best. You'd drink much more if you were actively social. The momentum would start to fade. But if you tipple at that same pace for a long time, then the quantity of beer no longer has any effect and sipping away feels like a waste—of time, beer, and money alike. All you feel is numbness and nothing seems to get done. In order to counter that feeling, you have to increase the quantities and switch up the beverages. Say, a bottle or bottle-and-a-half of wine in addition to the beer. Ah-ha! Then, you feel it again for a while. But only just a little. The cycle becomes shorter because before long, the wine doesn't have much of an effect anymore, either, though you don't want to end it just yet. You'd like to keep drinking and writing and just being. So, all you can do is add a little bit of hard alcohol to the mix. It gives you a short boost, of course, but then leaves you feeling exhausted and your innards start to ache. By then, it's clear that you have to take a break and get out of your intoxicated state soon. Things can get pretty hairy before that break and you find yourself not enjoying the buzz or writing or doing anything else. It ends up being no more than dull boozing, which, to be fair, can also be rather zen. Sitting around, listening to music. That's the break before the break. A break from thinking and being. But you also start to feel that your body is reaching some boundary it wouldn't like to cross. Then, it's over and you need to put the drink aside. That part's not too difficult, but it's best to find some kind of an activity to distract you from heading down to the shop. For in that state, there's no other activity. There's only lying around in bed, bouts of heavy perspiration, insomnia, and diarrhea. And agony. The agony is downright miserable. It's like a fear of death, even though your mind is telling you there's no death in sight. It's nice when you can hold onto someone. You can moan and groan for a while to console yourself, but that will wear anyone else down to death.

On those occasions, I lie awake at night and cling to you, damp with sweat and sometimes shivering. I try to hold you as delicately as I can so you don't wake up and pull away from me, because you find it annoying. I'm not feeling great, so I roll over onto my other side. Even with my back turned towards you, I try to press my bare behind against your body, preferably against your own bare bottom. Or I'll gently touch your buzzed scalp and listen to your soft breathing or snoring. It's not so bad anymore, being next to you. But in the morning when you leave and I've only slept a little and the sun wakes me up, the misery is oppressing. I don't feel like doing anything—not eating, not reading. The only activity I am able or motivated enough to indulge in is tossing and turning between the damp sheets, which also seems unbearable. Sure, I might take a bath, but I just feel sweaty again as soon as I get out.

One time, I stayed that way until you came home later in the afternoon, and you were livid when you found me. I couldn't understand why—I hadn't done anything wrong! But you were just silent and angry, so I—silently as well—got dressed and beat it. I headed to my studio, where I lay around missing you, though I couldn't go back because we were both angry.

◆

This time, it all started with drinking wine. I figured I'd buy a cheap bottle from Marks & Spencer. They sell budget wines that aren't so bad. There it was—a white wine with a handsome green label for just a little over three euros. It would be a little sour, but I planned to mix it with kvass anyway, to be easier on my stomach. I'd need to buy a big bottle of kvass so Siskin could have some, and there'd still be enough left for mixing drinks. On the other hand, one bottle of wine isn't enough to go with a two-liter bottle of kvass. So, I took three. And then I added a bottle of red for variety.

At the checkout, they said: "Did you know that there's a ten-percent discount if you buy six bottles of wine?"

I hesitated for a moment. So it goes . . .

"Fine, I'll take six," I said, and went back to the wine shelf. If I hadn't, then I'd just end up regretting it until I went back to the store and bought six more. "Sure is quite the collection," I mumbled when I shuffled back to the register.

The young man folded a little nicely-designed carrier for the six bottles and said: "Well, I'm sure they'll come in handy over time."

"Sure, over time," I grunted, wondering what that 'time' would be. Two days? Three? Maybe even four? *Over time*. And then, you'll be right back in the place where you have to switch over to hard alcohol again.

◆

Consequently, there's come a break from work and pointless meditation. Who cares. Though the Uus Maailm Festival was also coming up and I wouldn't be doing anything else during it, anyway. I'd just have a dumb, guilty feeling if I were to shut myself away in my room for the whole festival. Others had done a lot of work to make it all come together, and I wouldn't be showing any respect. And at the same time, you can't go to the events and not drink! There are even more parties like that in Brazil.

When the wine was starting to run out, I bumped into Andrei Hvostov, who was already working on a bottle of pepper vodka. We wanted to hang out, but couldn't think of anything better to do than sit side by side on the couch in Mihkel's apartment, stare at a spot on the wall five feet in front of us, and mostly not speak. Mihkel himself was away picking grapes with Ibsen and Marta in Italy. Merit was in the other room with Iti. She peeked in to check on us from time to time and see if we were even still there, because we were simply hanging around. It felt nice, having a comrade with whom all you do is sit around in silence. Although I suppose that special kind of seated silence is a form of communication, too. Leisurely conversation. A remark would occasionally be made, and then, after the long intervening pause, the conversation seemed to continue, or you sensed or imagined what your companion thought and felt about the issue. Even so, it would have been improper to ask or push him about it directly. I suppose he'll express himself in some way no matter what.

For I don't know how many days, I'd been in a condition where I kept having to go to the bathroom to fart. The bathroom was necessary because the gas would be accompanied by a spray of light red blood, which would also just trickle between my ass cheeks and needed to be wiped away every once in a while. Yet when that much blood was seeping out, then the acid that makes your crack ache stopped coming. I smeared baking soda and medicine over it. Many people have survived this before me, and some of them have held on for a very long time. Others never touch a drop of booze but still lose their zest for life.

I was flying high, in any case. I fried some potatoes with ground beef and onion. The apartment door was open, unannounced guests flowed in and out of my greasy kitchen, and I strove to feed them all as well as I could. Siskin's friends came around. Peeter Krull, whom I hadn't seen in ages, stopped by with his family. Kaarel stood and ate next to the fridge because my dusty stools had run out. "Has the cook gotten anything to eat, too?" he asked.

I wasn't hungry, even though the potatoes smelled delicious. I'd bought some big red potatoes, chopped them into fine slices, and rinsed them before tossing them onto the pan. Everyone complimented the taste.

"Oh, I'll eat soon," I answered. I enjoyed the smell but didn't want to shovel any down, even though I knew I should probably put something in my belly besides alcohol.

"Daddy, do you know what my most terrible birthday was?" Siskin asked.

I paused to think. No doubt it was the time she held her birthday party at the commune and, since I didn't feel like hanging around sober, I got roaring drunk. I suppose that made her pretty sad, but I didn't want to rummage any deeper in those memories.

"I don't know, honey."

"It was when you and Mom both drank," Siss informed me sunnily, "and then you argued the whole day." A split second later, huge tears started streaming down her cheeks. "And that was my birthday . . ."

"How old did you turn?" I asked, trying to sound casual.

"I dunnooo." Siskin was sobbing inconsolably.

"Come here, honey." And she did, obediently, and I hugged her and massaged her back for a while. There wasn't much point in talking. If only I could have come up with a way to change the topic! That can't be forced, however—Siskin would realize what was happening and might not go along with it. So, I was simply silent. My t-shirt became damp with her tears as I held her. It was sad, but also very intimate. I suppose Siskin could also sense the intimacy and needed it.

The boozing in the kitchen and the crying nevertheless had an effect, because Siss wordlessly put on her jacket and left as soon as Grettel went. She called only a few hours later and told me softly that she was staying at her mother's house that night, even though she was supposed to be with me for a while longer. It's good that she at least has an alternative. Whenever the bottles start opening in one home, she can just switch, and drinking usually doesn't go on in both simultaneously. I guess we'll see how she turns out. Probably a teetotaler. Or maybe the opposite.

I lay in bed, alone in the dark with Siskin's blanket and pillow still next to me. I'd wound down my drinking, having only a few weak shots and rationing the pepper vodka so it wouldn't run out before morning.

I couldn't sleep, so I called Laur. She picked up but was silent.

"What're you doing there?"

"Did you go to the festival? Are you there now? I guess you're not. It's so quiet."

Laur had said she would come and help to clean dishes. I'd watched her out of the corner of my eye but didn't approach her, as we'd been in dire straits lately. Neither of us probably knew who was presently feeling hurt because of whom anymore. Occasionally, one of us would call the other when they couldn't bear any more loneliness and had drunk enough. Still, it's not easy to get back on the same page when you're called by your drunk spouse at whom you're pissed. I'd hoped that Laur would come up and spend a little time with me and Siskin, which would help us make amends. We don't get into fights when Siskin's around. From another perspective, Laur was probably angry that Siss had been with me for a month already while she was just sitting around at home alone. We used to be able to do things as the three of us. Now that happens less and less, as if Laur can tell that I get something from Siskin that I can't get from her. Siss doesn't seem to have any problem with it, though. So far, at least, she can't even imagine that Laura and I fuck and she has no part in it. She doesn't know what fucking is. But what'll happen when she finds out?

"You're not talking again," I sighed. "Great stuff."

"It's not great. I didn't come. I'm sick."

"What's wrong?"

"I don't know. I've got a fever."

"Is it serious?"

"No, it's going down already. I had it for a few days."

"I can just imagine you at home. You don't eat. You don't pull the couch out or maybe even lay sheets over it. You're lying around in a dark room, alone and silent. Well, maybe the TV's on. But I can't hear it right now."

"I don't have the TV on. It's late already. I'm tired."

"That means you don't want me coming over. Am I right? I would have otherwise . . . You're not answering."

I didn't want to tell her that Siskin left for her mom's place because then, it'd be obvious that I didn't think of her much when my daughter was here, but now that she was gone and my home was filled with sadness, I was thinking of her. I felt like a little boy who wanted to hold his mommy's hand. It hadn't crossed my mind that she'd been sad for a whole month. All I do is drink and have fun with Siss and hug and kiss her. Well, I actually did think of Laura every now and then. When Siss fell asleep, for example. And not only because I felt like I wanted to have sex with Laur, though that naturally was the main reason.

"I'm tired."

"You don't even say that you don't know, because you're tired. You don't even leave the tiniest shred of doubt that you don't want me over. And now, I bet you're going to shut up completely."

She did. What could she answer, anyway? I was afraid she'd be the first to simply hang up, and then I'd be devastated. So, I spoke first.

"Bye, then."

I strained my ear in miserable fear to hear if she'd respond.

"Bye."

It was almost below a whisper and followed immediately by a click. Whew. At least that was something. Maybe we wouldn't be divorcing just yet.

I didn't stay tossing in bed for very long the next morning. The mixture of apple juice and pepper vodka, dosed in very small quantities for medicinal purposes, was starting to run out, regardless. I didn't feel like buying a new bottle. I had to find some activity to avoid feeling sorry for myself and thinking about drinking. I went down to the basement to shower. It's the 'writers' bathhouse' where you've got to pay attention to where you leave your slippers and take any step with washed feet on the muddy floor if you don't feel like looking for the mop to wipe up a bit. I went back upstairs and had to change to a fresh t-shirt several times before going out, because I sweat each one through in just a few minutes. Blood was coming out of my behind like earlier.

Laura wouldn't be coming home for half a day more. Maybe her apartment would be a nice change of scenery, as long as there isn't an opened bottle of wine in the fridge that I'd guzzle down before probably going out to buy a new one. Once you start, it's probably going to continue. Breaks must begin in the morning.

COMPLIMENTS

I WAS HANGING around Laura's apartment for the first time in quite a while. Orderliness and emptiness, as always. I wouldn't be getting anything done today, anyway. Tomorrow would probably also go by with me staring off into space and crawling out of the crater. It'll still be hard to get motivated or stoke a desire to do anything. I turned on Laura's computer and connected to the internet. Laura. I should ask her if I'm allowed to be here. I waited for the connection, then sent her an email: "Could I use the internet on your computer today?"

I felt I shouldn't surf around on her computer before she approved, so I sat in the armchair and stared at the white translucent curtain. It obscured everything from both inside and out. Only light passed through. I could have pulled the curtain away and stared at the treetops and the roof of the neighboring building, but I didn't. The basic white curtain made the room feel like a hospital.

Laura still hadn't sent a reply, so I called her.

"Do you think I could maybe use your computer today? I'm actually here already."

"Um . . . sure." I thought I sensed a note of pleasant surprise in her voice. A gentle tone.

"Okay, I will then."

My mood suddenly shot skyward, tensions began to fade, and I thought about going out and bringing back a couple of beers anyway. I resisted the thought for a while as I looked around online, but it came back again and again. I couldn't even find peace on the internet. Better to just go and get those couple of beers.

So, I did.

I occasionally checked the time to see when Laura would be arriving. The beer had softened my mood again and beaten back the despair. I didn't feel like being on the computer, so I went back to the armchair and stared at the curtain I couldn't see through. The thought of Laura and I fucking kept coming back to mind again and again.

I also decided that when she came home, we shouldn't dig up that protracted fight anymore—even though I knew what I was upset about and didn't quite know what had upset her. We should just pretend like it had never happened. Could I do that? We should also try to keep things good from that point onward. If I were to swallow that thorn, would it still jab back up regularly? And would those times be even worse? What choices did I have? Turning tail and running away? Arguing first and then booking it? Or somehow dismissing myself?

The thought didn't fully occupy my mind, but I had time. Images of us fucking occasionally resurfaced, followed by wondering if I'd be capable of not arguing. I took sip after sip of beer and I didn't leave. Then, she came home.

I stood up. Neither of us knew what to say or wanted to be the first to say it. I simply stood there and Laura did, too. *Yeah, haven't seen you in a while. Hey, yeah. Hey. We needed some time.* I sat down again. Laura took off her jacket and walked around, doing this and that. I stood up involuntarily and walked over to her.

"Should we fuck?"

Laura stared at me.

"No."

And she continued as before.

I sat back down. The energy drained out of me. Still, we gradually warmed back up to each other and I went out to buy us more drinks—a dark and a wheat beer for me, sparkling wine for her as always—and we later went back to the shop together to buy food for dinner and cooked. I could tell that she hadn't been eating much recently. Probably because she was out of money. Not that I had very much myself.

"Did you think you could just show up here and I'd come home and we'd just get right down to business fucking? Is that it?"

"I don't know. I wasn't thinking anything. I figured I'd ask just in case. I'd started thinking about fucking when I was sitting here."

Laura didn't respond. I thought with a grain of bitterness about how she'd given accounts of her earlier sexual encounters before. Many of them contained scenes where someone simply walked in and all they did was fuck. Were those men all somehow better than me?

I, on the other hand, hadn't really given many accounts of my own encounters to her. I couldn't remember them in great enough detail to describe any. Why try to paint them in broad strokes? Even so, I described them as well as I could whenever asked.

It felt like we really might manage to avoid digging up our old unresolved argument. For whatever reason, I didn't feel like bickering or doggedly pursuing my truth. It wasn't out of a sense of nobleness, but laziness. I was simply enjoying us. Voicing what had offended me wasn't worth throwing a wrench in the gears. On top of that, it was good to see Laura again. I had the urge to touch her, but was afraid she'd push my hand away or, even worse, freeze up like we were complete strangers and had zero connection with each other.

So, I kept my distance and sat in the armchair by the window.

"You compliment Siskin all the time," Laura suddenly said softly, "but you never say anything nice about me. Or do you? I certainly can't remember."

I felt a wave welling up within me.

"Excuse me?" I tried to stifle myself, unsuccessfully. "What are you talking about?! You're my wife. That's all I need to say. Full stop. I don't see any reason why I should go around trumpeting your praises. You wouldn't be my wife if you weren't praiseworthy, but I just don't see any reason to have to do it. That's bullshit."

The more I said, the more I was losing control. It was just the next injustice in a long line of injustices.

"Do you think you give *me* any compliments, huh?"

"I don't compliment anybody else, either."

"Siskin is a child. She doesn't live with me, for the most part. There's nothing making her be nice to me or want to hang out, but she is, and she wants to. And I'm glad that's the case. I'm thankful. Is there anything wrong with that?"

"You tell me."

We were both silent for a few moments.

"I was alone for a month," Laura said. "You were with Siss. You were having a good time. No other thought crossed your mind."

"What do you think I should have done then, huh?" What's more, I remembered that Laura and I had gone on two multiple-day trips over the course of that one month: to Tartu and Helsinki. Now, it was like they'd never happened. When Laura and I took a cab back from the ferry terminal, she grabbed her plastic bags of pretty new clothes from the trunk and disappeared into her own apartment without saying a word. It took me a few long seconds before I could tell the driver my address. On the way to Koidu Street, all I could think about was how I'd paid for that whole trip for you. And how I'd waited in McDonald's while you shopped. And how McDonald's is the last place I'd want to sit and wait for someone.

My stomach was churning. I got up and stormed to the bathroom. Nothing came out, though; not even a fart. I sat and waited patiently.

We were both harboring acute feelings of how unfair the other had been. And I still couldn't wrap my head around the thought that *I'd* acted unfairly. Raskolnikov didn't want to wrap his mind around it, either. Alas, there's no other way to live. Otherwise, you should just put a bullet in your head or voluntarily go to a Siberian forced labor camp. Sure—I did abandon you and do nothing but play with Siskin and hug and kiss her while putting her to bed. Now let me don my hat, go find myself a Russian Sonya, and head off to the Gulag. Sure—truth be told, you do look like a Nurse Sonya, but a little like a dour and poisonous Nurse Sonya, not boundlessly mild and kind. A strict nurse in the sadomasochist clinic. Tight-lipped. A judge and Pantocrator with an empty gaze.

I still couldn't shake my bitter feeling. Where had that blissful state of being gone?

Suddenly, I felt something spill into the toilet like from a tap one forgets to turn off. I sat there while longer before wiping, just in case. The toilet paper had turned a light shade of red. I checked the toilet, and it was the same. A long bout of drinking had made my blood thin and purified it to a strawberry hue. My beautiful martyr's blood.

"I don't know if it's good that I stay here," I said when I returned to the kitchen. "I've been leaking blood from my ass a lot lately. It comes out so sneakily sometimes that I don't even realize it's happening. I might get your expensive couch all bloody. I can go back to Koidu Street, it's fine."

The couch at Koidu was yours, too. Your old one. There was nothing wrong with it getting bloody now, though. You used to take stringent care of it.

You were sitting with your back towards me and looking away. Now, in the wake of our tiff, I felt much more at ease again. I took a book off your shelf, flipped through it arrogantly, and pretended not to notice you stewing your judgement.

"I can make up the folding bed for you," you finally murmured.

It felt like a ton of bricks. I hadn't been expecting that decision. I'd hoped you would either tell me to go fuck off so I could leave feeling smug, or you would self-sacrificingly take me by your side and everything would be fine again.

We left the conversation there. I seemingly had permission to leave, but was tired and didn't feel like it. There was also a lot of unopened drinks that I would've had to leave at your place, then go to the store to buy more.

Every once in a while, you'd go out onto the balcony to smoke, and I went with you. We stood close to each other but stared in different directions, just puffing away without speaking. Back in the kitchen, we sat as far apart as possible. Finally, you went into the living room and put sheets on the pull-out couch, but didn't set up the fold-out bed. Then, you fell asleep.

I stood in the doorway and asked again, if I should stay or I should go. It was demeaning, pleading for a judgement. On top of that, I already knew your answer. You'd say: "Do whatever you want." And if you said it in an especially indifferent tone, then I would leave, even though I didn't want to. I'd just hinge upon that nuance.

I waited for a few minutes, then quietly undressed and climbed into bed with you. I planned on not touching your body. But soon, my arm still wound around you and my hand clutched your breast. You didn't move. I stroked you and sucked on your nipple and slid my hand between your thighs. You looked away but didn't squeeze your legs together, either. After a few more moments, I went down on you. I've said again and again that I don't want to fuck if you don't presently want to. And I'd meant it.

"Should I put it in?"

"Do whatever you want. I'm not going to do anything."

That took the wind out of my sails. Still, I couldn't find peace and, after a while, I started trying again and finally entered you and started thrusting. You lay limp and stared at the wallpaper. After a while, you covered your face with your hand.

"What's that—are you crying?"

It came like a cue. Tears started flowing from beneath your palm. Now, you were the one suffering. I didn't know if you were suffering with pleasure or simply suffering.

"What now? What's happening? You told me to."

But you didn't respond, didn't move, didn't sob. The tears simply streamed.

I felt a little nonplussed, but still didn't want to feel guilty in the situation. I absently brushed away your tears. How long would this last? A long time. In the end, you turned to face the wall. I tried to figure out what was between my legs—sperm or blood? I went into the bathroom and wiped it off. No blood this time.

But in the morning, I spat light-red blood into the sink and a blotch came from my bottom when I farted into the toilet. It'll probably take time to pass. Abdominal blood was supposed to be black, wasn't it? Volkonski told me—he'd had it once. Where was this blood coming from, then? My innards and esophagus?

Not that that's anything special. One time, Laura said that, hey, there's blood coming out of my butt now, too. How dangerous could it be? I didn't look into it, though. Laura has a steadfast belief that we won't be alive for much longer. Maybe I'm just resisting it out of spite. How can we know how much longer we'll live? And what is long, and what's not? We've been alive for a pretty long time, already. Is a few dozen years so little? And long is never long enough, to be fair. So long as you don't tire out from it. *Tired of living, but afraid of dying.*

SEX

Fucking happens in waves. There was a period where Laura thought it'd be healthy to fuck a couple of times per week. I couldn't stay hard sometimes when I'd drunk too much. But I reckon I don't drink that much anymore. I feel like it'd stay put for sure, though we're already so used to each other's bodies that they don't stimulate each other as much as they did in the beginning. And now, Laura isn't as frisky. And I don't want to push for it, because I know that if I do and I climb on top of her, she usually won't orgasm. And nowadays, the most important thing is to get along well instead of fucking at any cost. But at the same time, will we really get along that well then? As if we didn't fight enough. And when Laura herself takes the charge, then she goes through the motions well enough and the result is more genuine, too. I guess I just have to trust her. And to collaborate, when she gives me the chance. Like a jazz jam session. Everybody's got to be willing to play along. Then, the outcome can be fantastic and you're tired at the end. Maybe a little bit happy, too. Why not?

But where this will all go—that, I don't know.

◆

"You see the signs, but you don't know how to draw conclusions from them," Mannu told me. I wondered why he'd suddenly turned so impassioned about the theoretical topic. "What you're saying is an old idea. It's not even your own."

"So what? I know it's not my idea, and I have no idea whose it was. Do you have any original ideas? Huh?"

"A woman doesn't just select a man. She selects an individual. Some enjoy a wider range of options, others not so much. No matter whether it's a woman or a man making the choice. Some men sleep with five women. Tell me who's choosing—the woman or the man?"

"Why should a man who sleeps with five women have to pick one? He'll want another fifty." I was several drinks in and getting into the swing of the debate. Mannu was completely sober. What gave him that zeal? Truth and justice? Who knows. Mannu wanted to do a story on me, though, and needed to wind me up.

"Sure, I guess that's his choice."

"I'm talking about prolonged cohabitation. When a bird is incubating an egg, she needs another bird to bring her food. But she also wants a strong, pretty companion who'll give her nice chicks. So, she tries to make herself visible and attractive to a rare male specimen like that."

"And doesn't give herself over until the male has put all his promises on the table."

"Right. How are humans any different? It's genetics."

"But we have a societal aspect in addition to the genetic one, and that's incredibly varied. Some females have a male who brings home food, others a handsome and proud father."

"Raven-dads and cuckoo-moms and all kinds of other parents. The line between male and female has been blurred lately, too."

"Now you're just contradicting yourself."

"That just goes to show that there's substance to what I'm saying."

"What kind of substance is that? You wring your words this way and that like an old sock and everything seems to have a grain of truth to it, but in the end you're no smarter than before and have no idea what's right and what' not?"

"As long as the conversation was interesting!"

"Maybe that's what those women of yours enjoy."

"Exactly. I don't know what tricks you use to get women."

"I don't. Not all that much. Not anymore."

"But before?"

"Back then, I drank. Then, it was no problem. Something would always work out."

"And that's what's bothering you. Not drinking anymore."

"I don't know. Maybe you're right. We all have a limited number of sexual encounters in our lives, just like breaths. You've got to keep track of how and with whom."

I realized Mannu was no longer being serious. The tension dropped. I reckoned he'd ceased winding me up for his story. He wasn't trying at any cost, either. I might've even gone along with it, though—seeing myself lose control. But there was no point to it anymore.

ROUTINE

I WONDERED IF the shower was occupied. What time was it? After twelve. Could it still be morning for someone, or would I be the last? I grabbed the bottle of shampoo off the dusty shelf in front of the mirror and my towel from the peg. It was sooty from the gas boiler. Should I start keeping it in my apartment? It'll just get dusty there. There are always dust bunnies rolling around the floor. Which one is better for the body: soot or dust? Or should the body be scrubbed with them in alternate fashion?

Lately, I've been wearing my slippers in the basement shower. The stairwell was being cleaned more often for a change and the floor was averagely tidy. I didn't pull on underwear, just shorts. That's the easiest way to go about your business. Otherwise, you've got to hop on one foot while pulling on your pants after coming out of the shower and choose between a muddy or a wet floor. Though I could also mop it up a little.

Should I lock my door or not? I did just in case, swung my towel over my shoulder, and stuffed the bottle of shampoo into my pocket.

Someone was coming up the stairs. I waited to see how far they'd come—all the way up to the third floor.

"Hey, Lilli."

Lilli was pink and flushed from a hot shower.

"Well, there you have it—boys do always have blue towels."

"Of course we do."

I don't know if there are still any monasteries somewhere in the world where the monks and nuns live together and drink and fuck willy-nilly. I bet there are. I don't believe ours is the only one. Most monasteries also have a boss—a deacon or deaconess. Do we have anything like that? I can't say. If so, then it's so secret that no one knows or notices. Or maybe the job is spread out between several people. That's feasible.

And friars do stop by sometimes, just like at a manor. Erko tends to be visited more by wandering nuns, which is also understandable. Who last stayed with me? Jaan Malin and Arno Oja at some point. But my cell has been rather empty and lonely as of late, which is also good. I've finally gotten used to it and wouldn't want anything else.

I'm hesitant to fix up my cozy cell. Maybe it'll mean I'm less lonely. And maybe the feng shui will change. I know several elderly people who live amid dusty bookshelves and won't hear a word about fixing things up, even though they have money. Nothing can change because it might redirect you from your mental riverbed. Your thoughts must be allowed to stand still or bubble along that route. I, however, don't need to consider that for long, because I have no money for renovations. But maybe that's also a good thing? Whenever I do end up having money, renovating is the last thing I'd think of. It occasionally comes to mind again once the money runs out.

◆

Siskin and her friends had somehow gotten the idea to ask for the same number of pelmeni as their age when I asked them if they wanted anything to eat around the house. It was because they had to say *something* when I asked, "Sure, fine, I'll make pelmeni, but how many for each of you?" Pelmeni were the first thing they agreed to eat, and was the simplest to make. I wasn't about to start forcing on them any strange new food I made for myself.

"Nine for me," Siss announced.

"I want eleven," Diana giggled.

"Six for me," Marta Maria whispered. She almost always speaks in a barely audible tone but stares you in the eyes as she does, so it's possible to grasp what she's saying from the gaze alone.

There are, of course, the occasional exceptions to the rule when the kids are starving. Or if they've just gorged on ice cream and candy. Or when I've forgotten to stock up on pelmeni.

One time, I'd absentmindedly bought raspberry pierogi instead. They gave the dish critical looks, but still politely sampled it. The pierogi just wouldn't do, so I had to eat it all myself. They were pretty gross, but I'm stubborn about not throwing food away. The next day, I deep-fried the leftover pierogi. The oil spattered everywhere. I think even Diana ate a few of them then.

Now, whenever I offer the kids pelmeni they ask: They're not pierogi, are they? No, no—they're not.

Diana lives a few houses down. Marta Maria is in the building next door. She and Siskin are able to blink flashlights at each other and make faces and hang over the windowsill to chat like Astrid Lindgren's Bullerby children.

Kaisa, on the other hand, rarely accepts anything I prepare in the kitchen. She's very picky about what she eats and what she doesn't, even though the girl just eats simple foods at home, too.

◆

"Nobody misses fucking like a married man."

"Jaanus's words started spinning around my head on the way home from the store. He did have a point. When had Jaanus said it? Years ago, I reckon. Before his divorce. How would I myself put it? "No one longs for tenderness and intimacy like a married man?" Maybe. And what about those married women? Do they want the exact same thing? Sex, tenderness, intimacy. Yet, neither the men nor the women get it from their spouses anymore. Why is that? Because routine things aren't enticing? Because you don't feel like being polite to whoever's closest?

"No," I mumbled to myself and suddenly stopped on the sidewalk. Jaanus had said something different. Maybe he'd worded it differently, too. Ah, that's right—"Nobody jerks off as much as a married man." Sounds about right. He and Annika had been living together for about twenty years at that time. Though he wasn't just masturbating, of course. He was fucking my wife, too, among many others. I suppose he's a handsome man. Am I jealous? I don't really know. Jealousy seems pointless. I'd actually like to feel a smidgen of jealousy, just to feel something. If not love, then at least jealousy.

And now, Jaanus was stroking Laura's head again. I suppose she felt a kind of tenderness and care. But whenever I touched Laura, she recoiled in disgust. Figures. And what do you know—I did get a little dose of jealousy. A tiny, delicate emotion. Soft pain. Not that I'd want to feel harsh pain, of course.

IMPROVEMENT

I KNOW YOU should spend as much money on food as you do on alcohol, but what about when you're out of cash? I don't want to give up drinking. I could buy cheaper booze, but that also has a worse effect. My intestines will just have to wait until I get bread money. For if I'm not drinking, then I'm also not working or wanting to do anything at all. There's just lying around and feeling depressed. Endless misery. Liquor at least keeps you moving like gas in a car. I suppose cars need repairs from time to time. It's a bit harder to repair a person. And you don't want to hear someone asking why you've poured in the wrong fuel. Or why the oil hasn't been changed.

◆

Who said that a person grows when they're sick? That sickness is necessary in order to grow? I've been sick for a while, but I'm just as dumb as ever. To be fair, I can't see myself. And maybe they meant that about kids. That kids who are often sick grow up to be smart. Who'd want wits that have to be paid for by being ill? How great is that wisdom, anyway? I bet it's tiny. And just like all intelligence, it's like currency. One day, there's a currency reform and it's ten times lower in value. Or switched out entirely.

But maybe I will get a little smarter. There's time, nothing but vacant time, and no need to rush my thoughts. And it seems like wisdom doesn't exist in the first place. Maybe that's a good start. Someone who doesn't reckon he's normal might not be crazy. Someone who doesn't reckon he's smart might not be very stupid at all. It's good to be a little stupid.

◆

"Do you really think this is going to help?"

"It might."

"So, you want me to sprinkle pepper over your back and then wrap tape over it."

"Yeah. But make sure to apply it straight to the skin at the edges, otherwise it might not stick."

Jaan seemed doubtful, but I'd been encouraging him for a while already.

There was a pain in my lung and it hurt to cough. I was lying on the couch at my studio and the pepper was actually chili that Jaan gave me once. It had been nice and spicy in meals, in any case.

So, he sprinkled it over my back.

"A real pepper bandage probably wouldn't cost much more."

"I don't feel like going out. And I've got a fever. I hope it's not contagious."

"Ah, no worries. I've been drinking pepper vodka."

"That's right. Honey on the inside and chicken shit on the outside."

"Or vice-versa."

"Exactly."

"Okay, I'm going to put on the tape now."

Jaan tore off a strip of tape.

"Go ahead."

"Is it going to come off afterwards?"

"I guess we'll see. If I die of pneumonia in this apartment, then don't go around explaining why I had this good tape on my back. Laura says that wrapping yourself in tape helps already. It improves circulation."

"I could've poured some pepper vodka over your back, too."

"Yeah, but then the tape wouldn't stick."

"I thought this was a quality role."

"It is."

"Well, if I ever end up breaking a bone, then I'll come to you for tape."

"I can give you half a broomstick, too."

Jaan finished taping up my back.

"You did put it over my lungs, right?"

"Where are they?"

"Don't ask me."

I sat up and pulled on my shirt, feeling the pepper slide down beneath the tape. None would stay on the upper part of my lungs.

Jaan was worn out from the effort and sat down in the armchair.

We stared at each other out of the corner of our eyes. Just as we usually do.

"Have a sip, too," Jaan said as he passed the bottle of pepper vodka, looking away.

"Alright."

I took a sip.

"That chili pepper you gave me really has a kick to it. Good in any meal."

"Yeah, I know."

"Though I guess you gave it to me years ago already. Back when I'd just moved in. When was that?"

"I've been living here for six years."

"I guess I'm at three. I recently read that Lewis Carroll or that Dodgson died of pneumonia. And I just wrote a short story where I'm dead, and I stole a name from him for the title."

"Which name?"

"Alice."

"There are Alices elsewhere, too. Who the fuck is Alice?"

"But he's the one I stole it from."

"Then I guess it's fitting that we put pepper on it. Have another sip."

"Just a small one."

◆

I was standing in the hallway and couldn't get in. I didn't have the key that opens the little door anymore. Why not? You didn't take it from me. At some point, you were holding onto my set of keys and I never got the little key to that little door back. The thought's crossed my mind that I'll have to return your apartment key someday. Thinking is dangerous. Still, you can't grab hold of a thought before bam—it's already been thought.

It was a little past ten p.m. Not late at all.

The last time I stood here in the hallway, it was somewhere around five in the morning. And I was knocking. You let me in pretty quickly that time, even though you had to get up and go soon. Maybe that's why it happened so quickly. You didn't say a word and disappeared to go back to sleep. I groped my way around the apartment and tried to curl up next to you as quietly as I could. I also tried not to snore, even though I knew it was impossible. Especially drunk.

But now, it wasn't too late and Laura still wasn't answering.

She'd called maybe an hour earlier and had unexpectedly sounded calm and friendly. This after a fight that'd lasted all day long.

The quarrel sprung out of a text I'd sent, asking: "What was so wrong about us waiting for you at Mickey-Dee's?"

Sure, the fight had actually started a while earlier when Siskin and I were waiting for Laura to finish shopping. She came to McDonald's, which was where we were all supposed to meet, and was in a bad mood. I couldn't tell why. Siskin was playing with her Happy Meal toy. The cartoon panther spun around and around her pull-up bar. The two of us were having a fun time sitting there together. We'd killed two hours walking around the mall before coming to the fast-food place a little early. Siskin was hungry. I didn't realize that Laura had spotted us enjoying ourselves from a distance.

"I don't want to sit here," Laur said without looking in our direction.

"Have some fries," I offered, trying to find some kind of a solution. Siss didn't feel like finishing them anymore and neither did I.

"No, thanks." Laura sighed as if she was saying it to someone else sitting next to us.

"Did you finish your shopping? Do you want to buy something else?"

Laura got up and left. I didn't know how to respond.

"But Laura's got to go to the stores," Siss murmured, seemingly to herself or to her panther. "I want to go to the stores sometimes, too."

My phone beeped, so I checked it. We were going to meet up in a couple of hours, but in a different place. At least it wasn't a message telling me to go fuck myself.

We had a good time hanging out together later. We walked around near the art museum and through the city. But when you tired out and we got a cab, I remembered that Laura didn't want us going to her place, anyway. The driver stopped at Laura's building.

"So, what're we doing?" I asked.

Laura just got out, grabbed her shopping bags of new clothes from the trunk, and went home without a word.

I reckon that was the beginning of the fight. Of that fight. Are there different kinds of them? I suppose there are, though they're fights all the same and it'd be better if they never happened in the first place.

The bickering had already tired me out and wound down by the time I sent the text. I was at home on Koidu Street. We hadn't spoken in days. Now, I was drunk and texted. I justified my action with the fact that it'd been spinning around my head for a long time. I waited a second before sending the message, suspecting it might make things worse. But then, I just hit send as quickly as I could. All about how I was an innocent martyr. How was I to erase it? What should I have done back at McDonald's? Let Laura tell me!

She called back immediately, also drunk. A long tirade followed. When she reached her peak, saying that she's probably just gone and done everything wrong and I've done everything to make her happy and she's done everything to ruin us and that I should call Siss and ask her if the whole thing made her feel bad, I abruptly cut her off, saying: "I don't want to air out any grievances. I don't want to fight. Let's end this now."

Laura was silent. She'd been in a position of power and I'd taken it away. I felt like adding that Somali pirates are commandeering ships and murdering people and dying themselves, and what were we doing here? Still, I imagined the scene where Laura didn't ask me if I wanted to go off commandeering ships or fighting pirates and was simply silent, because it would've all sounded so dumb, so I hung up instead.

Then came another bout of days of conflict and mutual silence, after which

Laur called and chatted in a kind and peaceful voice, and the thought subsequently flashed across my mind: What if we can just pretend everything's fine?

But now, I couldn't get in. I knocked and dialed her mobile and her landline over and over, wondering how long I could keep it up.

Suddenly, the door swung open. Laura was standing there, silent.

"Greetings," I said casually and walked past her into the kitchen.

I glanced back. Laura was still standing there, holding the door open.

"Is it best if I leave?"

Laura didn't move.

"Fine, I'll go. I don't want to fight. I just thought things were alright."

I strode out of the apartment. As I was walking down the hallway, I waited to hear the sound of the door either clicking or banging shut. I didn't hear anything. Neither did I look back to see if the door was still open. I turned and walked down the steps, never to find out how it closed. If she slammed it, then only a while later.

But maybe she was still waiting for me to return? Hardly.

I trudged homewards, ruminating. My relationship with Laura was one of the best I'd ever had. Still, where did I get that idea? I don't even remember those previous ones. It's just something I believe. I don't even remember my first fuck. Laura remembers hers. Fine, I can remember whom it was with. And sometimes it seems like once you've been in a relationship with someone, it lasts forever.

Scientists say that forgetting is necessary. There's no other way to live. I suppose there are several different kinds of forgetting. Like dreams. Sleep helps you to forget. It also brings memories back.

◆

"Why'd you come?"

Yeah, why had I?

"Why?"

"Walls, why'd you come here? Moon, why're you here at my window? Why did you all come?"

"Get lost."

"Already am."

◆

"I thought you were coming to check if I was at home and if I was alone."

"Why?"

"Because you couldn't get ahold of me and I was at Monika's and didn't hear my phone.

"Oh. No, that's not what I was thinking. I was just glad when you finally answered. And that you sounded calm and it felt like our fight was over."

"I said we're not going to start talking right now."

"That, I don't remember. Maybe I wasn't listening anymore. I was already on my way to your place."

VISITS

SINCE WE WERE fighting so much, fucking so little, and living separately, I started daydreaming about Carmen. She'd been at some gathering at Cabbages and I watched her out of the corner of my eye, but didn't strike up a conversation. I don't think she's seeing anybody at the moment. But so what? I knew full well I won't do anything about it. I just lay around in my studio, allowing my thoughts and feelings to unfold. Let all my thoughts and feelings do whatever they please—I'm not going to do anything about it; I'm married to Laura. But how long will that last? As long as it may. We're a couple of stubborn mules, and could stay just as mulish till we hit 100. Though would I really care to live to that age out of pure anger? And Laura would only be 80 by then. What's my realistic life expectancy, more or less? Sixty? Seventy? That's taking the age at which my parents died for comparison. But they both worked jobs for a living, unlike me. Did that help extend their longevity or kill them earlier? Like the Swedish king who gave one twin prisoner coffee and denied the other, we're just experimenting here. Though who can say whether my manias and obsessions are a lesser activity than my parents' ruthless labor? What did they ever enjoy? Am I better off for not building a house or gathering berries from the forest in autumn? Or does that make me worse off? Does it make no difference? Be you Kofi Annan or a Somali pirate, God still loves you. But does he embrace both?

◆

When did the Uus Maailm commune shut down? It did at some point. Oh, well. It did when it did. Now, they hang out here at the Poor Writers' House on Koidu Street. Or at least what's left of them.

"Hey, is that guy over there a Russian? Huh?"

What else could he be? And what do I care? What about it? And where am I even from?

◆

In the beginning, there was silence. That lasted a real long time. We were living in a Soviet apartment block in the Lasnamäe district. I can't remember how long it lasted. Months, I reckon. It's intriguing, of course, when you're sitting in the home of a beautiful girl, have brought some drinks and fancy snacks, and she's let you in but then just sits there silently staring off into nowhere. At the same time, she *is* drinking. I guess I sometimes supposed that she was just making herself intriguing and interesting on purpose. Mona Lisa *is* interesting, so long as you don't know her secret. Once you find out, you drawl: "Oh, so *that's* it . . ." And then, you start plotting your escape.

No, there was just a tiny window of time before that mutual silence where I couldn't stop talking. Though Laura was even quiet then. How long can you really go on when the person next to you won't talk? She's not criticizing, not disdainful, wants to be together, but is simply silent. And even so, she has no difficulty speaking up when she needs to buy groceries or a bus ticket. As ordinary as a person can be. No one realizes she's actually crazy. Though it is very possible that there are hordes of crazies around us who simply hide their craziness well. They've learned the role of an ordinary human being. I've seen their type before. For instance, there was an old man walking down the street, seemingly deep in thought. His legs were moving, but his arms were rigid at his sides. Then, he surfaced from his thoughts and apparently realized he might leave an abnormal impression by walking like that—that people might realize who he is. So, he suddenly began swinging his arms, too. However, he was so apprehensive that his arms didn't synchronize with his legs—the former swung faster out of excitement. He couldn't get the rhythm! The man's right leg and right arm swung together like a trotting camel. It took him a while to achieve the perception of a normal pedestrian. At the same time, he didn't dare to look up and around to see if anyone had spotted his predicament. I've heard that Jaak Joala could be in a vertical pose and close to blackout drunk before guest performances in Russia, but as soon as the chime sounded, he'd run on stage like a young shepherd, sing like a nightingale, and share his affection with the whole crowd from the front row to the back, and up to the boxes. As soon as he exited the stage, however, he'd collapse and was totally unaware that he'd pulled off the performance.

We pretend that everything's fine, that we're living a quiet, normal, and trouble-free life. Perhaps for some people, nothing is wrong and everything really is fine? That'd be quite a surprise. Does that mean they're callous, numb, or just so crazy that they haven't a single madness? And have they never heard that everybody's crazy to some extent? Robot-people. Perhaps they can robotically laugh and cry like people are meant to do.

And if that's the case, then who is more human: the crazies pretending to be normal, or the robots who don't know a thing about madness?

I thought that lobotomies were no longer performed, but Margit scoffed and told me they are, indeed. Some doctors are downright lobotomy fanatics, thinking it's the only treatment that can pull some patients out of the jaws of despair.

I wracked my brain over your silence but wasn't able to come up with a single logical explanation. When I asked you about it, your response was simply silence.

Why have I been drawn to crazy women again and again and again? Though maybe I haven't—I've just been drawn to women. Uncovering the craziness has just been part of the process. I couldn't tell they were at first, of course.

We still had sex during periods of silence. Silently as well. Laura only agreed to it when the sky turned dark and it was time to crawl beneath the covers, anyway. But I could tell she was far from innocent. I didn't know *how* far, though, and didn't really think about it. How un-innocent am I? I feel like I've done a bit of everything, just a little bit, but at the same time, I've retained some innocent. Doctors can't even check to see if a man's lost his virginity or not. If anyone can, then probably a psychiatrist.

I don't know why I kept visiting Laura, either. To fuck, of course. But I suppose I could've done that elsewhere if I'd really wanted to. Did I visit her to try to figure out her silence? No, because I was certain I'd never get to the bottom of it, anyway. Or was I waiting for the silence to end? Probably not, either. I had no expectations that it would ever pass. Why should it have? I reckon it was simply pleasant to be with a silent Laura. It was like going to school. Studying so you don't have to constantly chat. You can sit and be silent with a person, and there can be substance to that silence. Monks also meditate in groups. I suppose it's just more social that way.

Laura didn't even speak when she was drunk. She'd drink, wordlessly, her head drooping further and further at the kitchen table until her nose dipped into her glass. I felt like I'd seen a similar scene in some French paintings. I just couldn't remember which ones. It's clear that the man and woman in Degas's *L'Absinthe* have been sitting next to each other for a long time, are drinking, and are silent. And then there's the blue painting of a slender woman wrapping her arms around herself, a siphon bottle by her side. Whose was it? Old Picasso, I reckon. From his Blue Period.

I wonder if the time when Laura never spoke was our own blue period. I don't think it was. I've had blue periods before and know what they're like. That one was different.

I was afraid Laura might fall off her chair if she kept drooping further and further, but she never did. Only sometimes after returning from a longer spell in the bathroom would I find her asleep with her head on the kitchen table, just like a cat. Her own cat. That, in the sense that she never knocked over any glasses or slipped off the chair. I never did anything in those situations. I didn't bother her. I just sat back down across from her and continued drinking. And I was silent. It could last that way for half an hour before Laur suddenly sat up and was present as if she'd never nodded off. Her gaze clear, she'd take another sip, only glancing momentarily to see how much I'd drunk in the meantime. Perhaps she checked to gauge how long she'd been out—whether half a bottle's worth or longer. And maybe also to see how much more booze we had left.

There was a cheap grocery store right outside the building, visible from the window, which meant I could easily pop out to buy more booze until ten p.m. Which I always did. My unbuttoned coat flapping in the breeze, I'd unconsciously stop on the street to stare back at Laura's windows. There she'd stand as still as an icon, watching me go.

On my way back, carrying a bottle of prosecco or less frequently Lambrusco in hand or pocket, I'd wave. And what do you know—the icon would lift her hand and gently return the gesture. It was wise to immediately purchase a larger quantity of bottles and stick them in the freezer for a while, as they're not refrigerated at the grocery store. Often, we'd lose count of how many were drunk and how many were still in the freezer by the time we went to bed, already feeling tired, and the remaining ones would have burst by morning. Whenever a bottle of bubbly explodes in the freezer, it doesn't leave large shards like a frozen beer bottle, but a cloud of needlelike slivers, which are a headache to scrape out. You've got to thaw the whole freezer, which Laura did often. She's a pro at cleaning, though. I suppose it's her favorite activity. An activity that leads to no real result, but which can be done alone in silence. If cleaners were ever paid a proper salary, I bet she'd change jobs. We don't have any royal palaces where one could earn a decent living. Maybe at some mafia boss' mansion. But Laura is sensitive about criminals—I found that out later. I suppose I've also been drawn to the criminal world, but I've never had enough courage to dive in. Maybe I'm mistaken about thinking cleaning leads nowhere. It probably wouldn't for me, but maybe Laura would go far in the field. It'd lead her to a clinically clean room where she could sit back down and continue being silent. A room that is empty and silent, a person who is empty and silent. The cat is empty and also silent, for the most part. Satori in a Soviet apartment block with some bottles of wine at hand.

Anyway. Although I thought the period might never pass, it naturally did in the end. And I barely noticed. Did I domesticate Laura (it took a lot longer to domesticate Melissa to the point where she didn't reach out and bat me with her paw every time I walked past), or did Laura domesticate me to the point that she was able to speak a little? Maybe I'd passed silence school and completed my final silence exam.

Bit by bit and unremarkably, brief conversations sparked between us. It was mostly just small talk. Discussions about any sort of meaningful topics were out, because they were stupid. I figured that out pretty quickly. Still, meaningless talk would do. It came as a kind of relief. Occasionally, it even made me chuckle. Enlightenment doesn't have to come in one single form. Light itself can sometimes be one shade and other times another.

So, what was that small talk about trivial things, or even less trivial but unconditionally lighthearted and in no way meaningful topics, anyway? It was like passing along messages of goodness. *Moo*, says the cow, and licks the calf's neck—I like being with you. *Moo*, the calf replies—I like being with you, too.

What if there was a way to keep living as not-quite-acquaintances-yet? I suppose that's what we are—I don't really know Laura to this day. I've just forgotten that I don't. There's no longer those fascinating hours where we sat together in silence. It all turns to bickering and arguments. And that's saddening. We don't know what the world is or who we ourselves are—it's like we've forgotten. Still, I guess we don't have any truly awful fights. Our incessant squabbling is certainly tough to bear. But when a real fight flares up and we shout and screech and yell until our jaws hurt and Melissa flees, terrified, as far as she can get from us, and when we've tired ourselves out and screamed ourselves empty and finally shut up and I haven't stomped off yet—then. Then, it might take a day or two during which we're both still silent, but angrily so, clenching our teeth, until we realize that we don't want to be fighting at all. And when we find ourselves back in that benevolent state, the benevolence is perhaps just as great as it was after one of the silent spells in Lasnamäe. How many years ago was that? Three, or was it more? I can't remember. I don't know if we just have to get into terrible arguments every now and then to return to that blissful state of quiet benevolence. Isn't there any other way? Maybe we do have to; maybe there's no other choice. At least for us. Maybe some other couples have done better.

KOIDU STREET

I‍T WAS ALREADY dark out. Autumn rainfall. There was warm light seeping out from Cabbages. As I walked past, I automatically peered in to see who was there and what they were doing. A crowd had already gathered, including some familiar faces. I felt drawn inside, but I continued on my way. If I were to go in, then I'd take a seat and end up sitting there the whole night. Which would be nice, of course. So, why wasn't I going in? Why would I rather sit all alone in my empty, unheated room? Was I a bitter old man? My thoughts occupy that room, be they whatever they are. Down in Cabbages, where the atmosphere was pleasant, I wouldn't have a single thought in my mind. Did I not want that? I've thought and told people that I would. Have I been lying to myself and others? It's possible. And maybe I, myself, have believed that lie. Or did another version of me want it? A version that happened to be present at that moment. I'm not sure—I guess that means I don't really know him. That me who doesn't want any thoughts. That me is much chattier than the one who wants to think. It seems somehow contradictory. But let it be. Were those really words of wisdom? What did that wisdom concern? Was it that it doesn't pay to fight when you're married? I've always thought that way. But maybe Lennon meant something else. To be fair, I've never really listened closely to the lyrics or looked them up. Wasn't there some mother Mary? Mary the Mother of God? Or was it John Lennon's mother? I wonder if anyone would've given it much thought if Lennon hadn't been shot. McCartney wrote a lot of lyrics, too. Didn't he write some with Wings? No one's gone back to think about those yet. But maybe McCartney's ideas are more musical and Lennon's were lyrical. I do sometimes have McCartney's music playing in my head. Songs from *Band on the Run*, for instance.

Oh, fine. I'll go back and stop by Cabbages for a few minutes. Before going to Laura's, of course. Even though I know she's waiting for me. I like that she's waiting. I won't make her wait for very long. I'm waiting for the right moment to go to her place. And that expectation can be wonderful, too. Half of beauty. What's the other half? Fucking? It's possible. But even if we don't feel like fucking, it'll probably be good, too. Simply and without any reason. I suppose the good things that lack any reason are the very best; much better than positives with clear reasons behind them. For when there's a reason, you also know it'll soon pass and probably will never return again. When it's a perplexing good thing, then you have no idea how long it plans to last, and who knows—maybe it'll come back again.

◆

Did someone just knock? Or is the cleaning lady bumping around in the stairwell? If you're going to knock, then knock louder, otherwise it's impossible to tell. The house itself is always creaking and squeaking and groaning—that's its soft, agreeable way of talking. It's happened before that someone has knocked and then gone away, knowing that I'm home but reasoning that I didn't want to open up for some reason. Later, they tell me they knocked but I was apparently out. What's the point of acting so discretely? I don't have a doorbell, of course. Nor do I want one. There are a lot of things I don't have. There's no latch or hook on the bathroom door, and you can tell there's never been one. There's no hot water. No heating aside of the kitchen stove and heating oven. There's no light fixture on the kitchen ceiling where water drips through and the paint has peeled off in broad strips—only bare cables hanging where one used to be. And there's no electricity running through those cables. I reckon a puddle formed beneath the leaky roof once, causing a short circuit and something to properly burn out. It could've heated up that puddle, causing warm water to drip down. Tarmo Teder or Indrek Hirv, one of whom was living here at the time, would've been able to take a warm shower if the current had already left the water. Cold air blows in through the cracks in the windows. Sometimes it's nice; other times, it'll make your neck ache if you sit in the wrong place.

There's a lot of dust, too. I could start selling it at the Frankfurt Book Fair, for instance. A little box of dust from the apartment of the famous Estonian author Peeter Sauter. If Germans can sell bottled Trabant exhaust, then why can't I sell dust that I've breathed in and out several times? Well, sure—I suppose I should become famous first. There's no rush, though. The dust isn't going anywhere, either—there's more added every day. I've no idea who keeps bringing it. Probably when I'm out or asleep. The dust settles over the clothes I hang out to dry and has lined my hardworking lungs, which just overcame pneumonia. When I called my family doctor a week after my x-ray (I'd forgotten to in the meantime, but then my lung started aching as if it meant to leap across my liver and I was drenched in sweat 24/7), the otherwise immensely calm old Russian woman's voice went up a few notes.

"I was just about to start looking up your phone number here."

"Well, what is it?" (I hardly imagine she meant to ask me out to a café, but it's always flattering when a lady wants to know your phone number."

"You have pneumonia."

"Do I really?!"

I was nearly proud and delighted that it hadn't been a simple case of hypochondria that time.

"I just issued you a prescription for antibiotics. You can pick them up at a pharmacy."

"How long will I need to take them?"

"I can't remember how many I prescribed. A week, maybe. You'll see when you go and pay for them."

Cool. The doctor wrote down my number, just in case. I didn't ask for hers, although maybe I should have. All the same, if I was on the brink of death and called and said, "Doctor Rink, I'm dying now," then what do you reckon she'd say? "Goodbye." She probably wouldn't believe me anyway.

Maybe whoever it was didn't dare to knock harder because Siss and I were drawing giraffes on the door. Who goes around banging on another person's painting?

Ah, damn it. Somebody knocked. They're definitely gone by now.

I opened the door just in case. Button had been prowling around outside and darted in so quickly that if I'd wanted to catch his tail in the door and turn him into a Manx cat, I would've missed my chance. No one else was in the stairwell.

"Was somebody else out there with you, Button? You're not responding. I guess that means you were the one who knocked."

Button looked around, trying to decide whether to leap up onto the wardrobe to keep an eye on things or sharpen his claws on the armchair. No, first of all he needed to check whether anything would be served in the kitchen. He certainly wasn't starving.

The cat scampered into the kitchen, where warm patches of sunlight were cast across the scratched-up dirty floor coated in faded paint. Soft sounds of summer and people working in their gardens floated through the open window. The third floor really is the best. You hear just enough from outside. The soft radio of life is always playing. Like living in a watchtower.

Button and I checked the fridge together, then exchanged a helpless look.

"You're right, Button. There's nothing edible here. I don't know what to say. I wish I could offer you something. Maybe a little snack of condensed milk."

He wasn't excited by my offering, though he's licked it up before. I poured a little mound onto my plate, figuring I'd just stir it into a mug of tea if he didn't eat it. And where have all my plates run off to? The two nice, new white bowls I bought using coupons at the discount grocery store? Sanna's snail shell-shaped plate with her name engraved on it? And all kinds of other bowls of all sizes? Who's been eating out of my little dishes? Ah, I've just been carrying them off this way and that when I'm drunk and cook too much food and divvy it up among everyone else in the building. I do still have two plates. It's enough for when Siss and I are together. Things get a little more difficult when she's got a flock of friends over or when Siss and Laur are both here at Koidu, though that hasn't happened in a long, long time. Why is that? If only I knew. Laur doesn't want to have Siss over at her place anymore. She herself shows up here on rare occasion. The excitement and anticipation of engagement have been replaced by the tiring, blasé mundanity of married life. Huh. That sure didn't come out nicely. Am I any better, though? I'm not.

"I know you don't want to eat it cold, Button. There's no point in even sniffing. Just wait a little while, lie around a bit, then come back and have a little bite."

Button knew all of that already. He was already padding into the living room, his tail held out long behind him.

I sat down and did my own thing. Button would be silent for a while, then wake up in some nook and dash back and forth a couple of times or rustle around up on the wardrobe. A couple of times, he arrogantly leapt up onto my desk and walked right under my nose, pressing a few keys on the keyboard before I pushed him away. He'd probably enjoy curling up and falling asleep on the warm laptop, of course. But that's *my* spot to nap! I guzzle booze, rest my head on the keyboard, and snore. The screen then fills with an endless document that reads: "zzzzzzzzz . . ."

I wrote this and that on my laptop, but mainly just stared out the window. Just like I did in grade school when I was supposed to be doing homework. Most of it was never completed. What if I were to pull myself together and try to finish it retroactively? Ah, I don't know. I might still be able to do my first-class assignments, but would fail miserably somewhere around the fifth grade, anyway. Siska's in second grade. What was that word she asked about the other day? Something from her math class. I'd never heard of it before and suspected she'd made it up. But Grettel knew it, too. They found it funny that I didn't know. I guess math has changed since back when I was in second grade. Nowadays, they get more modern sums when doing arithmetic. Politically correct ones, too.

Would you look at what time it is, already! Almost four. Was I supposed to go there by four o'clock? I think I was.

I hurried to pull on some cleaner rags, leaving the papers on my desk the way they were. I pulled on a pair of shoes.

"Button, where are you?"

I checked the kitchen. The condensed milk had been licked clean.

"Button, I'm in a rush."

He wasn't in the wardrobe, on top of the wardrobe, behind the armchair, behind the futon—nowhere. What other places were there?

"I won't be gone long. A couple of hours at most. Be good while I'm away."

◆

Knock-knock. It was about eight p.m.

"Who's there?"

"It's me."

"Just a second, I'll put something on."

Lilli opened the door, looking drowsy. She waited for me to say something.

"Is Button with you guys?"

"No. Why should he be?"

"He was with me before, but I had to go. I couldn't find him. Now, I came back and he's still nowhere to be found. I figured that maybe he climbed out of my kitchen window and into yours."

Lilli turned around and walked through her apartment.

"Button-Button-Button. No, I really don't think he's here."

"Maybe . . . Maybe he fell off the roof."

Lilli gave me a concerned look, then went to her kitchen window. I followed her without taking off my shoes first. We leaned over the windowsill as far as we could.

"Can't see anything from here," I realized.

"Not really, no."

"I'll go outside and check."

I paused and turned at Lilli's doorstep.

"What do you think . . . If he fell from this high up . . ."

"I don't know. It's Button, at any rate. He can do pretty much anything. I've rescued him multiple times from different places up here. Got him down from the tree once, too."

"Okay, I'll look around. Go back to sleep," I said over my shoulder, though I knew she wouldn't. Lilli was already too wide awake.

There was no sign of the cat outside, so I went back in and knocked on Olavi's door. He opened it just a crack, light from a computer screen reflecting in his eyes. Apparently, he'd spent all day writing.

"Is Button home?"

"I don't know," Olavi turned his head back inside and called across the room: "Kaarel, you seen Button?"

"I saw him out on the street."

"When was that?" I exclaimed.

"Somewhere around an hour ago," came the muted reply.

"Anything wrong?" Olavi asked, as calm as ever.

"No, just he was locked in my apartment before and disappeared. I've got no idea how he got out."

"I guess he opened the door and left," Olavi said.

"Sure, but he doesn't have a key."

"Must have picked the lock."

"The door was locked when I came back, though."

"Then he picked it back. He's a polite cat."

"Okay, that's a relief. Well, good thing he knows how to pick locks. See you, Olavi."

"Bye."

I had difficulty concentrating for a while when I returned to my apartment. My mind kept going back to the cat. He couldn't have climbed down the drainpipe. He always gets himself into pickles because he doesn't know how to climb down. And he would never jump from a height like this. I think. I certainly wouldn't. If I did, then at least onto a car roof. Bang, and your legs would be poking into the interior. Pulling me out would be quite the task. Like the bum whose head got caught in a trash can in Aberdeen. It's a good thing they've made the openings on public trash cans so small in Tallinn that your arm can fit in, but not your head. If anyone's, then perhaps a very small-headed bum. One just a couple years old and trained by his father, who would lift the boy up to peek into a trash can fixed to a light post, and the boy would say: "No, Daddy, nothing here. Let's go to the next one."

HISTORY

THE SOVIET ERA never happened, just like World War II. I certainly can't say for sure it ever did. People write about it in books. Well, and so what? Lots of things are written in books. But I've never known it firsthand. How should I know what's true in books? And whenever I sometimes try, rarely, to tell a child about the Soviet era, I, myself, realize that it's all just a fanciful fairy tale. I don't believe it myself. The kids listen out of politeness and continue doing whatever they were doing. It's obvious they can't fathom it happened for real. There are some stories, but who knows what truth there is to them? And the stories range from one end of the spectrum to the other. Peter Bichel knew that America doesn't exist. I visited that America, but to this very day, I'm still not sure whether or how it exists. Well, I suppose I was drunk the whole time, too. Maybe it's a little comforting to imagine that I'm like a World War II and an America. I still exist a little right now, though one might doubt it on occasion. Just a little longer and I'll only be a picture. Just like a picture of America and World War II and the Soviet era.

◆

I hadn't seen Siskin in a long time. Every now and then I'd wonder what she was doing. The older she gets, the less business she has at my place. That much is clear.

She stopped by one day for no reason. I guess she was walking around the neighborhood. Or gathering chestnuts. Or she wanted to gather them but didn't feel like doing it alone and nobody else wanted to come with her. So, she came up to my studio. Just for a minute. She was a little hungry, too, but I didn't have much in my cupboards. She gladly chewed on a slice of dry bread. I sprinkled a little sugar on it and she ate it ravenously, washing the bread down with a mugful of cold tap water. I felt a little bad for not having more to offer, but then I remembered I ate the very same thing when I was a kid. So, it wasn't really that bad.

Suddenly, I remembered that I had a few banknotes in my pocket. Not much. "Hey, kiddo—do you have any cash?"

"Sure!" Siss thought for a moment. "But I don't have my wallet with me. Are you all out?"

"No, I've got some."

We sat there like someone who had just come home from the army or from college—somewhere far away. Neither of us wanted to talk. It was nice just being together. And I knew that Siss would soon be on her way. It was getting dark out and I had some work to finish up. Should I walk her home? Would she even want me to?

"Are you going home after this?"

"I dunno. Maybe to a friend's house."

"Where at?"

"I don't know which friend yet. I'll have to call around. I'm sure I'll find somebody. It's the weekend, you know. Everybody who's got a cabin someplace goes out there. That's why nobody's in the city."

I nodded.

"I wanted to give you some pocket money, but I don't have any change. No one- or two-euro coins. I've just got a little paper money."

"You don't have to. You've hardly got any yourself. Really, don't worry."

Siskin's in second grade but already seems more grown-up than I am. Maybe she'll start taking care of me and raising me someday. The bread ran out. Siss swept up the breadcrumbs and wet the tip of her finger to pick up the granules of sugar. The table wasn't too clean to start with.

"Daddy, do you know why I haven't come to see you in so long?"

"No."

"I thought you were mad at me."

"Why's that?"

"Well, we brought all those things of mine here to your place while we were fixing up the apartment. So many bags."

I could tell she was on the verge of tears. Back in the day, she would have been bawling already if she'd brought up something like that. She's really grown, even though she's been a miniature old person since the start. Maybe I used to be, too. But at some point, I started doubting myself, wondering if that was really the right way to be. I tried acting the way others did, instead. But I could never make it work. Nobody can take so many cues from others. And I was disappointed in what I'd initially tried to copy—the lifestyles of the wiser, older, and more successful. I couldn't even remember who I'd been at the beginning.

I studied Siska and couldn't help but smile.

"So, you're not mad then?"

"No, kiddo," I said, shaking my head.

Siss looked at me, wild-eyed, then rushed over and threw her arms around me. I was nearly thrown off my stool. We sat there hugging for a while.

"I felt like you were angry."

"Not at you, honey. How could you think that? Just at her. I couldn't wrap my mind around how she could think this was just some kind of storage space to dump stuff."

I caught myself and stopped talking, realizing it could go and ruin the good vibe we were enjoying.

We held each other until our arms tired out, then Siss sat back down and sipped water from her mug. A second later, it appeared that she hadn't gotten her fill of hugging, so she ran back over to wrap her arms around me. I hadn't gotten my fill yet, either. The next hugging session was briefer. We'd cleared the air already.

"Daddy," Siss said while still hugging. "I'm going to go now."

"Okay, sure. It's getting dark out."

"Yeah."

"Should I come and walk you somewhere?"

"No, you're busy. You stopped because of me. But I'll come back again soon."

"Any time."

"I could stay for a few days, too."

"As long as you feel like taking the bus all the way from here to school in the morning."

I knew things might go south with Laura again—I'd be at Koidu with Siska and Laura would be at Vindi alone."

"Maybe I could come for a weekend."

"Sure thing."

◆

Jessica living here did something good for our relationship. It added tension. Things were up in the air and I could have chosen her at any moment. The tension wasn't bad. You dealt with it swimmingly, except for on a few occasions. Like when you threw a fish at us on the bus. And when Jess sat there holding the big fish, you snapped: "You two have a beautiful child." I couldn't think of anything to say. Or when we were drinking at the pub and you found out and came to pick me up.

Still, that feeling that it could all go out the window kept the relationship feeling fresh. For a while, at least. There was a sense that it could all disappear, and it felt good that it hadn't.

I suppose that's a good way to live, too. Keeping in mind that death could come at any moment. Lots of people have said that, though I don't know if anybody's actually lived that way. It might drive you mad if you were to really live in constant battle-mode day after day, apprehensive of mortality. There'd be nothing good about that.

But now, we were married. OK—let's trust each other. Still, the relationship was numb and lethargic. But I couldn't just go find some new girl to move into my apartment. You wouldn't be happy then, either. It's no longer the same situation as back then. Now, we've got to come up with a different solution. Jess showed up at the same time as the relationship formed between you and me. Those two things were independent of each other. It wouldn't be now if I were to get somebody to move in. So, what's the solution? There are many, I suppose. Both good and bad. But which is a good one? I've asked you that repeatedly. You know as little as I do.

I guess we should just be happy about that—being able to search for a solution and having the will to do so. If we were to know the solution and things would be resolved in a cinch, what then? We wouldn't know what to do with ourselves next. There'd only be thoughts. Constructions. But what about reality?

PERCEPTION

I F THINKING OR witnessing creates the world around us (or, well, those particles or waves careening through slits and turning vainer when viewed), then I am what I think I am. I show off to myself, and that's just what I am. A king or a jester. Not that it always turns out right. And you're the person I think you are. If I think you're a witch, you're a witch; if I think you're an angel, then you are fair and gracious. Whether or not you can direct your thoughts is another thing entirely. I do try to think one way, but my mind lurches in an entirely different direction. I pray to be a saint, but sin lies deep in my body and soul.

So, if I want to have a good wife, then I've got to think that I have a good wife. Will that work? Hardly. But maybe it occasionally will. Even when she is the way she is, I just trust my thoughts and belief. Others saywhatever they may. Ruts Bauman persistently called his wife a princess. I called Laura "the beauty queen of Lasnamäe" for a while. When did I stop? You see, man—*you're* the reason why things tend to go sideways. You lost your beauty queen. Ah, that's all just old news. A Frenchman came up with it a century ago. Autosuggestion. Cultism. And how are those American positivists any different? It's all been invented again and again and again, anyway. Just another wheel. And I suppose one without an auxiliary engine.

◆

I peered into Cabbages. Nobody. I crept into their kitchen, thinking I might come across a missing plate from my kitchen, that I could use for cutting up a steaming hot dog. I felt like a thief. What would I do if someone came in? "I was, um, just looking to see if maybe one of my plates is down here."

"Oh, Peeter, Peeter—how are you going to eat without a plate?"

My ears pricked for any sound as I inspected the plates. Not one was from my kitchen. So, I softly crept out again.

◆

Visiting Alge and Viljar was nice. An old house renovated into a home, a cozy atmosphere and emotions aplenty. Nowhere to hurry, just sit back, drink wine, and let your mind wander. Blissful existence. It was wonderful to warm myself in the glow of a home that wasn't my own.

At the same time, I realized I will probably never have anything equivalent to that.

And even if I did have that warm home, then I might wilt in it. I might feel like my passion, my compulsion, lies elsewhere.

I suppose I'm just envious of those with a warm hearth. Who knows what I've got. I, myself, can't see it. Not that I want to. For I'll find out when I lose it.

◆

"When will your erection come back?" Laura asked.

Yeah, it's been a hundred years since you last asked; since you had any interest in the topic. Now, I could so much as call out: "Ahoy! I think it's back!" But then, you'd only get offended. Even worse, I could ask you when *your* interest in something like that might come back. Maybe I should just stay silent about the whole thing. Would that be any better? I'd still be thinking it. And even if I weren't thinking about it, would that be any better? I reckon it'd make me feel sad.

◆

"It made me sad when you told me to fuck off," I complained, but softly enough that Laura wouldn't do it again.

She didn't.

"But that's normal," she replied quizzically. "I've got friends who live together and tell each other to fuck off all the time. Every day."

I don't, I thought, instead saying: "I think I'll pop down to the shop. Do you want anything?"

"I think I'll come with you, instead. If that's alright."

"Sure."

"We'll shop around and see what we want."

"Okay."

We rarely go out anywhere else together, just sitting separately for days at a time. The grocery store is the only place we visit together like little kids on a mission to buy themselves candy. And we stand in front of the shelves and discuss it like little kids do when debating what candy they want, rolling their scant coins in sweaty palms.

Anyone who sees us might think we're happy. And are we, maybe? I, myself, just can't seem to be content.

HOME LIFE

"Hey, there."

"Hi . . ."

Who's calling, I wondered? I didn't recognize the number.

"I'm here now."

"Where?"

"In front of your building."

"Is this Juka . . . ? I didn't recognize your voice."

"I brought some stuff."

"What stuff?"

"Paintings and paints and some work stuff. A computer, too."

"Oh."

"Could you come down and open the door for me?"

"Yeah, of course. I'll be right down."

Juka was standing next to his old pickup packed with various items, smiling. Shyly, as always. A checkered cap was perched on his head and his windbreaker was unzipped. The tips of Juka's long blond hair drifted in the breeze. There were even a few things secured to the roof of the vehicle.

"Hey, Juka."

"Could you prop the door open for me?"

"Sure, one second."

I lodged a half-brick in front of the door while Juka untied the cord holding things to the roof.

"I was afraid they'd fly off. Looks like they didn't."

Juka was unusually chatty. He must have been in a good mood about something. I tried to keep the small talk going.

"Did you set your parking clock? They're always itching to fine people in this neighborhood."

"I did."

Juka pulled down a big roll of canvases.

"Hold on, I'll help," I said, grabbing one end.

We carried them up to my studio, then went back down for the rest of the mishmash: paint cans and an old cardboard suitcase and bulging black trash bags. A mattress. I grabbed the bulky computer system unit while Juka took the

14-inch monitor, which had seen much better days. He shifted the monitor to one arm and grabbed a brick from the truck, lodging it in one of his big coat pockets. Shifting the screen to the other arm, he stuck another brick in the other pocket.

"They go under my monitor," he explained. "I've always had them there, so I brought them along just in case." It appeared as if there was no danger the bricks might damage the coat and had been in those pockets before. Juka locked the pickup while still carrying the monitor.

The computer was the last thing to carry, so we went upstairs.

"I'll put my things in the corner for now and set myself up here on the floor where I was last time a little later."

"No problem. Do you want to park in the yard?"

"No, I'll take the truck back to Sindi Street and then come here."

"Oh, okay."

"I guess you'd forgotten I was coming?"

"No, I hadn't."

"I called last week and asked."

"Right, I'd been drinking then. I just didn't remember."

"I told you why I was coming, too."

"Can't recall."

"I've got to set up an exhibition."

"Where's that at?"

"The Tower Behind Grusbeke."

"And where's that?"

"It's one of the towers on the city wall."

"Huh, never heard of it."

"Nobody has. It's just in one of those places."

"But who'll know how to get to the exhibition, then?"

"I don't know. It doesn't really matter."

"What's the exhibition?"

"Paintings. "Grusbeke's Remaining Papers"."

"Great title. Who was Grusbeke, anyway?"

"Dunno."

We stood in silence for a few moments. I didn't know what else to say.

"Alright, I'm off."

"Sure. When will you be back?"

"Tomorrow. Or the day after. Or the day after that. Depends."

Juka just stood there. I did, too.

"I don't have any keys. I gave them back to you last time."

"Oh, right. Just a second."

I dumped the jar of keys out onto the kitchen table and searched through the mess, finding one extra set for the studio. Where were all the rest? I had at least three sets at some point. I handed Juka the keys and he stood there holding them, still making no move towards the door. He just looked around, smiling. Finally, he chuckled:

"Nothing here's changed."

It appeared he was glad that everything was exactly the way it'd been a year and a half ago. I suddenly felt uncomfortable about having gone on then about how I was going to renovate, but never did. That's not what Juka had meant, of course. Why should I be embarrassed? Nothing had changed, and that was that. Things were good that way. Let it be.

"Well, I'm off," he said as he strode out the door, not waiting for a reply. His head was tucked lightly between his shoulders. He hadn't taken off his cap. Nor his jacket.

CABBAGES

W E'D BEEN SITTING around Cabbages for a while. There was no special event going on, just an ordinary hangout. A fire was burning in the tiny luxury English-style potbelly stove Kätlin donated. From time to time, someone would get up, lift the red-hot cast-iron cover, and toss in a few segmented fence planks from the top. The coals reignited even when the fire had practically gone out already. Quite the effective little device. A draft streamed in through the window frames, of course, so it was only warm by the fire. You could curl up on the couch beneath the window once you'd downed enough warming drinks. Anyone who felt like it would change vinyls on the old record player. Short silences arose when nobody could be bothered to do so, but even those were nice. I don't know how to describe the atmosphere. The cellar in Gorky's *The Lower Depths*? The social club of a winter athletics camp? It reminds me a little of one at a pioneer camp in Elbi a long time ago. You're away from home and comfortable where you are. There's no point in doing much, and not much motivation to do it. Just whiling away with buddies is good enough. You don't even converse much anymore because the group has used up all the topics over the course of several nights.

It's nice to be quiet in each other's company. Whenever someone shows up who hasn't been seen in a while or has been gallivanting around abroad, there's suddenly a burst of fresh energy. Someone goes out to the shop and brings back more drinks. The only difference with athletic camp was that home was somewhere back in the city and you were away for two weeks, tops. Now, camp is all there is. There's no more home. Sure, there's a place where you spend your time, but it's more like your room at that camp. Or in a secular monastery. A soldier without a rifle, without an enemy, without drills, without a battle. A forgotten soldier. You could say it's like *The Tatars' Steppe*, but the characters there dined with white tablecloths like aristocracy. Although, who says there are noblemen among us? No, sure—now that I think of it, Mihkel is most certainly an aristocrat. Or Polish *szlachta*. Jaan is a Russian boyar, especially when he's growing out his beard. There aren't really any French. Or English. If, then the golden-locked Lady Grete. Erko, yeah—Erko's really hard to peg down. He's so mobile and keeps his cards close to his chest. Erko is completely open-minded and liberal and social, but still holds on to some kinds of secrets. I can't envision who I am. Certainly no Indian prince. Maybe a manor lord's bastard son, to whom the lord nevertheless magnanimously granted his family name (but not his property, because he was an impoverished lord).

But wait, but wait—there's Peeter Vihma, who's rarely around but could easily be counted among the peerage. What's more, he's fascinated by the travels of the Knights Templar, just like I am. Well, Laura is clearly an aristocratic lady—there's no doubt about it. I just don't know where she'd be from. A member of the court of King Charles II of Spain? Possible. There's something Spanish about her in any case. A proud and haughty beauty. Dulcinea del Toboso. There *was* also a baron in Gorky's *The Lower Depths*. Yes, one has to admit that we're all just poor noblepersons, and that's why we understand one another. Still, I believe we've only become that way in Cabbages. The atmosphere has endowed us with that dignity and magnificence and generosity in our relationships.

Pretty Laura was drunk off her ass. She was sitting somewhere between the stove and the couch, drowsing off with her mind floating who-knows-where. She would occasionally appear to come to, frown and think intensely for a couple of seconds, then either take a sip from her glass or go out to smoke. Every time, she'd solve that difficult conundrum with playful ease. If the solution didn't present itself immediately, she'd fretfully bite her bottom lip. However, she'd always come to a solution in the end. And then, she'd take a sip of the wine she'd poured herself or go back outside for a cigarette.

I observed Laura with delight from the other side of the room, never interfering. I was drinking beer that night. I had no idea how many I'd already had. I thought that if I tried to count them on my fingers, then I might be able to figure it out. That morning, at Laura's apartment, I'd set a bottle of light beer and a bottle of dark on the edge of the tub as I slipped in for a soak. I think those where the only two I had stocked in her fridge. Afterward, on my way to Koidu, I picked up two lagers from the shop because they were the only cold ones on sale and I didn't want to drink too much over the course of the day. But when Laura announced that she wanted to go to Cabbages that night and had already picked up some wine for herself, I realized that sitting at my desk in the studio just wouldn't play out, even though it was feeling cozy and writing was going well. So, I went down to the grocery store and brought back a whole bag of beers. But how many bottles were in that bag? I have no idea. I picked them out quickly and randomly, not wanting to have to go to the corner shop later to buy cold, expensive beer. The cash in my wallet was running out. I tossed the beers into Arvo Pesti's freezer and shuffled down to Cabbages with two in hand. But how many times had I gone back up for more? Oh, right—I took one of Erko's beers at first, too, because he had some extra cold ones. I realized I wasn't going to be solving that mystery today. Some things must remain a secret in life; otherwise life loses its charm.

Lilli and Kaarel were playing checkers. I don't know how many games they'd already played. It was Friday night, but still quiet in Cabbages. Time would tell if someone came back from downtown and was raring to go. It was still just eleven-thirty.

I involuntarily yawned.

"Laura."

She didn't hear me.

"Laur. Lauri!"

She looked at me, frowning.

"Hey . . ." I searched for the right words.

Laura knew what I wanted to say and answered immediately.

"I don't know about you, but I'm going home. Just a couple of minutes."

I knew that I had no other chance but to wait and see if she'd change her mind. There was no point pushing the subject. I yawned again and took a sip of beer. Did I have enough energy left to wait for her to decide? Most of the time when she's plastered, she ultimately comes up to my place. But what would she do if I'd gone to bed first? Would she come up all on her own? I haven't really dared to try it. Only once or twice. And on those occasions, she's arrived at some point. Did Lilli help her up the stairs, or did she awake from a nap and make the trek herself?

Today, at any rate, I didn't want to lie around on my own upstairs while knowing Laura was snoozing in Cabbages. I was just feeling so drowsy myself. Maybe I was sitting too close to the oven. I moved to a seat by the stairs on the opposite side of Laura and stared at her dozing from that perspective. It wasn't a bad sight from there, either. She's beautiful from any angle. Who was I in her court? A page? A steward making sure there's wine in her glass and food in the cupboard? I don't know, and I don't care.

Laura suddenly looked up again and spoke.

"I. I'm going home, anyway. Right now. I'm going to finish this, and I'm going." She then took a big gulp of red wine.

I really wanted to say that I actually hadn't asked her anything, but I managed to hold my tongue. I really wanted to tell her: "Go right ahead if you really want to!" But I couldn't. All I did was yawn. At some point, your bottle would run out and then you'd undertake some course of action. In some direction. As long as you weren't fast asleep, of course.

There was room on the couch. I flopped down onto it and tried to get a bit of shuteye, too. But the cold couch and changing places had dispelled my drowsiness. I still yawned from time to time. I was too tired to read anything, despite being surrounded by shelves and books. Oh, that one—I'd like to read that sometime. And that one, too. Murakami. Leonov. Myrny. But at that moment, I hadn't the energy or the motivation. The stove had sucked up all the oxygen. All the rest of us had, too. But it still felt nice. A little like when I would lounge around on evenings in the Sisters of Charity boarding house in Liverpool. Except there wasn't any beer there. There were sandwiches past their best-before date and tea with milk.

OBLIVION

THE DOOR WASN'T locked, meaning Juka was home.

I stepped inside, peering first into the living room and then into the kitchen. Juka had set his computer up on the corner of the kitchen table next to the window. The monitor rested on a pair of bricks on the floor. Juka himself was kneeling in front of the computer, working on something.

"Hey, there."

Juka glanced absently over his shoulder and replied, though barely audibly. The table was covered in peeled potatoes and potato peels. They were all dried and bluish. It looked like he'd started cooking, but had focused on other thoughts instead. It looked like it'd happened a while ago. The kitchen was chilly and Juka had a windbreaker draped across his shoulders.

"You haven't seen Siskin, have you?"

"Who?"

Juka looked over his shoulder again, a little irritated. He was fixing something in the computer stack.

"Siss. She hasn't been around?"

"I don't think so, but I don't know. I've been here. I haven't looked around. Maybe she's in the other room."

"No, her slippers aren't here," I mumbled. I didn't want to bother Juka, but I found myself in a strangely good mood and felt like chatting. "Can you get the net in that corner?"

"The internet?"

"Yeah. Kustas always sat by the windowsill there. He'd get the internet from somewhere."

"Um... I've got one of those USB-stick internet things" Juka drawled. "But I don't need it right now. I'm making an exhibition poster."

"Okay, I won't bother you, then. Where's it going up?"

"I dunno. Maybe right on the door to the tower."

"But you said it's somewhere nobody'll be passing by, anyways."

"Yeah, nobody really does."

"So put the posters up somewhere else, too."

"I dunno. There's no point, probably. I don't know where to put them."

"You're afraid that too many people might show up then."

"I don't really want too many, yeah. I'm going to keep painting there while the exhibition is open. It's hard to paint with lots of people there."

"But then you might not sell anything."

"Do you think any sales happen when people are coming in and out all the time?"

"I don't know. Maybe not."

"That's what I reckon, too."

I thought for a moment.

"Hey, these potatoes of yours. Did you want to boil or fry them?"

"I can't really remember. Fry, I think."

"I can do it for you. I've got time."

"I'm not sure," Juka sighed as if it were a complicated problem. Maybe he didn't want me bustling around the kitchen. But I felt like hanging out and doing something, whether it just be frying up some potatoes for Juka and me.

"Can you still make your poster if I'm cooking here?"

"I don't know," Juka sighed. "I guess."

"Aren't you hungry? Have you eaten anything?"

"I'm not hungry. Haven't eaten. Today. Maybe I actually am hungry. You can go ahead and fry them."

"Should I add onion?"

"Sure, if you've got any. But I'm going to keep working on the poster here."

"Yeah, definitely."

I managed to keep myself from talking. Juka continued working and didn't turn around. I wondered whether I should make us both tea, but Juka had brought his own special teas and had his own tricks for making it. There was no point in making plain old tea for him, he might not like it. I bet he'd still drink it, though. But I did have two beers I'd brought along for drinking with work. Maybe he'd want the second.

The potatoes had indeed turned blue. I wondered if I should just slice them or cut the blue part off first. Ah, I bet they're fine.

◆

We'd hadn't fucked in several months. Once when we'd made up after a fight and were both feeling congenial, I asked if we could have sex and Laura agreed. I stroked her for a long time and kept asking if it was okay. She acted extremely submissively and said it was at barely even a whisper, so I continued.

"Should I go down on you, too?" I asked.

"Okay." Again, barely a whisper.

I went down on her and then slid myself in.

"Could you get on top? Like you used to?"

A whisper. "Okay."

Laura got on top and fucked me, her face unsmiling and expressionless, until I finished. She waited a little, then slid off and lay down beside me.

I couldn't hold myself back from asking: "Did you get anything out of it?"

"No," she said very softly, exactly how she'd been saying "okay" before. I was at a loss for what to do. After a few minutes, I noticed big tears running down her cheeks, but she didn't wipe them away.

"What is it? What's wrong? Don't cry."

I wiped the tears away. She didn't make a sound, didn't stir. The tears stopped coming after a while. It didn't exactly give me a good feeling. A cruel thought entered my mind: Was it all for show? Why did she need to fuck me so submissively and then suffer so dearly and not wipe away her own tears? It certainly made me feel guilty. I hadn't even laid my arm across her, sleeping or not, in a long time, even though it used to feel so nice and made me feel secure. Like a child cuddling his mother as he slept. Over time, the desire to fuck had dwindled away, too. I suppose if we were now being celibate and that was your decision, then fine.

But today after emptying two bottles of bubbly, Laura reached out from under her own blanket, took my arm and laid it across her. Okay, sure. But it just lay there numbly like a log. Would I give into temptation in turn? How should I know what I could and couldn't do—if I slid my hand onto her breast, would it lead to more problems? And once my hand was already on her breast, it would involuntarily slide forward. Would that all end in tears and shame again? I didn't want it to.

I hardly imagine that we're unique in any of these issues. But how can we get past them? Are things just going to stay this way? Should I initiate a new beginning? Should we split up?

◆

I thought about an old relationship. It ended years and years ago. I wondered if it was wrong to imagine I'd loved her. That's what had led to the harassment and growing apart and breakup. No one wants to be harassed for love or anything else. You think you love someone, and suddenly there are such great demands made of you, all totally justified because you love that person so much? Fuck off with your great romance, then, if you're unable to simply be human and tolerant of them. I've had it with that kind of love.

◆

All Estonians are *poluverniki*, half-Russians. Laura has Russian blood. I've had multiple experiences with half-Latvian women. People say that Latvians are the most beautiful women in the world. But who am I? What kind of half-Russian am I? Can't say, and I probably don't even want to know. It's better to leave some things unknown. You don't want things to be too worked out. Whereas I would've wanted to possess the secret of life or some facts about time and space when I was young, I certainly don't anymore. But what if someone were to serve me the answers to those mysteries on a platter—would I ask them to leave and shut the door behind them? I don't know. I suppose I'm not that indifferent yet, though it's not impossible I'll get there someday. You can't take away my frameworks and little play space. So long as I'm buzzing around this world, let me just wear my jeans and have beer in my belly. Let me have my stupidity. Standing mute before some great wisdom might not cause me any joy at all.

The problem with wisdom is that it's hard to turn down once it's offered to you. How can you say no to a million dollars being handed to you with no strings attached? Even though you know that by accepting it, you'll be giving up all the life and activities you've been accustomed to until then. How do you plan on adjusting to the new circumstances? There's not much time remaining for doing so.

MARGUS

"HEY, DO YOU have a minute?"

I thought for a second. I hadn't been sitting at my desk for long enough lately. Things used to go so fluidly—I just sat down and the words started coming. I'm sure they could if they wanted to now, of course. That much is clear. But they just couldn't be bothered. What's the point of finishing up a huge manuscript, anyway? In the best scenario, you might get a cent or two more a minute earlier. Still, the difference is so small. It's nice to write slowly and drag things out. You don't want to procrastinate the entire day, of course, because then it's hard to get going again and you start feeling glum. A little delay to things is sweet.

"Are you still there?"

"Huh? Yeah. I'm here. Sure I've got time. What're you thinking?"

"I don't know. Something. Just to hang out. I reckoned I'd come to your place. If you've got time. Are you at Koidu?"

"Yes."

I wouldn't be going to Laura's place this early, anyway. What time was it? Already ten p.m. The shops were closed already, too, so I wouldn't be able to bring her booze. And what was the point of showing up empty-handed?"

"It's almost ten. The shops will be closing. I've got a couple of beers."

"That's okay, I've got some. I bought a bottle earlier. I didn't even know why. I just remembered I was planning to call you. I'll come over, then."

"When'll you be here?"

"I don't know. I'll come now? If that's okay."

"Sure."

I sat back down and suddenly felt a wave of inspiration wash over me. I tried to write an enormous amount before Margus arrived. My nimble fingers heated my thoughts to a boil, and my boiling mind set my fingers on fire. God knows if the writing turns out well or is just a load of shit—writing that feverishly can go either way. It's bad to write when your mind is numb, and bad to write when it's heated up too much, too.

I managed to totally forget that Margus was on his way until he called and told me he was downstairs. I checked the time—only half an hour had passed. It had passed nicely thanks to there being so little of it.

"I'll be right down."

Did he not have a pair of keys? Had he lost them? I certainly hoped he hadn't misplaced them somewhere. But so what if he had? Who would ever figure out whose keys they were? Margus had lived in his mother's office for a while when he had no other place to live. People would show up for work in the morning and he'd have to get lost. Afterward, he'd show up at Koidu to sleep a little longer, as he'd been up half the night already. Often, he had trouble getting in. The handles on the building's outer metal door and the semi-broken wooden inner door (which Tarmo once kicked down after he'd left his keys at work and couldn't get in) would sometimes get tangled. You'd have to slightly depress the handle and gently push the door open while it was halfway down. Margus had a different method. He was a whiz with any computer software, but anything mechanical didn't click with him. So, he'd simply grab the handle and ram the door with force until some combination finally worked out. One time, Laura and I were both in the apartment when Margus came. It must have been a Sunday morning. We had the door bolted from the inside and he couldn't tell that anyone was home. After unlocking the door, he started wrenching the handle angrily. It's possible that he was coming back from some all-nighter, was tired and annoyed and just wanted to get in and fall asleep as quickly as possible. Margus was rattling the metal door so hard that it looked as if he was trying to pull it off its hinges. Laura and I exchanged glances, but it felt better to not take any action and bother him. Finally, he got in and peered into the living room. "Oh, you're home." He didn't seem upset in the least. Not one bit. At least not on the outside.

Maybe some elements of Margus's personality reminded me of myself when I was young. Maybe that's why I was staunchly on his side. I also had a habit of doing stupid things and maintaining a carefree air as I did. One time when I was at Tiuks's summer cabin, I wanted to wash my feet, so I took a big, dented old aluminum pot down from the kitchen counter. I was sure that it was just old scrap waiting to be thrown away. So, I filled it with rainwater from the barrel outside, set it down on the grass, and started leisurely washing my feet in the sunlight. Tiuks walked past and paused for a moment to say: "Oh. Huh. We actually use that for cooking. I boiled some potatoes in it yesterday."

I looked up at her, wondering what to do with my muddy feet in their cooking pot.

"Oh, sorry. I'll make sure to clean it properly when I'm done."

"Mm-hmm," Tiuks murmured, not sure of what to say either.

But throughout that whole situation, I remained as carefree as Margus busting down our door. The memory is still clear, though. When did it happen? Over thirty years ago. Shame sticks with you for ages. Maybe even longer. Is it true that shame forms through the ego? Self-witnessing? Or is it all just another construction and simplification?

Margus was at the door, seeming as carefree as ever. His blond hair was grown down to his shoulders and the strap of a retro backpack was crossed over his chest. He just stood there silently.

I was still mentally surfacing from my writing.

"Are you coming in?"

"Sure."

We went into the kitchen so he could smoke by the window as we drank. Without a word, Margus removed a big bottle of vodka, a big bottle of Schweppes, and a package of cigarettes from his bag. I took glasses from the cupboard and mixed us drinks.

"How much tonic do you want?" I asked.

"Mmm. Half."

I made my own cocktail just as strong, calculating in my mind. A liter of vodka and a liter and a half of tonic. Drinking 50-50 added up. They'd only be getting stronger, anyway.

We sat and drank. Margus wasn't in a hurry to talk and I was also feeling unusually quiet and empty. I could tell that something was up, but no doubt he'd get to the topic whenever he felt like it. We simply had to drink our way there. Would there really be enough though? Ah, no doubt Margus knows the right amount he needs for talking if he showed up with one liter of vodka. It'd have to suffice.

I started pondering my own thoughts again while Margus sat across from me and did the same. Like two old boozehounds. The paint was peeling from the kitchen walls, the table in front of us was wiped clean but still old and dirty, its old white paint sticky for some reason and imprinted with color and text from scores of newspapers. The light fixture on the wall hung from its cord, the old Soviet-era fridge buzzed loudly. The silence and emptiness was bliss.

Finally, Margus got to talking.

"I can't get rid of her."

"What? Whom do you mean?"

"Liis."

"Who's that?"

"We were together for a pretty long time. You've seen her at some point."

"When was that?"

"A long time ago."

"Why should you have to get rid of her?"

"Because she sent me packing," Margus laughed, as if amused that I couldn't figure it out.

I thought for a moment.

"Oh, hey—was it that one with the red shoes? The one you had me sit down with at Tommi Grill one night and told me I should fuck?"

"Yeah, that's her."

"But there wasn't anything going on between the two of you. Otherwise I wouldn't have . . ."

"No, not then. It happened later."

"Wow, I had no idea. Was it really serious, then?"

"Maybe not so much when the two of us were together. But now it is."

"Well, shit. How serious?"

"I tried to kill myself."

"Cut the shit. Really? That's stupid. You'll get out of it. It just takes some time."

"I know. But I don't have it in me to wait. I'm just so tired of it."

"How'd you try to kill yourself, then?" I asked, already interested in the gossip. How exciting.

"I took a cab to the cliff by Rannamõisa to jump off, but there was no good place to jump. There were bushes all over below. I didn't want to get stuck hanging in some branches, either."

"When was this?"

"Just one night. I had a bottle of vodka with me."

"And the driver couldn't tell what was happening?"

"I don't know. Maybe he could. He didn't show it, in any case."

"But now you don't want to kill yourself anymore, I hope?"

"Well, kind of. I don't want to die, but I just can't stand living."

I thought for a moment.

"Where were you going to jump, exactly?"

"Somewhere past Tabasalu. Near the old Merepiiga Restaurant."

Something struck me as odd.

"Wait a minute. You used to live in Tabasalu. You should know there's no good place to jump around there. I bet you really wanted to live and were just playing with the idea."

"I don't know. I at least felt like I wanted to jump."

"But you were afraid, too."

"Of course I was afraid! Who wouldn't be."

"There's one good place there, actually. If it is still there. There's a rock that juts out. And a crack between it and the cliff. But it's a long time since I've been there. Maybe it's collapsed by now. But there were bushes down below it, too. People always go to commit suicide from Türisalu Cliff. Or drive off in a car. But that's a fair distance further down the road."

I could tell that Margus didn't feel like discussing the fine points of his attempted suicide. He just wanted to talk about Liis. About how he was tortured by her memory. And at the same time, he didn't want to talk, either. He didn't know which would be less tormenting—saying it all out loud and putting it into the open, or holding it in and hoping it didn't amplify the thoughts in his head. I didn't know, either.

"There's this line that I just can't get out of my head. The way the line of her jaw transitions to her mouth."

"A line?"

"Well, and a couple other parts of her body, too. Her legs."

"What the fuck, Margus?! She's not a sex doll. She's a person and a personality. Her body won't give you peace. Is that the way you treated her? It's no wonder she dumped you."

Margus didn't have it in him to argue. I apologized.

"Well, okay, I guess they're all intertwined. Body and soul."

"She's no personality. She's a wannabe babe."

"A 'wannabe babe'?"

"That's right."

"Then why's it bother you so much? What do you care about her anymore?"

"Exactly. I just can't get over it. I'm trapped. Can you take it away from me?"

I thought for a minute and suddenly felt that I could. I was probably drunk already, but I felt that I possessed that power. I didn't even have to ream Margus out or knock him around—I could simply take it away. But if I did? What would I do with it then? I'd have interfered in other peoples' lives. Wouldn't that strike a blow to me, too? And Margus. He's got that power in himself right now. I'd be taking it away from him. Sure, he's dying because of it, but it's a force that belongs to him and resides within him. What right do I have to go a yanking it out by force and messing everything up? What if he ends up becoming an even bigger cynic and loses the ability to fall in love ever again?

Maybe it was Margus's belief that I could take it away from him that gave me the belief I really could. But I chickened out. I'd be handling forces and things I can't consciously control. Like a motorcycle. It's fast-moving, but heavier than you, so you need to be cautious when driving it.

Both of us were moderately drunk, but the kind of drunk where we were still very sober and rational. The booze only made our anger and sober thinking more acute.

"No, Margus. I can't take it away from you. You might regret it later."

"No. I can't take it anymore."

"It's something that's inside of you. It's a treasure, even though it may be smothering you. Still, it'd be wrong of me to take it away."

"Oh, you don't have it in you. You're just saying that."

I thought for another minute. Now that Margus had said I wasn't capable of taking it away, I knew I no longer was. He'd given me the capability, I'd had it, and now I didn't. But maybe some little ritual would help him out all the same. Something onto which he could project his anguish. Maybe it'd make him feel somewhat better. Like what Konstantin Vorobyov wrote about his mother taking him to see a witch when he was just a boy and ill. The witch helped.

I went to get a big candle. I poured some water into a mug, floated the candle in it, lit it, then held the mug over Margus's head. He sat there indifferently while I held up the heavy mug persistently. The window was open a crack. Margus took a sip from his glass, picked up the package of cigarettes, and pulled one out but didn't light it. he waited to see what I'd do. I wanted a drink already, too, but I was holding the mug with both hands. I kept it there for as long as I could, then poured the candle wax into the water and blew it out. Holding back the congealed blob, I emptied the water and tossed the wax into the trash.

"It won't take everything away from you, but maybe you'll start feeling better."

Neither of us laughed, or even smirked. It was impossible to say whether either of us took it seriously nor not, but when the trouble is great enough, you'll give anything a try—who knows if it'll help. What matters is to just do something and believe in it, even just a little.

The whole scene was touching, moving. Margus in dire straits over a romance. I was reminded of my own low points. There was a nostalgia to it. Maybe that's also why I hadn't want to clear the whole thing away. Tragic romance. *Bozhe moi.* No music or literature would have ever come into existence without it. Why should I destroy it? I could sense how cynical I was when juxtaposed with much more cynical Margus. Perhaps it's self-defense. Margus himself gleefully made fun of me when I'd been at my wits' end a few years back.

SISS

S ISS WAS WITH me at Koidu for the first time in a while. I'd thought she was just grown up already—nine years old with all her own routes and girl-friends and no desire to come hang out with me. But Siss is just inert like me, lounging around wherever she presently is and rarely mustering the strength to get up and go anywhere. I suppose that's not too bad. This way, she has the time to adjust to everyone and every location. You say you want to hang around here? Sure! Let's hang around here. I don't know if it's any better to briskly hurry from one place to the next, never satisfied by any, but still having to constantly press forward. I suppose that's a bit of an exaggeration. Let it be.

Siss and I had gotten our fill of hugs and I made a stew out of everything leftover in the fridge. She'd been prepared to eat anything I made and we hung around in the kitchen and chatted on and on like classmates, even though there's a 41-year age difference between us. I guess I enjoyed turning on second-grade behavior. Then Siss pulled out a copy of *Mio, My Son*, which she had to read for school and was nearly finished with, and read a couple dozen pages aloud. I made a few sarcastic jokes and both of us giggled, but we did both enjoy Lind-gren's slightly overly sentimental writing. Why shouldn't we? Siss soon tired of reading and took a juice break, but then dove back in and finished the book, which I enjoyed, too.

Kaisa would call her from time to time. The girl had seen us walking to Koidu and was waiting for Siskin outside. I kept expecting her to want to leave, but she kept delaying it. I was glad that my daughter felt like spending time with me despite the fact that her friend was waiting for her outside, and even though we weren't doing anything special. There was competition for Siskin's attention and this time, I won.

"Hey, honey—do you feel like walking to the big grocery store with me to buy beer?"

"Sure, I do!" Siss beamed like a pioneer, which made me want to be a cheerful and spirited pioneer, too, and do everything in my power for us to have a good time. It was already getting dark outside. Autumn in the north.

"Don't you have a reflector?" I asked. "You know police check for them some-times."

"No, I don't. I don't know how I lose them all the time. They disappear every year," Siss replied, unconcerned. Well, I wouldn't worry then, either. No matter what might happen to us, it was always carefree and nice to be together. I don't know if it could ever be that way with a woman. There's always something about men and women. Otherwise, women wouldn't say that hanging out with homosexuals is the most enjoyable. Male homosexuals, that is. That they can always just be friendly.

Siskin remembered that she needed a red colored pencil. And a brown one, too. I'd once bought her a fistful of felt-tip markers and Lilli gave her a bunch for her birthday. That must have been a year ago. Thick-tipped colored pencils hold up well and make for quality time when Siss, biting the tip of her tongue in the corner of her mouth, draws, be it alone or with a friend. That gives me an opportunity to type with them somewhere in the background, behaving quietly.

The office-supply store in the mall had a big shelf full of loose pens and pencils for sale individually. There were tons of them. Siss found a scrap of test paper and started trying them out, simply making zigzags or drawing a little dog or a star. She collected a bunch in one hand, then exchanged them for new ones. I stood and waited next to her. There weren't any other shoppers. The two saleswomen were busy at the counter and didn't even look in our direction. I looked fondly upon my daughter's endless doodling and pen- and marker-testing, though it was taking a very long time. I stole a glance at the saleswomen every now and then, but they didn't care about us scribbling and trying out markers for an eternity.

"Maybe we should buy you some drawing paper, too, honey. You don't have any thick sheets left."

"It's okay, I don't need it. I can use your old papers. Those'll do."

"But what if we got you a pad of thick paper?"

"No, that's alright. Daddy, which brown do you like better? Look."

"I've got no idea. You can get both."

Markers were outrageously expensive and Siss knew it. She always stubbornly tried to avoid racking up big costs for me.

"There's a silver one over there, too."

"I know. Wait, I'll try it."

She did.

"Pretty. But I can't do anything with silver. Maybe I'll try this pink one. And this green one. And this other green one. Tell me when you want to go, Daddy."

"No, go ahead. Try as long as you like."

I started thinking about all those times that are completely pointless and seemingly just idle activity, but are still simply so fulfilling when they're spent together with Siskin, just the two of us. They're amazing and somehow always memorable, too. Much more than any exciting encounters I have—any party or fuck. Afterward, once you're feeling normal again, you can't remember any details of the ecstasy or how it really felt. Like how you can't remember a narcotic high. But passing the time away and feeling nice all the same somehow sticks with you. Siss is nine years old already. She even has little breasts. Tiny, but her glands have started working. I wonder if they sting already, too. She hasn't mentioned it.

I used to wonder what the point of living would be if you couldn't fuck anymore for some reason. How do old people live when they can't have sex any longer? Maybe some do, no matter how old they are, but probably not all of them. Why keep living? But who the hell knows—Laura and I don't even fuck now. Simply watching Siss and spending time with her is a high in and of itself. Maybe that's something I experienced when I was young, too—feeling good while hanging out, with no other motives. Like hanging out with an old person.

We'd started to leave several times already, but Siss always turned back and said: "Wait, I'm going to try that one out one more time. Last one, I swear."

I waited, trying to hold on to the happiness of the moment, though it was starting to annoy me a little, too. Like how a very long fuck would start to get annoying. You just can't finish and can't finish and that's how it ends. I doubt I could pull off that kind of long fuck that ultimately annoys you anymore.

MARTA

FOR SOME REASON, I'd started daydreaming of Marta. I have no idea why. She's big-boned and beautiful. And when she's only wearing a shirt, you can see the deer that's tattooed on her abdomen with its antlers going up to her breasts, its head stuck between them.

I could come up with all kinds of theories about what was behind it. Marta and Margus had broken up. Laura and I hadn't had sex in who-knows-how-long. She'd floated the idea of having sex with others and then clarified that, no, she'd meant *I* could have sex with someone else (an explanation that I seriously doubt). I hadn't had a drink in a while because of the antibiotics, and I tended to get unexplained erections. Who knows—maybe the reason lay somewhere else, or somewhere other than that.

In any case, I was lounging around my studio and felt like doing something and suddenly noticed thoughts of Marta pouring into my head. Thoughts about her body, mainly. I felt pretty helpless. It was hard doing any work like that. I didn't feel like lying down and just daydreaming about Marta, either. Neither did I want to masturbate to thoughts of her. I wasn't about to rush out anywhere to deal with it. Dear God—what's one supposed to do in a situation like this? What would Adam do? Sure, I'm no longer in the Garden of Eden, but still. You haven't abandoned me like you abandoned your son.

Fine. What's the point of resisting. Would that make anything better? I imagined having sex with Marta. I fantasized about having a kid with her and the four of us living together: Laura, Marta, the baby, and me. I suppose it wasn't a very reasonable daydream. I suppose I thought that if I didn't fight the thoughts and let them flow smoothly through my mind, then I'd be able to do something else, too. Not to say that the daydream wasn't pleasant. And absurd. If I make it to the age of 70, what will I dream of then? Still the same old things? Maybe it's even better than dreaming about having great wealth or a business empire. And to tell the truth, I hadn't dreamed of anything in a very long time. What would I like to dream of? I could mull the question over for a very long time, but I wouldn't come up with anything better than Helju Rammo's story about a girl named Blockhead Triinu who dreamed of having a multicolored pen. I suppose that's ideal—having a useless dream that won't hurt anybody if it comes true. But just you try to dream of having a multicolored pen, then. What if fucking Marta is my own multicolored pen? Dreaming gets your endorphin-machine running just like little Karlsson-on-the-Roof's steam engine somewhere in his belly. And then, you can adjust the safety valve to get more endorphins trickling out. There's not as great a risk of the engine exploding like how Karlsson blew up Little Brother's machine, either. It was sure disappointing to read about that when I was a kid, even though I'd never seen a machine like it. Does one even exist anywhere outside of Lindgren's Karlsson books? The kind of Marta who exists in my head doesn't exist anywhere else either, I suppose. But what about the Laura? The me? The who-knows-what? God? And all kinds of finer garbage?

JUKA

WHERE ON EARTH was this Tower Behind Grusbeke?
I walked along the city wall. It was supposed to be somewhere behind the Tallinn City Theater. Tower after tower loomed before me, none of them with any signs identifying which was which. How was I supposed to know?

Then, I noticed a little sheet of paper on one of the tower's lower doors. I looked closer. This was it. Juku had pinned up a poster the size of a sheet of notebook paper. Maybe it *was* a sheet of notebook paper. There was a drawing in pencil. What it depicted, I had no clue. But there was also the word exhibition and an arrow pointing upward.

The stairs seemed endless.

Finally, I made it to the top. There was a huge wooden door. I tried the handle. It was locked. I knocked.

"Juka, are you in there? Juka?"

Nothing. I was still out of breath from the climb. I leaned against the handrail, staring out at the roofs of Old Town. It might have been about four stories up.

The door opened a crack with a loud creak and Juka peered out cautiously.

"Oh, it's you."

"Hey, Juka."

"Did you come to see the exhibition?"

"Yeah."

"Come on in, then," Juka said, pushing the door open wider.

I went in. Juka's paintings were hung on the wall, but it didn't look like he was still painting anywhere. A cloud of smoke hung below the ceiling.

"I smoked a hookah. You're not really allowed to smoke in here."

"Are you painting in some other room?"

"No."

Juka walked over to the hookah and got it going again.

"I'm just looking around and thinking right now. I'm not painting."

"Got it."

"I'd offer you something, but I don't have anything. There's nowhere to even make a cup of tea."

I sat down in the arrowslit recess. I hadn't brought anything with me, either. I could have.

"Well, do your paintings like it here?"

"I don't know. I guess so. But I can't really say. They don't talk to me."

"Why not? Do they just not talk here? And they do other times?"

"Well, yeah. On rare occasion."

"Have you had much of an audience?"

"A couple of tourists came. I think they were lost."

"Just a couple of tourists over all these days?"

"Yep."

"Did they like the paintings?"

"I don't know. We didn't talk. Much. Didn't really understand each other."

"And they didn't want to buy any?"

"I don't know. I wouldn't have sold them, anyway. They're unfinished, too. Most are unfinished."

I fidgeted, not knowing what to do.

"Hey, let's go have lunch somewhere. Or a drink or two."

"I don't know," Juka said doubtfully. "I agreed to be here during opening hours."

"Well, put a sign out saying you went to lunch and will be back soon."

"I don't know. I actually brought along something to eat."

"What do you have?"

"Porridge. Are you hungry?"

"No, not really. I was just wondering."

"Yeah. I just sit here all day long."

"Are you pleased, otherwise?"

"Yeah, I suppose I am."

We sat for a little while longer, not really knowing what to talk about. I peered out each of the tower's tiny windows and inspected Juka's paintings.

"Okay. Well, I'm going."

"Okay. I'll get my stuff out of your place soon, too. I take the exhibition down on Saturday and I'll clear my things out on Sunday."

"Hey, no worries. Take as long as you need, it's fine."

I left. Juka didn't appear to know what to do with himself, either. He started refilling the hookah as I walked out.

FAMILY

Would I even want us to have a child? I've never really thought about it. Though I never thought about it before, either. Not when I did have kids. And what's there to think about? It's not my place to think. It's like tomorrow's weather.

But sure, I suppose things would be a little different then. How, I can't say. Right now, it is how it is. Let it be. I suppose I've just got to spend time in the present.

One time when I pressed you on the topic, you finally said you could have one child. Back then, I didn't know that you had trouble conceiving overall.

But late another night, I even had to trot out after a pregnancy test. It'd been a long time since I'd been to a pharmacy to buy one. I couldn't remember when it'd last happened. Ages ago. And especially late at night at the 24-hour pharmacy on Tõnismäe Hill. It was a nice errand. Like the possible start to a new life.

Early the next morning, I woke up for a moment as you were going to work.

"So, are you pregnant?" I asked drowsily.

"No," you replied softly.

I fell back asleep.

◆

"Hey, let's go after you finish watching that, okay? I said to Siss. "Laura has some sort of plan and I don't want us to run very late."

"Okay. I'll finish this one and then search for the other movie I wanted to watch earlier, but I won't watch it yet."

I'd curled up and fallen asleep next to Siskin, feeling utterly exhausted by midday. We'd only walked around downtown earlier, visiting Ojaver's exhibition and Lapin's exhibition and a photography exhibition. And then we hung around Freedom Square for a bit. At first it was to wait for the rain to pass, but then the sun came out and we didn't know what to do next, so we just stood there. Siss didn't really feel like standing and doing nothing, but I'd lost the urge to go anywhere else. The square was empty. Almost. Siskin and I were enjoying the warm sunlight on the corner.

"Where're we going now?" Siss asked repeatedly. Every time she did, I ran through all the places we could go in my head, and every time, I replied: "I don't know."

Sometimes, I'd switch it up and ask her: "Well, where would you *like* to go?" But she didn't know, either.

Siss was wearing her Heelys, so finally we walked to the big ramp going down to the tunnel under Kaarli Boulevard. She picked up a little too much momentum and fell on her hands and knees, but she didn't cry, just looking back over her shoulder to see if I'd seen her fall. Perhaps that's why she didn't break into tears—I'd seen. I checked her palms after she ran back up, but there wasn't any blood.

"I dunno what to do, really. Let's go home, maybe, and make some pelmeni before we go to Laura's place."

"Okay."

"Maybe that'll make it a nice little Sunday for us. A lazy Sunday."

"Huh?"

"But the weather's real nice, and we can just spend time together. I'm sure having a good time."

"Me, too."

We got on a bus. Siss and I usually held hands on rides. I automatically reached out to grab her hand, but only noticed she hadn't reached it out once I felt empty air. I didn't want to take her hand intentionally.

After we got to my studio, we sat in the kitchen for a while.

"I'm going to watch some cartoons. You can come watch too, if you want to," I said.

Siss was drawing, biting the tip of her tongue.

"When's it starting?"

"In five minutes. No, three fifty-five. So, seven minutes."

"Okay, I'll come when it's starting. I'm going to finish this picture first."

I went into the living room, flopped down on the sofa, and turned on the portable DVD player.

"When's the cartoon starting?" Siss called out.

"I don't know."

"Just tell me when it is."

"Okay. How's your picture coming?"

"I'm drawing myself a movie ticket. What's the name of the cinema?"

"Barn Swallow."

I was feeling drowsy, though. I set the DVD player on Siskin's pillow, pulled up my knees, and closed my eyes.

"Is the news on yet?"

Siss was standing next to me holding a drawing of a movie ticket and looking slightly worried. The ticket was incredibly detailed: Ticket to the Barn Swallow CINEMA for: 3:55 p.m. Showing: cartoons Row: any Seat: any. I checked the ticket before allowing Siss to snuggle up under the blanket beside me. I'd gotten warm and cozy already.

"Honey, is it okay if you watch alone for a little while? I just suddenly got so tired. I'm going to take a little nap."

"Sure, go ahead. I'll watch."

I wrapped my arms around her and blissfully dozed off for a few minutes, but the cartoon music penetrated my dream and woke me up again, so I cracked one eye open to watch. They were film-school art projects by students of Priit Pärn, all reminiscent of his style. Natural.

It was nice to just lie there. Like living childhood again.

"Hey, honey. We should get going to Laura's soon. She wanted to go shopping."

"Okay, just a little longer."

"She's kind of particular about these things. About the way things should be. You've got to do everything at the right time and should never run late."

Siss's attention was focused on the cartoon and not my moaning.

"When it's quiet time at kindergarten, that means it's quiet time. You've got to respect that, isn't that right, teacher?"

"What?"

"Oh, nothing. Go ahead and watch, I'm going to close my eyes for a little longer."

"You mean the one eye you're watching with."

"Exactly. The one eye I'm using to watch you and the cartoon at the same time. Both are pretty nice."

"Let me watch the cartoon now, Daddy. There's no talking in the cinema."

"Right you are."

I drowsily considered that Laura might be pissed off if we didn't make it to her place by the time she thought we'd make it. But when was that supposed to be? We hadn't agreed on any specific time. I'd told her that Siss and I were going to hang around for another hour or so. How long had we been hanging around for already? I had no clue.

"Siska, let's go soon."

"Okay, just a minute."

I couldn't tell what had made me so tired. The empty day behind me? Life as a whole? I was only able to get maybe another minute of shuteye before worry started gnawing at me again.

"Siss, honey, let's go, really. Time to move."

"Okay, Daddy," Siss murmured, continuing to watch the cartoon. "I'm just going to finish this one."

"You do that."

The cartoons weren't long, maybe about five minutes each.

"And then I'm just going to search for that movie I actually wanted to watch. It won't take long."

"Uh-huh, sure."

I sat up and watched with her. Random thoughts rolled through my mind. I'd been spending time with Siskin here on the couch, worrying about whether Laur might get mad if we were late. Those are all the worries we've got. Nothing else. I suppose that should make me a happy man. I'm not worrying about spiritual redemption or the hundreds of thousands of people killed in the Syrian resistance movement. I was watching a cartoon with my daughter, worried over whether it might make Laura angry. I'm living in paradise. If only I could realize it.

"What do you reckon, Siss—are we living in paradise?

"Paradise? What's that?"

"I don't really know."

"Is it something from the Bible?"

"Kind of."

"We haven't learned about it at school yet."

"Makes sense."

"I'm you'll explain it to me sometime."

I sluggishly watched the cartoon to the end. What was it that Brautigan was trying to describe? In *The Abortion*, for example. Was it about how simply accepting everything makes you feel nice and free and high? Did that help or save him? As if. He still ended up shooting himself. But there's no need to be critical. Maybe it did help and rescue him, at least for a while. Though *A Confederate General from Big Sur* was better. I should translate that to Estonian someday. If I don't die first. I formed it into a full mental sentence—As long as I don't die first, I will translate Brautigan's *A Confederate General from Big Sur*. Does life have nothing else to tell me? To be fair, however, was that really a 'little' piece of information? Aren't I content? I am. Life doesn't tell you very many things just any old day, you know. Today it has one message, tomorrow another. Just like newspapers.

"Honey, we really have to get going."

"Mhm. I'll just check really fast to see where that movie is. The one I wanted to watch."

Finally, I heaved myself onto my feet.

"Siss, time to go!"

She looked up.

"Okay. Can I just watch the beginnings of the other ones on the DVD first, too?"

"No, honey. Let's get going. I can't keep track what time I'm supposed to be where."

"Fine . . ." Siss sighed, her eyes still locked on the screen as she shut the DVD player and set it on the floor next to the couch. "I guess we'll just watch the rest next time."

"Yeah. And next time, we'll pick up right where we left off living this life."

Siss slowly crawled out from beneath the blanket.

"Do you leave a lot of things off, Daddy?"

I'd never thought about that.

"I might, yeah. I suppose I do. Maybe I even like not finishing things."

"Because, like, when we're together and then we're not, we can pick up where we left off the next time."

That seemed wise. I started pulling my coat on and kept an eye on whether Siss was also getting her things together. I started thinking about whether it's possible to leave bad things off, too. Hardly. Who fails to finish anything bad? You carry it out to the end, as far as it'll go. Though you're unlikely to leave a fuck unfinished. I suddenly wondered: Do I love you? There was no immediate answer to the question, but I was glad to have had such a silly thought. A nice little silly notion. Still, I didn't start considering whether you might love me. Better not to think about it. And I suddenly remembered that Mart died. Just recently and out of the blue. Younger than me, even. I wasn't going to dwell on it now.

"Come on, honey, let's go."

"Hold on, let me get my things."

"Sure."

My phone rang when we were outside. It was Laura.

"Did you two change your mind?"

"Huh? No. We're on our way. I'll call when we're downstairs."

Where were we supposed to go after that, anyway? Oh, right. Laura wanted to go shopping for some things before Tuuli came to visit her. When were we supposed to have showed up? There hadn't been any firm plans.

I called Laura when we got to her building and she came down, seemingly untroubled. But when I started off briskly in the wrong direction, it took me a few seconds to realize she wasn't coming. I stopped and looked back to see her standing by the door, glaring. Siss had walked a short distance behind me as well and now stood between us. I was going the wrong way.

"Oh, right. You didn't want to go to Rimi. You wanted the bigger Prisma. I got mixed up."

I walked back. Laura didn't say a word, wondering why I wasn't at the top of my game.

So, we went to Prisma.

Siskin was walking funny.

"What is it, biscuit?"

"It's just—my foot's wet."

"And soot's a pet."

"What?"

"Show me where it's wet."

"Here."

Siss stood on her left leg, lifted her right, and pulled the rubber sole. It went all the way back to the balls of her feet.

"Well, I think we've found the problem. Don't you have any other shoes at home?"

She shook her head.

"Come get on my shoulders, I'll carry you."

"You're not going to let me fall, are you?"

"I may be drunk, but not that drunk."

"I'm not so drunk that I'd fall over, either."

"Ohohohohoo!"

"You said it."

Laura stood, watched, and waited as I hoisted Siskin onto my shoulders. I tried to make it look natural. It wasn't easy.

We plodded on toward Prisma and I felt like sitting down somewhere several times along the way. The bus stop we passed would have been one possibility. I even glanced over at Laura, but abandoned the idea of asking. I staggered a little with Siss high on my shoulders, but she didn't seem to pay it any heed. Her confidence gave me determination, too. When had I gotten drunk today? Had I been drinking somewhere? Where would that be? I must have, but I couldn't remember where."

"Do you remember, honey?"

"Remember what, Daddy?"

"You know, just in general. Things that happen in life."

Laura gave us a lengthy sidelong stare. I started to get the feeling like a train was barreling towards us and we were standing on the tracks but couldn't escape. Like in a dream. The anticipation of an impending disaster rumbling towards us hung in the air. That kind of silence coming from Laura had ushered in crises before. But I didn't know what to do about it. I hadn't done a single thing wrong. Why should I have to go and tremble before her? And it felt like I'd only make things worse by trying to apologize or explain things. So, all that remained was to try to ignore the impending doom and carry on as if nothing was wrong. No matter that I could tell such a carefree attitude only made Laura even more irritated.

"I remember some things."

"Like what?"

"I don't really know."

Laura glanced at us again. I had the urge to say that Laura certainly remembers a thing or two.

"Could we just . . ." I asked Laura, stopping in the middle of the sidewalk.

"Just what?"

"You know, be okay."

"But everything is okay."

We carried on our way. I started singing out of nowhere: "Everything's o-kay, everything's o-kay, everything is ok-, ok-, ok-, ok-ay."

"You're singing it wrong, Daddy," Siss teased. "You're out of tune."

"How's it go, then?"

Siss belted out the ditty just as loudly and off-key as I had, but tried to do it in a very deep voice: "Everything's o-kay, everything's o-kay, everything's ok-ay, ok-ay, ok-aaay!"

I started laughing hysterically and had to stop to prevent myself from bucking her off my back. Laura took a couple more steps, then stopped and half-turned for a moment.

"I'm going to the grocery store. I'll see you there," she said, then turned on her heel and walked briskly away.

I called ahead to her: "Siskin and I have to stop by the mall's shoe-repair place. Her sole's come loose."

Laura didn't react. Siskin and I quietly followed.

"Daddy," she said at some point, "I can get off if I'm too heavy for you."

"No, you're fine," I said, and for some reason, I sighed. At that moment, I resolved not to sigh any more.

The cobbler's booth was at the opposite end of the mall from the grocery store, which was quite a trek. I decided to keep Siskin on my shoulders, even though there weren't any puddles inside. How many more opportunities would I have to lift her onto my shoulders, and how much longer would I even be able to? She's already nine. Siss had stopped talking, too. She held onto my head and looked every which way. I could see our reflection in the store windows. It was heartwarming, like in a film: a drunken dad and his rather grown-up daughter on his shoulders.

Laura was standing near the cobbler's counter. Her head drooped like a sad little girl and her purse dangled long and forlornly from her feeble grip, almost brushing the floor. I suppose it's not easy for her to be with a guy like me. But suddenly, I balked at the idea: she was the one who wanted to be with me and get married! I hadn't pressured her or anything. Or had I? I couldn't remember anymore. I suppose I was just a persistent guy, and probably not as persistent anymore. It's not something you can do every day. Maybe sometimes when the weather's nice. Or was the problem that I obviously tried harder to be nice and accommodating with Siskin? It wasn't out of the question. How had Laura put it that one time? "But *I'm* your daughter, too." She'd been in a good mood when she said it. Jokingly, of course. Even though there was a grain of truth to it. A pinch, even. A pinch of salt.

Laura didn't even look up when we came and stood next to her. The cobbler was making spare keys at the back wall of his space. A sign stood on the counter, reading: SHOES MUST BE CLEAN AND DRY. Heh. We wouldn't be standing here if her foot was dry.

The cobbler noticed us out of the corner of his eye, but finished making the keys and wiped his hands clean on his apron at a leisurely pace before coming to serve us. I could read Laura's mind as we waited. She was thinking: We're running late and need to go meet Tuuli at the bus station and we don't have any time to buy all the things I planned to serve at the party. She'd long since given up on the idea to make wraps before Tuuli came, as they would need to stand for a little while. Even though she'd come up with the plan days ago. I almost joked that Muammar Gaddafi was in a much bigger pickle right now than any unmade wraps, but I luckily caught myself. I don't know what would've happened if I'd said it. Divorce? It certainly wouldn't have lowered the tension.

He'd sized up the situation before he walked to our side of the room. At least that's what I thought. Laura had lost all hope by the time she'd stepped up to the counter, and Siss was wearing a wet sneaker with half the sole peeled off. I believed the cobbler had also resolved to save our marriage and then send me on my way in as mild and carefree of a mood as possible. I, for my own part, agreed in advance to receive his wisdom.

"The thing is, I'm sorry, but our shoe's not dry and clean. The rubber came off just now and we've still got a ways to go," I explained, pulling the sole of Siskin's shoe as far back as it would go.

"I see," the gray-mustachioed cobbler grunted. "But I don't have that kind of glue. Synthetic. And it'd need to dry even if I did. Otherwise, the glue won't stick. You'll have to dry the shoe and then take it to the cobbler down the street. Endla 33 is the address."

"It's a sneaker," Siss specified.

"You said Endla 33?"

"Yep. Endla 33."

"Siska, try to remember that address. Endla 33."

"Endla 33, Daddy. I already remember it."

Laura didn't make the slightest movement to show her impatience. She was frozen from head to toe.

"Thanks," I said to the wise cobbler, then turned to Laura. "Okay, let's go to Prisma."

I started walking, fighting the urge to look back and check if she would follow. What if she went straight to the bus station to wait for Tuuli instead, and then they went out to drink somewhere and there would be no going to Laura's apartment? What would Siska and I do then? There'd be no more cartoons.

I fished through the coin pocket of my jeans once I reached the line of locked carts, Siss still on my shoulders. Oof. I was running out of steam. It would have been best to just lift her into the child seat, but I was beat.

"Time to get off, kiddo."

"My legs were already starting to get stiff, anyway. Especially the wet one. The other one, too, though."

I lifted Siska down onto the ground. There was still some strength left in my arms. Enough to lift her up. I really have drunk myself away. The only strong, exercised part left is my abdomen. My arms do nothing, my legs do nothing, my head does nothing. Sumo wrestling could be my thing. I could rise through the ranks in a league of drunk veteran *rikishi*. It felt promising. I kept searching for a coin to stick into the cart and unlock the chain, but couldn't find one.

Laura appeared beside us. Relief.

"Laur, do you have a coin on you?"

She didn't hear me. I wasn't sure if she was pretending not to hear, didn't feel like hearing, couldn't bring herself to hear, or was just so tuned out that she genuinely didn't hear at all.

"I don't hear you, you don't hear me." What band sang that? Some young guys, boisterously and without a care. In a major key. I suppose that's the mentality of these days. Though back in the old days, there were also tough guys who'd say: speak, speak, my ass will hear.

It's nice that Siska and I hear each other, always and immediately. We'll see how long it lasts. What's that attitude say about a person? That you're more important than I am when we're together? That it's nice that way and that's the way I like it? And I like how you're capable of acting the same?

I kept searching my pockets but couldn't find a coin, so I went and got change.

Siss stood and waited next to Laura, though she didn't look in her direction. She's learned to switch herself off and not interfere when grown-ups are bickering. Perhaps she just realized there's no point in trying to get a word in.

Siskin is already so big that jamming her into the child's seat of a shopping cart takes time. It's hard to fit her feet through the holes, especially when she's wearing puffy sneakers.

"Take off your kicks, kid."

Siss pulled her sneakers off and I finally wedged her into the seat. I used to push her around in the cart itself and had fun careening around the store, but somebody usually comes to put a stop to that now. I squeezed her foot.

"Honey, your sock is soaked through."

"I know. It's super nasty."

"Let's go."

I started walking at a brisk pace, though I had no idea where to go. Laura hadn't said anything yet, either. I stopped a pretty employee. She looked Russian.

"Chyildryen's saks?"

She was Russian.

"Kam, let's go."

As I followed her, I wondered if maybe she only seemed attractive because of her makeup.

I grabbed the first pair of socks I spotted and stopped the employee before she turned to leave.

"Sorry, hold on—we need shoes, too. Children's shoes."

The woman stared as I pulled off Siskin's wet sock and replaced it with a dry sock, its pair dangling from the white plastic piece they'd remove at checkout. She made no comment. I held myself back from mumbling: "*Nu*, lyets go."

Children's shoes were in the next aisle.

"*Spasiiiba*," I said to the young Russian employee in heavily accented Russian.

Someone had been trying on shoes there before us and one hefty-looking boot was lying right next to the stool.

"This one looks great, let's take it," I said, tossing it to Siskin. We were in a hurry to track down Laura and save what was left of our marriage. How did these marital crises arise so easily? We hadn't even been married a full year yet. What led to Uuno Turhapuro's crisis? And how did he resolve it? One should know the classics. If you don't, then where are you going to find the meaning of life? Or of love?

"Do you like it?" I asked, trying to put it on Siska's foot.

"I dunno. There's only one of them here."

"But you've only got one wet foot."

Siss giggled.

"I don't think they'll sell us just one. Anyways, it doesn't fit."

Siskin's laughter calmed me down a little.

"Come on, get out of the cart and put it on yourself. Here's a horn, too."

"A horn?"

"A shoehorn."

I dropped the boot and started tugging Siska out of the cart. I was a little too rough.

"Ow, Daddy."

"You still have your foot?"

"I don't know."

"Better if you do, otherwise this whole shoe hunt would be a waste."

I could tell Siss wasn't too badly injured.

"Did you get hurt?"

"A little, but it's fine."

It took me a long time to get the shoelaces undone.

"See if this one will fit. What's your shoe size?"

"I've got shoes in all kinds of sizes. Kid's 11 and 12 and women's 2."

"Well, it's on your foot. Stand up. How is it?"

Laura suddenly set the boot's pair down next to us. She had followed us. Just in case, I didn't look in her direction or say anything.

"Is there space by your big toe?"

"I think there is, Daddy. And I think my toe's scrunched up."

Out of the corner of my eye, I noticed Laura walking down the aisle. Whew—maybe she'd gotten over her mood.

"Honey, take that Spanish boot off now."

"Spanish?"

"Yeah. Do you remember when we were in Spain together?"

Siss was working on pulling off the boot.

"Not really, but I know we went there. You've talked about it a lot."

I acknowledged that was probably true—my world is so tiny, and the things I know and I do are so few, that I no doubt end up talking about them over and over again. Everything I bring up in conversation is always simple and primitive, too. *I am just a simple man, trying to be me.* Who sang that? There wasn't much to the song aside of the same words on repeat. It might have been Bad Company. Well, what's wrong with singing Bad Company songs? They should suit me well. Sometimes, I wish things were even simpler. The more simply you go about life, the purer and prettier are the things you get from it. Like the crumpled shoes in that painting. Whose was it? Cézanne or Van Gogh? I suppose both painted crumpled shoes at some point in their lives, whenever there were no good models to be found. They were forced to simply find friends around them. Friends like a pair of old shoes.

I wonder when Siska will get tired of me sounding like a broken record? Perhaps she wouldn't if I could just manage to talk about the same things in a more interesting way. If I could see those trivial things, beer bottles, pines, and familiar faces better all the time. But maybe being able to see and understand better is no more than an illusion. Maybe you can't even really grasp what's been. Or it just no longer interests you. Laura had disappeared for an awfully long time already. And she was the one in a hurry! What time was Tuuli's bus supposed to arrive from Tartu?

Siss kicked her newly-socked foot back and forth, in no rush to go anywhere. She was prepared to sit there for as long as it took. How wonderful! You could learn a thing or two about passing the time from her. Siska had no idea what was to come, but it gave her no concern at all. Like an old Aboriginal or Indian chief.

"Daddy?"

"What is it, honey?"

"Do you love Laura?"

"I don't know. Sometimes it feels like I do, but sometimes we just can't seem to get along. If we were to have a hundred years to get used to each other, then . . ."

"You'd start loving each other."

"Or hating each other. Either way is possible. Now, I bet you want to know whether I love her or hate her more than your mom."

"Yeah, I did want to ask that."

"You go and try to answer a question like that! What do you think? What's the right answer? You're actually smarter than I am and I bet you could teach me something."

"Okay. But one more thing."

"Something just as simple?"

"I dunno. You were talking about that horn."

"Shoehorn. This one."

"Yeah. And it got me thinking about that horn all filled with fruit and stuff. A corn . . . cornucopia. And now I'm hungry."

Did I really have to go and make that mistake? It'd be a while before we could stop to eat somewhere or make anything.

"We're in a supermarket. There's food everywhere you look. Grab whatever you'd like. And pour some food into the shoe with its horn, too. Stick half of a candy bar into the toe. I'm sure the next person who tries it on will be delighted."

"They'll think St. Nicholas put it there!"

Laura walked up carrying a heap of boots in her arms. She dumped them on the floor next to us—all the same style but different sizes.

"Did they have to get more from the back?"

"Yeah."

Oh-ho! Laura was talking to me. Oh, happy day.

I measured the sole of one against Siskin's foot, adding a little extra room for her to grow. Size 2.5. Those should last her till high school.

"Here, try this one on."

Siss worked her foot into it. The pair wasn't connected by any plastic bits. She stood and thought for a second.

"Well?"

"They're kind of big. But I think we'll take them."

"Good job, Pippi Longstocking! Try walking in them, too. See if you can go backwards."

Siss did, flawlessly. Then, she sprinted away through the aisles.

I left the pile of boots lying there and turned to Laura.

"Alright, come on. Let's quick grab something to eat, Laur, and then hurry to the bus station. Should I call us a taxi? No, never mind—there's always some waiting out next to the gas station. We'll take one of those."

I strode away in Siska's pursuit.

"Siss!" I called out across the supermarket. "Don't go disappearing. We've got to leave in a minute."

"I'm just trying my boots out!" she yelled back over her shoulder, and immediately took a spill. She lay still as I abandoned the cart and ran over to her. How badly had she banged herself up?

Siss looked up at me. There didn't appear to be blood anywhere. I reckoned she was more shocked than anything. I knelt down next to her and helped her to sit up.

"These are really good boots, though, Daddy. I like them. So what that I fall down in them sometimes. You don't have to take them back."

"Okay, honey. Let's get up. We're in a little hurry."

"Is it my fault?"

"No, honey, it's not."

I stroked Siskin's head and she flung her arms around me. I closed my eyes and we stayed that way for a few long, wonderful moments: she sitting, I kneeling in the middle of the supermarket.

When I opened my eyes again, I looked around to see where Laura was. There were heads turning away and people starting to move and Laura standing next to the cart, her head drooping. I scooped Siskin up in my arms and shuffled back, peeking to see whether Laura's tears were dripping onto the floor. There didn't seem to be any.

"Laur, let's go. Time to skedaddle. Hey, toss some fruits and veggies into the cart here—whatever you want. What else? Should I grab a number for the ready-to-eat counter? I'll grab some wine, too. Does it make any difference what I get, or is it all the same?"

Laura slowly lifted her head but didn't fix her eyes on me, or on the far wall of the supermarket. She just stared off into space.

"Hey, come on, let's go now, please . . ."

I lifted Siskin back into the cart, trying to seem unconcerned. It took me a while to get her new boots wedged in through the gaps.

Laura took a few steps backwards. I could feel more than hear her heavy breathing.

I was about to try one more time, but decided it was better to wait. Siskin briefly glanced at her, but then looked away, seeming not to be worried. We've got similar traits. Has she learned them from me, or are they genetic?

Laura's head was now arced up and nearly all the way back, her face scrunched up. She was inhaling and exhaling through her nose at full force.

I waited. I can't say how long the situation went on for.

"I can't. I just can't."

Laura spoke very softly, but for some reason I felt I could hear or sense her words perfectly. Was I maybe reading her lips, too?

"I'm so angry. So angry that I just can't."

We stood and waited. I was silent, Laur was silent, Siska was silent. I tried to keep any expression from forming on my face. No wrinkling of the brow, no smile, no smirk. I froze like a store mannequin, waiting for Laura's decision.

She approached us again, now quite calmly and unemotionally. The incident had passed.

"I don't know. Let's just get some kind of fish and maybe shrimp and a selection of different cheeses."

"Okay."

I wanted to ask what time Tuuli's bus was supposed to arrive, as I'd completely forgotten. But I didn't. I supposed she'd call if she arrived and we weren't there to meet her.

PRESSURE

I WAS HALFWAY through writing when I became worried. Where was the springboard? The conflict that maintained pressure? I didn't want to simply imagine one. It would've seemed bland with that kind of a piece. I hoped life would deliver one to me.

But things had been generally quiet, lazy, and happy between us for quite a while. We rarely bickered, rarely engaged in chilly silence, and fucked even more rarely. Things were pretty good. All I wanted to do was hang around the studio all day long and plug away at writing. But when you can't get the ball rolling with a piece of literature, then things are pretty bleak. How long could I keep working away at it that way?

I thought for a while and realized that the outcome could only be negative. Laura having a baby wouldn't do the trick, so long as it didn't throw her into depression. On top of that, Laura didn't want kids. She thought she couldn't even handle herself. If she were to die, as she's threatened to do, it might be alright as a short story, but not a novel. Why can the topic only be negative?

Seeming to intuit my problem out of the blue, Laura came to the rescue and unexpectedly transformed her lifestyle. Whereas we used to just hang around at home or drift around town (and there was a period when Laura said that, just like me, there was nothing else in the world she'd rather do), she now got down to serious business and started partying five times a week in places unbeknownst to me and without extending an invitation.

First, she disappeared for an entire night without saying anything. I couldn't get a hold of her.

Then, she went to a birthday party and double-locked the door, which prevented me from getting into her apartment to wait.

I huffed and I puffed, feeling pissed off and shitty.

Laura just put on a fresh layer of makeup, sneered at me a little, and disappeared back into the night.

I was at a total loss.

"Someone recommended that I don't just go out with you, but spend time with other people, too," she said. "I can't during the day because I'm at work. Ergo, I've got to go out at night."

I felt my blood boil. How arrogant! We'd managed to go out and do things during the daytime frequently before. But whenever it was starting to get late, Laura would often say: "I can't, I'm so tired. I've got to go to work tomorrow." Well, there you go. The difference was where she went and with whom.

We argued and shouted obscenities at each other. Laura was no worse than me in the art of vulgarity. We gave no thought to the neighbors, or anything else for that matter. I slammed a knife into the cutting board, snapping it in half. At least it was into the cutting board. In the early morning hours after Laura came back, I lay in bed next to her, staring at her body and knowing that if I were to attempt to touch it, she'd push my hand away.

Then, I tried a conciliatory approach. I spoke calmly, blamed myself and absolved her of all guilt, spoke about how I was a slave to love and unable to be alone and hugged her, and Laura put up with it numbly and indifferently. Still, she did put up with it. At the same time, I realized it was better not to go any farther than platonic hugging. *Me, her husband*, I thought bitterly.

I felt like we'd been living some kind of a life together before, but now, I had stayed behind or been abandoned while Laura had moved ahead somewhere else. Where, I didn't know. In any case, she was having the time of her life elsewhere, while I was sad, miserable, and alone here in our former life together.

I explained to her how I felt.

"That's your problem," Laura snapped.

"I guess so. I thought I was taking a wife, but I got a problem."

"So, I'm your problem?"

"That's what you're getting at."

I somehow got the impression she enjoyed being my problem. Like a new role in her new life.

Ah-ha! I thought. I'd hoped life would give me a springboard for my writing, and it had. It was just wound so incredibly tight that I could only mope around home, depressed and apathetic, unable to really do anything in my precarious position.

On top of that, where was my original textual springboard? Should I write about exacerbating jealousy swelling into a great, menacing passion that drove the object of affection far away? For who'd want to be the subject of a psychopath's delusions? Nobody. It's been written about a hundred times.

Right, and what hasn't been in terms of relationships between men and women? Were you hoping that your romance would be somehow original, Peeter? Not really. I didn't know what to hope for—it was nice to just let things be.

I demurred. I didn't want the springboard that had been delivered upon my request. If trouble and misfortune alone were fit to be a springboard, then I didn't even want that anymore. I'd simply write without any inner conflicts or tensions or fights or development. Just give me my happy life back. It's nice to occasionally write and have no greater desires, but literature doesn't matter more than life. Old uncle Fyodor Dostoevsky knew that well. But what did that old guy do? He continued to write and torment people with varying degrees of success. I suppose he loved, too. Sadomasochism. If there's no black-latex-costume sadomasochism, then it's still there in some form. Maybe the style with whips and those black latex costumes is better. You get your roleplaying fix and are free to live another life. I just torture and love here day and night without any kind of whip. It's exhausting.

◆

I was waiting as the pharmacist bagged my aspirin and a bottle of Alka-Seltzer Plus.

"What do you know—Peeter's out shopping!"

It was Kaku, grinning from ear to ear.

"Yep, only the best."

"Attaboy."

I was glad that those were the only two items on the shopping list, not more potent stuff. Though what medication could really be so compromising? Antibiotics can be used to treat STDs and pneumonia alike. And who cares if I were to buy condoms or a pregnancy test from the pharmacy? It wouldn't be the first time.

"Take a look at what I'm getting," he said, unlocking his phone and showing me a note he'd typed as a reminder: Perskindol. It almost looked like *persekindel*—ass-sure. My mood immediately improved.

"Would you look at that. They've included a little joke with the drugs."

"Right?"

I wanted to wait and hear Kaku ask the pharmacist if they sold Persekindel, but Siss was waiting for me with her cough and runny nose, so I left. Even though the drugs weren't even for her.

TIME

"DADDY, CAN I come to Koidu and pick up my things?"

"Of course you can! There's no need to ask."

"Okay. Mom is going to drive with me and get them. I guess you don't want to be home then."

"I'm not, actually. I'm at Laura's. When are you going?"

"I dunno. Soon."

"Okay, then I'll stay here. I wasn't going to go there before this afternoon, anyway."

"We'll be gone by then."

I didn't understand why she'd called. They'd come and gone to get things and drop things off when I was home before, too. I'd even gone there to haul off an old cupboard she no longer needed, piece by piece. Though to be fair, no one was home at the time. We'll see how many more times I manage to carry those pieces from place to place. Just some tired old possessions that occasionally need to be moved until they're abandoned. They were once new and precious. Or simply functional. How can they be made old and precious? You've got to want to make a home with someone, or at least play home. But I haven't done that or played that game in a long time already. Who knows—maybe I never will again. I'll remain an impartial witness on foreign soil.

But when I went to my studio that day, there was a note on the table: Daddy i Sissi, cam got all the things. We get tugetir In June ok. I kant wait. LOTS LOTS HUGS AN KISESES LOVE SISSI

I was amazed at how much she's grown up—capital and lower-case letters, and even a few commas and periods. She wasn't the same kid who had sent me an SMS when I was in London, reading: DADDY IM O SAT. That was after the divorce. How many years has it been? Who knows. And do I really even want to know how many? And how many years has it been since everything was last great? Siss was already born. Or at least on her way. It's a good thing she waited around.

◆

It was such a meager time in Estonia that I asked the salesclerk for two eggs.

There wasn't much on the shelves overall, of course. Bread, I think, and flour or some other kind of milled cereals. Maybe even milk. There were ration stamps for other stuff, but not eggs.

"What do you mean, two?!" the chubby and cheerful clerk asked. "Take a whole dozen, make yourself a nest."

"No, just two eggs, please."

I brought them back to my studio and cooked them for my girlfriend. We ate. Whether fried or hard-boiled, I can't remember.

How could that kind of a time have existed? How could it be that everything was so natural and ordinary? As if things had always been that way? What if that sort of a time were to resurface? I'm sure it'd seem the same way before long. Otherwise, I wouldn't stand it. One has to adapt. And maybe by adapting, you can manage to be happy and content. No matter how or where.

I suppose the girl and I were happy and content rather frequently in that studio. Twenty years ago, more or less. I can't say those emotions occur all that frequently anymore. We were probably content so long as we took care of each other. But at some point, that ended. Who messed things up for the other? I suppose we both did, taking turns and with varying success, which makes such things increasingly difficult to right.

◆

What's something I haven't done in a long time?

It's been years since I last rode a bike. I think I haven't fucked in several weeks. No, more—over a month. Or is it two? Time is hazy. I haven't watched TV in a while either, luckily. Why do I say 'luckily'? Because the situation would be even worse if I had. I haven't stayed sober in who-knows-how-long. But it's been ages since I last wanted to kill myself, too. Since I last told you I love you? And have I ever said it without acting ludicrous or as part of some dark humor? I haven't considered the existence of God. Exist or not, my pondering isn't going to change much about it. Oh, right—I haven't had ice cream in a long time. No, wait—I asked for a bite of Siss's one day and she gave it to me. I haven't bought new clothes in some time, a clear sign of mid-life crisis. I've been sick, just recently. I haven't been entirely drunk, strangely, even though I'm buzzed all the time. My body can't handle drinking much anymore. Moderation has arrived.

But what would I *like* to do? Good question. There are actually a lot of things. I'd like to get along with you. Arguments are boring. But what can I do to make that happen? We both want it, but at different times. Why can't our intentions coincide? Every time you express the desire, I feel like—great, you've got it. Which means I don't need to hurry; no doubt I'll get there. But by the time I finally do, you've run out of steam or lost interest and have lost it. And then, I take offense. I approach you so things can finally be pleasant, but you no longer want it. And then I say—fine, if you don't want it, then there's no need, either.

Do I need to fall in love with someone for there to be a spark to life? I don't think I can fall in love with you anymore. Did I ever even fall in love with you before? We've just been close companions. Relatives. You don't fall in love with kin. Ergo . . . Sure, but what if you fall in love with someone else? Death and destruction, even though both of us have other loves in our past. And neither of us probably misses those woes. You can want to be slightly in love sometimes, just to feel somewhat happier. Without actually doing anything. But who can guarantee that it won't blossom and bury everything beneath it?

So, I haven't been in love in a long time. And I don't know if I want to or not.

If only spring would arrive. It hasn't been spring in over six months. Though I suppose it's not coming anytime soon.

APPOINTMENT

"WOULD YOU COME to a job interview with me? It's tomorrow at ten."
I was puzzled.

"What am I going to do there? Do they want to see your husband? I'll just leave a bad impression. I've done a lot of work to achieve it."

"I don't know how to get there."

"Look up a map of Tallinn online."

"I did. There are so many streets. I don't know where they're all at. And I don't have money for cab fare. And you don't have any to give me, either."

"How long have you been living in Tallinn?"

"A few years. You don't need to come if you don't have time, okay?"

Damn it, I thought. *We didn't use to talk this way. That is—I didn't talk to you this way.*

"Of course I'll come with you. I've got nothing else to do, anyway. When is it?"

"I just told you. Tomorrow at ten." At least you didn't say it in a pissed-off tone. I couldn't tell if you were still hoping I'd come even when you continued: "You know, no—please don't come if you're going to be this way."

"But I want to come. I like going out with you together. We haven't been anywhere together in who-knows-how-long. What's the job?"

"What difference does it make . . . I told you yesterday already."

"Can't you repeat it?"

"I don't want to."

"Fine. I'm coming. I'll come with you, no matter what the job is."

"Okay, fine. But could you wait for me there? I don't think it'll take too long."

"You can't get back on your own, either?"

"I don't know. I get afraid. And I don't want to call you if I get lost."

"Little girl in the big city."

But I knew you were right. You only moved along specific urban trajectories that you'd practiced and learned. Lines between certain shops, or certain bars and cinemas. Or beauty parlors. And maybe a handful of people's homes. Tallinn isn't a metropolis where you feel lonely among masses of people, but you can cultivate the feeling if you try. There's loneliness in the crowd, but just not the 'crowd' part.

Have blithe flirtation and hitting on other men become a sort of soft nagging, the next phase? Dishes fly across the room and doors slam. The doors have already slammed, but there've been no flying dishes yet. I wouldn't quite dare to throw you. You're more fragile and delicate than porcelain. On top of that, me cracking your skull on the ground probably wouldn't upset you more than if I smashed your heirloom teacups. I've accidently broken a few when drunk before, but not your skull. So, how do I know that the former would be worse than the latter? Because you don't care much for yourself, even though you're abhorrently self-centered. I can't understand how those two things can be true simultaneously, but they are. A lack of self-care just made others care for you more and fed your love for yourself. You didn't deny it yourself.

I knew I'd have a hard time getting up early enough to accompany you somewhere by ten o'clock. That's usually when I'm just getting out of bed. And it's not *my* job interview. Could I even come up with a place where I'd like to work? It's just as unlikely as thinking of a place that would want to hire me. Could I be a mailman? What about you? Would you have the strength to haul a mail bag around? Would you feel like making sure that every single letter went into the right mailbox? Could I be a building caretaker? What about you? Do you know what time a caretaker wakes up at? Around six. *You* don't have hangovers so early in the morning. Others have been no better than me, of course. Juhan Viiding was only good at disappearing into the dewy grass and Salinger at catching kids on a field. True, he was pretty good at it and managed to snag several young college girls. If you can still call them kids.

"Wake me up in the morning then, please."

"But you won't get up."

"Try it several times."

"You'll get angry."

"I won't."

"You get angry every time my alarm clock goes off repeatedly."

"That's different. I didn't have to get up those times."

"You don't have to tomorrow, either."

"No, I want to."

I knew I should try to go to bed by midnight at the latest, but I couldn't fall asleep. I wasn't used to trying that early. I scrolled through Facebook and read an old newspaper and solved a crossword puzzle. Slowly, slowly. As slowly as the tenacious snail climbed Mount Fuji. Only where was my mountain and where was its peak? At the same time, who says the snail can even glimpse Fuji's peak and knows it's climbing a mountain in the first place? It's just what that poet said—what was his name again? Had he even ever seen the snail ascending the mountain? I doubt it. The poet was only speaking to himself. He had some peak of his own that he wanted to reach. Ambition. But if he saw himself as the snail, then maybe he didn't quite believe he'd ever make it to the top. Maybe he was simply poking fun at himself. Still, which of us is happier: the poet with his unreachable peak, or I without one?

You'd been asleep for a while already. I'd gone to lie in bed with you for a bit and just hold your hand, not even harboring the faintest hope of it leading to sex. But it was also nice to just feel your presence and hold your hand. Call it a sense of security or an energy flow. I drifted in and out of sleep, too, but kept finding myself wide awake. A clock ticked or a cat softly prowled in that quiet, dark room. Getting up seemed pointless. Lying awake seemed pointless, too.

So, it was better to sit behind a half-finished crossword puzzle. I then managed to fall asleep and be obstinate and ornery when you got up in the morning.

I hadn't needed many drinks to fall asleep that time, either. Port wine. Or pepper vodka. Only a few beers. I milked them for as long as I could so that the beer only ran out once I felt tuckered out, not before. I managed to time it pretty well. The situation was in the right place by two-thirty in the morning. And then, I plummeted into a black hole.

Even so, I sat upright on the edge of the couch the moment your telephone alarm went off. You hit snooze and rolled over. As always, you'd set a backup alarm. I glared at you, feeling like a pulp. I wanted to flop back down to a horizontal position, but I knew it would make the next attempt awfully difficult. It is every time that you tell the first attempt to take a hike. Squinting through swollen eyelids, I dragged myself into the shower and turned on the faucet. Cold water would've gotten the blood flowing and woken me up more efficiently, but it also would've felt terrible. My eyelids drooped under the warm stream of water and I waited to hear your phone alarm go off again.

Hmm. Were you planning to take a shower before your interview, too? You usually didn't shower on weekday mornings. But if you had planned on taking one now, then the warm water would soon run out and you'd be pissed off. I closed the faucets, mechanically dried myself off, and trudged into the kitchen, peering into the living room as I went. You were asleep. Your second alarm hadn't gone off yet. How were you able to count them in your sleep and get up when it was the right one?

I sat down at the kitchen table, last night's unfinished crossword puzzle before me. I picked up a pen, squinted at it, and wondered what the hell I was doing.

◆

I stood outside on the sidewalk.

You'd gone in and said you'd likely be done in no time. Job interviews—how long could those take? I'd accompanied you there, so I reckoned I could go ahead and split. No doubt you'd find the way back on your own. But we'd forgotten to work out those details. You said you'd be right out, but half an hour had already passed.

I'd left my phone at home.

It felt weird just standing there on the street as if I was waiting for a date. But you never agreed upon a random spot on the street to meet. There was a café just around the corner. I went there.

"One meat pastry, please."

"Should I warm it up?"

"Just a little. But could you pack it up in a doggie bag?"

"Sure."

I trotted back to the spot, clutching the pie packed in a paper bag. You don't like it when I disappear or run late anywhere. Not that I do it on purpose. Though it does happen all the time. I suppose I'm absentminded. Maybe you think that shows that I don't care. Still, it could also show that I hold you near and dear to my heart. It's like I'm going on a date with myself. You can always run a little late to those. How are you going to up and leave yourself?

I crossed the street to eat the pie in a park. There were two Russian girls there pushing a stroller. They took turns at the helm, glancing at me out of the corner of their eyes. I had the urge to go and tell them I was no suspicious perv and was just there to eat my meat pie. It had to be as clear as day to them, too. I don't know how I could tell right off the bat that they were Russian. Some tiny details gave it away. Clothes, makeup. They pushed the wailing kid back and forth, shushing it one after another, all while I walked back and forth with my pie, keeping one eye on the sidewalk. The girls were pretty. I had a mind to chat with them a bit. But that was impossible.

How can a job interview last for forty-five minutes? Did you get pissed off when you didn't see me and booked it? You'd sure have it in for me then. You'd be in a bad mood for ages.

It felt incredible to just stroll back and forth without any purpose. There was nowhere for me to go. I had a duty—I was allowed to stroll. I'd be a great mailman. Maybe I could even stand guard in front of the presidential palace. I wonder how long they have to stand there? Twenty minutes? Half an hour? How long did a *dnyevalniy* stand guard in the Soviet Army? I can't recall. But they'd never have me at the palace. The ones there belong to some elite squad.

It's a good thing I left my phone at home. Now, all I can do is stand and walk, walk and stand. I should leave my phone at home on purpose next time. Though I suppose that trick doesn't work like that. It wouldn't be genuine solitude and silence anymore. A little fake and intentional. I used to have a phone that turned off on its own all the time. Broken. It made for a lot of silence, but was a little worrying, too. Leaving your phone behind somewhere is better.

Fine—I'll eat my pie, wait for a full hour to have passed, and then go inside. Even though it was nice to just stand around and I felt like I could do so for hours. It'd be a stupid thing to do if you'd already left, though. I couldn't just lie to you and say I stayed waiting because that's what we'd agreed on. You would be able to tell there was something fishy. Neither could I deceive myself if I'd already thought that you might not be coming anymore. Waiting wouldn't be that nice, mere waiting anymore then.

Why do you get pissed off whenever I run late? Waiting is pretty great. Waiting for a good thing, at least.

I ate my pie slowly, savoring every mouthful, but it ran out in the end. I had to take a few steps towards the Russian girls to throw away the wrapper, which seemed to make them stiffen up and be more on their guard. I quickly disposed of the trash and hurried away at a guilty man's pace. Ah-ha! The flasher simply lost his nerve. Now, they'd have something to discuss later and tell all their girlfriends. They'd made a flasher in the park get lost! Some unshaven dude in a filthy jacket, probably Estonian.

You were nowhere in sight.

My obligatory hour wasn't up yet and I wouldn't leave before it was. It was my time, an hour allowed by God himself for me to simply stand around.

A middle-aged woman approached the Russian girls, cooed at the stroller a bit, and then took it over. Oh-ho! There's an explanation for everything. One of the girls must have been the woman's daughter, the other her friend. But in that case, one of them would've showed the baby a little more attention. Hmm. Maybe neither was the older woman's daughter, but a couple of relatives or connected to the family in some other way. We've a little more work to do here, Watson.

Eleven o'clock rolled around, so I went in. My head hung a little because I sensed that you'd beat it a long time ago. Probably when I was buying the pie. And that meant my meditative time was stolen.

It was a big office building. Where had you gone? Something that started with an A, I think. I couldn't ask from the security desk. I read the directory on the wall. Lots of businesses started with the letter A. Most of them, in fact. It's good when a company name begins with A. Then, you're at the top of all kinds of alphabetical lists. The two older women at the security desk stared at me suspiciously. Go ahead and stare. I wanted to be on my way. I picked one familiar-sounding A name and set off looking for their office. It took a good amount of searching.

A young secretary was seated right behind the door I opened.

"Hi. Did a young woman come here for an interview? An hour ago?"
I could tell from the secretary's mild confusion that I was in the right place.
"She left a while ago then, yeah?"
"I believe she's in the restroom."
"She been there for a while?"
"Let's go have a look."
I walked after the secretary. Another beautiful woman. You don't become a secretary otherwise, though. And there she went solving the problem in a jiffy. Right here in the bathroom!
The secretary held open the door to the women's bathroom. You were putting on makeup in front of the mirror and glanced over at me.
"Just a minute. It took a little longer than I expected."

INTENTIONS

T HINGS HAD SEEMED to be a little miserable lately. It wasn't the arguments—we'd fought since way back in the beginning, I think. We were
both tough and stubborn as mules. But so far, we'd always had the will to grind
that wheat into flour. The quality itself was debatable. It was just that we no
longer cared or wanted to resolve the fights anymore; to make concessions, forget the bad things, focus on what was good, be kind to one another. Over and
over, we pried open old closed-up scars and wounds. I suppose it's far from the
first time, feeling like if they won't make the effort to be nice to me, then why
should I return the favor? Why should I try harder? I, mysel,f have been giving
it my all, but all I get in return is a punch in the jaw over and over again. I can't
live as someone's punching bag. I knew I had to make things absolutely clear: I
don't buy it. If you want to keep this relationship going, then you're going to
have to pull yourself together and change. Though I suspect we both felt pretty
much the same way about each other.

I took a second to consider what kind of an email I was sending you—pure
nitpicking. At the same time, I hadn't been happy bumming around alone on
Koidu Street for who-knows-how-long. True, you had occasionally tried to be
a little nicer. But I don't know. I suppose I was convinced that you owed me
an apology for the last few times you'd told me to fuck off, and so long as I
hadn't received that apology, I wouldn't feel like you also realized you'd made
any kind of a mistake and didn't plan on acting like that again. Of course, you
had absolutely no intention of apologizing and would rather I fucked off for a
long time more. It would just drag on and on that way. I suspect we're not all that
original in terms of that.

These things are trivial. We could spend more time thinking about, oh, I
don't know, the meaning of life and human happiness, or even North Korea and
civil wars in Africa, but good luck with that. Nothing pleased us more than snapping at each other's throats day after day. Maybe it gave us some kind of energy.
Why else do people care to spend decades acting the same way? Nagging and
bickering one day after the next. Is that really our future? Oh, shit. Am I going
to suddenly become good tomorrow, like Albert Schweitzer or Gautama Sid-
dhartha? Fat chance. It'd all get too mushy. All the same, I wouldn't mind it
being a little better and cheerful for a change. Even if it just meant having sex.

There's the catch. I can be a good person, but if I don't get sex, then I slam the door shut again. I'm nice to you, but you don't even fuck me! There hasn't been any in ages! You don't even let me into your apartment if I haven't gone shopping for groceries and booze. Is that a classic marriage? What was I even expecting? For things to be different between us somehow? I suppose I did. Come to think of it, I didn't know what to expect. And now that I have my assumptions, what next? I suppose there's one option. Though I don't really feel like restarting the whole fiasco from square one with someone else. Even though it probably would be pretty great for a while.

Who was the French actress who said that love lasts for three years? Why three years, specifically? Is it biological? Because that's how long before a baby finishes breastfeeding and the mother can go out on the prowl again? And does that mean you should live in three-year stints with separations for a breather and beer? Though, nowadays, lots of people don't have kids. Then, your genes are the ones who are confused. They sit around your body, putting their heads together and shrugging. Humans don't want to yield to us anymore!

How many years have you and I been a couple? Four and a half? Almost forever and a half, which makes me feel a little loopy. But what's wrong with being loopy if it gives you bliss? There used to be hope that ignorance is bliss, but I've started to seriously doubt it. And it's already too late. You're not going to get any smarter after fifty. Maybe you can try and get a little wiser, but I also haven't observed intelligent people being much happier. Perhaps they're just better at hiding their unhappiness out of politeness. The ability to bear living is equally plentiful or scant among the intelligent and unintelligent. Intelligence must be more differentiated. Even if you divide wisdom into street smarts and book smarts, it doesn't adequately describe the situation. Funny—intelligence can be classified, but ignorance can't. There's no street ignorance or book ignorance. Ignorance is just freely accessible and identical in the eyes of the intelligent.

One time, my brain shorted out over the fact that you use name-brand laundry detergent and I use generic, and whenever your kitchen sponge looks a little worn out, you immediately throw it away, whereas I would have kept using it for several more months. And I, for the most part, buy all that higher-priced junk for your place and make do with the cheapest I can find for my own, because you don't have much money. Even though you work a nine-to-five and I'm officially unemployed. I also take your old things and put them to good use. You got a new couch and the old one came to my studio on Koidu Street. I sleep on it when we're fighting, and I remember the times we slept on it together. Armchairs, too. And your old stools. I'm your trash can. Maybe you'll start resenting it at some point. You buy new clothes in Helsinki; I go to the dollar store. You call me a dollar-store bum and we both laugh. And you say I'm stingy because, back when you lived in Lasnamäe, I'd buy you Lambrusco and Prosecco, but now opt for much cheaper sparkling wine. You don't come here to Koidu all too often and don't want to, either. It's dusty in every corner and strips of paint are peeling from the kitchen ceiling. There's only cold water and a shower in the chilly cellar and a wood-heated stove, but you've got hot water and a bath at your place. You threw out your old Soviet-era fridge and bought a state-of-the-art one, even though you don't have cash for groceries or wine. I've got a fridge that Arvo Pesti threw out and Tarmo Teder picked up off the street. It runs like a tractor engine and is dear to me. You eat and drink astonishing amounts. Why am I thinking about all this now? And why am I wondering how long it'll take for you to find a new chambermaid to replace me, one who does everything you want, if I start complaining? A bleating butler and a picky princess.

"Whenever my dad bought cheap toilet paper, I said something about it," you informed me.

"What'd he do then?"

"He stopped buying it."

When will you switch me out for someone else if I can't buy you things anymore? Only time will tell. When the Moor has done his work, the Moor can go. I'm sure it wouldn't be hard to find someone to deliver food and drink to you daily. Still, who knows. I can't say why you picked me for the job. There's not much hope for a severance fee, though. Probably not even a single fuck.

◆

I did a little side job in Viljandi. Luckily, I got a ride there and back and didn't have to take the bus. It was only for a day and the round-trip would've been grueling but I drank the whole way, because what else are you going to do when you've got to sit in a car for over two hours?

On the ride back, I realized it was almost ten o'clock and the shops would be closed by the time we arrived. So, I called you.

"I'm on my way. What do you want from the store? We're getting in sometime after ten."

"Sparkling wine."

"Okay. I'll stop somewhere and get some." I hung up.

"Hey, Marju?" I asked the driver. "I'd like to stop at a grocery store, please." Marju looked at the clock. I'd already asked for stops in several places to buy more booze, but she didn't comment. We pulled into a parking lot in Kose and I hurried into the store, trying to be quick.

The only sparkling wine they had was Sovetskoye Sladkoye, basically a fortified soft drink. Pricey, too. They didn't have a decent selection, and pepper vodka seemed like the only reasonable option. Pure and not too expensive. I decided not to buy beer for myself or wine for you, but we'd share a bottle of pepper vodka, even though I'm not the biggest fan.

I called again, just to be sure.

"Hey, they've only got Sovetskoye Sladkoye. It's shit and stupidly expensive. I'm getting a bottle of pepper vodka instead, okay?"

Marju was waiting. I hung up and paid for the bottle. I didn't open it in the car—I could wait for us to drink it together in Tallinn. Instead, I cracked open the literary magazine I'd brought along and had another sip of beer.

When we were getting into Tallinn, I could tell that Marju was unsure of where to drop me off.

"Take me to Vindi Street, please."

"Vindi?" she asked hesitantly. Why Vindi? Didn't I live on Koidu Street? What was wrong? Was I that drunk? Not that that was unusual.

I tossed the empty plastic beer bottle into the trash can next to your building before marching up the stairs and knocking, because I didn't have the key to your front door anymore. I'd returned it to you at some point and you hadn't given me a new one, which meant I couldn't get into your place if you didn't want me there.

You opened the door, looking rather cheerful. It cheered me up to see you that way, too.

"I got the pepper vodka. There was nothing else good there."

"Did you get the smokes and juice I asked for, too?"

"Smokes and Juice? You asked?"

You gave me an odd look.

"Do you think I'm just going to drink pepper vodka straight or something?"

I felt like saying that we'd drunk all kinds of different vodkas straight before without any problem.

You stood in the doorway and waited. I didn't know what else to do but take out the magazine and read you the last few poems I'd read in the car. Anything but argue. You just stared at me, smiling and taking a step back. But I was confused, as you swung the door shut at the same time.

"What's wrong? What are you doing? Aren't you going to let me in?"

I can't remember if you replied. Probably not. But I do remember your tight-lipped smirk showing through the crack in the doorway. I was filled with warmth and booze and didn't feel like pleading or hammering on the door. If that was the way it was, then fine. I zipped up my coat and stomped home, not taking a single sip of the vodka. It's not a very long walk, only about ten minutes or so. You were the one who moved close to me for whatever reason.

I've been home alone for a long time, though. How long already? Five days? Six? Pretty snow is falling outside and I don't have proper firewood for heating.

I suppose neither of us are feeling all that great. And yet, neither of us can make the first move to get together, as that would mean giving up and retreating from our just position. Maybe even apologizing. But neither you nor I are capable or willing to do that.

One day, I emailed you: "You proposed that I fuck somebody else, since you yourself don't want to anymore. A girl who I think used to like me came to mind."

"Go, Peeter, go," you replied. "No need to talk so much about it."

Huh—I seem to remember that you were the one who talked about it, multiple times, I thought.

But two days later, you called and asked how I was doing.

"I don't know. Not great. You?"

"Not too great, either."

"Should I come over to your place? I'm going to finish up a couple of things first. Can I come then?" I checked the time and saw I wouldn't make it to the store first if I didn't leave soon.

"Mm, no. I dunno. I haven't thought about that yet."

And that's where we left it. Like school kids. Though I am 50. What do I even want? Don't I *want* life and love to be like it was back in school?

◆

Siss hasn't come around in a while. Does she have better things to do? Or is she just too grown-up? Did I offend her somehow? Occasionally, you find yourself having lots of friends, a companion, and a wife. And then, suddenly, you have none of them. It's sad. I'm sure they'll surface again sooner or later, though. Maybe.

◆

Eeny, meeny, miny, moe,
  Catch a tiger by the toe,
  If he hollers, let him go,
  Eeny, meeny, miny, moe.

Is that how the rhyme goes? Why did it sound so deep when Siska sang it once? Because if you catch something and it wants to go, you shouldn't stop it? How philosophical. The thought came and went, and things are still pretty much the same.

◆

"But I'm your daughter, too. I could be your kid!"

It recurrently came to mind after you said it. What did you mean by it? Aren't your parents parent-y enough? I suppose you did curse them while you were dying and banged your fist on the table, wailing: "Why are you all just letting me die?!" At the same time, you loved them and they loved you back.

Were you jealous of my children? Possibly.

Were you simply trying to say that I should care for you and show you tenderness as if you were a kid? Just like your parents did? Maybe. But I've never really been all that tender with my children, even though I certainly believe I've shown them love.

I can't love you like you were my child. Maybe I could learn some other way to love you. What other types of love are there, anyway? I've no idea. Or I do know something in theory, but not in emotion. I don't know what the criteria is. I would probably die for one of my kids. I'm not sure if I'd die for a parent. It's weird to say that I might even be prepared to give up my life for Estonia. Just not in war or by killing others. I'd just hand my life over for Estonia somewhere if I could and believed that it would help. Not like that will ever happen. So, it's just safe idealism. But what about giving my life up for you? I don't really know. Maybe if I was drunk. I seriously doubt you'd give up yours for mine any other way, and that's a good thing. If you give up your life for too many things, there won't be anything to give it for before long. I can at least buy you some groceries and wine today, though. There's still money left for that, I think.

DEATH

I CAN'T WRITE about my own death, unfortunately. But would I if I could? Would I describe how it happened?

What does that say about me? That whatever I'd like to write about is the ultimate? I can't imagine what that is, though, and even if I try, I just realize it's impossible to detail.

It's Blockhead Triinu all over again: the girl whose only idea for the essay on what she dreams of is a multicolored pen.

The vicious thinking cycle. Still, it's not bad that they're around: the multi-colored pen, infinity, immortality, or Blockhead Triinu.

The notion of wanting to describe death after dying is somehow comforting and assuages mortal fear. Just a little.

◆

Laura strode over to the door, opened it, and stood there.

"Get going!"

I glanced over my shoulder to see what the weather was like and whether a frightful wind was howling like in a Priit Pärn animated film where a man is thrown out of the house. Even though I'd only just come in. Still, it was dark and I couldn't tell if it was windy or not. I had no desire to venture back out into that darkness from whence I'd come, a couple beers clinking in my pocket. I'd much rather have waited for the sun to rise again.

"Okay, just a minute. I'll drink these beers first."

"Did you show up just to check on me?"

"What do you mean?"

"To see if I was home? If there was someone else here with me?"

"The thought didn't even cross my mind. Why? Should I have?"

Laura didn't reply.

"I just wanted to see you. To be together. I can check your ticket if you want. Even clip it. Ticket, please."

"Get going."

"Just a second. Sorry I only brought beer and no wine for you. It was late already, and I only had beer at home."

"Now."

"Okay, okay. I'll just work on this crossword a little and then I'll be out of your hair. Who's a six-letter Estonian writer?"

Laura retreated into the living room, leaving the door standing open. I realized my time was up either way, then figured out the puzzle all on my own.

"It's Kallas. Teet Kallas," I called out.

I hoped Laura would snap back that I'm Teet Kallas, but she just turned the radio up to full blast to avoid talking or hearing me.

Her cat Melissa stared at me, bemused. I felt the very same way.

♦

How could I manage to enslave you? Occasionally you're a slave, and we get along well when you are. Whenever you're totally broke, that is, and want me to bring you the best the grocery store has to offer (not that Maxima has anything of the sort) after we've had a drawn-out fight and you've been starving for days. I don't have the cash to buy you the most expensive things, of course. But I can scrounge up enough change for a couple bottles of sparkling wine for you to drink over the evening. And a couple bags of chips. A rotisserie chicken. A kilo of potatoes. Cucumbers, tomatoes, bell peppers, olives, cheese, and a few other little things.

If things go well and we don't get into another tiff, we might have sex around midnight in exchange for my offering.

How's that for life? Marriage. As beautiful as can be. Happy. There are no wars raging anywhere near. The flies aren't biting. The government's paying me unemployment benefits. I've just got to clean myself up once a month and show my face at the office, saying: "Hi, it's me again. I'm hunting for work night and day, honestly. Please give me my benefits."

"You are? Where do you plan on being in five months?"

"Right here at your desk, because you're so pretty and it's nice to have this rendezvous once a month."

No, that's not how I'd reply. I'd say: "Oh, I don't know. I guess it all depends on chance." What was that written on the wall of the toilet in grade school? *Õnn on juhus, junn on õhus.* Happiness is chance, a turd's in the air. I won't say that to my counselor. Though maybe that's a mistake. Perhaps she'd like it. On top of that, what could be better than being a floating turd, moving however you please? Freefall. But Salinger complained he was just falling and falling and getting nowhere. Or was that me in one of my last books? I can't remember. I tend to mix myself up with various writers. Not that there's really much of a difference between us.

Well, okay. There's two options. One is getting you pregnant. But that's not so easy. You'd sit at home then and be a slave, indeed. Depending on me. Only then, you wouldn't drink and maybe you'd get fed up with me drinking all the time and stinking in bed. How does Sergey Shnurov have such a beautiful wife? He drinks nonstop, too. I suppose St. Petersburg has a wide selection of women. Every day, they shout: "Women selection!" into a bullhorn on a street corner, you pull on a polyester jacket, and head out into the city to pick one out (if you feel like it).

The second option is to get you unemployed. But that's not up to me and you wouldn't want to be unemployed, either. Even if you did, you'd just mope around and not want to fuck, even though you'd depend on me even more.

◆

It's autumn, but the weather is spring-like. The wind is biting. Evening darkness. Thaw. Spring is in the air. I sit by the window, listening to the gusts. Winds come and winds go. The windows rattle a little. Softly. You, you old fart, can feel a couple more springs in your autumns this way. Don't fret. You won't be dead by tomorrow. And you can still get erections, too. On occasion. Snapping to attention. It does just lounge around, for the most part. Out of formation. Up, two, three, four, which leg do you wear it on? That's the whole meaning and philosophy of life these days. Uno Loop had that song that went: "May began in March," but here March happens in October and November. It's comforting in a way. Christmas snow fell in October and everything was beautiful. A couple days later, however, somebody said they couldn't wait for spring. Well, here it is.

I'd like to make a little springtime in winter, too. To travel somewhere. To go drink by the Mediterranean. I suppose I don't have the money for it, though.

Why do so many people die in spring? (Huh—didn't they used to say people fell in love then? And are the reasons the same?) Maybe our vital juices start flowing then and shriveled-up old bodies just can't take the internal movement. We'd have dozed on for a while longer if we hibernated, but once there's a demand for living, something cracks. Or the person just has such a great desire to see one more spring. When my mother had cancer, she told me she wondered how many more springs she'd be able to see, and every time spring rolled around once again, she was afraid it'd be her last. Life and desires become simpler when death is near. And I've always wanted life to be simple. I suppose you can't fake death being near, though. It doesn't work the same way. Maybe it'd help if you worked as an undertaker or a gravedigger. Something that kept the memento mori constantly in front of your nose. And in it. Though I reckon you get used to that over time, too, and soon no longer have the slightest whiff of death in your mind as you wash the corpses. A slaughterhouse worker doesn't think about death; otherwise, they wouldn't have it in them to kill anymore. I bet the former guards of concentration camps were also scratching the backs of their heads in Nuremberg and elsewhere later, also. Wondering: Did I really kill all those people? Did I gas and execute them? I'd never have believed it. So many of them. And they were all people. People just like me, really?

If you were to talk to someone who's been waiting on death row for their sentence to be carried out for years and years and years, just like they do in America, then would they be as indifferent about death as Jaan Kross was of his long-awaited Nobel Prize? The proximity of death won't make life sweeter like sugar in tea anymore, either. You dump in more and more, but everything is tasteless.

◆

I'm older and stupider than you. At least that's the way I feel. But will you also end up turning older and stupider someday? I don't know. And maybe you don't want to. I can't rule out you even starting to enjoy it.

I told you once about how Monica doesn't think about anything—she just sits around and smokes like an old lady, even though she's only twenty. You shot back with a resentful reply: "Well, *I* don't think about anything, either." I considered it for a minute and had to admit that you honestly didn't, even though I'd never noticed it before. Or hadn't known how to praise you for it. I should probably praise you more. I just don't seem to have the guts, because once I do, I'm going to have to start doing it more and more. And then I'll have to trump my last compliments, because repeating them would just seem uninspired. So, I just don't. And then I see some other guy coming and stroking you and giving you all kinds of compliments and you listen like the *Mona Lisa*. Just without the smirk. You are smiling, but it's an inner smile. It's not like I can pop up in those situations and say: Hold on! Wait up! I can compliment you, too! I can flatter you even more sweetly and with a kick! You wouldn't believe me. And you'd be able to tell I was jealous. Still, it's been that way for ages and you don't really care much anymore. A new guy's praise is always more intriguing. Naturally. It's the same when any new woman praises me, though that happens pretty rarely. What a life.

CHORES

S OMETHING WAS CLINKING in the washer. I wondered what it could be. Was there something with metal snaps hitting the glass?

I'd gone to Anne's apartment to do some laundry. She herself went out after I arrived, carrying a big black bag of clothes. Her washer is in the kitchen. I had a couple bottles of beer with me. I loaded it full and started a cycle.

"You can have whatever you'd like from the fridge while you're waiting," Anne said from the doorway.

"No thanks, I brought a couple of beers along," I said as I squatted next to the appliance.

"Well, beer's one thing I don't have. Have some kind of a *zakuska*, then. For your health."

"A *zakuska*," I repeated, grinning. "For my health." I couldn't tell from Anne's expression if she was joking or not. She must have felt good about being a good Samaritan and letting me do my laundry there.

"Alright, I'm going," she said, but still lingered. "Just let the door close on its own. You don't have to shut it yourself. But you know that, don't you."

I nodded.

There was nothing more to say. She left.

It's strange—I suppose the thought of us as a couple has never crossed Anne's mind. Is it because I visit her to do laundry and hold a debt of gratitude and that just won't do? Coming, washing my dirty underwear, and then wanting to climb into her bed to boot? I have made myself a sandwich on a couple of occasions, however, while I wait. She herself has offered it. And it's always a wonderful time, sitting and waiting in someone else's kitchen. There's no point in going out anywhere for an hour and a half. There wouldn't be time. And I couldn't, anyway—I don't have a key to get back in. I don't even have the desire to read anything. I just sit and stare out the window for the most part. Yep, back to childhood. The washer makes one sound, and then another. And then, it's silent for a while. It does its own thing, lives its own life. Idle time. Pleasant. I can't just sit around at home that way. I get restless, criticizing myself for not doing anything. But here, I am doing something. Laundry. I have the right to just hang around and do nothing. I have no desire to go into Anne's bedroom or living room and poke around her things. I've seen them before, anyway. We've sat and chatted. But since I'm just a clothes-washing visitor, I've never made any advances. Maybe I'm afraid of losing the chance to do my laundry there if I make the wrong move. Better the opportunity to have clean clothes once a month than an uncertain fuck. And I wouldn't cheat on Laura, anyway. It's just an obligatory thought that must be wondered so it isn't silenced and repressed and doesn't cause any frustration.

I hunched down next to the washer. What a television. A spinning world. Atoms, electrons, planets, stars, and a washer. Little in the great and great in the little. The triviality of abstractions, the metaphysics of trivialities. If only I knew what metaphysics is. I suppose it's something there used to be and no longer exists. Something from Immanuel Kant's household that he didn't want and sold off to some traveling salesman. And now, it's lost for good. Maybe it's since been recycled into a McDonald's burger that we've digested and shitted out without knowing it.

A few coins had settled near the washer's glass door. I'd forgotten to take them out of my pants pocket. I wanted it back. The coins were now nice and shiny. Washed with good old Ariel detergent. I doubted they'd end up going down the drain. Maybe they'd just block the pipes or break the washer and flood the apartment. Probably not, though. Whoever designed it had to have accounted for people not bothering to take coins out of their pockets before doing laundry. I wonder what amounts of money have been washed. Can you still take washed bills to a bank and exchange them for new ones?

I returned to the window. Thoughts are still inferior compared with what's outside. Even though the view wasn't very impressive. The backyard of a dilapidated wooden house, laundry lines, a collapsed garage, not a single person. But you just try to beat that with thinking. Then again, best to not even try.

It's too bad I have to leave once the washing is done. But there's no other choice. I can't stay sitting by the window with my clean laundry and Anne coming back as if I'd moved in to live with her. It's true—there were probably more random, vacant, pointless pauses back in Soviet times. The buses ran less frequently. You weren't able to appreciate them then. They had no value.

I can already recognize the residents of the neighboring building. The woman who stands by the window in the afternoon and stretches, wearing nothing but a shift. I don't think she can see me. Her light is on, mine isn't. And she's so far away. I can't make out her face or tell her age. Two little girls play behind another window; sometimes they fight and I glimpse their mother. But today, I saw a man there whom I haven't seen before. He got dressed. The kids were nowhere in sight. Who knows what'll be showing at that cinema the next time.

Maybe I should play out an episode by the window on Koidu Street, too. Even if it's fake. I could hang a noose from the hook of the light fixture. Or jump up and down, naked. Just to offer a little variety. But no one can really see into my window there. At least not without binoculars. I have no audience.

The drum started turning again, making the coins clink. I should put more money into the machine next time. I wonder if the sperm in my pants was still alive? Last time I was at Laura's place, I came right into them and then beat it. Even though I usually don't really feel like having a quickie right before I have to go somewhere. Old age. I could try to get myself into the mood, but there's no hope for Laura orgasming when it's just a quickie. And I don't know why, but that's becoming increasingly important. Some human aspect of sex that hasn't much to do with sexuality. Maybe in the end all we'll do is lie around, stroking each other's hands or shoulders, and that'll be it for eroticism. Otherwise, we'll be afraid of doing something wrong; something wrong for the other person. An orgasm doesn't outweigh her having bad sex. Quite the injustice. Sliding into middle-class decency. If you don't have anything nice to wear, you don't end up needing it.

There's something spinning around the brain like in a washing machine. Going around and around, even though I wasn't the one who sent it spinning. At least I think I wasn't. Ah, let it spin.

◆

I keep food between the windows in winter. It stays fresh even when the sun shines on it. The sunlight isn't warm enough to melt butter before spring. And I usually don't even have butter. I also usually don't have enough food to make getting to the bottom layer difficult. Food just goes bad if you have too much of it. Even in winter. It's only annoying when two people are trying to smoke, because then you can't open both sides of the window and have to hunch together by a single opening. In summer, I keep food under the kitchen table. And some other things in the Cabbages fridge. Most of the food I have there goes uneaten, though, because I rarely feel like going down to the basement to get it. And then Erko will ask: "Hey, Peeter—are these your leftovers? They stink."

"Show me. I can't remember. But I guess they must be. What's in there, anyway? Cheese usually doesn't stink."

"We ate the cheese one night, sorry. I'll buy you a new block."

"Oh, don't worry about it. I eat your guys' food all the time."

I peeled back the plastic wrap a little. It did smell pretty foul.

"I can't tell what this is. I'll throw it away. Maybe I'll flush it down the toilet. Otherwise, it'll stink up the dumpster for a while."

"Probably a good idea. Just don't . . ."

"I know, I won't flush the plastic wrap."

"Great. Good plan."

Whenever there's a crowd of people drinking at my place, I scoop the food out from between the windows so I can pull both open and everyone can fill their lungs nice and full of smoke.

But do you know why I stuff food in there in winter? The kitchen's usually just as cold as it is outside. I suppose I've seen it somewhere before and am trying to copy some Soviet scene. Nostalgia.

◆

"Could you please remind me tomorrow that I need to do things?"

"What things?"

"It doesn't matter. Just remind me tomorrow, then I'll know. I'll remember I'm supposed to do something.

"Tomorrow."

"Yeah. In the morning."

"If you don't tell me what things, then you might not remember them."

"You're right, but I don't really feel like talking about them right now. They're boring. And if I don't end up remembering them, then they must not have been important."

"We should get groceries tomorrow."

"Remind me of that then, too. My memory's shot."

"You sure have a sharp memory whenever I do something wrong."

"Memory is very specific. I always remember anything I've done wrong, too. Only childhood memories can be shameful sometimes. Not stuff from today."

"And you get a kick out of that shame."

"Maybe. It's shameful all over again when you remember. I guess I do get kind of a kick. The shame mostly comes from childhood. You know what? If you remind me tomorrow and I can't remember what I was supposed to do, then say we were talking about shame. Maybe that'll jog my memory."

"So, it's something tied to shame?"

"No. Just if I want to remember details, then remind me of the situation where we're talking about right now. It's a memory technique."

"Tie a knot in a handkerchief."

"I don't have any."

"Yes, you do. In your laundry basket."

"Do I really?"

"Yeah. You just haven't used them in ages."

"Oh, now I remember. Someone in my family got a whole box of handkerchiefs for Christmas. There was a picture of Mount Fuji on the box. It was yellow. The sun was shining on it."

"Were they silk?"

"No, I don't think so. I was jealous. Maybe that's one of them in the hamper."

"Go check."

I didn't feel like getting up and figured I'd look later. But I didn't.

The next morning, I immediately remembered that I'd asked you to remind me about something. I waited for you to say it, but you didn't. You'd forgotten. And then, I also forgot the things I'd planned to do.

◆

Sometimes, I'll kneel in front of the heating oven and chop firewood into kindling with a tiny axe. I enjoy it, chopping away like a little boy.

Mihkel brought it up one time (he lives in the apartment beneath me).

"What's all the banging going on up there? You chopping firewood?"

"Yeah. I make kindling. I like not having to burn too much paper. Or any at all." In reality, I just enjoyed splitting wood. Whenever I'm tipsy, I often miss and put dents into the metal sheet in front of the stove. I make sure not to strike myself, but the axe does sometimes hit the floor.

"Hey, I'm not keeping you up at night, am I?"

"No, no," Mihkel reassured me, scratching the back of his neck. "It's not that at all."

I realized there was *something*, but he was so damn polite that he wouldn't give it to me straight. There was a pause in the conversation as I pondered. Then, still grinning as if it was a funny story, he said:

"There's a crack in my ceiling there and the paint's coming off the wall."

"Seriously?" I'd been impressed by the retro renovations he'd done in his place.

"Yeah!" He chuckled.

I didn't know what to say, just wondering how I was going to start fires in the future. Maybe I'd buy those fire-starter blocks we used to use with Jessica and Kusti? I never felt like making kindling back then. Or would I take my banging to the kitchen?

But then, Mihkel went off traveling for a long time, it slipped my mind, and I started chopping splinters in front of the stove again. It was a shame to give up the activity. I guess I got in the habit out at the summer cabin once. Or it's a throwback to when I was a boy. Why is chopping kindling so calming? It's a pointless activity, but you can somehow convince yourself of its purpose. And I couldn't be bothered to start exercising or knitting or crocheting. I don't want to do anything that results in something being made or any kind of self-improvement. What other hobbies are there? Darning socks? No, that would never do. Cleaning? Sure, cleaning is also nice. Though it'd be better to clean somebody else's place and leave my own dust alone.

♦

A ping-pong table showed up outside a while back. It's on the street-side of the yard, right by the Cabbages window. It's endured the autumn rains pretty well. When the first snow fell—a proper, thick Christmas blanket—Diana swept the ping-pong table clean and continued playing. I can't say how well the balls withstood sub-freezing temperatures.

I'd bought a bag of fried herring from the cheap grocery store and devoured most of them immediately. But then, I thought it might be nice to jar some of them. I didn't have any vinegar, carrots, or onion for boiling the marinade, so I reckoned I'd pop over to Laura's place.

Laura had just arrived to walk me over to her apartment. I can't remember why. She buzzed from downstairs. I tried to quickly get my things together and change clothes so she wouldn't have to wait long outside. I don't know why I didn't just let her in. It was cold out. She must have been smoking. And I always dawdle and make her wait forever. It was as if my subconscious was telling me: Oh, don't worry. You're fifty and she's thirty—you don't need to run after her all the time. As if I was doing it on purpose. It's no wonder she was getting sick of it.

I trotted down the stairs, panting. Laura was in a good mood. The wait hadn't affected her at all.

My phone rang as we started walking, the bag of herring dangling in my grip.

Joonas started giving me a speech about how I should come to some political event and pull on a security vest, as they needed someone for the job. It sounded like they were planning on overthrowing the government. Sure. Great. I wandered around our yard, talking to him for a while and insisting that I didn't really feel like toppling any governments. It's just an endless cycle, I explained. Plus, there was no better government to be had in Estonia for the time being. If you don't just let politicians do their job, then all you get is headaches, and in the end, they'll still be in power but lots of work will be left undone.

By the time we got to Laura's apartment, the herring had completely slipped my mind.

I remembered them two days later. Laura recalled that I'd hung the bag on the corner of the ping-pong table when my phone rang. We both figured that if no one had taken them, then some animal would've probably eaten them already. The fish were in a light-green Marks & Spencer plastic bag. I'd just bought a discount sauce there.

Meanwhile, I visited Pärnu and Laura and I just hung around her apartment drinking. I reckoned my studio was pretty cold, as I hadn't been there to heat it in a while. I knew I should go and get the oven warmed up. So, I did.

The Marks & Spencer bag was lying on the ground under the ping-pong table. The herring were still there. No animals had touched them. I guess the stray dogs and cats in the area are living quite well. It was damp from rain that had recently fallen as the snow melted away.

Marko's Volvo was parked next to the ping-pong table, the door standing open. It was packed with a television and all kinds of other stuff. I tried to close the door, but it wouldn't shut.

I sniffed the herring. I couldn't smell anything. So, I took them up to my studio and stuffed them between the windows, planning to still take them to Laura's and jar them later.

◆

I'm unable to work whenever Laura and I are fighting. As soon as we make up, I get busy again. I suppose reconciliation comes from neither of us being in a good place and wanting to return to our previous state. Not forgiveness or reevaluating what happened. Whatever it was simply loses importance, because it's worse not being together. *Swallow your pride.* It's a good thing we have no assets that would prevent us from ever divorcing. Divorce is then impossible, because things would be even more miserable then. Fighting makes that instantly clear. Our disputes arise in nearly certain intervals. Whenever we're together, we want to be apart, and being apart, things quickly turn sour and we want to be together again. It's particularly great when we can have sex—work goes swimmingly then. Fighting gives me a chance to do things that aren't work: baking pies, painting the heating oven, and taking trips I otherwise wouldn't take. Those are fine breaks, indeed.

When Friedebert and Elo Tuglas got into a fight, he'd slam the door and sit down at his writing desk with pleasure. I wonder if he had problems writing when they adjusted, reconciled, and stopped fighting? And if I were to have to choose between impotence and an inability to write, which one would I choose? Luckily, that's not a decision I'll ever have to face. If anything, then writing is a sublimation of sexuality and you enjoy one fuck left with every page. Oh, what bullshit. You almost start believing Freud.

◆

The wood-fired oven was starting to rust and paint was chipping off in places. The aluminum is pretty thin. One of the kids had made scratches in one place; someone had tapped tiny dents in another. There were no holes, but you could tell how thin and soft the metal was, and how crumbly the bricks were behind it. Like plastic glued onto putty. But I still need it to work. I don't want to heat with an electric radiator.

Tarmo reckoned it should be demolished and another, smaller one built in its place. Standing next to it, he showed me what it should be like—how tall and how nice and tubby. I realized he was envisioning an entirely new, handsome heating device. Probably not aluminum, but ceramic. He stroked it and smiled like it was his son. Tarmo was drunk too, of course. I couldn't see his oven, but it was starting to take shape in the distance. Then, the conversation turned to other topics.

Tarmo occasionally takes an interest in how strong the draft is in the chimney. It *is* his old apartment. He nearly died of carbon monoxide poisoning once when he closed the flue too soon one winter while crashing, drunk, in his studio. I admitted, slightly embarrassed, that the chimney sweep made two more vents and removed a bucketful of soot.

"Oh, sure. That's not bad at all," he crowed. "Vents in and soot out. And now I bet the draft's pretty swell."

"It's better."

"Better, better—of course it's better now."

I was relieved that Tarmo was content with the new state of affairs. But that's just Tarmo. He gives good, friendly advice and paints you a picture of the way everything should go smoothly. And if you do things differently, then he'll approve of that, too. Everything is fine. Now, that's my kind of guy.

I don't know if he manages with himself that way, also—suggesting a good plan but nevertheless deciding to act differently. And if it goes a third way entirely, then he's okay with that, too. He's considered going sober and enjoyed it before even beginning, because it's never lasted long. Soon, he goes right back to drinking again, and even that's terrific.

I'd been meaning to paint the oven for half a year already. The chimney sweep had said there's some kind of paint that can be sprayed. And I'd repeatedly made myself a mental note to go and get it. The store was just on the opposite end of the city.

Once I dragged myself there, it took me a long time to find the right paint. Siss was with me and we browsed through the pretty, colorful paint cans together. She was fine with me buying any of them. The more a can seemed right to her, the more I doubted it was really the right type, and I began to suspect that maybe we weren't in some Zen story where all the cuts of meat at the market are the very best. Ultimately, I asked a salesperson for help.

Then, the can just sat on top of the cupboard for a while longer. I was hesitant to paint the oven with Siskin around, even though she would have liked it. I just wanted to do it all on my own, like Tom Sawyer's slave. I pulled the couch away from the oven and taped old newspapers over half of the room. I opened the window, but then shut it again—it was frigid outside and the cold air gave me a hacking cough. I've been coughing for a while already, to be honest. It started after the pneumonia. It just refuses to go away. Chronic bronchitis? The early stage of lung cancer? I've seen lung cancer before. Not pretty.

Now, I was ready for the oven operation. I'd only been drinking for the last couple of weeks, not doing much of anything. Just sweeping the floor sometimes. A man must build a house and plant a tree. In reality, sweeping the floor makes you feel pretty good, too. Doing a big number two in the bathroom has about the same effect. At least you've accomplished something.

The paint was black and the air full of chemicals when I sprayed it. My lungs would be a nice matt black tone, too. Do the bronchitis germs find the paint tasty? I guess I'll find out soon. They seem to enjoy nicotine and smoking paper, in any case. When Pirandello said he was one hundred thousand pieces, I doubt he meant the bacteria living in his body. Though not all plaque and sperm are called Pirandello, either. Maybe some don't even have a name. Not even a scientific designation. Peeter Selin collects butterflies and hopes to discover a new beetle that'll be named after him. There are untold numbers of beetles and new species are determined by the shape of their genitalia. Selin himself doesn't check their dicks—he's got helpers for that. But some scientists could search for new species inside their own bodies. You don't really need to wander so far. Searching for new ideas within yourself is somewhat harder. They can't be named after you and won't be recorded in scientific catalogues, either.

I wrapped Kusti's old scarf around my face to filter out the chemicals and sprayed away. The paint ran out before my fascination with spraying. Afterward, I kept returning to the stove to check on it. I had lunch in the kitchen and paused to go look at the stove. I sat down to read, but soon got up to check it again, seeing how the coat had turned out and whether it covered everything. The room reeked of paint, and I was happy. I'd accomplished something for the first time in years. I'd spray-painted the oven. Antti Hyry is right—working is a wonderful thing. I can't say it's redemption, exactly, but certainly oblivion and a way to pass the time. I probably shouldn't show the books I write to anyone. Or better, at least, if I just don't see someone flip through them, read, yawn, and then toss them onto the cupboard. Toss them, I don't care. I'll read my books myself. Someone should.

I opened another beer and considered posting on Facebook that I'd painted my oven. But I don't know how to upload a picture. And would I care to look at pictures of someone's painted oven? Not really. The only painted oven I care to admire is my very own. And I won't show it to anyone else. I can't be bothered. If anyone knocks to see what the smell is and asks if I painted the oven, I'd rather not let them in. They might make a comment about how I've painted it all wrong or not be sufficiently impressed.

Once you get accustomed to working, it might become boring and monotonous, just like drinking.

I opened another beer to sip between the dark one and the German lager I already had open.

I should do more activities. If I drank as rarely as I work, then maybe drinking would be fascinating, too. But what other activities are there, anyway? Fucking, sure, but aside of that? I'm not about to go to war. Some kind of exercise? As if—even Churchill said: "No sports," and drank Armenian cognac. I can't be bothered to heat up the sauna regularly like Tarmo. TV's a bore. Newspapers are irritating.

Fine, I'll just repaint the oven once a year. Even though the whole can of paint hisses out in just five minutes. If the activity makes me feel good even once a year, then there's no need to underrate it.

◆

I opened the door at Koidu. What was that sound? Where was it coming from? I dropped my things in the hallway. Warmth seemed to emanate from the kitchen. I pushed open the kitchen door. It really was balmy. There was a tin cup on the gas burner, and it was lit. I quickly shut it off. The inside of the cup was charred black. How many days had I been away? I didn't show up yesterday. What about the day before? I couldn't remember. Scatterbrain. Booze-addled brain. I grabbed an oven mitt and moved the cup to the porcelain sink. It hissed. The basin wasn't completely dry yet. That meant I must have left the burner on two days ago. Where had I run off to? I was about to turn on the faucet, but stopped myself. Maybe the temperature difference would make the paint peel off the cup. At the same time, it must have been pretty durable if it didn't catch fire. I'd have to wait and see if I could scrub it clean later.

When am I going to end up burning the whole house down? Or someone else? What happens if I'm guilty of starting a fire? If I'm not burned alive first, of course. Who knows. Is that a crime? Criminal negligence? Maybe punishment would be lighter than the lack of it. Otherwise, you're left carrying that lousy guilt around for the rest of your life. Maybe you get used to it. Some people commit murders and continue living as if nothing ever happened. Others speak an insult and bear the burden for years. It might not even be an insult, but just something a little conceited or the wrong word. How can things be so different for different people? "Sorry I gave you a hard time for murdering that guy. Ten years ago—you remember? It was no big deal, actually. He was a huge asshole.

You're not mad at me, are you?" "Oh, definitely not. I didn't even remember it anymore. Don't worry!"

Living is terrifying. I could end up creating some fiasco just about every day. It can happen the second you step outside.

PERMANENCE

I'VE BEEN SAVING a lot recently. Another fight. I don't have to go to Laura's at night or buy her two bottles of sparkling wine and a basket of smokes and groceries. It's a relief, because I'm short on cash anyway and expenses stress me out. But now, I'm stressed by sitting at home alone. Perhaps it's because reconciliation is entirely possible and my subconscious keeps on nagging me: What the hell's your problem? Why don't you just make up? You might get some sex and cuddling and all of that. If we're to split or some other fatal fissure forms, then I'd no doubt learn how to be alone again. I've learned it many times before. It's never easy. No doubt it'll be like other arts I used to know. I've forgotten how to write on several occasions and then remembered again.

◆

Why did I start tugging the fridge out of the corner? The Soviet-era appliance had been there ever since I moved in, formerly belonging to Arvo Pesti and dragged into the apartment by Tarmo Teder at some point. Tarmo once lit a fire in it when he was plastered, thinking it was the stove. Luckily he couldn't get it going, so the next day he just scraped out the firewood and kindling and scrubbed it a little.

Maybe the notion crossed my mind that although I've been living here for several years, the space beneath and behind the fridge is a shadowy corner into which I'd never peered before. A place that wasn't yet my territory, my domain.

Who knows what I'd hoped to find there. Lots of crap and dust clumped up by soot from the gas boiler. Maybe a dead bug or some other creature.

Would I break the fridge if I fully tugged it out of the corner? It was so old.

There were old plastic bags wedged between it and the wall. I'd stuffed them there myself to use as trash bags. I tried to pull out as many as I could, but couldn't get all of them. They were out of reach.

The fridge rumbled like a tractor, but I didn't dare to pull the plug from the wall. It was surprisingly heavy, as I'd just stocked it with beer. I didn't feel like unloading all the cans and bottles first. I tried tipping it and the door swung open. Something smashed. A beer bottle had fallen out onto the filthy wooden floor. Beer flowed along the boards and disappeared into the cracks. I quickly grabbed a rag, but most of the contents flowed into the spaces before it got too far. The floor was so thin—was it already soaking through into Marten's ceiling? Oh, shit. He'd just painted.

I gathered the shards into a plastic bag, trying not to cut myself. Nevertheless, a tiny sliver jabbed painfully into my finger, as it always does whenever you're cleaning up broken glass. Still, it's odd that one prick is enough. After that, you take extra special care to prevent getting another, which is usually a success. But there always has to be that one.

I managed to mop up all the beer. All there was left to do was wait for the floor to dry, as the hardened crust of grime could be slippery when wet and I might easily slip and fall.

So, I decided to have a beer in the meantime.

I opened one up and drank it.

Then I went back to tugging on the fridge, trying not to rock it as much. I still couldn't be bothered to take out all the beer.

On the floor behind the fridge, I found straws and a few old one-kroon coins that someone had probably accidentally swept off the top of the fridge. There was also a box of matches, dusty and dirty but relatively dry, nonetheless. I tossed it onto a stool and threw away the straws. The coins went into the trash bin, too.

It took me a long time to scrub away most of the filth, but it was cleaner in the end. Then, I rinsed the rag and washed my hands.

What do you know—I *had* accomplished something today. Whether there was any point to it, who knows. I'd at least spent my time doing something, like a bird weaving a nest. No, wait. Birds have a specific plan in mind when nesting. I had none.

The fridge was still standing in the middle of the kitchen. I certainly wouldn't be pushing it back today. Let the floor behind it dry first. I'll lug it back another day.

◆

Temporary things last the longest. What are they, anyway? Something I've stuck somewhere just for a while, resolving to put it away properly later. Something I'm planning on fixing, but am in no hurry to do so. Like the high sills over which Krõõt had to lift buckets of pig feed in *Truth and Justice*—sills that were never lowered, that were still never lowered, and ultimately, she died. The most precious shirts are the ones full of holes. Even when the collars are stretched and tattered. But shirts like those aren't sold at the dollar store. A broken lampshade installed temporarily on a light fixture. Temporary relationships in your mind and your heart. It's hard to figure out if I, myself, am temporary, too. I guess I'd like to be temporary. Fleeting, impermanent. But is that simply so I'd be lasting?

As soon as you attempt to give something the slightest bit of thought, you hit a mental block. Words lose their meaning, opposites are interchangeable. Some people have killed ages worth of time on such things, though. Kant or others like him. I suppose that means they played the game well and enjoyed it. Not all kids are good at playing alone that way, you know. I suppose it takes practice.

Does that mean the opposite should also be true? Lasting things are impermanent. Like national borders. Vseviov says they're drawn for all time, but their endurance is a glimmer at best. They might last for a couple measly human generations, and even that is quite the accomplishment. And our Heavenly Father, who is eternal, and truth, which itself is also eternal. That means they are also temporary. And I suppose it's not far from accurate. Occasionally credible, usually not. The Heavenly Father has to keep an eye on humans to keep track of when He's being taken seriously and should open up his mouth. Then, I might even listen. But when God starts talking when nobody is taking Him seriously, there's only a big old grin. Not that there's anything wrong with that, either. Sometimes you get more of a fill off of a grin, other times off of something serious. Every now and then off of tears, too. It's not often, but sometimes on occasion, you also need those tears to get a full belly. Or at least some kind of spiritual comfort.

"I'm just going to sit for a minute," Jaan Toomik said. He took a seat and chatted with me and Margus before the two of us moved on to another café. In my mind, he's still sitting there now. That temporary act of sitting for a minute took hold somehow. Why, I don't know. Maybe it's because he's going in a hundred directions at once all the time with a hundred different thoughts in his head, even though his demeanor is calm and he doesn't make any grand speeches.

COMPLETION

I WENT DOWN to see who was making a racket in the basement. The banging was coming from the backyard side of Cabbages. I peeked in through the window. Erko was pounding at the stone walls with a crowbar. He immediately realized someone was looking in and came to the window to chat.

"Holy moly—you're really going for it there."

"I'm upgrading Ruitlane's storage space a bit."

"And all on your own?"

"Yep."

Erko had been chipping away and cleaning all day long, but still wore a wide grin on his face as always. Ruitlane's storage space took up nearly a quarter of the basement already. It was spacious and looked impressive, with fieldstone walls. The past stares back at you. And it wasn't just for storing Ruitlane's firewood. Logs made up a tiny portion of it. I don't know what else he keeps down there.

An electrician showed up to string simple white cables along Erko's wall. No need for anything fancy. He already had new kitchen appliances installed. Why don't I have energy like that? For years, I've been sitting around an apartment that's in the exact same state as it was when I moved in. All I do here is mope. No, that's not fair—I relish hanging around on better days. But enjoyment smoothly transitions to moping, and vice-versa. I'm afraid of changing anything, for some reason. For who knows whether it'll be just as good as it is now. A fear of changes. Maybe a fear of living. What if I get hurt? It's happened many a time before. Sometimes, you dash straight into life, but then scream: "Ow!" and shuffle back to your den.

I remembered that tomorrow was Kristo's birthday party. He'd made the event on Facebook a week ago and kept reposting it. Laura and I discussed whether or not to attend. *Shit,* I thought, *if I show up at six or seven and start drinking right away—because who are we kidding, I will—then I'll be out for the count by the time night rolls around and useless in the morning.* It didn't sound very appealing. At the same time, I felt I would like to spend time with the rest of the house. What to do.

Laura and I were lounging around the studio. Siss had been around earlier, but had gone off somewhere. Probably to her friend Maria Marta's place.

"Should we fuck?" I asked.

"Now?"

"If you want to."

It was still light out. Laura usually didn't want to have sex during the day. Even now, after however many years we'd been together. How many was it? Three and a half? Or was it four and a half? On top of that, it wasn't home. Even though we've occasionally slept together here on Koidu Street over these three- or four-and-a-half years. At the same time, I knew that if she didn't feel comfortable, then there was no hope of her orgasming. And it feels miserable to enjoy yourself while your partner couldn't care less. Laura didn't reply, so I dropped the topic. I'd just thought that if we were already spending the day hanging out together, which was nice in and of itself because we hadn't been together here in ages, then maybe we could give sex a little go, too. Simply lazing around and daydreaming in bed in the middle of the day was nice, too. Just being together, at long last. Like lazy kids.

Laura was contemplating something, but I couldn't tell what it was.

"Something on your mind?"

She didn't reply. I'm pretty used to it already. What can you do?

"I'll have a smoke in the kitchen, then okay."

I was surprised. I waited for Laura to get up and have her cigarette, but she kept delaying and delaying. So, I rolled over to my other side and started dozing again. Sleepily, I felt her get out of bed and go to the kitchen, though I tried not to let my thoughts drift to fucking. Who could say what direction things would take? And now, the sleep coming back over me almost seemed sweeter and dearer.

I sensed her return to the room more than I heard anything. I peeked through parted eyelids. She was taking off my red t-shirt and pulling down her panties.

"Should I close the curtains?"

"Sure."

I was suddenly wide awake, though I tried not to look too excited. Laura needed time to gradually get into the mood. To feel comfortable.

"Should I lock the door?"

"I already did."

"Did you leave the keys in the lock, too? Siskin might come back."

"No."

"Ah, fuck it."

It wouldn't really matter to Siskin, but it would to Laura. She couldn't keep going if Siskin came into the apartment, even if he just waited patiently in the kitchen.

Once Laura was already in bed, I really started going at it in spite of wanting to hold back. I guess I don't know how to do it any other way, or it just never turns out. Why drag something out when the momentum's already building? That's no good, either. I couldn't tell if Laura was motionless because she was feeling good and focusing on the pleasure, or because she was tense. It's hard to tell with introverts like her. Though I suppose I'm also an introvert with varying success. Are we both mentally unstable? Probably. Depression alternating with hyperactivity. What's that PC polarity term you're supposed to use now instead of psychopath? Multipolar behavioral disorder? You start feeling better the moment you can name your illness.

Laura remained motionless, but that didn't surprise me.

"Should I go down on you?"

She didn't reply, so I did. She tasted strange. Strong, in a way. Had she not showered in a while? It didn't matter. It bothered me at the moment, but maybe I'll start to miss it someday if we can't have sex anymore for some reason.

I'd been going at Laura's corpse-like body for a while already. A proper lesson in necrophilia. It'd been going on for so long that I lost my erection.

"Would you hold on to my dick?"

It took a while before Laura finally any sign of movement, but she finally gripped my penis tightly, which helped.

"Hey, would you get on top of me now?"

"Fine," she replied almost immediately and without any intonation, as usual.

I still had a weak erection and the whole thing went quickly.

"Go fast now, I can't take it any longer."

So, Laura sped up and I couldn't hold myself back any longer and huffed and groaned like one should, or at least like in a cheap porno.

Laura realized I'd finished and just sat motionless on top of me for a while longer. I couldn't tell what was wrong. I'm an idiot. And I'm not getting any smarter.

"I didn't even get close," Laura whispered with anger and bitterness in her voice. She slid off and stretched out with her back towards me. I was at a loss for what to do, but couldn't help feeling my body filled with a sense of satisfaction from ejaculating. Do I have to be the one to blame now? I had no idea. I didn't want to get the sheet too moist, hoping that maybe we could lie around a little longer, so I shuffled into the kitchen to rinse my dick with cold water in the kitchen sink. I scrubbed it as well as I could, feeling mixed emotions. I dried my dick, first with a kitchen towel and then with the hem of my shirt, then checked to see if there was anything to drink in the fridge. A little wine and a warm beer. I took a couple sips of the beer.

I didn't try draping my arm over Laura in bed. It seemed like she was trying to nap a little. I rolled over with my back to her and tried to doze off for the afternoon as well.

What did we do when we woke up? I reckon we tried to find some activity to keep us from going straight to Kristo's birthday party and start drinking. But I can't remember what it might have been. I think we went somewhere else for a few drinks first. Or had dinner at the Chinese place. I knew that we would have to show up and congratulate Erko at some point. He'd renovated a whole new room for Cabbages and everything. Pretty impressive.

Or did we just get drinks from the shop and hang around my studio? It's possible. That way, you drink at a slower pace than you would at a party. On top of that, I was feeling blissful with Laur around and us just hanging out and doing nothing all day.

Suddenly, she roused from her thoughts.

"Aren't we going down to that birthday party? Kristo's?"

I preferred for it to just be the two of us. Hanging out in a group would mean just that: not having a close connection with anybody and just mingling as a whole. Being in a crowd is terrific when you're alone or the whole situation is routine.

"I dunno. I don't really feel like it today. I don't want to drink much, but I will if I go down. Though I don't necessarily have to. You want to go?"

Laura didn't reply. Fine—neither would I. We sat in her old armchairs that we'd moved here when she got new furniture, silent and contemplating. I thought it was the best option for the evening—just sitting in each other's company, drinking and not speaking. Even if there was no point in considering sex.

"Aren't we going, then?" Laura abruptly said, looking up.

I also looked up from my newspaper.

"Uh . . . You mean . . . Sure, let's go. Just a second." We were still only half-dressed: I in underwear and a t-shirt, Laura in panties and one of my t-shirts as well. Both of us were wearing socks. I sleep in them and Laur's learned to do so, too. She's learned it so well that we don't even take off our socks during sex, even though we're otherwise naked. I get colds if I don't wear them. I get colds when I am wearing socks too, of course, but less frequently. Or at least it seems that way.

"I'll get dressed."

We said nothing else to each other. Both of us had a good buzz going on, too. I felt like we'd drunk enough to just sit together in silence, but now we were letting all that cultivated coexistence slip away for empty banter in a bigger group. But the decision to leave had already been made. There was no point in dragging it out, because confirming we'd go had put a definite end to hanging out in the studio.

I took my bottle of dark beer along. Laur didn't feel like dragging her bottle of bubbly around. We walked down to the basement.

The atmosphere in Cabbages was as nice as it ever was when a party was going on. There'd been rather few of them lately. Simple sitting around—sure. Though those also swelled to become parties every now and then, too. Somebody put on old records, people drank, played chess, sometimes somebody would start dancing, and the drinking would continue however people wished. Today, there was one new face after another in the crowd. Young guys who had cracked open the vodka bottles early. Some were swaying, others already dozing off. Not that it mattered. The New World commune had a strong positive vibe. Their overall good will spread and melted everyone around them together into a kind, supportive whole. Katharina was chatting with her friends—I hadn't seen her around in ages. I wondered if she'd already talked to Siss, her favorite. Where was Siss, anyway? Had she already passed through? She'd been excited about the party.

"Hey, Katharina. Was Siskin here, too? Did you see her?"

"Yeah, she and Maria Marta went somewhere together."

"Oh, okay. I'm going to have some of your celery here. And the cold stew. Mm, it's delicious."

I grabbed a handful of celery from the coffee table next to them. Why haven't I eaten celery much before? You can feel the vitamins simmer away inside you immediately. A sure hangover-prevention tool. I mercilessly went after more. Laur had acquired a glass from somewhere and I peeked to see what was in it. She hadn't switched to the hard stuff yet, had she? It'd put her right to sleep.

"Here, have some celery, too. What are you drinking?"

There I went again, giving her a hard time. But why should she nap through most of the party like she usually does?"

"Celery's good," Laura said, chewing. "Wanna dance?"

"I don't know. I should drink first. Otherwise I'll try too hard and hate it."

I couldn't just hang around a large group of people sober. It made me so uncomfortable. Pure agony. The only way to make it work was to try to put away a formidable amount of booze as quickly as possible. At the same time, I didn't want to drink hard liquor and get wasted. I haven't mastered the complex art of dosing in my fifty years of living.

I drank myself into an adequate condition while leaning against Ruitlane's heaps of firewood. Laura made her rounds of the room, occasionally coming to hang out with me for a while before setting off again. At some point, I moved to the other room. I grabbed Vahur Linnuste's book of theater stories off a shelf as I left—a copy he'd given me right there in Cabbages—and read about Artaud and Grotowski and who-knows-who-else to pass the time. Sure, I'd heard lectures about those guys and their plays at the theater school before. But Linnuste himself attended the plays. I guess they rubbed both of us the right way. I realized I hadn't seen Laura in a while, so I went to get another drink.

I peeked through the doorway into the other room before I left. Laura was standing and chatting with a guy I'd exchanged a couple of words in English with earlier. I softly closed the door. I needed to pee, too.

I made my way upstairs, took a piss, then rummaged through the fridge for my next beer. I uncapped it and stopped to think for a minute.

How 'bout that—Laur came upstairs, too. She also needed to use the toilet. I stood in the stairwell and waited. I suspected that she glimpsed me in the doorway when she was chatting with that guy and came to see if everything was okay. That filled me with gladness.

The two of us went back downstairs together. We drank for another hour or two. As usual, Laura flagged at some point and fell asleep in an armchair.

I was talking to Markus Vihma.

"You know, you gave me some real Christian first aid here the time you put up with my rambling till the early morning hours. I didn't bring it up, but Laura and I had just gotten into a fight," I said, peeking over at her dozing next to us. "She'd thrown me out and I'd never have fallen asleep if I'd been forced to mope around my apartment all alone. But you made the effort. It never even crossed my mind that you've all got a code where whoever's opened Cabbages doesn't leave until the last guest leaves, and they can't just kick them out."

"Oh, I had no idea," Markus remarked, grinning. "Are you coming out to the hot tub Erko rented?"

"No, I just got over pneumonia."

My gaze came to rest on the guy Laura had been chatting with earlier. He was leaning over her as she slept and whispering something.

"Whoa—how'd you get that?"

"Right here when we were having a sauna. I came into Cabbages to sit between rounds and guess I got a cold." I knew I was flat-out lying, like I do so often.

"Really?"

Markus looked surprised.

"No. To tell the truth, I've got no idea how it happened," I quickly corrected myself, all the while eyeing the guy still bent over Laura. A second later, he straightened up and went into the other room.

"Laur. Hey, Laur. Did you know that Markus stayed and listened to me blather till three or four a.m. that time you threw me out?"

Laura looked up drowsily, but immediately remembered.

"Yeah, you told me."

"Alright, I'm going to soak in the hot tub, Peeter." And Markus left.

"I'm going to get myself something to drink," Laura drawled very slowly and softly.

"I can get it. What do you want? Wine or something harder?"

"No, I'll go."

Laura stood and suddenly appeared totally sober. She can go through big swings like that. Good metabolism. Drunk and swaying and swooning, then sober as a judge after just a five-minute nap.

I stood by the record player like a security guard, even though there was no one to protect. I suppose I was trying to protect myself, though I realized I'd be unqualified for the job if things should get serious. I was getting very drunk. Things were progressing. The situation was becoming tolerable. Soon, I'd be capable of conversing.

I decided to fetch myself another beer from upstairs. I had no idea what Laura was doing. Probably talking to that guy. He was putting some serious moves on her. I passed through the other room on my way up. Laura was standing next to a big bowl of food, holding her own bowl and scrutinizing each individual macaroni before placing it into her mouth. I think she'd stationed herself there to be close to the source for seconds. The guy was sitting by the wall, alone and focusing his gaze solely on Laura, even though the place was packed.

I walked past Laura.

"I'm going upstairs for a minute, Laur."

"Huh?" She'd gotten very drunk again in that tiny window of time. "Upstairs? I'm coming, too."

I paused for a second before walking towards the door. I glanced over my shoulder. Laura was watching me leave. She set her bowl down on the edge of the table and took a long step, mayonnaise smeared around her lips, then froze in the position, wobbling slightly. I had the urge to help her, but I knew she didn't want it and it'd be best if I just went on without her. So, I did.

I flushed the toilet, pulled up my pants, and zipped them, then heard a strange noise. It seemed to be coming from somewhere very close, and at the same time very far away. I opened the door. Laura was leaning against the wall in the stairwell, bowed over like a wounded samurai, crying. Tears streamed down her cheeks. Although nearly silent, she emitted strange squeaks and creaks like a rusty machine. Laura seemed to be present and somewhere very far away simultaneously.

"Laur, cut it out. What's this now? What's wrong?"

She pressed a hand against her thigh. Her thin, bony thigh.

"These pants cost a hundred euros. I bought them myself. With my own money."

"And what's the problem?"

"I bumped against a nail. There's a hole in them now."

"Did it puncture your leg?"

"I don't know. I don't care."

"Hey, we need to look at your leg. It might have been rusty. You could get tetanus."

"I don't care. There's a hole in them now."

I noticed that Laura's tears had dripped onto the entryway floor and it was now damp and sprinkled with droplets. How could she squeeze out so many tears? Or was there some other source? Had she peed her pants? I craned my neck to see. No, they were dry. But the floor was wet. It'd get all muddy before long if we kept walking back and forth to the bathroom. I got a mop from the kitchen and swabbed her tears into the dirty fabric.

"Laur." She didn't respond. "Laur?"

"What?!"

"We don't have to go back downstairs."

"I want to. I don't want to be alone. But if my pants are torn. I can't go. I can't go if my pants are torn."

"So what if they are? Lots of people walk around with their pants in tatters. Big ole holes in their jeans."

"I know. But these aren't those pants. These shouldn't have holes in them."

The tears kept coming and coming. I mopped the floor again.

"How can you cry this many tears?"

The mopping seemed to help clean up the dirt from our shoes, too.

"I don't know," Laura sighed tragically.

"Well, what are we going to do? What do you want?"

"I don't know. Let's go downstairs. I'll wash my face first. And put on makeup. Will you wait for me?"

I sipped my beer as I waited. Laura had the ability to switch off the tears in an instant so she could rinse and put on fresh makeup. That's not her only skill. She could get drunk and fall asleep and start partying all over again fifteen minutes later, cry herself dry and then go right back to heavy partying. Is it learned wisdom or an inner autopilot? Or a tenured partier's wealth of experience?

We went back down. I felt my buzz had faded a little bit, even though I'd continued swilling beer upstairs. I looked around to see what else was available. The boys had several open bottles of vodka and would certainly share. But no—no vodka tonight.

"Hey, Erko—could I have one of your beers?"

"Yeah, sure. Take one from the fridge."

I opened it.

"Hey, you're out."

"Really? We've got those festival beers, too. I'll go grab you one, Peeter. What brand do you drink?"

"Whatever."

"I don't know if we've got that label."

A chorus of other voices echoed from around the room: Erko, bring me a beer, too . . . And me, too . . .

Erko counted the show of hands and was gone.

Laura switched hats with Kristo. She pulled his wool beanie down over her hair and he slid on the wide-brimmed hat she'd gotten off Jürgen Rooste. The switched hats looked nice, respectively. Both have slender frames. Laura wrapped her arms around Kristo and demanded that somebody take a picture. The guy who'd had his eye on Laura before was still staring.

"Here's your beer, Peeter."

Erko handed me a Carlsberg and carried an armful of Saku Originaals to the fridge, distributing cans left and right on the way. I knew where he kept his stash—on top of the stack of firewood on the other side of the basement. Even though I knew they might be freely available, I wasn't just going to go ahead and help myself to them as I pleased.

Beer in hand, I shuffled into the room facing the street and took another random book off a shelf. It's nice to crack one open without seeing what the title is or who wrote it, just reading a page or two for fun. Still, I suppose all the books here in Cabbages are good and filled with good stories. The shelves are stocked with various local authors' personally-curated personal collections, free for anyone to browse. It doesn't matter what the work is about or who wrote it—you're going to find something good. People were dancing, some in pairs and others in larger circles. They threw one another up into the air, squealing and laughing. Erko performed a particularly impressive leap and crashed down onto a low table, knocking a glass onto the floor. But that only added to the fun and someone casually swept up the shards.

I read until I finished my beer, leisurely and unhurried. It was a pleasant and unusual experience to read amidst the melee, even though I couldn't really process whatever it was. Words, no doubt. Words.

I lumbered to the fridge to get a fresh beer if any were still left. Hell, I shouldn't need to ask for permission every single time anymore. Maybe I could restock the supply a little from upstairs, but how much beer did I have there? I'd like to slurp something while sitting in bed before I fell asleep, too.

Kristo had dozed off on a bench next to the wall. Laura was sitting next to him and also asleep, still wearing his hat and resting her head on his shoulder. I watched them for while. Like two drunk, innocent kids. Hansel and Gretel. The Russian guy appeared to enjoy it, too. He plopped down next to Laura and started whispering softly to her again, though I couldn't tell if she heard. The bench wasn't very long, so the guy was pressed close to her. Laura was sand-wiched between two men. I felt rather befuddled.

Laura told me recently that she didn't know what's wrong with her. That she doesn't want to have sex with me anymore, even though we'd sometimes fuck several times a day just a year ago. She couldn't say what was different—maybe my appearance had changed and I often moaned about one pain or another and she didn't find it attractive. She admitted that she enjoyed flirting with men at parties and allowing herself to be flirted with, even though she didn't want to have sex with the suitors, who surfaced every time and in ever-increasing num-bers. But she didn't want to have sex with others while married, and she didn't know what to do. Life was just like a movie. And I in turn didn't feel like fucking if Laura only did so reluctantly. Ergo, we didn't have sex anymore. Almost never.

Still, I also felt like I didn't want that guy to start stroking Laura as she slept, so I went over to them and addressed him in Russian.

"You like Laura?"

"Yes. You're here with her, yeah? She's got a problem, you see? She wants to go to sleep."

I was about to say: "And you want to help her go to bed," but I caught my tongue.

"You're the one with her?" he asked again.

"She's my wife."

"Oh, so everything's alright with her? It's all good? Well, fine then. I just thought she might need help . . ."

The guy stood up a little unwillingly, but vanished swiftly into the other room. Maybe he felt like a stranger in our company and was afraid people would gang up on him if there was any conflict.

I took his place next to Laura and sipped my beer to pass the time. I couldn't tell if anyone had watched the scene—two men's shift change at Laura's side. I didn't feel like ruminating on it, either.

At some point, Laura awoke and we went upstairs to sleep. She cried a little before drifting off again, staring silently at the ceiling. I was tired and didn't ask her anything, just watching the tears roll down her cheeks. I reckoned her pil-low would soon get wet, but no doubt she'd just flip it over. As long as she didn't dampen both sides of the pillow with tears. Though I reckoned she didn't care.

In the morning, Laura herself made a proposition.

"Would you go down on me?"

I was sleepy and didn't really feel like it. And there'd been such a weird tang yesterday, as if she had vaginitis.

"Sure, if you want."

So, I sat up briskly like I was preparing for morning exercises. I wasn't very energetic about it. Afterward, we fucked to Laura's rhythm and I quietly hoped that maybe she'd orgasm that way. But after I finished, I rolled over and didn't ask. I tried to get a little more sleep.

NIGHTMARE

MIHKEL TOLD ME his worst-ever nightmare. It wasn't the first 'worst' he'd had, of course. In the previous one, he was in some city in the south of France or Italy and nuclear war broke out. He and Ibsen, that is. This time, the two of them were driving in a VW Passat and heard some alarms going off, but ignored them, figuring it was just some kind of a test or training. But gradually, some kind of gigantic centrifuge or tornado started spinning and swept everything along with it. Mihkel realized this was the end, there was no escape, and he'd never see Ibsen again, either.

As I listened, I couldn't understand what was so terrible about the dream. To me, a great catastrophe like that wasn't at all frightful. My nightmares are personal and directly involve my life. I've murdered someone, for instance, and am afraid I'm just about to be discovered. Or I'm in prison or the army and start getting harassed and there's nothing I can do to stop it. Maybe Mihkel wouldn't find dreams like mine so harrowing.

I started wondering when I'd have an abstract dream that would be a worthy partner to Mihkel's. And a couple nights later, I had a long one. I was in Tüüne's apartment. There was some kind of hullaballoo going on, but I can't remember what it was. Then, I was standing among the apartment blocks in the Mustamäe district. There was a bench and a small table. A few Russian-looking guys sat down, and I was seated between them. Some were wearing uniforms, though I couldn't figure out what they were. I checked a newspaper to see what the place and date were. It appeared to be written in Russian, but at the same time, it wasn't. Some similar language. The date was somehow fuzzy and obscure, too.

"What year is it?" I asked.

That made them laugh. They were good-natured, but it was a stupid question. It started to dawn on me that for them, there was no definite year. That wherever we were, it was multiple times or years all at once.

I looked back down at the black-and-white newspaper.

"What's this place we're in?"

They laughed again, but in a kind way.

I felt like the place was rather similar to Tallinn many years ago, back in the end of the Soviet era, but also not quite. I'd ended up in a parallel world. I was an alien there, and had no idea how to return to my own.

Still, it wasn't really all that frightening. And by that time, Mihkel was already traveling in Mazzano and I couldn't tell him about my dream.

"Ibsen's coming to Mazzano, too," Mihkel had told me. "We'll be together there for the month. And then, our paths will part."

"How do you know? Did you two agree on it?"

"No, but I just know."

I was perplexed and didn't know what to say. It was a like someone telling you when they were going to die. Like Salinger's "Teddy". What can you really reply?

◆

"I have a doctor's appointment tomorrow," you said.

"What kind? A dentist? Your dentist is in Tartu. Oh, right—she had a baby."

"A gynecologist."

"What's wrong?"

"I don't know. I go once a year. Or twice. I had the papillomavirus that time when I was in Haapsalu. They burned the cysts out of my ovaries. There are a lot of those kinds of viruses. Only a few of them are dangerous and can lead to ovarian cancer. Mine was the dangerous type."

"How'd you get it?"

"I don't know."

"Did you get it from someone else?"

"I don't know."

"Is it the thing that men can carry and still never get infected with? It'd be good to know who you got it from in that case. So you can tell him he's got it."

"There's no way I can know."

You were standing in the doorway.

"Did you tell me because you're going to be later today? And we're not going out?"

"Yeah."

I fell back asleep. I reckoned I'd look up the disease later, but by the time I woke up, the name had escaped me. Was it ureaplasma and osteoporosis, which that girl I used to date had? Or was she just afraid that's what it was? I scrolled through web pages and researched ureaplasma. Pretty confusing. Diseases exclusive to women. I suppose men have their own, too.

You'd mentioned a risk of cancer. I couldn't help but wonder what would happen if you died. You've talked so much about it before. I almost started dreaming about it, which made me feel uncomfortable in turn. Like how I dreamed about my grandfather's death after he promised to bequeath his watch to me, then felt guilty when he died. But things with Laura and me were weird. I suppose we were tired of each other, though we knew neither one of us would

cheat or dump the other. Death was the only way out of that exhausting relationship with nearly no sex. Quite the difficult thought. And if Laura really did die
of cancer, I'd feel guilty once again. I, myself, didn't want to die, though. And
Laura didn't, either. I don't think you should talk about your own death. Your
loved ones will start thinking: Fine, but when? And they'll unconsciously start
making plans for what to do afterward. I could immediately come up with several girls to pursue if Laura was dead.

One night before I really thought it through, I asked: "Were you really serious about that?"

"About what?"

"You said once that if you die, then I'm not allowed to date anyone for a year.
That I should have a year of grieving. Did you mean it?"

At that moment, I realized that Laura realized I'd been thinking about her
death. Alas, the little bird had flitted right out. Laura considered it calmly for a
moment, then said tonelessly.

"No, of course not. I can't demand something like that of you."

"Ah, forget it, Laur."

I wrapped my arms around her in bed. But what good would that do? Something inside of me made me press further.

"Did you find out anything at the doctor's office?"

"No, I have to go back again. They need to do more tests."

"When?"

"Next week."

"Why're they dragging it out?"

"I don't know."

◆

I'd been alone at Koidu for several days. The solitude was nice. Like a silent party.
Being home alone and doing nothing. The best childhood option has returned.
I cheerfully mused that I was saving money, too, by not having to buy Laura a
kilogram of ground beef and two sparkling wines every day. Okay, not a full kilo
every time. Sometimes, I stingily buy just half, figuring that should be more than
enough for her. Then she pouts a little, because it isn't.

We were in another fight, naturally.

That night, I went to the pub alone just to pass the time. I hadn't gone solo in
a long time. The pub had been moved to a new location. I used to be a regular at
the old one.

I ordered a beer and read the newspaper.

There was that waitress who used to have her eye on me and would blush. I'd
decided that she liked me. Maybe it was total bullshit. Those were different times

and I was trying to hit on a different waitress. Nothing came of it, of course. That was years ago. The first waitress was still working there and stared at me absently from across the room. I was now a void. But maybe this was the right chance to hit on her. Laura *had* told me to go and fuck somebody else. What would happen if I did? A whole fiasco, that's what.

I read through the whole newspaper and downed my beer. Still, I couldn't start chatting up the waitress before talking to Laura and getting her express approval.

Once I was back at Koidu, I emailed her: "Hey. I randomly saw a girl I think used to like me. If you still don't want to fuck, then can I give it a go?"

The reply came promptly.

"Go, Peeter, go. All you ever do is just talk about it."

Reading the response, I felt that now, having permission, I didn't really feel like it anymore. Age and laziness.

Laura called me the next night. And even though we didn't talk about the elephant in the room, I felt like she was interested in whether I was pursing the woman or not.

So, I went to Laura's place and we made up again for a change.

Our fights seem to be happening very often as of late. *Tired of living and afraid of dying.* Tired of being together and terrified of separating. And it certainly wouldn't be easy, learning to live alone again. It's nice for a couple of days, but being alone all the time? You start chasing women around town and acting silly all over again. And even if you don't pursue anything, you feel like shit.

◆

Laura's words were spinning around my head: "I want to want to have sex. I'd like to like to have sex with you again."

I guess they left an impression on me. And yes, I would like that, too. But what if it never happens? What then? Something else will come around. We can still be nice to each other. Or at least try to be.

The carousel of Laura's words going around in my mind will certainly stop at some point, too. It always does. And for the most part, the sentences spinning around there don't matter.

NOVEMBER

I've BEEN FIGHTING a persistent runny nose and cough because the draft through the cracks around the windows is strong enough to move the curtains. I taped them up at one point (what year was that?), but it's long since fallen away. Maybe I could find some window seals somewhere. It's a pain to get to the hardware store, though. Do any buses even run there? Not that it's far to walk, of course. I could if the weather was nice, but I'm afraid that thought will be delayed until spring. The weather won't be improving before then, and by that time I'll no longer need it. You can't build a roof in the rain, and you don't need a roof when the weather's dry.

But when I'd lazed around for half the day and could tell I wouldn't be writing or reading or doing anything else, I figured I should probably go out to see what life was like in the great outdoors. So, I pulled on my old boots and set off towards the hardware store on Kaare Street. Walking got the blood flowing, too. Before long, I had the stride of a man who is off to be productive and plans to do some proper renovations. I wasn't sure I'd find the right stuff there, however. Nobody has windows with such wide cracks in the frames like mine anymore. They're all upstanding and have replaced all their windows. I even still have a cracked pane that's simply been taped over for years already. And so what? Do I get a kick out of the filth that surrounds me and the way I live? It's possible. Or is it self-defense? Puttering around, moving this here and that there, but doing very, very little. Just a smidgen of work. Because there's not really much of a point in doing anything. Activity just interrupts taking in the atmosphere. And where will that lead? Nowhere, obviously. Still, is there anything more genuine than that? Activity is oblivion—fine, then let's all get a kick out of that. Or maybe it's a different state that can be taken in, though you don't have the time for it when you're busy.

The wind spattered raindrops across my face. November. The nastier, the better. *No dusk, no dawn, no sun, no noon, November.*

"Do you have any window seal?"

Was that even the right word?

"Next department."

They came in every color and thickness. If Siskin were along, then I bet we'd buy the pink roll. It was pretty. But the pink part was only the paper you pull off the back. The sales assistant was busy stacking something at the other end of the store. How could I bother him with something as trivial as window seal? Maybe he'd come to cut sections off the big roll himself. I waited, but he didn't notice. The cashier wasn't busy with anything. Maybe she would come over.

I ended up walking to the register myself.

"Could you cut me off a length of window seal?"

She stared at me quizzically, then left the register, faced the other end of the store, and shouted: "Hey, come and cut this young man some window seal."

Strange that I can have such a hard time with such things. I sit inside for days at a time, then step outside once and fail at the simplest human behavior and act weirdly. It's also strange that it bothers me so much. As if competently asking for window seal is so awfully important. Acting the way you're expected, never drawing attention to yourself. And what would happen if I were to go to the hairdresser or put myself into a situation where I have to speak immediately and at length with a stranger? Outrageous.

The sales assistant, perhaps because he hadn't noticed me earlier, was incredibly kind and pleasant.

"How much should I cut and which one?"

"If only I knew," I sighed. He stood there patiently, holding pair of scissors and in absolutely no hurry. I had to make a decision.

"Is there any difference? Like which one goes to what kind of window?"

The sales assistant didn't reply to my dumb question. It was obvious that some were wider and others less so. The selection was too big. You don't hem and haw so much when picking mushrooms out in the woods—why should you with window seal? Sure, you did have to pay for the latter and wouldn't want to buy the wrong one. Mushrooms can be picked and thrown away. But why couldn't you throw away the wrong kind of window seal, too? Maybe you'll get used to it. You buy a meter every day and simply toss it, all to free yourself of excessive indecision.

"I guess I'll take ten meters or so of this one. And some of that, too."

"Ten meters?"

"Sure, why not."

How many windows did I have? Three. And two smaller ones. But how many of them needed new seal? Who the hell could say.

"I won't get ten meters out of this one."

"Just give me however much you have."

I felt drained by the time I made it back to Koidu Street and tossed the rolls of window seal on the kitchen stove. And that's where they stayed. For weeks.

◆

The weather was nice today so I happily went out, not fearing being in public even though I hadn't left home in a long time. I felt confident and carefree. I strode along the sidewalk as if I was a regular person and did so every day, instead of lurking around my studio, dreading human interaction. Ah, walking down the street? No big deal! I'm a pro. Child's play.

I walked downtown. Quite the big adventure. People walked by and didn't even glance in my direction. Consequently, there was nothing weird about me. I was aware that my gaze darted around restlessly and my gait looked forced, but no one seemed to notice. I suppose that meant my awkward way of walking wasn't so out of the ordinary after all. Or they were just wrapped up in their own worries and awkward traits.

I reckoned I should put an end to sitting around at home and acting sick. That I should get active again. It's absolutely impossible to be out and about and stay sober. What can you do? I'm not going to apply for any job. Where and as what? It was an absurd thought. Who would hire me? Where would I even want to go? Nowhere. Unless it was putting together cake boxes at a loony bin. Maybe. Somewhere with a little workshop where guys like me could just show up and put together a few without being noticed.

Where was I even going? Into town, sure. Maybe to some store? But which? A café? Which? I ambled around for a while, my lack of confidence slightly fading. But I didn't go in anywhere. What was I going to do? I decided to just shuffle back to Koidu Street.

Nevertheless, I just kept walking. Luckily I didn't see anyone familiar and didn't have to stop and make small talk. The longer I walked, the more pointless ducking into any doorway seemed. I'd only browse through books and that would be a sham, because I didn't want to buy any books at that moment, much less haul any around. I could sit down at a café, but that would also be phony because I'd be uncomfortable and simply waiting to leave again so I wouldn't have to stare blankly at people and watch them staring blankly back.

So, I ultimately went back home to Koidu. It was a nice walk, all the same. An adventure. Maybe I'd go out again someday. Maybe even farther than downtown. But where? The woods, I guess. But the woods are too far away. And I'd feel alien in a forest, too. Still, it doesn't really matter if a squirrel or a hedgehog sees some weird guy wandering around their home and not even knowing how to act there.

And then on another day, Siskin is in trouble and calls me crying because she's wet her pants and isn't brave enough to get up and keep going, so she's sitting in a public toilet. I promise to come immediately and I drop everything at home and quickly get dressed and leave at a canter, and have no problem being outside, and then run back home to grab her some dry clothes and then make it to the Kristiine shopping center panting and out of breath. I call her outside the women's bathroom and she still doesn't dare to emerge because she's naked and she peeks out of the stall door and there's nobody else in the bathroom so I casually go in and help her wipe dry and insist that she rinse off in the sink, too, so I lift her up and wash her bottom and someone else comes in and looks surprised but doesn't say anything and goes into a stall to pee and I'm confident and happy and proud, mainly because I'm suddenly not afraid of life, and reckon I can manage to do anything, just give me something to do, I'll get it done. I roll up her pee-soaked pants into a plastic bag I brought along and we go to BabyBack to eat because they've got the best food, albeit a little expensive, and Siskin's spirits lift pretty fast and all of a sudden she's looking carefree,too, and we sit in the restaurant as if we've won the lottery, boundlessly cheerful together. I call out to the waitress at the opposite end of the room whenever I feel like it and manage to tease her and compliment her, and she wags her finger at me but you can tell how pleased she is anyway, and Siss gives me a little kick under the table so I don't go too far with my flirtation, and we're happy. I don't want to ever leave BabyBack and end the good time, but my energy is starting to fade, and ultimately, we keep the bravado going, artificially, but also not too strained. The good mood simply exhausts us and we fall silent, holding hands like young lovers—I with a mess of unwashed gray hair, my beer belly pressed against the table, different-colored shoestrings on my boots, and a slightly stinky plastic bag by my feet, and Siskin almost as dirty as I am, her hair matted and unwashed, but an eight-year-old beauty all the same. And in the end, it can't be helped—it's late and Siskin has to go home because she has school early the next morning. I walk her to the bus stop and wait with her, hoping it will take its sweet time arriving even though it's rather cold out.

"Don't you have a hat?"

"No. I think I lost it somewhere. I'll find another one at home, though."

"Pull your hood up, then. Your nose is as blue as a boozehound's."

"Is it? Yours isn't."

"Not yet, but I'm sure it will be soon. Every proper boozehound has a blue nose."

"Or purple."

"That's right. How did you know that?"

The bus pulled up.

"Daddy, what're you going to do with those pants?"

"Oh, I'll wash them at home. Don't worry, I'm happy to. It's not the first time."

"Okay, I'm going," Siss sighed.

I managed to give her a kiss and a quick hug before she hopped into the bus, the stinky bag dangling from my grip. I waved to Siss for as long as the bus was in sight, and she waved back. I took a deep inhale and exhale and felt a little like you do when you leave a cinema, having experienced something great that is now over. I walked home, the positive emotions still lingering. I still felt good in my studio, though I couldn't bring myself to do anything for a while because it would be a shame to interrupt the ecstasy. Was there any difference between that and being in love back in grade school and having a chance to do something with the girl, like homework together? It made me so happy. I reckon it's pretty similar.

INTOXICATION

"LET'S HAVE A Christmas truce," Laura proposed.

"What's that?"

"We've had a fight every single Christmas and New Year's. Maybe let's not have one this year."

"It's just because we've gotten really drunk. That's when we argue."

Laura didn't respond. I hadn't immediately approved of her proposal. Laur wasn't going to repeat it, either—she's sensitive about those things when someone makes a comment or doesn't praise her idea. So, I whipped up some swagger.

"Hey, no, that's a fantastic idea! If I start getting under your skin, then just remind me that we've got a Christmas truce. Just interrupt me and say: 'Christmas truce!' Then I'll remember and can take it down a few notches."

It really was a great idea. I mulled over whether it would actually work and wondered when the first time we'd have to jog the other person's memory might be.

It didn't take long. Things started getting heated between us just a half hour later and I had to bark: "Laura! Christmas truce!"

I can't even recall what the fuss was all about. Just regular bickering. And who started it, I can't say. The reminder worked that time, even though it felt stupid to say. But why not utilize dumb tricks if they can produce even the tiniest change and make life better? Prayer, for instance. Childish or indigenous magic. Or some other game between me and people and me and God.

At the same time, I knew I shouldn't start thinking or expecting it to have any effect. And even if it did work just a little, then fine, move on and don't cling to it or pray for half a day, and don't be mad at God if He doesn't have a second to hear your prayers and solve your problems on the double. "Dear God, you didn't have time for me today, but so what. We'll talk again tomorrow. I'll just try to be good in the meantime and not get you too angry. Well, sure, I am going to get drunk tonight and I can't promise not to get angry at Laura when she ignores me, but I hope I won't make too big of a mess."

Bukowski wrote that nature and God pull mean tricks. They don't give a single shit when somebody messes something up. He didn't like that sort of thing—God's and nature's indifference.

Fine, but would it be any better if there was a god who reassured you the second you called: "Hey, Peeter—don't worry. We'll get that worked out for you straightaway." Life would be messed up in that case, because the benevolent god would receive a constant flow of contradictory requests. I suppose he has to pretend not to hear or harden his heart every now and then, even when his own son is getting weak on the cross.

Deals were always done and trades made with gods in the old days. Even in the Old Testament. But it doesn't appear to work anymore. God's no longer such a close and familiar business partner. You don't know his face or acts, or even his address. He's like a distant relative with whom there's still a glimmer of hope that they might help you out of a pickle or leave you some kind of a minor inheritance. But who knows—maybe that inheritance will be a burden of worry regarding the world and humankind, and who would ever want to be left something like that? Nowadays, lots of people inherit their elderly relatives' bank loans.

Maybe God has a handful of closer relatives who will get hit with those inherited burdens first. Stan, for instance, or any one of those five hundred fallen angels. Not to mention the whole lineup of archangels. And it's foggy with Gabriel, Michael, Immanuel, Nathaniel and all the rest in turn—who's in the gang and what it's called.

Still, close relatives have the right to refuse an inheritance.

When I'm last in line to be asked if I'll accept that inheritance, if I'll take the dear Lord's load of worries as my own, then what will I say? Turning it down would be a little uncomfortable, too. Who'll be left with it? And all in all, God & Co. has been so nice.

I'll have to see if those problems can possibly be simplified or divided or transformed into something else somehow. I doubt they can be made into joy, but . . . Perhaps they can even be turned into something like recycled metal or paper. Recycled and reused concerns.

The Syrian civil war has been going on for two years already. God knows how many simple folks have been killed. That doesn't make it an old problem, of course. And there's nothing that any of us can do about it. Joking doesn't help, either. Neither does whining about it. What other options do we have?

The indifference of God and of nature. I'm a part of nature and of God, and yet I'm nonchalant about piles of corpses in Syria? Pretty miserable.

◆

"Bedtime? It's almost midnight."

I was feeling sleepy.

"I'm sure not going to bed yet. What time did you get up?"

"One."

"And you already want to go to sleep."

"Yeah."

I myself couldn't understand why, but I was afraid that if I allowed that sweet drowsiness to pass, then I'd be wide awake until morning. It'd also be nice to get up earlier the next morning. Maybe that could happen if I hit the hay now.

"Fine, go to bed. I'm staying up. I don't have to go to work until ten tomorrow morning. That leaves more Metaxa for me."

We'd gotten bored of wine and beer, so we bought something else from the cheap liquor store on St. Tony's Hill after the Johanson Family concert. Calvados. The show was like a gust of air straight from childhood, as they hadn't performed together in a very long time. Not in years. That made it something special. I spent half the concert thinking about what liquor to get for home afterward (the bar was closed during the performance so noise from the automatic coffee machine wouldn't interrupt). I cycled through different types of booze in my head and daydreamed a little about them. Still, nothing exceptional came to mind. I'd been a fan of calvados at some point, but that was a while back already. I'd also drunk the local grocery store out of all their dark and wheat beers. Or they just couldn't be bothered to restock.

"What drinks should we buy on the way home?" I asked Laura when the concert ended.

"You have any ideas?"

"Calvados, maybe?"

"Sure. Where do you want to get it?"

"That shop on the hill."

"Do we have to walk there?"

"It's not far. A little walking is good for you, too. I haven't done anything all day." I was aware, of course, that you'd gotten up early and been at work all day and were nodding off during the concert, as always.

A photographer walked by and took a couple pictures of us. I hazily remembered that he used to live in Keila and drove a Nissan, but I couldn't unearth his name from my dusty mind. Andres Teiss? Probably.

"Who are you working for nowadays? I've got no idea," I asked him.

"I don't really know. I used to contribute to *Nädal* all the time, but that's gone. Merged with *Kroonika*. Can't say what will come next."

"Does that mean we'll be in the next *Kroonika*?" Laura asked.

"No, I'm not good enough for them."

We walked towards the coatroom, not swaying a bit. The photographer grabbed my arm and held me back for a moment.

"Who's that woman I just took a picture of you with?" he asked.

I hesitated and wracked my brain for a moment. Recently, I'd tried for two days, unsuccessfully, to remember the title of my yet-unpublished and -unprinted novel. In the end, I had to look it up on my computer. Huh, that's right! *A Tight Knot*. Good choice.

"That's Laura Sauter," I finally replied after I beat back Alzheimer's. "My wife."

Suddenly, looking at Laura, I was surprised to have a wife like her. Had I married her? Or had she married me? I suppose that's a nice way to live, though—constantly surprised. You open your eyes in the morning and think: Look at that! I'm alive. Look at that! The world. Seemingly familiar and still a little surprising.

The photographer kept haunting me for a while. What *was* his name? The liquor store on the hill didn't have calvados and it cost an arm and a leg at the little 24-hour shop down the road, so I ended up walking down the slippery sidewalks holding a bottle of sparkling wine under one arm and a 0.7-liter bottle of Metaxa in the other, debating which hand I would brace myself with if I fell. I decided that I wouldn't use either, but would hold both bottles over my head if it were to happen. Luckily, it didn't.

At home, Laura poured herself a little drink and I got sleepy and laid down in bed.

"Ha, ha! More Metaxa for me," she called out.

Fine, I thought. My liver had been aching for days. Märt has told me before that your liver can't ache, of course, because it doesn't have a single pain-sensitive nerve. However, my old alcoholic relative, who is a medical worker, figured out that the pain comes from the membrane surrounding the liver—when it expands, it causes a slight ache.

But then, Laura came to bed and wanted to fuck. She proposed it all on her own, for the first time in ages. I did the best I could, and afterward, she fell asleep.

I was as wide awake as could be.

So, I finished off the whole bottle of Metaxa. I was too drunk to do anything else productive, anyway.

To pass the time, I googled the photographer at the concert. I tried finding him by browsing pictures, seeing whose face was familiar. I'd have to tell Laura the next day that it wasn't Andres Teiss—it was Sven Tupits. I was pleased to have figured it out and lessened the Alzheimer's a little more.

Laura was asleep and the 0.7-liter bottle of Metaxa was emptied, so I went out onto the balcony to smoke and irritate my liver a little more.

Today at the pub, Taivo told me about how his father sometimes won't recognize him, but if someone calls him by name, then his dad snaps that he knows full well who he is. He'll also show off his old Zhiguli 2106 in the garage and say: "Take a look at my new car. It's half a meter longer than the old one." When

Taivo looked, it did seem a little longer than before. Maybe it was just the light or something. He told me he hopes his old man will wander off one day and freeze to death in a snowdrift.

"How do you get Alzheimer's, anyway?" I asked.

"It's genetic. Forty percent is if someone else in your family has had the disease. Or something like if someone in your family has had it, then there's a 40% chance you'll get it, too."

I wondered if any of my relatives has ever been diagnosed with Alzheimer's, and realized I didn't know. There've been cases of insanity, but what family doesn't have those? Taivo and I sipped our beers and tried not to look directly at each other for too long. I wondered how sharp Alois Alzheimer's own memory had been, but decided not to ask.

Nobel invented dynamite, not the Nobel Prize, and Darwin didn't discover evolution, though he did write a book about it. What Dynamite discovered, I have no idea. Maybe he just lived a quiet and peaceful life.

I spotted the name Delilah Samson online, but didn't look her up on Facebook to see what she was like. If your last name is Samson, then sooner or later, someone's going to name their daughter Delilah. Though maybe she got the name through marriage.

◆

It was kind of a silly reason to get together: checking to see if we could get cheaper booze from a bulk warehouse. Laura had left early for work and I'd lounged around her apartment till noon, taking a bath and drinking the rest of the wine left over from the previous night along with two half-bottles of beer. I read a couple pages of Ivan Bunin in the tub, then a few of Henry Miller and Juhani Aho.

Siss called. She wanted to stop by Koidu and hang out with her friends in the studio.

"I'm at Laura's. Do you want me to come there, too? Or are you guys alright on your own? Are you just there for the day?"

"Just the day, yeah. You can come. Without you, it's kind of. Well. You know."

"It's cold right now, too. I'll come and heat up the stove and bring you something to eat. What would you like?"

"I dunno. You don't have to get anything." Any time Siss says she doesn't want anything usually makes me go and get something I hope she'll love.

"Would you eat some potatoes if I bought some?"

"Okay. Or those wedges mixed up with fries."

"Sure, no problem."

Suddenly, I had something to do. Life had meaning. I hurriedly cleaned up the kitchen. The bed still wasn't made. I checked the time.

So long as Laura didn't come home to see a messy bed, everything would be fine. Otherwise, we'd get into a fight.

It was also good to clear out before she returned. Otherwise, the logical next step would be to go to the grocery store and make dinner together. But if I told her I was going to heat Koidu for Siskin and bring her some food instead, she might turn dour again.

So often, I failed to catch myself and ended up doing or saying something that put her out of sorts again. Then, she's simply silent. In the worst case, she might pretend not to see or hear me at all. Still, I try to be cheerful and confident and act like nothing's gone sideways. At some point, it seems so unfair that I do everything in my power to make things right again, but Laura is relishing her feelings of depression and indignation and refuses to lift a finger to put the relationship back on track, so I slam the door and get lost or do something else that's stupid.

I haven't been able to figure out the right way to act in those situations. Maybe I should slow things down, calmly focus on doing my own thing, move on to other issues and hope the conflict will simply blow over.

Have I ever tried that before?

But what if we *need* conflict? And if we manage to work our way around one, then neither of us is satisfied. What's there to do—we failed to fight.

And do we then go right back to seeking out another conflict? All so we can bicker and go our separate ways and be alone for a little while so we can focus on our own things and think our own thoughts? If things go well, then we get back in the mood to be together again after a short time and lose the desire to lay blame and pout and be silent and ignore each other.

If I hurried, I could still manage to pop into the store to grab a few beers. Saku Dark and Saku Stuttgart were about twenty cents cheaper here at the Maxima than they were in the little bodega. Money was tight.

Whenever Laura and I were together, something made me throw around as much nonexistent cash as I could. Being stingy was no good. But then on the days I'm alone, I use a knife to split matches into four pieces. True, that was a thing of the past. They no longer make matches like they did before the war, when you could parsimoniously slice them into four usable pieces on days between benders, the way Juhan Viiding wrote about.

My liver had been aching for four days already. The thought crossed my mind that I should take a pause from drinking. A liver holiday. Still, the ache was minor and my thirst greater.

I decided to make a stop at Maxima. Otherwise, I'd later end up buying more expensive beers anyway.

Why did I think about us arguing when we'd already smoothed things out? Were we preparing for a new one? Which one of us? Ah, but we had a Christmas truce, and we'd made it early. Back at the beginning of the month. That should hold up for a while, then. It was wearing me out.

When he and Elo got into a fight, Tuglas would slam the door and sit down at his desk with pleasure, even if he didn't feel like writing much at the time. How do I know that? I didn't make the fact up myself, did I?

Reality and imagination are all mixed up. Before long, I'll start confusing strangers' kids for my own. And talking to the television set. Even though I don't have one.

You don't go talking to radios that easily. You've got to see another person's face. Maybe it'd work better if you taped someone's picture to the radio. But people talking on the radio don't take pauses that would let you interrupt. They just go on and on.

TV news anchors pause when they show pictures. That gives an Alzheimer's patient the chance to chime in.

A mere picture on the wall that doesn't talk back wouldn't work well either, for some reason. Not unless you're extremely drunk. And then there's the question of who you'd like to talk to in the first place. You're not going to go chatting with an image of Jesus. The old picture I have of Viivi Luik on my wall might do, but I'd be bothered by the fact that it's a photo of her when she was young. Would I be an idiot for talking to a youthful Viivi Luik in the year 1968? I myself was just six at the time. But who knows, maybe little six-year-old me would have been able to hold a conversation about life with Viivi back then. Kalju Suur, the photographer, managed to snap that picture of her. I don't know if he'd want to nowadays.

I do occasionally say a few things to pictures of my late Kustas. But only a few.

I'd gotten lost in thought while still sitting at Laura's kitchen table, one pant leg pulled up, the other wrinkled on the floor, and a beer glass in hand. I needed to finish it off, otherwise it'd be stale by evening. Last night's half-finished beer, still with a bit of fizz in the bottle by morning. Which beers preserve best when they're only half-drunk? Dark ones turn syrupy; wheat ones stay lively, more or less.

Alright, time to go.

Have I finally made it to the life I've wanted to lead? I walk around in a daze for days at a time and my most productive activity is daydreaming. I'm not only stuck on teenage-era music, but lethargy or a leisurely rhythm. And it's something to which I've returned. *Back to childhood*. I arrived here relatively early. I might have regressed to childhood by the age of seventy, but I'm almost there already.

Okay, okay—on your way.

I wiped down the kitchen counter and rushed to make the bed, suddenly full of vim and vigor. How can I be so mercurial? Like a firefighter. Though maybe most people are this way. Drowsiness alternating with manic activity. What could be better? Going about life slow and steady all the time. But then you wouldn't have those flights of fancy that give such a high. And you can't be *Raging Roland* all the time. You run out of steam.

I hadn't yet zipped up my coat by the time I stepped outside. I jogged to the dumpster and glanced behind me to make sure no potato peel or scrap of paper had escaped the garbage bag. Bam—I slapped the bag onto the stinking heap. The metal lid refused to shut. Oh, you'll get yours. I would have heaved myself onto the lid to press it down with my weight, but the dumpster was too high. Fine, let it be.

Slipping and sliding down the sidewalk, I made my way towards Maxima. I started patting my jacket pockets to find the crumpled-up plastic bag I'd grabbed from Laura's place to avoid paying the ten-cent bag fee.

Okay, just to the beer aisle and that's it; no need to waste any time. Actually, no—I should grab a couple of snacks for Siskin, too. And I was almost out of toilet paper.

Got it. Snacks, toilet paper, beer. Faith, hope, love. And the greatest of these is love. Was that Paul the Apostle? Did they really have any right to talk about love if they didn't even fuck? Maybe they did. Is that the point when true love finally arrives? And who said that Paul never fucked? I wonder who had more sex: Paul or Saul? And if a person should first be able to love themselves before being capable of loving others, then did Paul ever love Saul? Did he even have a grain of sympathy for him?

So, shopping. I knew I didn't need a cart—that would just take time. No, wait—I would, because you shouldn't carry much if your liver is aching. Livers are sensitive to heavy loads. Good point. I paused for a moment. I would be carrying the beers back to Koidu, all the same. So, I just couldn't buy much. Not ten. Eight. All in the name of my liver. Because if my liver stops letting me drink, what then? Love comes when you no longer fuck—if you no longer drink, then what? Maybe that very same love. The fewer things you do, all sorts of things, the more time you have for simply observing the world and loving it. I suppose that means you should love the very most when dying. But who says I won't die as a bitter old man? Even though a bitter old man can also love in alternation with bitterness, or even at the very same time. I'm going to love you, fuckers! It *sounds* believable.

Trotting had made me perspire. I unzipped my jacket again. Snacks—got 'em! Toilet paper. Damn it, the cheapest was the biggest pack, 24 rolls. I couldn't waste money and *not* buy it. Was I really going to shuffle all the way from Kristiine to Uus Maailm with the big pack of toilet paper in tow like it was the Soviet period? Well, why not? Even though it was a little bit of a hassle. Hey, liver—are you up for some TP? And liver, you're the reason I have diarrhea all the time. Let's not be so shy about tramping around town with a big pack of toilet paper.

I hobbled down the un-shoveled sidewalks towards my studio, the bag of beers clinking in one hand and the pack of toilet paper knocking against my knees from the other. The quick pace sped up my mind for a moment, but then shut it down completely and set a single thought spinning. What kind of a physical state results in fluid thought? One that doesn't send your thoughts into such a storm that you can no longer catch up with them, unable to follow or notice or register any train of thought. One that doesn't switch your mind into automatic or set a chorus or phrase repeating? Sure, okay—the right amount of proper booze. Even so, booze should somehow fit your current physical condition to prevent it from extinguishing entirely. Where is my brain and regulator of bodily chemistry? The reader for my physical chemistry that tells me what kind of chemicals I should add to feel absolutely divine, receive enlightenment, and be hit with the idea for a genius novel. Why hasn't something like that been invented yet? No, it's good that it hasn't. Thousands of geniuses surrounding you? That'd be too much. It would get tiring and annoying. Keep your genius to yourself, please—it's enervating. Give me your ordinary, average ego; I can probably cope with it somehow. God's thought everything out pretty nicely, or else chance is simply a fantastic god.

I splashed down the narrow, muddy footpath towards the soccer field and passed through the filthy tunnel underneath the railroad. An old lady walked past. Neither of us were inclined to step off the path into the snow. I spread my arms wide like I was nailed to the cross, the bag of beers dangling from one hand and the toilet paper from the other, to take up a little less space in profile, and we edged our way past each other. I could have hugged her on that snowy expanse. But maybe she would've had a heart attack and I'd suddenly find myself holding a tiny old deceased Russian woman.

"Good day," I said instead in Russian.

"Good day, sonny," she replied in a strong accent, and I realized she wasn't actually Russian. Huh. She must have also realized that I wasn't either. Even so, she replied in Russian. Best not to get a big burly drunk man angry when you encounter him in a wintery wasteland. If he wants to speak with you in broken Russian, then let him.

"Maybe you want a bottle of beer? I'll give one to you. My bag's too heavy, anyway."

"Thank you, but I don't drink beer."

"Oh, well then. Have a nice day."

"Have a nice day."

Maybe she would've preferred a roll of toilet paper instead. Who knows.

We need pointless tasks to be upbeat and hardworking like a builder of communism.

When I used to have a job a long time ago, I was sometimes given tasks, but I never dared to regard them as pointless. That was a mistake. Taking my responsibilities seriously didn't allow me to treat them lightly and with relish like mundane absurdity. Is mundane life absurd at all, though?

When a bear poops in the woods, no one regards it as absurd. However, I can have that attitude towards myself doing the same act. In the end, what's the difference? Sure, maybe if a bear found itself sitting in my toilet, then it'd seem a little strange to him as well.

I paused for a moment. Why had I read with such fascination about Juhani Aho having children with two sisters and it coming out into the open only thirty years later?

Was it because that somehow made Aho an impressive guy? Still, if I hadn't enjoyed his writing, then I probably wouldn't have cared about the sisters-thing, either. You could certainly guess he was the melancholic type judging by his novel *Juha*, but maybe he wasn't.

Would I want to have kids with two sisters? Laura doesn't have any sisters. Have I ever been with a woman who has? I can't really remember, so maybe not.

What is it, then? An urge to be sinful and immoral? To seek guilt so as to have an impulse to write?

Oh, come on. That's just Märt's nonsense about me having a guilt complex. The authors of the Bible had one, too.

I don't have the same kind of envy for an African king with a hundred or so kids. It's not some selfish gene that wants to have as many offspring as it can at any cost.

So, what *is* it? Courage to flout conventions? Free will?

Aho wasn't so free at all if he pursued having a kid with Tilly and Venny both. And Venny ended up leaving him because of it. Then, there was another old flame of his who had a motto from his book printed in her husband's obituary. So much drama and heartache. I suppose it's necessary. Or is it? Do all those fiascos make life livelier?

Aho didn't woo those women without purpose, of course—I suppose he liked them all. Yet another romance, so much fun and laughs and joy once again. My ass.

I realized I'd continued walking. A bitter old man. I had all the right qualities to become one.

Yet, those who preach about great romance are also often egocentrics, womanizers, and stubborn sourpusses towards nonconformists. Nonconformists themselves are often most bad-tempered towards their own kind. Towards anyone who doesn't think differently the way they do.

And who are those nice old geezers, then? Moderate miscreants? Sin and let sin a little, too. Is that the real point of that saying?

I suppose it's harder to be virtuous and come to terms with the idea that others can act virtuously, too. And where do I belong? Where do I want to belong?

Fine, that's enough thinking for today. The great philosopher is going to the corner shop to buy his daughter some snacks. Or wait—what was I supposed to buy?

My phone rang.

"Daddy, how far are you?"

"Not far. I'm actually pretty close. Do you want to come to the shop with me? Where are you now?"

"Sure, I'll come. I'm at Koidu."

"You don't want to be alone there? I bet it's awfully cold."

"I'm alright being here alone. But I can come with you to the shop, too."

"Wait a minute. I'll bring my beers upstairs and then we'll go to the shop together."

"Okay, I'll wait."

I considered whether Siss might be afraid because others have mentioned that my late Kustas might haunt the apartment. I suppose she isn't too concerned, though. There've been times when she's been fine with going to sleep alone there when she's tired. She's simply lonely. She simply doesn't want to be alone. Just like me. There's no ulterior motives.

I could try to pick up that trait from her. But how?

Salinger asked an editor to accept a skimpy-looking book like how eight-year-old Matthew Salinger held out a cool lima bean at the lunch table in the hopes that someone would take it. When I read it, I couldn't tell if it sounded beautiful and sincere or fake and phony (which Salinger hated).

I should just leave the late Salinger in peace. Ha! Good luck with that. Salinger also chased around the schoolgirls who flocked to him for half his life. I wonder if he ever got any of them?

All these thoughts could've been left unthought if I'd just stayed soaking in the tub. But would that have made anything better? I doubt it. Stupid thoughts and footprints or soap bubbles and an underwater fart. Is there really any act that could change a life? Sure, there are bad ones. You kill a person and suddenly, life is different. But nice acts don't change all that much in life. Just as little and just as much as pointless deeds. So, what are you to do?

The only thing you should keep in mind is not to kill anyone and get into any kind of mess. Is that really it?

My door was unlocked.

"What do you think, honey—is that really it?" I asked to finish my inner monologue.

"Is what really it? What do you mean, Daddy?" Siss asked, skipping to the door.

We hugged and kissed.

"You know, even if that really is all that life really is, then I suppose it's not always so bad. Especially when you're here."

Siss ignored me. She was used to me saying things like that.

"Let's go pick up some things, honey, but then I'm going to try to get a little work done. Can you find something to do then?"

Sure—now that Siss was actually here, I had to go and turn my back on her. Now I couldn't just laze around with her because it would've felt like wasting time. I was certainly good at lazing the whole day away alone. Even though that would've felt like wasting time, too.

"I think I can. I'll call somebody, or I'll play with my Pet Shop toys."

HPV

"So, what was it?"

"Human papillomavirus."

"And what does that do?"

"It can cause cancer."

"Lots of things can."

"Sure. There's a lot of them. Some are dangerous, others aren't. Mine is. Ovarian cancer is the second-most dangerous type for women. I got a mammogram, too."

"What then?"

"They removed the warts or papillae by freezing them."

"Did it hurt?"

"No."

"Does that mean I have the virus now, too? Or could you have gotten it from me? I know one woman I slept with who was afraid she had it."

"I don't know. I can't tell you."

"You don't want to talk about it anymore."

"I don't know. I don't care."

For a while after our conversation ended, I couldn't get my mind off how I tend to get awfully worked up about the tiniest things and be afraid of getting sick. At the same time, you've got a serious illness and act like it's nothing. Maybe men and women simply act that way. Men are touchier.

I researched HPV on the internet for a while. There was a lot of information available. Men are generally just carriers, though it can also lead to testicular, anal, and who-knows-what other kinds of cancers. How many viruses are living in me? I suppose I'll never know. And perhaps that's a good thing. But afterward, I started drinking and when I tried to remember what I'd read the following day, I couldn't come up with much. For a while, I even forgot what it was called. But then, I noticed an empty bottle of Papidoux calvados on top of the fridge and remembered it was the papillomavirus. If you can't even remember the name of your own virus, then what will ever stick? It's strange, but sometimes a certain mood comes to mind—something recent or a childhood shame or a scent. Feelings of happiness never come to mind. Or how to be happy. Instead, I remember some specific, insignificant smell of fresh pancakes or a toilet. Not that I can even describe them. There's no point. I can't bring them up in conversation, either. They only exist inside me, and I won't give them to anyone else. I can talk about them if any of those instances have done something to me. But I reckon none have. If, then in such a complex and imperceptible way that not even I realize it.

SLEEP

SISKIN WAS SITTING up with us, but was noticeably nodding off and sliding closer towards the couch. Even so, she couldn't bring herself to admit she wanted to go to bed. I'd lit two candles in empty wine bottles. Laura was slowly but surely devouring a bag of juicy drum sticks we'd bought on sale from the grocery store in the Solaris Center just before they closed, washing it down with red wine.

"Come on, honey. I'll make your bed."

"Okay, sure," Siss whispered. "Where am I gonna sleep?"

"I'll put you on the pull-out couch for now, but we'll see where you end up when we come to bed. I'll blow up the air mattress and set it next to the couch, just like always."

"Okay."

"Just don't roll off. Or if you do, then roll back on, because the floor's cold."

"Okay."

"Get undressed for bed while I make it up."

Siss climbed into the armchair and lazily pulled off her clothes. I pulled open the couch and took out the sheet and pillows and blankets. There was nowhere to stack them, so I piled them onto Siskin. She was buried.

"They're not too heavy, are they? You can breathe?"

Siss played possum and was silent. I reckoned she was fine.

I made the bed, slowly and neatly. Laura was sitting and staring at the chunk of chicken on the plate in front of her. I supposed she was working up the strength to finish it. She was determined to eat it all, and I knew she would. Even if she had to vomit it all out later. Overcoming anorexia had made her bulimic, though it hadn't added any weight. Anything she gobbled down came right back out in a hurry. I bet I've still got sausages from last Midsummer's Eve in my intestines. At least that's the way I look.

I lifted the linens off of Siskin one by one. She stayed lounging in the armchair, her limbs akimbo. A scrap of white paper lay just between her legs, as if it were the tip of a tampon. I wasn't going to mention it or pull it out. Let it be.

"Come here, honey. I'll lift you into bed."

Siss stretched her arms and legs luxuriously. I tucked her in. The cool sheet work her up a little, but only so much that she opened her eyes wide, staring off into nothing. It looked as if there wasn't a single thought in her head.

I dampened the mop in the kitchen sink and squeezed out as much water as I could manage, then wiped down the floor next to the couch. I couldn't see very clearly, but I knew it was dusty. Dust collects in a single day. Dust bunnies form in two. It comes from somewhere through the walls of this old house. It's not bad dust, of course. I'm not mad at it. The house is simply dusty. It's in my lungs and my hair and on my books and my manuscripts and my computer screen.

I stuck an old cassette into the tape player. I'd recorded whatever was playing on the radio a couple decades back—quite the blast from the past. My cassettes had been misplaced for years, but it was nice to finally listen again. They contained more of the past than old pictures do. You get too used to photographs and they stop speaking to you at some point.

I lounged in the armchair, scrolling through Facebook and news sites. The internet was moving at a snail's pace. No matter—it allowed me to contemplate things leisurely. I took alternating sips of light and dark beer, as always.

Laur had bested the plate of meat and slunk over to my desk, where she stood staring at the picture of Kustas on the wall.

"Do you have copies of that picture?"

"I don't know. I can check."

I pulled a stack of pictures out of the cupboard and started flipping through them.

"No, none of that one. But I can make more. They put them all on a CD."

Laura was staring absently as if she hadn't even heard me.

I poured myself more beer.

"I want to go home but I'm too tired," Laura finally sighed. I didn't know what to say to it.

By the next time I looked up, Laura had sat down on my desk chair and fallen asleep, not leaning against the desk. I'd heated the stove and the room was warm and stuffy. I wondered how long she'd sleep that way today. Usually, it was for about an hour. But I couldn't just go to bed on my own and leave her sleeping in the chair. Not even if I lifted Siskin onto the mattress and left space for Laura next to me in bed. Ah, no big deal. I wasn't tired, anyway. I'd been staying up till five in the morning the last few days. If I got up at one the next afternoon and spent a couple hours easing into the day, it'd already start getting dark again. What can you do? That's just the time of year. The season. And that time of life.

PRIDE

"**B**UT I *AM* a proud girl!"

Every now and then, I remembered you saying that. What had it been in response to? I think I'd been whining and asked if you didn't think you were acting a little proud. Your response left me at a loss for words. I still don't know what to say to it. Nothing can counter pride. The declaration itself seemed somehow . . . I can't say. I don't know why you said it that way. You were proud of being proud. Sure.

Have I been finding more and more things about you to be critical of lately? Or did I notice them before but didn't wish to think about them? You also don't find me to your liking anymore. I'm not the way I was when we first met. And I've got all kinds of physical disorders. And I don't buy you as much to eat and drink as I used to. I'm tempted to say that back then, I'd only come over to your place a few days a week, so each time was like a party and I never scrimped. Still, I wouldn't have had the cash to bring you the best that money could buy every day. Now we're together every day and everything seems to be going south. I don't hold back my farts anymore. That must be it. You behave more respectably at home than I do, too. My gut hangs out and I've a bad habit of scratching it and picking my nose. You've got to be respectable alone, too. But when you sleep, your mouth drops open and your jaw hangs and you snore. More softly than I do, certainly. All the same, I've never sighed "Jesus Christ!" when you do.

Siskin can have terrible breath when she doesn't brush her teeth for weeks, and even a little kid can sometimes appear out of shape. Nevertheless, we somehow rediscover our fondness and care for each over and over again. Will you and I? Do we even want to? Is it a good or a bad thing that we don't have any shared assets or a home that would keep us together? It'd be extremely easy for us to split. What effect would that have on us?

◆

Laura and I were talking on the phone and . . . I don't remember what I said, but I had to wait and wait for her response. In the end, she said nothing. She's a master of silence and can keep it up for ages sometimes. I've tried to learn to be silent in response as well. If we don't talk, then we don't talk—so what? Why persist?

All I could hear on the other end was background noise. She must have been in a pub. Clinking glasses and dishes and soft Russian conversation. I listened for a while. It was like a soft radio drama. You couldn't even tell if they were acting out a murder or a high-level European summit. I don't know how long I listened. Long enough until the call finally ended.

I set my phone down on the table and thought for a moment. So what that you occasionally got calls that seem to halt or brake your train of thought? They always launch a new mental chain-reaction in turn. One that's either better or worse than the one before it. Do I know people who are better or worse than me? I guess I don't. Maybe only some who are dead or I've read about in books or on the internet. Like Mahatma Gandhi. Though if I'd known him in person, then maybe he *wouldn't* have been any better. Or worse. *What if God was one of us? Just a slob like one of us?* Or related to us somehow?

My phone rang again. It was Laura. She was confused by what happened to our call. All of a sudden, she could only hear silence. And then the call ended.

We had nothing to say to each other this time, either. Just the usual: oh, okay, mhm. And we ended the call again.

EVENT

"DO YOU KNOW where Siss is?" Kristo asked.

"I think she's out of town. With Grethel."

"So she's not coming to today's piano concert."

"I suppose not."

"My daughter's down here at Cabbages already and keeps asking where Siss is."

"Yeah, they're in the country."

"When are you coming down, then? You're today's main act."

"I know. I won't be long."

I realized it was almost eight o'clock. I felt a little reluctant to go. I couldn't say why. I'd felt ready for the party when I showed up to Koidu that morning. Erko had made a piano concert Facebook event a while back already and sent out several reminders. As I approached the building, I could hear him softly plinking on the upright in the sauna dressing room. There were certain melodies he enjoyed improvising and switching up. I don't know what they were, exactly. He'd written in the event description that lots of people would be playing and I'd be wiggling my ears, too. Now, I wondered if someone would come up to me and ask me to wiggle my ears, or if Erko could call me up to wiggle them for the audience, and what I'd do then. It was like waiting to see Santa at the mall when you were a kid, and when you finally got to him, you were terrified and wanted to run away. I'm 50 years old already. Nothing's changed. Maybe I should be glad nothing has. I'd like to run from my own birthday. I don't know if I want to run from death, but probably.

I decided that if it were to come up, then I'd say I can personally move other people's ears or read some poems in a corner. Not that I really wanted to do that. I did feel like hanging out, though.

I'd stopped in a couple times to check out the Christmas market he'd organized earlier in the day, too. All three rooms in the basement were packed—the sauna dressing room and the kitchen and the library. There were several different tables and books written by residents of the house and our friends were on sale at discount prices. I patted my pockets but was out of cash. That meant I could browse without worrying if I had enough to buy anything. I fingered the handicraft earrings and sock puppets, then pulled on a pair of giant mittens. Pretty neat. But before long, I ran out of things to chat about and didn't know what else to do, so I left.

I didn't know if Laura was coming or not. I couldn't say how we were getting on. She'd been tight-lipped, as usual. I couldn't even tell if she had any interest in checking out the Christmas market. All in all, she was out of money, just like me. What would be the point of showing up? Perhaps it was actually nice to have no idea how we were doing; to be in a state of perpetual ignorance. Ignorance also causes stress, but it keeps you fresh. Like hiking through the desert without a map. And what are you going to do with a map in the desert, anyway? Sure, there was a dune here yesterday, but I don't know if it'll still be here tomorrow. Our life is no desert of romance. I reckon we occasionally express hope that some kind of love will spark between us someday, but if it doesn't, then no matter. It's a good thing if you're crossing a desert and prepared to accept that you might not come across anything other than that very same desert before you. And even if you do, you'll just have to wait and see if it's a positive discovery or not.

I drank a little and brought the bottle down with me, as always.

Erko had dragged the upright piano into the kitchen space and set up various stools and chairs gathered from different apartments. Quite the Villa Villekulla. And who wouldn't want to live in the Villa Villekulla, or at least visit? Before the kitchen space was finished, the library at Cabbages was always packed during parties. Now, both rooms are equally jammed with people. I don't know if there's a line between a good crowd and a crowd that's too big. I certainly keep clear of festivals.

We sat around and chatted. We drank, each according to personal taste. Some had brought their own booze, others borrowed. I spotted Heidi sitting at the opposite end of the room. I called out to her.

"Hey, Heidi! Is Ülo here, too?"

"Somewhere."

"And Peeter?"

"I think he's coming."

I'd already seen Markus. Peeter hadn't been around much lately. He and Artur were making movies. And when I was somehow unexpectedly expected to do TV with Artur, things turned a little rotten. I didn't mind. Peeter and I were supposed to make a movie at one point, too, but nothing came of it. I suppose neither of us had enough content. Not that I really cared. The unfortunate part was that things have kind of fizzled out with Peeter, too. You could simply reconcile with the fact that friendships come and go, and so what? But it's not like there's an overabundance of good friendships. How many do you end up having in life overall? I suppose people have more these days than they used to, but what about the *truly* good contacts? How much room would I even have for them, anyway?

A couple of guys were playing a few instruments softly. Guitar and percussion. Erko did vocals and kept spirits high. I wound my way to sit in the back row. A girl I didn't quite recognize said hi. That's become normal. Probably partly due to the drinking. People greet me and I don't know who they are. No doubt they realize, for the most part, that I don't recognize them, even though we've met and drank together sometime. I don't remember all that much these days. So what? We'll see how bad it gets. In the end, I'll only remember my childhood, like Aunt Helmi. But I'll start a sentence and forget what I was saying before I finish. Maybe that's an even better desert of ignorance to walk through and enjoy. The world becomes new and unfathomable all the time. There's no misleading sense of understanding everything.

Erko called Jaan to the front of the room and he played a couple of minimalist Jaan Rääts melodies. I reckon they were the beginnings of longer pieces. Haunting and surreal. Atonal, even. The audience hung on every note.

"So now, Jan Uuspõld should be arriving at any minute and play us some piano, too, but he just doesn't know there are so many people waiting . . ." Jaan Pehk announced.

"Yeah, I put up a big poster over the door: 'Jan Uuspõld in Concert—SOLD OUT!'" Erko joked.

"If Jan doesn't show up, then can we get our money back?" one drunk guy asked. Entry had been free, of course.

"I ask that when Jan gets here, then I'll give you a sign and let's all be really quiet so he thinks the place is empty. But when he walks in, we'll all give him a big round of applause," Jaan continued excitedly.

The crowd was abuzz. Several more people took their turns at the piano. Ülo played. Many appeared to have prepared and practiced. It was nice to see. So what that we were all just a big group of friends doing it for kicks? Things are always better when you make somewhat of an effort.

Next, Markus sat down to play.

Not everyone was a virtuoso, of course, but the audience clapped and cheered fervently if they gave it a sincere go.

Erko emceed and tried to keep things from getting out of hand. The room was packed, people were getting tired of sitting, everyone was drinking, and some started heckling. Things had to be kept under control.

Jaan kept coming in and out of the room.

"Well, Jaan, is Jan here yet?"

He was holding his cell phone and continuously checking it.

"Jan'll be here in five minutes. I'll tell you when he's outside and then please be quiet, everybody. He doesn't know there's such a crowd. And when he comes in, then clap as loud as you can, okay?" Jaan was grinning amiably from ear to ear. He was reiterating it for the fourth time already, and he knew it, but continued because it was genuine and had turned into a fun, silly joke.

How is it that anything Jaan or Jan say or do always comes off as effortlessly jovial?

Suddenly, I glimpsed Laura. She'd walked in together with a crowd of other people. I was glad. I stood up as tall as I could in the throng and waved. She spotted me, appearing to be in a good mood and content to stay where she was. I debated whether or not to push my way through the crowd to stand next to her. Ah, maybe later.

I can't remember who was plinking on the upright when Jaan entered again. His 250-pound appearance was significantly more noticeable than Laura's 80-pound arrival.

We were sure that Jaan would repeat the same lines he had had before, but he just stood there silently and lifted both arms above his head.

"What is it, Jaan? Is Jan outside?"

Jan is outside. Silence, please, he mouthed.

People didn't care much to quiet down, however. Neither did the man at the piano. Erko stood up and gently repeated Jaan's request.

"Hey, guys, let's shut up for a moment please, okay?"

I can't accurately describe the atmosphere. It was kind of like a school party. We were having fun being silly together. All you do is give somebody a thumb's up and it's already funny because everybody's so wound up.

Jan appeared in the doorway to raucous applause. His presence was a loud metaphorical clap that declared the party's true commencement. Jan looked a little edgy, as always. I can't tell where to draw the line between him genuinely being a little edgy and simply displaying an accustomed edgy appearance, which implies that everything is fine. Egon Nuter ushered him in dramatically. Peter Strand made a few quips. I wondered—*does* Jan know how to play the piano? I supposed we were about to find out.

It seemed like he was a little reluctant to sit down at the piano, but he no longer had much of a choice. Maybe he was just good at working up the crowd's anticipation. When he did finally take a seat, total silence filled the room—a silence that was absent when he entered. The silence was filled with people wondering what he was going to do; with how he'd handle the situation. It was obvious that he had to come up with some kind of a trick, but what was it and how would it work?

Jan played a couple of pensive chords, closed his eyes, and concentrated. His chin fell to his chest, then he flung his head back proudly. His fingers rested on the keys and his foot depressed the pedal, allowing the notes to reverberate. The audience was already in awe, as if he'd performed something extraordinary. He thought. Everyone was silent. I don't know what we were expecting. A joke? Doubtful. We were simply waiting, and that air of anticipation itself was half the show. I suppose that inspired Jan, too, and he started singing in a mellow voice.

"There's a teddy under the bed . . . and Barbie's holding back . . . she can't understand why I'm fucking . . . a dusty . . . teddy under the . . . bed. Oh, I feel bad, oh so bad for the teddy, but the sex . . ." he sighed and played a couple more chords, ". . . is so savage . . . my dearest teddy bear . . . and Barbie, you prude, I plead, try to understand . . ."

I couldn't figure out if he was purely improvising. In any case, the mood was suddenly tender and silly. You didn't know whether to laugh or cry. I eyed the children in the audience. Their eyes were all glistening. It was naïve and shameless, and Jan's expression was dead serious. That also made it more comical, though it was hard to say why. Maybe because he was making absolutely no effort to be funny. The absurdity of the farce made it hilarious, as absurdity was what we'd all been awaiting and when it finally arrived, the nature of it was totally unexpected.

Jan ended the song and stood. He took a deep bow, pressing one hand against his breast. The audience replied with a long and wild standing ovation.

Nuter, who'd arrived with Jan, realized the night could go on endlessly this way, so he came to the actor's rescue and proclaimed: "Jan will perform three songs tonight! Three!"

So, Jan continued and the lyrics grew more and more ridiculous.

After finishing his third improvisation, Jan seized the chance to finish and bowed deeply once again.

"Thank you, thank you, from the bottom of my heart!"

Nuter quickly stepped in and declared that Jan's concert had officially ended, but the applause rolled on and on.

"Jan's finished, but the concert hasn't ended yet—it's just getting started!" Erko called out. "We've got a long list of performers here, and guest performers as well!"

But it was suddenly obvious that outdoing Jan's set would be a staggering task for anyone to accomplish, even if they were a professional pianist. No one cared to listen anymore.

Things really kicked off then. People got up and moved about the room, starting to pluck at various instruments in different corners of the space. I shuffled over to Laura. It was nice to see her, especially close-up. I realized that she was completely plastered. It didn't matter, though.

"Hey, Laur—what do you want to drink?"

"I don't know. What is there?"
"I've only got beer. But I think Erko has some wine."

ILLNESS

Pus seeped onto the pillow. I'd had an earache for over a week already. It was a change of pace, at least. I hazily recalled that children's mental capacity develops when they're sick. Why is that when their minds grow? Because they're just going over thoughts in their head? At the same time, you usually don't have any great flights of fancy when you're ill. Maybe some delusions. Do we also grow when we have good or bad dreams while sleeping? Maybe.

The pain is worse when it's dark out. Then, it's just the two of us together. And it's worst of all when your drowsiness lulls at the witching hour and you've got to take sleeping pills to carry on.

My first real ear infection. How about that. And only by the age of fifty. I should make a mark in a calendar somewhere. In God's calendar. Because I don't have a calendar that runs for my whole life. Why haven't those been printed? It should be all too hard. Peeter Sauter's life calendar. Here's where it starts, and here's where it ends. I'd certainly buy one to hang on the wall. It could also have what's going to happen on any given day. Nice to check in the morning. Today, I'm going to the doctor's office and she'll give me a prescription for antibiotics. I'll get it at the pharmacy but won't start taking them yet, because today's the opening of Kurvitz's exhibition, which means I'll probably have to be drinking for a couple of days. And there's no point in wasting antibiotics when you're drinking. Thus, I'll just have to suffer through my earache for two nights before getting sober and starting the treatment. I share my existence with a body, the interests of which I need to account for to a certain extent. It's my body. And actually Laura's body, too. And even her psyche. There's actually quite a lot of things you've got to account full. Don't even bring up how 12 hostages have already been killed in Algeria and 250 bloodthirsty French mercenaries are making their way into Mali.

When the Pentagon invented the internet, I wonder if they took pointers from the Islamic world, where a similar thing has been running for ages without electronics. No central administration, but a type of mentality that runs all on its own, spreading info and resulting in activity that benefits the whole population.

For a while, I considered whether an ear infection could develop into meningitis. Is there much of a difference between dreams and fears? I'm not sure if they're handled by the same area of the brain—i.e. if you're dreaming, then you can't feel fear, and vice-versa. It's certainly true when you're dreaming. Nightmares offer no pleasure, and pleasurable dreams aren't scary. Sadomasochism is something different.

◆

Treating illnesses. As soon as treatment advances, then so do the diseases. Both in my day and throughout human history. You occasionally treat me for this and that, sadness and a fear of dying, and then offer me new melancholy and angst for a change. It's still progress. Medicine has undoubtedly advanced over centuries. Viruses, too. And humankind—I don't know how long. But have I developed over these few decades? Or my illnesses, psychological and other? I'm not sure. And if I haven't, by chance, developed, then maybe it's only an illusion that humankind and medicine and viruses have advanced as well. Maybe they just shift like an image through a kaleidoscope. Sure, the picture becomes a little bit more refined, but maybe the kaleidoscopic image simply fractures into many such images, none of which are significantly more complex than the original when observed individually. Just as how the genes inside of me wish to duplicate, so does the world gene wish to diversify and duplicate as well. Well, go right ahead. Good luck. And I'm just a cog in the machine. Though cogs can be slick young minnows. I suppose I'd like that, anyway. As long as you're another cog. Would you like to be one? Wasn't there some song about that?

The trivial and the abstract should be together. God should be sitting on the john, smoking a Camel, and reading yesterday's *National Enquirer*. Otherwise, He isn't credible.

And the more treatments I have, the more illnesses I get. I suppose that's alright, though, because we do learn to love our illnesses.

REALITY

SOMEONE PINNED A scrap of paper on the message board by the front door of the building, which read: "WELCOME TO REALITY." You can't help but stop and think whenever you walk past. It seemed arrogant at first. Check it out—*these* guys live in reality! They know what reality *is*, but none of the other jerks do. Jerks like me, because I'm arriving from outside of reality whenever I read the note. But I guess they themselves read it, too. I should ask them where this real reality is located and what it's all about. Does it mean not having a conventional lifestyle? Not going to work? At the same time, I was irritated by my nitpicking.

I suppose I've gotten used to the note since then. I'll come home in summer or winter, arriving from different places but always entering reality without fail. True, life in the building never changes much. Not even when I, myself, have changed. No matter whether I'm pissed off or in a good mood, penniless or flush with cash, fighting or blissful, I always enter that reality. I can't claim not to like that arrival. Hopefully no one takes down the note. If they did, I'd be left staring at an empty spot on the board and wondering: *Huh, so where have I ended up now?* It would be the very same place as before, but no longer called reality.

One door used to have a label scrawled in marker that read: *Dom Krasnava Komandira*. Home of the Red Commander. I always paused for a moment before knocking. He used to make pants for half the hippies in the town. Dormidontov. There were always a bunch of hippies from Russia hanging out at his place, too.

The note also made me think about the saying: "Be realistic: demand the impossible." Who said that? And what does it even mean? I can't remember. The words stuck and I know I figured it out once before. Just like you when you're silent, it's better to just sit and stare straight ahead and not try to figure out whatever you're thinking.

Alice Cooper sang: "Welcome to my nightmare." I hardly reckon the nightmare I'm living would scare him much. Before long, he'd say: "Fuck off from my nightmare!"

When I walk past the message downstairs, I suppose I can occasionally muse that I've gone and visited reality and it was a pretty nice stay, but now it's time to head back to my studio. Or to Laura's apartment, where I can stare at my initials on her ass and debate where that road leads.

◆

I sat and admired your navel. I can't say it's beautiful, but certainly dear to me, because it's familiar. And attached to you.

Whenever I admire your navel, I'm admiring my own as well. Because your navel is mine. I actually haven't looked at my own in a while. I don't know if I can bend far enough to see it. I've actually got more than just ours. There's Siskin's navel, too.

Nombrilisme. Naval gazing. There are other things that can be admired for a change, too. But what? Nature? Culture? The world in general? There's not much more in life. And I wouldn't like much more to begin with, so what that I'm not interested in other people's navels. I can't say what interests them, either. Probably their own navels if they hide them, too. But it could easily be true that our navels and navel-gazing are similar as well. One navel reflects another; is kin.

And who says my navel doesn't contain nature or my navel-gazing an encounter with culture and other people?

I'm only justifying myself, which means I must have ended up in a poor position. I should duck out quickly. I should slip around a corner and stare at my navel there in silence.

If you write about anything other than your navel, then it's still navel-gazing, just more refined. Those lines you write are the navel and are there to be appreciated. Or despised, which is basically the same. (For there's no difference whether someone writes in awe of their navel or writes about how they hate it.) One cannot escape the navel because the navel is writing itself. It's the center of the world, too. I'm having a nice time writing, my face is glued to the screen, so consequently, I am the center of the world and what matters most to me. Why else do I write? If what I write didn't concern me, then I'd never pen these pretty lines. But maybe refined admiration is more respectable somehow.

Eroticism also derives from hidden qualities, not display. So maybe self-admiration should be concealed to be enjoyable. Though even that is transparent. When I tell you how much I like you, I enjoy giving you the sweet compliments and using flattery to wrap you around my finger. It's the same with the entire world or anything outside of myself that excites me. I wouldn't do anything if I didn't hope to benefit from it.

◆

The dissolution of romance begins with marriage. But what are you to do? It also starts when you don't get married but the thought has crossed your mind, because direction changes. You no longer strive to please the partner, but you've taken them under your wing and try to hold on to keep them from leaving and to make them however you want them to be. Which in turn increases their desire to skedaddle.

I didn't bother you much before we were married. You could have sent me packing then. Now, it's like you're no longer allowed to. Back then, I knew that it was a stroke of incredible luck to be hanging out with a young woman, and knew I should hold on to you (not cling to you) and that no one could say how long it would last. I'd at least enjoy it while I could.

When we got married, I made the mistake of taking the status seriously. Laura has been legally declared as mine, is counted among my assets, and if someone steals my possessions, it's a crime. It never crossed my mind that your wife getting fed up with you isn't a crime.

It's the same bullshit with life itself—what right do you have to take away the life I've received as a gift?

Hey, life wasn't given to you as a gift—it was lent!

Maybe my wife is also only borrowed. At any time, her real owner could show up and say: "Alright, dude. You've had her for a while and I hope you took good care of her. Now, it's time to give back the wife."

A borrowed life with a borrowed wife. Even writing could simply be lent and not belong to me. A life full of loans. Pretty nice.

Borrowed things can't be used as collateral for new ones. For example, you can't use your wife or your life as collateral when signing a car lease or a bank loan. That's certainly a good thing.

◆

Sex going away somehow brought eroticism back. Eroticism excites and torments. When sex returns, it quickly becomes unerotic. Wild animals don't fuck all the time, either. People try to but never manage.

So, what other option do you have? If you want to fuck, then don't get married. Is that what Aarne meant when he said: "Better ten lovers than one wife."? That would get a little boring, though. You'd have passion, but not warm intimacy and tenderness and softly stroking each other.

To be fair, those no longer exist in marriage, either.

◆

I checked the fridge for food. Onions. Butter, too. And two pieces of dark bread.

I'd fry the two onions in the butter, no matter that it'd fill the whole apartment with their stink. Only I'd be smelling it and eating it.

I estimated how much butter I should slice onto the pan. Most of it would just fry into a brown film on the pan anyway. Fine, let it. I dropped a generous heap on the pan. Why should I skimp with butter, eh?

The butter crackled and I stood watch like a soldier who's stealthily crept into the canteen to fry a secret onion in the dead of night. I checked if the underside had browned yet—I didn't want to burn it. Oh, damn it. A nice ring broke apart. It wasn't even brown yet, either.

I debated if I should butter the bread, too. No, no need. It'd all get too buttery.

As I fried the onion, I remembered the last time we cooked at your place. We had barley porridge with beans that was a little cold, so I decided to fry it with semi-smoked sausage and onions, but the leftovers smelled sour and you suspected it'd gone bad.

"I can just make you fried sausage and onions," I offered. "I'll finish the porridge myself. It should be alright if I throw it on a pan for a bit."

"What, *just* fried sausage and onions?" you asked incredulously.

"Sure."

I could already tell you didn't see that as a proper meal. I hadn't brought enough decent food from the grocery store. My performance hadn't met expectations and I'd only brought you a bottle of sparkling wine. You'd had one in the fridge already, though it was starting to run out.

Those were the spiteful thoughts that rolled around my mind as I fried onions at my Koidu Street studio. Was there any point in dragging myself over to your place if those were the things I was thinking? Would they surface somehow, even if I didn't mention them? Such thoughts always make their way out somehow, like in an unusual form of criticism. How can I shake the habit? The only way would be if I loved you specifically because you don't regard fried sausage and onion as any kind of edible food. But I can't. It's as good a food as any, in my mind.

I have repeatedly said that "The Princess and the Pea," is my favorite fairy tale. A princess who wasn't fussy, was just born with such a fine taste that if there was a dried pea hidden beneath seven layers of feather mattresses, then it was impossible for her to sleep, and all her sides would be painful and bruised. It's natural. I praise that fairy tale, but I mentally curse your fussiness. I'm a pharisee. People have told me that before. The one who drove Jesus out of the temple. Where did *I* go when Jesus drove me out? Right here, that's right. To the studio on Koidu Street and to your place. I don't know if I'd even want to return to Jesus. Maybe he'll get bored and come to check up on the old pharisee from time to time:

"Well, how's it going here, you pharisee? Would you like to come back to the temple?"

"No, thank you. Not right now. Maybe another time. But would you like to have a bit of fried-onion sandwich? I can offer you some beer, too. Unless you'd like to make yourself a glass of wine."

"Fried-onion sandwich? Well, sure—let me have it."

Then, Jesus will eat and I'll watch, hoping that in his mind, he's thinking: *Huh, I guess he isn't such a bad pharisee. Maybe we need pharisees in the world, too.*

"Are you still mad at me?" Jesus will ask.

"For flipping over my money-changing table? That was my grandmother's table, you know. And one of the legs broke off."

"Oh, really? Huh. That went a bit poorly, then."

"Don't worry about it. I just took it to your dad's shop. Joseph's a tip-top carpenter, you know. He had some great superglue lying around and fixed it in a jiffy. He didn't even want any money for the job. He'd heard that you broke it. I hadn't said anything. So, I bought him a couple of drinks. You know, it really wasn't right of you to toss your mom and dad out when they came to see you?"

"You think so?"

"Well, yeah. They were pretty down about it. They hadn't seen you in so long."

"Sure, I mean, but we were having a party. I guess I felt a little ashamed. I was kind of tipsy and there were a couple of whores with us there, too."

"Oh, they knew that already. They simply wanted to see you. It's something parents do."

"Yeah, I guess so," Jesus will say, sighing heavily. Even so, he'll eat every last crumb of the sandwiches and I'll be pleased. I'd actually eaten my fill earlier.

"I actually liked you, you know; no matter that we worked every day and all you did was party and destroy things. It was just your style. And if you ask me, I think you're a good young man."

"What kind of work is money changing, anyway?"

"Are you trying to say it isn't? Sitting at a table all day long, trying to make sure no sly thieves rip you off? As soon as you flipped over the table, all the coins went rolling around the floor and bums flocked there left and right to grab them. That sure made me blue. It wasn't your money, you know."

"But you were making such an insane cut with every transaction!"

"How do you know that? *You* didn't come to change any money. People just paid for you wherever you went! And people only ever cursed us. I got used to it, of course."

Ah, crap. I burned the onions while I was floating around my thoughts. I quickly turned the gas burner down and sprinkled salt over the pan. It's strange how I sometimes get lost in some vapid daydream that ends up leading nowhere. Still, I don't want to ever lose it—daydreaming is a nice time. Maybe one of the best times there is. I can't say if literature can produce the same effect. Perhaps that's what the beginning of the Bible is referencing: "In the beginning was the Word." God was bored and ended up telling himself some story just to pass the time. He was a daydreamer, too. Maybe the world *is* the story that God tells himself as a pastime. One he imagines to not be so miserable and lonely.

EXHIBITION

"WE WERE SUPPOSED to go to that exhibition opening."

"I know."

"But I'm at work and have to be here until five-thirty. Somebody's coming to the salt chamber. A customer. I have to be there with them."

"I don't know if I want to go to that exhibition in the first place. I might get a cold."

"It's not that cold outside."

"Well, then, I don't know."

"Think about it."

"Okay."

"Does that mean Marta is back in Estonia now?"

"I don't know."

"I just saw that she invited you to the exhibition and you replied that you were going."

"Right, but I don't know if she's in Estonia."

I'd told you about my dream of fucking Marta back when she and Margus had split up and you and I weren't getting along well, either, and you never wanted to have sex. You'd asked me: "But does Marta want to fuck you, too?" "I don't know," I'd replied. It was true—I hadn't even thought about that part of it. I'd just guessed that maybe she would. Though I suppose it wasn't much of a smart idea.

Marta had a proud look to her. She was usually filled with bravado, which I liked, though the way Margus talked about her, I could tell she was fragile and delicate on the inside.

I'd had an ear infection for a while. Sometimes it was annoying, other times enjoyable. Small pains and self-pity. But when the pain swelled late at night, it no longer left room for self-pity. Then, I just had to swallow an ibuprofen and wait for the pain to quiet down enough for there to be a point to crawling back into bed and hoping for sleep to come.

Our call ended. I knew I actually did want to go to the opening. I'd been planning on it for ages. Suddenly, I found myself in a hurry. I had to close up the heating stove. I washed my beer glasses, stuck antibiotic cream into my ear, and swallowed a pill to keep my belly in shape for drinking. I figured I'd stop by the cheap liquor store and grab a big box of wine. Margus mentioned in the email that guests could bring any beverage they wanted to the opening.

I quickened my pace, but then slowed back down. It was just an exhibition opening—who cares when you arrive? There weren't going to be any grand speeches or ribbon-cuttings. So, what wine should I get? Dreamer was cheap, sweet Romanian slurry—that wouldn't do. Everybody drinks that Fine Chile brand, though. I've never seen anybody turn it down. I didn't want a bag. Box of wine in hand, I strode through the city—let everybody see and be jealous, and let Laura see how much wine I've bought for her and rejoice!

I threw open the door to Hobusepea Gallery and stomped in. Jüri Ojaver was standing right at the entrance and eyed me. "Who's this imbecile?" he grunted, but he was grinning and I could tell he was drunk and just being friendly. Still, I didn't know how to respond to the abrupt welcome, so I did my best to keep up the banter.

"An imbecile, huh? Well, thank you—that's sure a nice greeting. Haven't gotten a compliment like that in quite a while."

Ojaver had been waiting expectantly for my response and appeared disappointed when it came. I would've like to tell him how both Siss and I were enthralled by his artwork where he sat naked on a bicycle, pedaling tirelessly and occasionally sticking his head out the trapdoor of a cuckoo clock to shout: "Cuckoo!" It was cute. A good work of art should be enjoyable to kids and adults alike. But now wasn't the time to discuss it.

The whole exhibition was splendid: glittering white crosses on the floor, some standing and others flat. It left an impression and was laconic through and through. There was no point in discussing what it meant.

I found Margus in the crowd and congratulated him. Laura was supposed to arrive a while later when she got off work. People were drinking cheap vodka. Margus had delicately wrapped plastic wrap around each of the one-liter bottles. The film was transparent and the Laua Viin label could still be made out, but at least it didn't pop. I hesitated for a moment. I didn't want to start drinking vodka, but if I started guzzling wine instead, then half the box would be empty by the time Laura arrived and it wouldn't be enough for her. So, I grabbed a plastic cup of vodka.

"Hey, Peeter—do you know Gabriel?" Jüri called down to me from the curator's office, waving a bottle of aperitif.

"Never have," I retorted.

"But you've chatted with Agnes before, haven't you?"

"Nope. Nobody's introduced us. And she's with another man, anyway."

"You want me to pour you a shot?"

"No thanks."

I immediately regretted turning it down, however. What could be better than sipping a nostalgic drink with Jüri Ojaver? Why just stand around discussing culture? Though that was unavoidable in any case.

I fetched a shot glass and Jüri filled it. Just as I was about to take a sip, he pulled it away from me.

"I thought you brought *me* the glass!" he said with a twinkle in his eye. I was surprised by his trickster mood.

"Oh, I did!" I answered. "Drink to your health. I'll go get myself another, bigger glass."

I did, and Jüri poured generously.

Some Russian girl from Moscow was drinking French cognac and asking strange questions, such as if we weren't disappointed in our Estonian Republic. It wasn't the republic we'd hoped for, was it? I was turned off by the attempt at conversation and suspected she'd been sent from the Russian Embassy around the corner to recruit assets. I made a mental note to ask when I got the chance, but realized the conversation would have shifted to something else by then and that I enjoyed chatting in Russian for a change. Let her spout her Russian propaganda—I've got no problem hearing it. But neither did I care to debate. It all seemed so pointless.

"Hey, were you the one who brought this box of wine? Can I open it?" a young guy asked me.

"Of course! It's there for drinking," I said.

Laura called and couldn't remember how to get to the gallery. I was baffled. We'd been there drinking together multiple times before. I was about to say it was between Lai and Pikk streets—how hard can that be? It sounded like she was in a sour mood, however, so I felt it best to hold my tongue. Softly and succinctly, that's enough.

"I can come out to meet you. Where should I go?"

"I'm on my way on the #17. What street do I take?"

"Well, you'll go across Town Hall Square. Get off at Freedom Square and I'll meet you next to the pharmacy."

I abandoned my chat with the Russian girl, still unable to figure out why a Moscow girl should start bellyaching about Estonia with a grin on her face. To hell with her. Laura was coming to meet me. I hurried to get to the rendezvous point before she arrived.

Laura wasn't on Freedom Square. I started walking towards the pedestrian tunnel under St. Charles Boulevard and suddenly wondered if we had passed each other without noticing and she was already waiting for me on Town Hall Square. It'd be a sad state of affairs if she was still in a bad mood and had to wait for me to boot. I dialed her number, but then spotted her emerging from the tunnel and searching through her purse for her phone to answer. I hung up and she saw me. Suddenly, I felt wonderful. I hoped her spirits might lift a little, too, because she seemed pleasantly surprised and said: "Oh, you're here. I thought you'd be waiting for me on Town Hall Square."

Christ, how easily we miscommunicated and had mismatching ideas about the simplest things each day! What about loftier things like love and fidelity—I don't even dare to bring those up. How are we to guess what the other person is thinking and feeling in regard to those ideals? It's a miracle that we've managed to stick it out for four and a half years already. Still, you never know how much longer it will last, no matter if you have four months, four years, or four decades behind you. Raivo told me he had a grandfather who'd been living on a farm with his grandmother for nearly his whole life, but then rode to the city one day and announced he wasn't going to live with that old hag any longer. And refused to explain further. The man lived in the city for a week before getting on a bus and heading back home to the farm. But that was the only occurrence, I think.

Laura and I walked towards the gallery in silence. A group of people were smoking outside the door and Laur immediately joined them. I went back inside and continued to drink and small talk with this person and that.

Laur came in and stared at the cup I was holding.

"You're drinking vodka!"

"Mhm."

I wasn't going to start explaining that I'd brought a box of wine for her and left it there.

"What would you like?" I asked her.

Laura didn't say a word but poured herself a glass of wine. Marko Kekishev and I were in the middle of a conversation that needed to be finished. He was going on about the peculiarities of the Mustamäe district's Soviet-era plumbing system, which didn't let warm water go up. I could tell that Laura wasn't interested in the subject, but it'd been so long since I last talked to Kek and I didn't care what we talked about. It was the conversation with him that mattered, not the content. There was a kind of energy- or information stream coursing back and forth between us—words were merely the filling or the vehicle.

Laura drained her cup and set it down on the windowsill.

"You can stay here, but I'm leaving," she said curtly.

"Hey, wait—you just got here," I protested.

The men smirked as they watched, thinking: Well, Sauter, what are you going to say to your wife now? And I didn't really know what to say, of course.

"Well, if that's the way it's going to be," I sighed, "then let's go together. What's gotten into you? Wait one second, I'll finish our conversation and finish my cup."

Laura stared at the ground as she waited, dour. I couldn't figure out what was wrong. Waiting was torment for her. I made a quick trip to the toilet.

Margus noticed we were leaving and started pouring out the rest of the vodka into people's cups. Mine was filled three-quarters of the way. Laur watched out of the corner of her eye. I suppose I was already pretty wasted. I was unsure what to do with my glass. I couldn't just leave it there—Margus had just filled it. Neither would I be able to down it in a single go.

"Okay, let's go," I grunted, cup in hand.

"So you're coming, then?"

"Yeah, sure."

Ojaver glanced over.

"That's right, Peeter: if your wife says you've got to go, then you've got to go."

I didn't feel like answering or squeezing out some kind of a joke, but did anyway.

"You said it, Jüri."

We left the nearly full box of wine there. It would've come in handy back at home. Neither of us had any money.

Still holding my cup of vodka, I trudged after Laura through the Old Town. No one I knew walked past, but that was fine. As far as I could remember, Laura never had a problem drinking anything while walking down the street or hanging around anywhere else. Now, she seemed somewhat annoyed.

My cup still wasn't empty by the time we'd marched quick time to the #77 bus stop. It pulled up after just a few seconds and I clambered through the back door after Laura. The stench was no doubt wafting around me and I tried to keep the vodka from spilling whenever the bus rocked or shook (good cheap Laua Viin is to be cherished), but enough of it was already swirling in my belly that I wanted to wait a while before taking another sip. We were just about halfway to Laura's stop. She'd been standing, her lips pressed into a narrow dash, and staring in the opposite direction. Suddenly, when the bus was about to reach the next stop, she leapt from her starting blocks, darted through the other passengers towards the front section of the bus, and disappeared. I craned my neck to look, but couldn't tell if she'd gotten off.

There was no point in me waiting around, so I stepped off the bus, careful not to spill my drink. Laura was nowhere to be seen. Maybe she'd used her head start to disappear between any of the tall apartment blocks. The fact that some women are expert at shaking me off their tail is no news to me.

I abruptly felt there was now room in my belly for the remainder of the cup's contents. I leisurely sipped it to the last drop and tossed the cup into the trash bin next to the bus stop. Somehow, suddenly, I felt relatively sober.

There was no longer any point in going over to Laura's place, so I spun around and started strolling towards Koidu Street. These things tend to happen rather unexpectedly. You reckon you might see them coming, but you don't. And they seemed to happen more often than they used to.

As I walked, I remembered thinking that something should happen in our lives—otherwise, our marriage would never make a decent novel. But what should the event be? A child? A divorce? A kid was nowhere on the horizon and I doubted now would be the right time for one. Divorce did seem to be somewhat of a possibility, though I didn't want that, either. Had I been subconsciously starting to manifest a divorce so our novel would have a twist? Could it really be true? I couldn't say, but that would be awful if it genuinely was the case. And aren't novels written about quiet, even-keeled, pleasurable lives as well? Not that I could think of any. And Laura wasn't writing any novel, so why did she need to go and run off? I seriously doubted that she was attempting to write along with me. I did used to joke that I went boozing around town to bring writing material back to you. It sounded cruel because I was blackout drunk when I did and didn't want to hear a word about writing.

◆

I started praying. I'd wander around the city and recite the mantra: May things go well for everybody, and for me was well. I used to pray when I was a kid, but I can't remember how. I wasn't about to start composing any longer prayers now, in any case. I couldn't analyze why I began doing it. Maybe I was in some kind of a panic. I'd been unemployed for a while, sure, and it was a new situation for the first time in ages. Did that make me afraid? I don't know. Or did I feel guilty like Märt believes, and was trying to rid myself of the guilt?

At some point, I realized that prayer is self-programming. Like a motto on a family crest. A statement for which I stand. If I repeat it, then my identity strengthens and my acts will hopefully correspond to the motto. Like some kind of a mission. A secret task I was assigned here in the monastic school, or which I chose myself. The head boy wipes down the chalkboard and counts the missing students.

But I also knew that Helmi was praying for me, and sometimes that made me feel good. Whether even because it simply meant she was thinking about me and cared. And then I wondered: if Helmi dies, and death is something she wishes for, then who will pray for me? Nobody. So, why shouldn't I pray for Helmi, too? So I did: May everything go well for my Helmi. Then, I counted up all my acquaintances and realized there was no escaping it: I needed to wish good upon everyone with whom I've ever had any relationship. Otherwise, I won't be getting any As or Bs. I'm not sure I even will now.

Standing by the Pskov-Pechory Monastery is a man who has calculated how fast a spoken prayer travels around the globe. I guess he has scientific background. He stands there and prays day after day because there's nothing else in this world for him to do anymore. When I heard that story, I reckoned it was probably some means to escape depression or some other spiritual woe. No doubt it is.

So, who or what am I running from? If I could find out what it is, if I could see that monster, then would I need to run anymore? The monster would lose their terribleness. Or I could fight it. Would I even want to? Like an ancient knight and a dragon. Whatever pursues me is probably just a part of myself. If it comes to battle, then who will triumph over whom? One part of me over another. Then, I'll be less. I'll be purer and stronger. Poorer?

Or is prayer meant to avoid thinking, to clear one's mind of thoughts, to keep certain thoughts from buzzing around your head? So, right back to fear. What thoughts do I fear? Or am I afraid of feelings? Afraid that if I walk across a narrow footbridge, I'll lose my concentration and splash into the water? You aren't likely to keep your balance if you overconcentrate, either.

There are quite a lot of people around the world who pray every day and finger prayer beads. You'd generate tremendous electricity if you were to attach a dynamo to them. What would we do with all it? Something, I bet. As long as the prayers don't tire you out, endorphins will help to get it running. I doubt my prayers would do any good. They're pretty dull. Mediocre prayers.

Then there's the story Raimo told me about a boy who broke a mug and prayed in church for it to be whole again. Afterward, it was still broken. So, what good is it? There's only a point in asking for what can be done and makes any sense. For instance: the mug may indeed be broken, but what if it didn't matter? Well, there's still that sense of guilt. If an athlete prays before competing, does it get them fired up? Hemingway prayed for bullfighters. It certainly might have helped them. The bullfighter himself could've prayed for the bull, though. Maybe he did.

Now that I've gone and said it, then is prayer made pointless? Is it null and void? Or does the prayer now carry on in this writing like a machine of perpetual motion, praying on and on in the computer? There are a lot of unanswered questions, and none will ever be answered. Does that mean they shouldn't be asked? Maybe we should just be a little more selective. Would you like some tea? Should I get a bottle of bubbly from the shop? Right, I did ask you that earlier today. Maybe that means our relationship will get just the tiniest bit better.

MATRIMONY

A M I MARRIED to you or to Cabbages? I relish hanging out there, too. And at Cabbages, there's no routine. We both act the same whenever I'm at your place.

No, that's a boldfaced lie. Of course I'm married to you. I just wanted to make myself seem a little more interesting.

At the same time, I'm not so sure about whom you are or wish to be married to. I feel like you, yourself, don't even know. You once had that guy named Aram, whom you loved. I don't know if I've ever experienced that type of boundless love. Perhaps I did at one time, though I later regarded it as a mental illness or some kind of mild insanity.

That doesn't mean I can't occasionally sit around Cabbages and enjoy it, though. I actually spent awfully little time there. Why is that? Am I afraid that hanging out with others will rob me of myself? I'd dearly like the company of others, but at the same time, I don't really feel like wasting days away by hanging out. Solitude is so exquisite. Still, it's only like that when you also have the opportunity to spend time with someone else. Like the chance to run over to your place at night.

Or am I married to you, but Cabbages and the people who hang out there are like lovers? Everything's fine and dandy then. They're lovers, but I'm not cheating on you. And you give me permission to socialize with the regulars down there. I guess you just need some small alternative to marriage.

Still, marriage itself is an alternative to solitude.

As soon as you get an alternative, you start searching for variety from that as well and ultimately flee back to being alone. It all goes full circle.

There are board games where the pieces move around in a circle to reach home—a place you leave, and to which you must return. There are a lot of different variations. And then there are board games where you travel from start to finish, sometimes leaping forward and other times falling back. *Chutes and Ladders* and the like. Not to mention a wide range of military games like chess and checkers and one Chinese-style game where you jump over your opponent and use them to get home. And there are money-collecting games like *Monopoly*.

Has anyone ever studied why and how different people have invented different board games?

I suppose there isn't a game that lacks competition or fighting, is there?

Maybe there is. When I was very young, I remember there being games that simply required you to stack patterns on top of one another. I can't recall if it was played in groups or individually. And what pieces were used? Drinking straws? Bits of plastic?

There's also the game where players have to pull wooden blocks out of a stack.

Are shogi and similar games any model for living? Ones meant for different people? Or is one model adopted sometimes, and other times another?

Dominos is pretty fun, laying the pieces crosswise.

There are games where the player who gets a lot of things wins. And there are games where whoever gets rid of everything wins. Are there any where you collect things until the sand in an hourglass runs out, then turn it over and reverse the process? That would never end. I suppose I'd like to play it—to alternate between gathering and destroying. Sometimes winning and sometimes losing to an opponent. Maybe I'm playing it now. Am I playing it with you? I want to beat you, but then I want to lose as well. Are we two sides to the same coin in bed?

◆

I was sitting at the kitchen table and suddenly heard a key turn in the lock. Shit—you were coming home in the middle of the day. I quickly looked around and gathered up all the snot-filled balls of toilet paper from the table. Crap. Half-finished glasses of beer and a dirty salad bowl. The cutting board covered in crumbs of bread, cheese, and sausage. Shit, shit. Oh, right—I also hadn't made the bed yet. What time was it? One-thirty. True, I was sick, but I'd also been lounging extremely lazily and had only taken a shower about an hour earlier. I'd thought I had time aplenty to hang around. Why were you coming home so early?

There was obviously no time to make the bed, so I apologized.

Once before, you'd come home from work early and found me drunk and sitting in my underwear, not having made the bed. That fight lasted for days. Your home wasn't in the condition you wanted it to be. What can I really say to that?

You stood in the doorway, looking around the room, expressionless. Was something wrong? Something else?

I felt like it was now a competition to see who could make the bed first. I didn't want to lose in the name of competitiveness, but neither did I want to win. It was clear, in any case, that we wouldn't be making it together.

◆

There came an unexpected period where you flirted with other men at booze-fueled parties. In truth, you weren't the one who flirted—they came to flirt with you and you simply allowed them to stroke your arm and you went outside to smoke together. And I, just as drunk as you were, observed the whole scene from the opposite corner of the room, at a total loss for what to do. It felt stupid to make a scene, but it felt just as stupid to merely sit and watch.

Sometimes when we left to go home, you told me to fuck off as soon as we were on the sidewalk. One time, we got off the trolley and were still a fair distance from your apartment. You simply stopped and let me keep walking, and when I noticed and waited a long time for you to follow, you finally told me to go back to my studio alone. Other times, you vanished on the way. I knew that you hated it when I suspected you of being up to no good, but I wasn't suspicious. I believed you were honest with me. All I felt was that neither of us really knew what was going on between us.

You'd said you didn't want to have sex anymore. I'd already figured it out somehow, but it still baffled me. In a way, I'd grown accustomed to your body and could tell it no longer had the spunk it had in the beginning. That much was clear. I'd made it through such situations many a time before and reckoned there was no point repeating them ad infinitum. I reckoned it was best to just stick to one. But now I had, and that one no longer wanted me.

I knew I also didn't care about you the way I had a couple years earlier. Or I wasn't as determined. At the same time, I was saddened by the realization that I wasn't just unattractive to myself and most people in general, but to you as well. In the beginning, I'd been comforted by the thought that I suited you. Had I stopped caring much to be attractive because I thought we fit together either way? Now, that was over.

◆

I lay in bed, simply staring at Laura. I couldn't sleep; I'd been plagued by insomnia lately. Too much drinking, what else could it be? I tossed and turned at night, sometimes only falling asleep by morning. I didn't feel like swinging my leg off the bed to turn off the light with the foot switch. Laur looked beautiful in the silence. I knew she didn't want to fuck. She was wearing white gloves and looked like Mickey Mouse with them resting on top of the blanket. Laur had just gone to the doctor and gotten a handful of anti-allergy creams and pills. Her hands were red and covered in scratches. The chemicals used at her job were to blame.

Maybe the fraught situation between us was a factor, too.

Her estrogen levels had finally risen for the first time in years, too, so there was a danger of getting pregnant. She was haunted by it. Not that she wanted to have sex, anyway.

That night, Laur told me she hadn't want to fuck me years earlier, either.

"Well, sure, but I often couldn't get it up back then. Now, I'm hard all the time. I've got a chubby most of the day. And I can't do anything about it, because the only thought in my head is how we used to fuck and how much I'd like to now. I just drank a lot back then."

"You drink a lot now, too. It's not just that."

I knew she was right. There was a period where I'd become overly accustomed to Laura's body and it no longer aroused me. And sometimes when I looked at her face, it wasn't the same face I could once gaze upon for hours. What was so alluring about it then? The fact that I didn't know what was going on behind those eyes. Now, the thought never even crossed my mind anymore. I noticed a couple of wrinkles and a couple of hairs and wondered how I'd failed to notice them before. Her skin wasn't so smooth at all. At least not close-up. Sure, I was aware that there's not a person in the world who's that smooth. Not even babies. If you study people from up close and aren't filled with sexual desire, then you won't find anyone too smooth. The ideal life exists only in your head. And in Photoshop.

But now, I was lying in bed, filled with that desire once again, and had already made peace with knowing that desire would remain unfulfilled. We weren't going to have sex. Still, I could just lie next to Laura and, if I was lucky, hold her hand. Or simply watch her, although I couldn't actually see her body. We slept under separate blankets. Staring at her slightly parted lips was more than enough for me, however. She wasn't snoring at the moment. Her breath was soft, almost unnoticeable, like Snow White. I don't know if it was because the light was so dim or I was in some kind of a state again, but Laur looked so damned beautiful at that moment. I kept staring and staring and even when I grew drowsy, I resisted falling asleep. I didn't turn the light off, either. Let it burn. I knew that if I did doze off, I'd be opening my eyes again before long because my sleep cycle was off kilter. And then, I'd be able to continue watching her in the half-light. The light wasn't bothering her, anyway.

I did fall asleep and wake up again before long. Laur had tenderly wrapped her white-gloved fingers around my wrist meanwhile. I couldn't say if she'd done it consciously or while asleep. She knew I didn't dare to rest my arm over her body while she slept. I was afraid she'd push it away or sleep restlessly. Still, she'd gripped my wrist all on her own, though her head and body were in exactly the same position as before.

That hand kept me from falling asleep again for a while. I felt rather happy for the first time in a while. It meant we'd gotten over our miserable fights. We hadn't gotten together in a while, but we were still together. And we wanted to be. In some way, at least.

♦

Learning how to love takes time. I've insisted that crap to Laura since the very beginning, urging her to be patient. Let's just hang out and maybe we'll learn to love each other—it takes time. "How long?" Laura asked. I didn't have the right answer, of course. I suggested that once we'd been together for two years, then perhaps we could get married. Still, I had no idea what clocks were ticking inside of her. Biological ones? Her thirtieth birthday? Her fear of dying soon? And it turned out that was no joke. Several years earlier, she'd been told exactly how much longer she had left to live. I can't remember how long it was. A few years, I suppose. But that was long past by now. Even so, I reckoned it could easily haunt her. I certainly couldn't smell death on her.

When we'd been together for two years and several months on top of that, Laur reminded me what I'd said about getting married if we managed to stick it out that long.

My feelings hadn't grown any surer.

"It'll take more time," I insisted. "I need to feel absolutely certain. There's got to be loving support. And trust. And . . ."

"How much longer, then?"

"I don't know. A decade, maybe. Or maybe it'll never happen."

I could see how pissed off that made Laura, not that she ever expressed it candidly. She was simply silent and gloomy. I myself started wondering: shit, what if I'd been giving her a load of bullshit and my words meant nothing? That wouldn't do, either. And she might let me go for good before long. So, I pulled myself together.

"Okay, fine. If you want to, then let's get married."

Laura didn't reply, as if she'd lost any interest in the topic. But judging by the way in which she was silent, I suspected it still did matter to her.

"Marriage is one thing, but I'm talking about love. It takes a long time for it to bake, and you never know if it'll turn out nice and ready or will be ruined in the process. You might burn the bottom or it could go sour. All you can do is wait. But in my opinion, it's worth that wait. You can't just dive in headfirst. Falling in love can happen and you may be in love for a while, but that's all about chemistry and endorphins. Love itself is a slowly simmering pot."

I knew what I was talking about, as far as I believed. I'd once lived with a woman for 17 years, and that *still* came to nothing. It dissolved sometime after I believed I'd just begun to love her.

I can't remember what the theory was: how long you should practice a field before you start to master it. Some number of hours. Ten thousand? Maybe it'll take about the same number of hours for Laura and me to master each other. Ten thousand isn't all that much. How many years? Who knows—we aren't involved in each other all day, every day. And what about sex? Can I ever have the time to even begin to master that? I don't feel like adding up all the hours. Arithmetic isn't my strongest suit, either. I certainly haven't worked on it for ten thousand hours.

"And when you're learning to love, there are setbacks and fights that might take you to the brink of splitting. But if you can get over them, then I suppose you and your partner will fuse more strongly together afterward. I guess; I don't know."

"You keep on saying, 'I don't know,'" Laura scoffed.

"But I don't. No one knows."

"I *know* that nobody knows."

I realized I'd been spouting drivel. I'd been saying things that Laura knows better than I do. And for her, they didn't encompass the point at all. But whatever that point was, she wouldn't tell me.

It crossed my mind that I should get down on one knee and ask for her hand and her heart. But I didn't want to; I wasn't good at that. I can't even say why. Was I afraid of being a liar? Was I a coward?

At the same time, Laura wasn't going to go down on one knee or ask for my hand and my heart, either; even though she'd already nearly done it, in a way. I was just too thick to realize it. Is that any way to treat a lady? Not that I was much of a gentleman, myself.

◆

A year and a half had passed since then; we'd been married for just about a year. And we no longer had sex. Why, I couldn't say. It started drying up right after we exchanged vows. Was it because Laura's estrogen level had risen? Because that was what she'd said: "I'm not having sex right now—I could get pregnant. I can't even take care of myself, much less a . . . Anyway, my estrogen has risen to that level now. You can Google estrogen and see what it's all about."

I didn't feel like looking up anything with her talking that way. Estrogen, huh? I seemed to remember you being worried earlier about your body being in such a poor state. About it having been for years. Menstruation was an infrequent guest. Who could say why it had suddenly gotten better. We'd been drinking heavily together, but maybe eating more often, too.

You'd also just told me that you no longer felt attracted to me. And you'd started flirting with other men. Does that come with a rise in estrogen? Does it make women want to start scouting around for better partners? I wouldn't be surprised. Who's the best guy around? The best candidate for childrearing? I was penniless and homeless. All I had was my studio and debts. I didn't even have much in the way of clothing. What kind of a man is that? I was tempted to ask why you ever bothered wasting your time on a sad sack like me. But who was really wasting time on whom, anyway?

What does a male creature do when he's impregnated a female? Biologically, I suppose he brings food home until the baby is capable of surviving on their own. But when are humans ever capable of surviving independently? And what does the male do then? If he even does anything at all. If he's been diligent about dragging food to the den for his offspring, then perhaps another female will track him down and stick up her tail. But if he's overly diligent, then he'll end up looking like a worn-out old slipper after all the hard work, and then nobody will want him anymore. Not even the original female. What's all this wrangling between males and females for? The foxtrot and the waltz and what-all-else. And then there's the tango—heaven forbid. It's a good thing I've never learned the steps. Not every female cares if a man knows how to dance or not; some will lead you out onto the dance floor anyway. Or at least hint that she'd like a twirl.

◆

The bread tasted moldy, but I was hungry. It was the only bread I had, anyway.

I also had cheese, sausage, and peas.

I was wary of mold, but I wanted the bread.

So, I ate it.

I heated the second slice on a pan, hoping it might kill any mold. What might mold do to the intestines? I supposed it would simply live on. Who knows. There are endless armies of bacteria in the stomach. Symbiosis. Why is it okay to eat moldy cheese, though? Are there all kinds of different molds? I suppose there must be.

Aren't I giving you my *Helicobacter* whenever we kiss?

I suppose I am, though it doesn't do you any harm. I bet I've passed on a whole heap of my previous partners' bacteria to you. No matter that I haven't given you any STDs. But since several of my former partners had multiple sexual partners in turn, and those probably fucked a lot of people, too, then we've got a fine force of bacteria between both our bodies.

We're kin to all Estonians, but our bodies share bacteria with countless other humans.

Genetics tell me where I came from, and bacteria must say something as well. Who ever listens, though? Or maps them out? Nobody pays them any mind.

◆

What was it that Aarne said? "Better ten girlfriends than one wife."

He'd certainly gotten around in his day. And his wife recently left him, to boot. Is a man like that all that credible? Though I suppose philosophers and others who lived life to the fullest and shared their wisdom with others, Schopenhauer and the like—they also had issues that led to them speaking their minds. Jesus among them. Well, at least they had a body and a soul with which to wrestle.

◆

"Do you even want to be with me?"

I was as surprised by the question as you were. You gave me a quizzical stare. I quickly tried to elucidate.

"I mean, what I meant was—do you want to be with me at all? I know you don't want to have sex anymore. But I don't know if you still want to be together. Maybe we're just a couple out of habit."

Why was I pestering you? Habit was fine, too. Can't there be nice moments in being together out of routine as well? Are nagging and urges to split up simply a part of it? You can't have the pleasure of making up if you don't bicker and stomp away in the meantime.

"And did you ever sincerely want for us to be together? We did both doubt it constantly."

"Hey, I've got your initials tattooed on my ass. I didn't do it just for kicks."

I continued sullenly reading the newspaper and pretended as if you hadn't said anything. But in fact, I was overjoyed. I cherished that comment for a long time. Shit—you hadn't gotten my initials tattooed on your ass just for kicks. I can't imagine you ever saying anything more beautiful.

You told me once that if you were to die, then I should get your initials tattooed on my ass, too.

I didn't really know how to respond.

And what would've happened if I'd lost the bet, not you? If I'd have gotten your former initials inked into my big, fat ass? Would you have kept your last name when we'd married? That would have been a shame. Or would you have taken my last name in addition to your maiden name and had me tattoo a third initial, my own, onto my right buttock? Hard to say.

I don't want you to get anything tattooed onto your tits, though.

And I wouldn't especially like it if you got Michael Jackson tattooed anywhere, either. We'd be having sex and I'd be staring at the image of a pop star you sometimes dream of fucking. Though who's to say that would have any negative effect on me? Maybe it'd be a sobering reminder that none of us are all that pure, transparent, or unique.

I can't remember having ever thought about or imagined someone else when we were fucking. I reckon I never have. And I've never asked if you have, either.

What was it someone said? "Man is the most complex organism. It's been determined that we can never fully analyze ourselves, anyway." Sure, then I suppose there's no hope of us ever fully understanding another person, either. You're lucky if you can figure out just a little. Whenever I try my hardest, I end up over-thinking and ascribing things to you that I, myself, have falsely imagined. I credit you with my worst thoughts. I never suspect good things. There's always the fear that festering inside of you are negative things that you refuse to say. I don't suspect that you secretly have infinite love for me and you simply never say it. But you probably don't suspect that of me, either. You don't harbor any suspicions about me. That's nice of you.

I enjoy being with you because you already bid farewell to life at some point. You don't have any particular demands or expectations of it. But what do you want then, really? To be surrounded by cleanliness and order. And at the same time, you want smelly, chaotic me to be a part of that tidied world. Maybe your life would otherwise be too orderly and sterile. I was lucky that you desired such an addition to your life. I have a function. I haven't latched on to you and won you over for naught. Still, I reckon you don't want me to get even stinkier or more chaotic or any poorer. I reckon you'd much rather prefer me to be a little more orderly, at least in terms of appearance. And to wear nicer clothes. I don't know how I can get over my filthy clothing complex, if I can at all. Why do I want to be filthy? I can remember why I once wanted to: as a means for preventing myself from having flings outside of my relationship. A handsome, well-trimmed, polished appearance is like a bird or a beast raising a flag to declare: I'm looking for a partner! But now, I suppose I'd like to shed my filthy nature. I just can't seem to keep it up.

SISS

SISS HAD A dance recital coming up and she called me repeatedly throughout the week to see if I'd be coming. It was taking place early on Saturday morning. I'd have to leave by eight and make my way to the opposite end of town.

"All the other kids' parents are coming, you know. But I don't know if you want to. I know you don't get up that early."

Siss hadn't been to see me at Koidu in what seemed like ages.

"No, no, I'll come. As long as I get up in time."

"I'll call you in the morning and ask if you're coming."

"Sure, sounds good."

I'd gone to see her dance recitals and gymnastics routines before. A pedophile's dream. A group of girls in tight-fitting clothes flinging their limbs about and dancing. And they're immediately followed by others, ranging from first grade to high school. For hours on end. Why didn't I feel like having a front-row seat to that? I suppose I was shy, afraid that someone would look over and see a solitary old fart ogling young girls. I'd certainly watch Siskin's performance, though. It was strange to think of her leaping around in a costume as a spectacle for all. I'd probably have liked to keep it to myself. A private show. Still, the recital was an opportunity to spend time together. Time that was diminishing the older that Siska got.

I sent Laura an email (we hadn't been talking directly for a while) telling her that I was going to watch Siska on Saturday, and that she could come and spend the night at Koidu if she wanted and Siss would be staying for the weekend.

Laura replied: "I'll consider it."

So, I spent a long day with Siska at the athletic building. And it was a good day. I carried a book around with me, even though I didn't read it. The object just gave me a small dose of confidence in the alien environment.

Both of us were worn out by that afternoon. Siss, from all the horseplay with her friends, I, from the drinks I'd drained in the cafeteria. Even the new book looked a little swollen by the end of the day.

"Hey, honey, let's get a cab. I don't feel like going back another way and don't have the energy."

"Whatever you want, Daddy." Siss is nine years old already, wearing a bra, and our conversations have grown more succinct. At least compared with when she was four and a half and came to save me and care for me after the divorce.

I remembered during the cab ride.

"Siss, Laura and I were talking and she might come to spend the evening with us on Koidu Street. Could you give her a call?"

Siss called, they spoke.

"Daddy, she's tired and was sleeping and thinks she probably won't come over."

Several more blocks went by. The neighborhoods really were at opposite ends of the city. But there was a blizzard raging and it was nice to ride through the drifting snow. Like in an old Russian film.

"Hey, Siss—I just remembered I was supposed to give Laura something. Is it okay if we stop by her place so I can give it to her, and then we'll go to Koidu together?"

"Sure. I haven't seen Laura in a really long time."

The taxi drove between the towering apartment blocks on Vindi Street, bouncing over the mounds of ice on the street. Someone was walking in the opposite direction, traversing the slippery pavement with a determined gait. It was Laura.

"Hey, stop for a second here!"

"Right here?"

"Yeah."

I jumped out of the car and shouted: "Laur. Laura!"

She was staring at the ground and didn't hear me, so I stuck two fingers between my lips and whistled.

"Laura!"

She looked up. I figured she was on her way to buy a fresh bottle of sparkling wine.

"Hey, Laur, I was supposed to give you this thing. You know. That's why I'm here."

"Oh. Okay. But I don't need it right now. I thought I'd go over to Piret's place. I wanted to watch the *Estonian Song* competition. The weather's pretty terrible, though."

"We can take you there in the cab. We're driving around, anyway."

"I can just take the trolley, too."

"However you'd like. We can take you."

"I wanted to stop by the shopping center first, actually. If you could take me there ..."

"However you'd like."

"Okay."

So, Laur got in the cab.

"Hi, Siss."

"Hi, Laura."

I wondered how long it'd been since they last saw each other. Months, maybe? It had to be around the last time Laura and I had sex.

"Take us to the Magistrali shopping center, please," I said to the cab driver.

Everyone was silent during the drive. As Laura was getting out, I repeated my offer to drop her off at Piret's apartment.

"It's right across the road here," she said. "I'm just going to buy something first."

"As you wish."

Laura paused for a second to think. I waited.

"Fine. But it might take me some time. I'm going to look around a little for what to get."

"No worries. We'll wait. I'm not in any rush. We've got nothing else to do later, anyway."

Laura went inside.

"Daddy, do you have any paper?"

I searched my pockets. There was a Saku Brewery invoice in my breast pocket. They'd given us free drinks for a book release. Le Mans beer and cider. Some new product of theirs. Nobody who attended had seen it before.

Siss accepted the document and studied it.

"Doesn't Laura need this?"

Oh, right—the invoice was made out to Laura. She'd placed the order.

"No, not anymore. Do you have a pen?"

Siss pulled one from her pocket.

"I've got this *Revenge Office* pen I found at your place. It's my favorite. You didn't know who left it there, you remember?"

"I guess it was a warning from the *Revenge Office* crime squad. One of them must have broken into my place at night and put it on my desk as a warning to reconsider my life and mend my ways."

"Well, are you going to?"

"I don't know yet. I'll have to think about it. I'm fresh out of ideas about what to change, exactly."

"Maybe you could just drink a little less."

"That's a good idea. I think I have been drinking a little less lately, too."

Siss was already drawing.

"Would you be drinking even more if you hadn't gotten the pen? Say a wild animal."

"A flea."

"That's not an animal. It's a bug. I don't know how to draw a flea, anyway."

"A bear."

Siss drew a bear.

"And now say a pet."

"A bear. But a different kind. A teddy bear."

"What's the difference?"

I glanced up at the front seat. The driver was staring off into the darkness like a mannequin. I reckoned he was daydreaming about home construction or a woman who left him.

"One stinks and the other purrs like a kitten."

"But their paws are the same."

"Are they?"

"You've got to say another animal."

"But I don't know any others."

"A dog or a cat, you know? Something in Estonia."

"A frog?"

"Can you have a frog as a pet?"

"Sure. I've got friends in Berlin who raised frogs at home. They didn't even keep them in an aquarium. The frogs just hopped around wherever they pleased. I've no idea how they avoided stepping on any. Claudius hoped to start selling them. My friends were unemployed and didn't have a lot of money. They ended up getting a divorce. I don't know who got the frogs. In any case, the frogs were gone after everything was said and done. I suppose Claudius took them with him. Or they managed to sell them and used the money to cover the divorce fees."

"Say an animal."

"A kangaroo. But it's an Estonian kangaroo. Someone's probably got one of those at home. Or a bison. People *definitely* keep bison in their apartments. I've seen it in a film."

"I don't know how to draw a bison."

"Can you draw me?"

"Does that mean you're a pet?"

"I guess so. Though I bet if Laura sends me packing for good, then I could become a wild animal myself. A feral pet. Dingo the stray dog."

"I thought you wanted to be a bear."

"There's a bear living under our bed already!"

"You talk silly all the time."

"It's just because I'm sad. And because I love you."

"What are you sad for? Because Laura didn't want the thing we went to give her?"

"Not really. Hundreds of people die in Africa every day. Isn't that a sad thing?"

"Is it?"

"Not really. Can not being sad because Africans are dying make you sad?"

"No."

"You're right, as always."

Suddenly, my eyes came to rest on a tall woman leaving the shopping mall. She was carrying a heavy bag and seemed to be walking in the direction of nothingness, head down and determined.

"Hold on, Siska—that's Piret."

I jumped out of the cab and shouted to her, but she didn't here. I trotted after the woman, doing my best not to slip and fall on the ice.

"Piret! Piret!"

Finally, she stopped and looked back.

"Hey, Piret. Laur just went in to buy some drinks and stuff for your place. We've got a taxi here to drop her off. Would you maybe like . . ."

Piret's long arm was stretched even longer by the bag.

"No, I'm just going to go straight home," she said curtly, and left.

I walked back to the cab.

"Daddy, look."

Siss had drawn several creatures, all with different limbs. One had an elephant's trunk and a mouse's legs. I felt it was the perfect kind of drawing for people like us.

"Those are really nice."

"But you're still feeling sad."

"It's my calling."

"I think you're just bragging, Daddy."

"Yeah. It's the only thing that's keeping me afloat."

"Bragging's kind of dumb."

"I know."

"And the way you brag is kind of whiny, too."

"I know. I'm just trying to draw out compassion. People have told me that before."

"Oh, Daddy. I don't know what to do with you."

"You could just love and support me, I guess."

"I do. But it doesn't seem to help much."

The driver was tapping an SMS into his phone. Maybe he loved someone, too. He certainly loved his car. But maybe somebody else as well.

Laura came back carrying a bag bulging with goodies, as silent as ever.

"Hey, Laura? I know it's somewhere across the intersection, but I can't remember where."

"I'll give directions. Cross here to Vilde Street, please. I'll tell you where to turn."

We wound through apartment blocks until we finally arrived at Piret's stairwell.

I was quiet and in a state of despair. Before getting out of the car, however, Laura rummaged inside of herself for a few words.

"Um, yeah. I don't know. I'll see how it goes. Maybe I'll come over to Koidu afterward, if I'm not too tired. I can't say for sure."

"Okay," I said, trying to sound emotionless. What a mess. I was certain she wouldn't show. They had such a well-stocked bar up there. Logically, Laura would get drunk and pass out. As always.

There was a young guy in front of the door trying to call up to some apartment and get in. As the cab drove away, I looked over my shoulder to see if he and Laur were chatting. They didn't seem to be. I was never jealous before—why did I suddenly feel that way now? I was treating Laura like property. When had she gained that status? Treating people that way doesn't make anything better, obviously. But how should I treat her? Who on earth could explain to me the right way to treat a woman, honestly. The same way she treats me? But what way was that? I couldn't really say, and hadn't known for a while. I can't adopt her game and copy her patterns if I can't perceive or discern them.

But wait—I did know a good way to act. As if we'd just met and I really wanted to hit on her, politely and persistently, casually and cheerfully. But that's something you can't fake or falsify. Or can you? You can if you're capable of making it work. Maybe it's a good thing if your wife constantly gives you the cold shoulder, because it gives you a reason to woo her time and again. The meaning of life is elusive and keeps on changing its form and face. I can't grasp my own wife. She's one thing in the day and another at night. I suppose that must be a good thing.

Siss was starting to nod off in the taxi. She turned in her seat to lean against me. I wondered if I had the strength to carry her up to the third floor. Along with her gigantic backpack, of course. She'd brought along her school things. Siss walks around like a soldier in full gear because she never knows where she'll be spending her time until the next school week.

The cold air roused Siskin as soon as I opened the door, though she looked around as if she couldn't tell where we were.

"Hey, honey, can you make it upstairs yourself?"

"Are we there already?"

"Did you fall asleep?"

"Mhm, no, I dunno."

"I can grab your big old bag."

"No, I can do it."

The cab driver was immersed in his phone again. He had to be working on either fixing or building a relationship. Peeter, you're not the only man with complicated relationships in this town. Maybe the majority of people are in messed-up romances. That's just the way we live. Things being good is an exception, not the rule.

The studio was chilly. I piled blankets on top of Siska and started a fire in the stove, drawing the last match in the box and sticking it under the heap of firewood. It caught fire.

But then I didn't know what else to do, so I simply sat and listened to the firewood crackle and burn. I took alternating sips of light and dark beer. Sitting there and doing nothing quickly lost its appeal. It was clear I wouldn't be able to fall asleep in such a state. The only chance I had was to get good and drunk. But I didn't feel like doing that, either. Stinking and snoring next to Siskin in bed? Not my first choice. I'd sleep in till noon anyway, no matter if I sat around until daylight or got sozzled enough to fall asleep.

What if I went to the gas station to buy cigarillos? Walking to avoid having the same thoughts running around my head? And I did need to buy matches! Otherwise, I'd be unable to light a fire in the stove in the morning and Siska would get cold while playing and waiting for me to wake up. It'd be good to be vertical for a few minutes in the morning and light a fire, then go back to sleep for a little while longer.

Ah, Laura. My darling wife. An unearthly poem.

So, I swayed my way to the gas station and stood there staring at the cigarettes.

"Why's your selection of cigarillos dried up so suddenly? It used to be a lot bigger. And these all have filters like regular cigarettes."

The chubby girl behind the counter was calm and kind. Yes, their selection had dried up. She didn't seem to mind a drunk old man like me bellyaching. I immediately felt ashamed for having made the comment and tried to act more politely, though I couldn't seem to come up with any good quip to make up for it. The attendant was there all alone. It was late at night and she had several more hours of standing behind the counter and putting up with guys like me ahead of her. Even so, she graciously lined their entire cigarillo selection up for me.

Hm, I thought, *the ones in tins definitely have filters. Maybe the soft pack of Ritmeester doesn't.*

I plodded home, a familiar nighttime journey.

And my phone rang. And it was Laura. Well, what now?

"Um, so, I'm taking a cab home. I can come over to Koidu if you're not asleep yet. Are you?"

"No. Siss went to bed. I went out to buy cigarettes. Come over. Please. I'll be waiting."

A wave of endorphins and energy washed over me. I wanted to gush about how much I was looking forward to it, but I held myself back to stop from sounding like a silly little schoolboy. Laura was coming!

I knew there was no need to hurry, but I started jogging back to the house anyway. My legs quickened their pace. I knew it'd be amazing to see Laura again, but more importantly, she'd be saving me from late-night loneliness. I wouldn't have to struggle all on my own. Purely my own interests were at stake.

Now, if we could just keep from fighting. If she's drunk and I start feeling dejected again about how she didn't come to hang out right away, but went out partying first and didn't even find it necessary to tell me—if those feelings start to churn, then it won't be long before I lose control and make some comment about it. That would only set the ball rolling.

As I jogged, I tried to quickly program myself to only be cheerful and in a good mood. It doesn't pay to hide or repress your sadness, though. You've just got to accept it and foster greater happiness beside it. That way, you deprive those grim thoughts of their chance to dominate. Having a bit of sadness and melancholy is fine, so long as they're not the only things you feel.

Laur arrived and sat in her old armchair in my untidy living room. She hadn't been here in ages. I was sitting on the couch next to Siskin as she slept, adjusting her blanket.

"Are the three of us going to sleep on the couch tonight?" Laura asked.

"I don't know yet. We can't all fit too comfortably. I'll blow up the air mattress for her like always. Do you want to go to bed already?"

"Not yet. Soon. I'm going to check what there is to eat in the fridge."

"Go ahead, but there's nothing in there. And there's only beer to drink. I wasn't sure you were going to . . ."

That was a lie. I'd been almost certain that Laura wasn't coming. But if I'd known she was, then would I still have bought her a bottle of sparkling wine? I'd been rather miserly as of late. I was honestly low on cash, too. Laura somehow seemed to have money, even though she usually has unpaid bills lying on the kitchen table that she should pay but can't bring herself to take care of. How long do women keep penniless suitors around? And who coined the phrase: "No one shows a poor man pussy"? It's crude, but probably true. I haven't seen one in a long time. Such things outdate culture. If you drag a mammoth home, you can count on feeding an offspring. If you don't feel like chasing mammoths around, well, then I suppose the woman might keep you around for a little while if she's already grown used to it. But generally, she'll have her eyes open for someone else.

I shuffled after Laura into the kitchen just to be near to her.

She pulled a cucumber and a package of cheese out of the fridge and sliced them, then tossed a couple fish sticks onto a pan. It was a good thing my fridge wasn't totally empty.

"Hey, do you still have any of those zefirs left?"

"Zefirs?" I wracked my brain and dimly remembered there being some in the fridge. I poked around the back of the shelves but couldn't find any.

"I must have thrown them away. Yeah, sorry, I did. I figured no one was going to eat them."

I'd brought a big bowl of macaroni down to the local top-notch Korean chef Kyuho when he was sitting with some other people in front of the house one time, and he, later, gave me the treats as a gift. I still had his thank-you note pinned onto the wall. I suppose it would've been nice to eat them all, but I wasn't in the mood to eat sweet foods for a while. I doubt my own cooking was on par with his. The zefirs had just been a polite gesture.

"Do you have any ketchup?"

"I think so."

I checked. I didn't.

"I've got a bit of Heino Kiik's homemade apple sauce and some adjika, if that will do," I cautiously offered. I reckoned I'd offered them to Laura before, albeit unsuccessfully. This time, however, drinking had made her hungry. She dropped a dollop of butter onto the warm fish sticks and poured some of the red sauce over them. I was glad to see her eating. I watched her like a timid schoolboy who's astounded to have the prettiest girl in class come over to hang out unexpectedly. Only this girl wasn't promising anything and I was baffled by why she came. Was it out of pity? Boredom? Maybe she'd allow me a pity fuck.

"All I've got to drink is beer, unfortunately. But you drink beer sometimes, too. Wheat beer, right? I've even seen you drinking dark."

"I actually brought my own."

"I can help you carry those plates into the living room."

"No, I've got it," Laura said as she skillfully picked up the two plates, cutting board, and a small glass all at once.

She pulled a can of Sinebrychoff Long Drink and a flask of pricier Aramis brandy from her tote bag and poured a thumb of the latter into the glass.

"Have some, too."

I took a little swig of sweet brandy. A kid's drink. It would certainly make a ruckus with the beer in my belly later. Laura took a sip of long drink. Sinebrychoff is a little expensive, but it's the only kind that will do for Laura.

Laura was unusually talkative as we sat. She hadn't been like that in ages. She talked about how everything was going great for her. About how she was happy. About how she liked work and felt cared for and appreciated there. With minor exceptions, of course. About how she works with autistic children and if one of them speaks even a single word by the end of the day, she feels it's all paid off and is a tremendous gift.

I tried to be upbeat and supportive as I listened, even though I was thinking about how we'd spent long, mute, downbeat evenings so often. I knew you were only cheerful when you've gone out with your other friends. Why? Would it be that way forever?

Laura said I was the reason she was tired all the time.

True, she only ever felt exhausted when we spent time together at home, and never felt like going out anywhere when I invited her.

I felt as if I were having déjà vu. Where'd I experienced this before? In books? In my own life? In a film? Only the person closest to you can be the most intolerable. Or a person who used to be close and now, there's a wall between you and zero inclination to break it down or overcome it. It's terrifying. The wall is crucial to have some peace. To take a break from the exhausting . . . What? Love?

I considered how we drank rather sizeable portions every single night. The constant flow of alcohol has tired me out. At first, it gives you a boost. For a while, maybe. But then there comes a period where you need to increase the doses more and more to reach that same state. And in the end, it becomes unattainable. You just find yourself exhausted the next day.

"Maybe," I began cautiously, "you'd be less tired if we drank less. Not totally sober, but with little breaks here and there. Otherwise, it's like two of your favorite songs go: at first, it's *push it, push it to the limit*, and then it's *take the pill that makes you weaker, take the pill that makes you sick.*"

The ensuing moment of silence was icy and acute. Something surged its way through Laura. I could instantly tell that I'd said the wrong thing and now, everything was fucked. What 'everything'? The whole mood. Those songs are Laura's girl power, so to say. They're sung by rebellious young women. They were off-limits.

"I haven't been like that."

I tried explaining that wasn't the point I was trying to make; that I wasn't trying to insult her.

"Sure, but you've taken yourself to extremes before. And you've ended up in the hospital."

"I didn't take a single pill there. I spat them all out."

Now, I couldn't hold back.

"Not one? Over a whole three-quarters of a year?"

"Not one."

"You, yourself, told me that you had some kind of an issue and got over it in the hospital. That you really were sick."

Laura didn't reply.

"I think that *push it to the limit* is about sexuality. About fucking that you've got to go to the extreme to do at any cost. And then there's a hangover. You know it. Casual sex with pretty much anybody, pretty much anywhere. That's an extreme."

I was aware that my spiteful words weren't true, and that I was suddenly filled with jealousy and resentment. Jealousy over your past before me. What an idiot. I'd never have believed myself capable of turning out this way. Maybe Laura hadn't either.

She looked down and didn't take another sip of either drink.

"And *take the pill* isn't meant literally. It's about being in a situation where you're surrounded by doctors and they're harassing you and cramming all kinds of different pills into your mouth because they don't know how else to keep you alive and bring you back to life."

Laura shot to her feet and started getting undressed, though she only pulled off her pants. She also removed her bra without taking off her top, unfastening it and yanking the straps off through her sleeve. As she did so, her gaze was fixed on the ground intensely. It appeared as if her intoxication had abruptly evaporated as well.

Without uttering a word, Laura slipped beneath the blanket in bed next to Siskin.

I sat there, alone in spite of everything. And I was the one responsible for this mess.

I'd lost any desire to drink. I continued to sit, staring into nothingness. I'd just done what I knew I shouldn't do. What had driven me to it?

I pulled the dusty air mattress off the top of the cupboard and inflated it, thinking I should probably be the one to sleep there. At the same time, I knew my weight would be too much for it and I'd end up on the floor. But if I crawled into bed next to Laura, there was the danger that I wouldn't be able to resist touching her while she slept, even just gently. And if she were to feel it, then I'd just be pushing myself farther and farther away from her.

I glared at the dusty air mattress on the dusty floor next to Laura's old futon. I glared at the drinks on the table, then grabbed the bottle of Aramis and guzzled a bulging mouthful. About a quarter of the whole bottle.

I lifted Siskin down onto the mattress. She didn't stir.

Eying the empty spot next to Laura, I kept drinking and drinking. The booze gradually started to take effect. I knew I'd stink later.

Fully, tipsily asleep, Laura started taking up more room and covering almost the whole futon. I couldn't lay down without touching her anymore. The only choice I had was to keep lounging and drinking in the armchair.

I woke up to the sound of Siss scribbling at my desk. She'd apparently been up for a while already. Laura was asleep next to me.

I pushed myself out of bed, took an aspirin, and lit a fire in the stove. I tried to be as quiet as I could.

"Hey, honey—what would you like to eat?" I whispered.

"What do we have?"

"Pelmeni, macaroni, beer. I can make a cucumber-and-tomato salad, too."

"Okay. And some pelmeni, too, please."

"How many?"

Siss held up eight fingers.

"How'd you sleep on the mattress?"

"I dunno. Like normal."

"Did your butt press against the floor?"

"Yeah."

"There's got to be a hole in it somewhere. I don't know what to do. Maybe I should grow a big old pimple and you can sleep on that. Anyway, I'll make you breakfast. Put on some clothes, okay? You'll freeze to death in that old nightshirt."

"I know."

The fire was slowly growing and crackling in the stove.

I made Siss a salad and boiled pelmeni, then brought a stool from the kitchen and we ate together. Occasionally, I peeked into the other room. Laura was motionless. I wondered if the mild smell of pelmeni was unpleasant to her.

Out of nowhere, Laura sat straight up in bed. She got to her feet, dressed, and left without saying a word. She didn't even wash her face in the kitchen.

Siskin and I were both astonished and made no mention of what had just happened. Siss has seen all kinds of things and knows it's better to just stay quiet when men and women are in some kind of a dispute.

RECONCILIATION

LAURA AND I had made up and I managed not to be pushy in bed. But then one night, I attended a book release and ended up guzzling a fair amount of vodka. Laura didn't feel like coming out. At home, all I did was admire her and sense how full of passion I was. All kinds of passions. Sexual, too. But merely watching her felt like more than enough. I got my fill. Even so, I'd certainly have wanted more. To touch her, stroke her. To be close. To be together.

A couple of times, Laura glanced over uncomfortably as I stared, then quickly looked away again.

I was quiet. I didn't know how to explain myself. And I was afraid that anything I said would only create a new rift and lead to a fight.

Until we went to bed.

I stroked Laura gently. First her shoulder, then her stomach. She didn't push my hand away, only protesting a little when I stuck a finger into her belly button. I stroked her breasts beneath her t-shirt. Laur didn't ask me to stop, but was lying with her back to me and didn't roll over. She didn't make the slightest movement to expose her chest a little more. Lying on her side that way, Laura's breasts were a bit sad and saggy and didn't have the same sexy effect as they did when she was straight-backed with her chest arced out, or when she pushed them up on better days. Even so, I continued to stroke those precious, familiar breasts in their forlorn, limp state.

Since Laura didn't say or do anything to stop things from progressing, I pulled down her brown sweatpants, delicately rolled her onto her back, and caressed her between her legs. It seemed to do something. The crack became wider and softer. I felt she was with me, and I was mindful to concentrate on her pleasure. Ultimately, I couldn't hold back any longer and rolled on top of her, though I realized I wasn't erect. And yet, I was so aroused.

"Laur, can you hold it a little?"

She remained motionless, her head turned to the side and her expression dour and impenetrable.

I worked to insert myself into her and managed somehow, though I didn't have time to do much before it was all over. Laur had put a hand over her face and was sobbing.

I watched for a few moments, remembering that one time, way back when,

I'd feigned crying when in bed with someone. I can't remember why. I guess I was guilty of something and hoping to find some compassion. I genuinely had been on the verge of tears and tried to push myself over the edge so they'd start flowing. But the girl reached out and touched my face in the darkness to see if my cheeks were wet. They weren't.

I wondered what Laura was doing and why. Was it a sure-fire way to make sure I'd leave her alone and do no more harm?

Or did she feel demeaned and insulted? Did it remind her of her past?

I lay next to Laura, silent. After a while, I could tell she'd fallen asleep. But even then, I didn't dare to stroke her anywhere.

In the morning, she went to work and I had time to lie around. I reckoned I was still drunk from the previous day. Sex scenes from bed kept spinning around my head. I couldn't stop thinking about them. Should I be pleased that I imagine fucking Laura and no one else? I suppose. At least that gives me a chance to be close to her. I restlessly tossed and turned in bed. I reached down and touched my dick. It wasn't hard or growing, by any rate. But after rubbing it against my hand and the bed a little while longer, I finally managed to cum. All without an erection. Look at what I've come to. I took off my shirt, wiped the sperm off my belly, and knew I shouldn't do something like that again. I can't start living that way. At the same time, it'd have been a shit situation if I hadn't. I'd just spend the whole day in distress. Was it from drinking? Was it because I'm unoccupied every day and end up pestering Laura and she keeps distancing herself more and more? Or some weird psychological state? I should find something to do. I should travel somewhere. But I really don't want to. All I really want to do is struggle like this.

◆

Laura once changed her Facebook profile picture to one where I was kissing her. Afterward, she asked: "Hey, can I change your Facebook picture?"

"What are you going to put?"

"The same one I've got."

"Sure, okay."

They stayed that way for about a year. But now, someone mentioned to me that Laura changed her picture.

I checked. It had changed. Now, she had a black-and-white profile picture with her looking mournful.

Before long, we were fighting again and I yelled into the phone: "You changed your Facebook picture! Why didn't you change mine?! I didn't put it up, you did! And now, that picture with me kissing you doesn't suit you anymore. Why don't you scrub it from my Facebook page, too? You're the one who put it there!"

Shortly after, I started wondering if I really wanted her to change my picture. That would only drive us farther apart. Laura was drifting further and further, and I was clinging on with all ten fingers. Why should I try to push her even more?

Still, there are two sides to it. You hold on, but when the other person keeps moving away, then there are times when you'd like to propel them even more rapidly because you're tired of it all—you can't take the endless drift that will never lead to a relationship. One wave seems to draw the woman away, another brings her closer. Alas, you'll never meet again, though neither does she disappear from the horizon. She simply remains far and unattainable. I've already played that game before and told myself I'd never do it again. But what choice do I have?

An old, gray-haired man in dire straits with a young woman. I've had issues with older women before, too. They weren't any better.

PANIC

I HAD THE chance to use someone else's office for a while. It was a better environment for doing certain things. There was also a big computer screen, which I, myself, don't have. I was able to keep several windows open and adjacent simultaneously, which is good for comparing a translation to the original or scrolling through several parallel web pages at once. Not to mention the lack of internet at my studio on Koidu Street. Still, I don't feel like getting it. I just use other people's Wi-Fi. The connection often fails, which means I probably end up spending less time online. I just sit and stare at the glow coming from the stove or out the window for a while. Koidu's Windows hasn't changed much in years. It hasn't had any upgrades. And that's nice. Only the seasons change in my personal Windows.

It was Saturday and I suspected that if I spent too long out and about, then Laura would be pissed off at night because I'd failed to bring her sparkling wine and groceries. Nowadays, Laura was drinking Rocca-brand bubbly, which cost €4.75. She usually didn't have the money to buy it herself. How much did those Lambruscos and Proseccos cost back before we switched to the euro? Somewhere around 60 kroons, I think. And even those seemed expensive. And we never had the money, though I now know that booze was cheaper then and I actually had more cash. All things considered, the differences aren't so great.

There was a concert coming up at Cabbages. Erko had been organizing them ever since the commune shut down. Which is to say it was only the second. People from the house played songs and regulars showed up. Some took it seriously, others went for the surreal and the absurd. But last time, the atmosphere was incredible. We all crowded into the slightly mildewy back room of the flagstone cellar. The place was packed. There was silence and expectation, followed by patient listening and laughs, and later simply dance and debauchery. I think Laura enjoyed it. She was hammered, of course. I was afraid she wouldn't feel like leaving when I'd had enough. I can't remember if she ultimately came up willingly or just wanted to grab some drinks from my fridge. Maybe it was both.

I checked the clock. Less than an hour until the concert began. Would I have time to dry off? I'd taken a shower at the office. Random showers can be nice. Sometimes they clear your head of intoxication, other times they're just good for taking a break. I'd had all kinds of different colds lately. Where do they come from? Was it because I just hole up in my studio and barely engage in physical movement? Easy prey for viruses. I could've taken a shower earlier, but I lost track of time on the computer.

I called Laura.

"Hey. There's some concert at Cabbages tonight. I don't know if you saw it online. Eight o'clock. Would you like to come?"

"Okay."

Laura's verbal replies had become just as laconic as her electronic ones. Okay, and that's it. *U matrosov net voprosov.* Sailors have no questions. Melissa the Cat and Kot Matroskin. All my cats. But are they really mine? Cats don't belong to anyone.

My fingers flew across the keyboard faster and faster because time was melting down. That always gives me a burst of motivation. Does every instance of time running out have the same effect? Would someone on death row write with ever-increasing speed before getting their shot? I doubt it. I beat the keys mercilessly, though they paid no heed to my anger. Not that I was actually angry, of course. There was just fervor spouting from my fingertips.

It was always possible to show up late to the concert, of course. I could go at any time. I just wanted to get a seat with Laura, otherwise, I'd never find her in the crowd. And if I ended up spotting her far across the room, I'd be forced to watch her sitting and watching next to someone else.

I slammed my laptop shut, even though I reckoned it meant leaving the best unwritten. That was just my opinion, of course. Maybe there was nothing special about it in the first place. Who knows.

I could hear the music from a couple blocks away and quickened my pace. There was a crowd gathered around the door to Cabbages, so I used my key to go through the front door of the building and walk down the stairs straight to the back room of the cellar. The audience was sparse enough there to elbow my way through the kitchen. Some people were seated, and others stood along the wall. There was one free three-legged stool next to a young woman.

"May I?"

"Sure."

Jaan was playing the piano. It was pleasant. It'd been a long time since my last beer, however. Maybe several hours already. I couldn't see Laura in the crowd. Did I have any beer in the fridge upstairs? I thought I did. Most people had brought their own drinks and I didn't notice any box of wine anywhere for sharing.

So, I crept back out and up the stairs.

The floor in the stairwell was covered in a thick layer of drywall dust, as Kristo was renovating Jaan Pehk's place. Still, I didn't bother to take my shoes off in the studio. I was in a hurry and wanted to track down where Laura was. Instead, I just wiped my shoes as clean as I could on the mat, took one step inside, reached out, and managed to grab hold of the mop. I stepped on the damp rag wrapped around it, massaging it with the soles of my shoes, then tossed it back into the blue bucket. Finally, I could tiptoe into the kitchen. There were several kinds of beers in the fridge. Should I take two at the same time, a dark and a light? Ah, hanging around with both hands full is annoying. And I might not get my spot on the stool back. I was halfway out the door, holding one open beer, but stopped and spun around. What a bother. Two at once it would be. I'd alternate, just as always.

I returned to the kitchen, opened a second beer, and went downstairs.

There, I managed to get my seat on the stool back. The concert was running pretty long. Erko was aware of it. There were simply lots of performers. I walked back and forth between the two rooms whenever I saw the chance. Laura was nowhere to be seen. She must not have come. I checked my watch. Almost ten. The store would be closing soon, cutting off my chance to buy Laura dinner and sparkling wine. That would only lead to trouble.

I stuck my empty beer bottles into the big bag of recycling. Better I go straight to her place. I'd stop by the store and gather up whatever I could. She was probably out of most things, wasn't she? I hurried to make it in before ten.

Once between the aisles, I tossed groceries into the cart as fast as I could. I knew more or less what she liked. Smoked sausage, savory jellies, bubbly, butter, salad ingredients. I couldn't think of anything that might surprise her. And beers for myself. Two bottles of dark beer, maybe a Stuttgart and a Karl Friedrich lager from the refrigerated section to sip on while the others cooled in Laura's freezer. Nothing else decent was already cold here. At least there was something.

I paid and left just seconds before closing, then walked to Laura's place at a brisk pace. Maybe she won't be too ornery about me taking so long. And I won't be mad about her not coming to the concert, even though she didn't say she wasn't.

Laura's windows were dark. I figured she must be so exhausted that she'd fallen asleep already. She couldn't be drunk yet. It had just been a hard week at work. Totally understandable.

I panted as I climbed the stairs, two at a time. I couldn't wait to be together and at the same time was afraid of meeting. Maybe she'd be angry about something. Or simply silent. And I won't know how to act, so I'll start pressing her to tell me out of guilt, which will only make her shut up more. And then, bam—we'll be fighting like we occasionally do. And I'll end up leaving. That was a situation I certainly didn't want.

But maybe everything would be fine! She's simply napping, and she'll be glad

I came. I'll stick her bottle of Rocca bubbly in the freezer to cool and snuggle up next to her on the couch and just watch her and wait for her to wake up. And if she's snoring away in deep sleep, then I can just sleep in my clothes next to her. We can even eat and drink past midnight if she wakes up late. Tomorrow is Sunday.

I cracked open the door, trying to enter as quietly as I could. I made sure the bottles didn't clink in the bag when I set it down in the kitchen. They still made a little noise. Damn it.

I peeked into the living room. Nobody. I checked the bathroom door to see if it was locked. It wasn't. I looked into the kitchen again, but she wasn't passed out in the armchair as she sometimes is. I went back and opened the apartment door to see if she was smoking on the communal balcony and I'd just failed to notice. Empty.

I turned on the light in the hallway.

"Laura? Laur, are you here somewhere? Answer me."

I supposed she wasn't playing hide-and-seek. She certainly wouldn't be curled up on a pillow in the cupboard with Melissa.

Casually, I removed my shoes and coat. Maybe she was just out drinking somewhere. Though she usually let me know. Had I turned my phone off before the concert? I pulled it out of my picket. It was on.

No doubt she'd just popped out for a minute and hadn't felt the need to tell me.

I went into the kitchen and stocked the fridge with groceries, putting the sparkling wine in the freezer. The beers as well. Cottage cheese, sausages, *kama*—all in the fridge. The cucumber and tomatoes went on top.

I decided not to call her yet. Not to bug her. Let her have a good time at the burger stand or wherever she might be. Out with girlfriends. I could just sip on my beer and wait.

I opened the Karl Friedrich. Ah, it's nice that there's beer. I suppose I'm almost always drinking. It's a good thing my body puts up with it and my stomach doesn't act up too much. Maybe I should switch to wheat beer for a while. Maybe semi-active yeast would cause problems in my gut. Wheat beer is nice for a change, though, as long as you have several a day. Otherwise, the menu gets boring.

Should I turn on the radio? No. The TV? No. The computer? No.

I was sure Laura would come home before long.

Nevertheless, I picked up my phone and called at eleven. It rang, but no answer. Typical. Laura usually called back before long. All I had to do was sit and wait for it. I wondered what I would say or do if it turned out she was partying somewhere. Would I ask whom she was with? Why she hadn't told me she wasn't coming to Cabbages? I tried to remind myself to be calm when she finally called. Not accusatory. Still, I suspected that the more I told myself to be calm, the more tension I'd ratchet up and the more nervous I'd get. And how would that all pan out? It'd happened time and again before. I'm calm at first, forcing myself to keep my cool for a while, but am merely tamping the gunpowder tighter and tighter and when one spark finds its way in, I explode. And if the spark is delayed longer and longer, then I feel like the other person knows exactly what could happen and is keeping a low profile on purpose, which leads to me exploding without any spark at all.

It'd happened so many times before, but I still didn't know how to resolve the situation. Sure, it'd be nice to watch TV or read, or even go back to Cabbages and party. But I hadn't the peace to do any of those things. I might look like I was having a great time if I headed back to Koidu Street, but I'd be a raging fire inside. And on top of all that, I'd feel like I was doing the exact same thing that bothers me about Laura. What right did I have to be pissed off and moaning?

I checked my watch and my phone. Nothing had changed since the last time I looked at either. Time was inching slowly but surely onward and not one SMS had arrived. I considered making a rule for myself to not call too often, but there'd be no point in the end. How would it be any better to call ten times but not one hundred?

Maybe you'd decided to go to the concert anyway and were walking through the dark down a path you were usually afraid to cross alone—through the grimy tunnels beneath the railroad tracks, past the soccer stadium, down the unlit streets of the slum—and something had happened to you? I couldn't bring myself to put what it could be into words.

I picked up my phone and called again. Your number usually doesn't ring too long—five or six beeps before instructions on how to leave a voicemail. That meant your battery wasn't dead; you simply weren't picking up. If somebody had harmed you and then taken your phone, how would he behave? He'd probably switch it off. The police could use the signal to pinpoint its location. Can you find a phone with GPS when it's turned off? I've no idea. I don't know much about life. If you rape and kill a person, then there's no need to take their phone with you. A mugger might hide it somewhere and go back for it later, though the police could set up a trap. As if Estonia's police had enough resources to spend days and nights waiting in ambush for a mugger, though.

What the hell was I thinking? It does no good to think such thoughts. Still, it doesn't help to stop thinking once the thoughts have already appeared. They only grow stronger in your subconscious once they're repressed. Just like any fear.

I sat down on the couch with all the lights on. On the coffee table were two small glasses of beer. I took little sips from both and got up to refill them every now and then. I stared at the wall, which I'd stared at many a time before, and it never spoke to me. Laura had a few paintings hanging there and none of them contained any emotion. I contained no emotion, either; at least that's what I thought. I tried to refrain from getting drunk so I wouldn't cause a scene when you finally came home, plastered and brooding. What could I even do in that situation? Make the bed in silence and lay down next to you to sleep, I suppose. Not that I was likely to achieve that. No doubt my mood will be buoyed when you showed up unscathed. Still, that joy would soon melt and I'd be left staring at old, familiar annoyances. I suppose people aren't original when they're happy or miserable or pissed off. When *can* they be original? When they're simply lazing around? Thoughts that are either happy or unhappy and simultaneously propelling don't really exist. I reckon that not even criminals are all that original, though some may see themselves that way. Like how a drug addict's hallucination is always extraordinary, though I suppose it only seems that way to them, and so long as it lasts.

Is our relationship original? Definitely not. Maybe just to us. I suppose the word 'original' itself has become trite and meaningless, too. Originality is impossible. So, why is the word still used? Sure, I guess if I continue thinking that way, then soon, everything becomes impossible. Escape, creativity, oblivion, happiness—ha, you could write half a dictionary of impossible words. Has anyone ever tallied to see if the dictionary contains more abstract or concrete words? Pygmies and Aboriginal peoples use very refined language, and the more refined they are, the more abstractions they have. Extremely refined people barely have any nonabstract concepts. That is until they get tired of all that abstraction and start coming up with tangible things again. Tangible art and music and language and thought. Though it may turn out there's no going back.

Laura's return home didn't have to be original in any way, but return, she could. Would you look at the time—I managed to daydream my way into the future. Fun little mental escapades like those help me to keep from going bonkers. Self-admiration saves the world and humankind from going crazy. Even so, being pissed off at you and trying to prove to myself that I was simply worried is a part of egotism and self-admiration as well. The desire not to be cheated on and to have you with me at home is probably a form of self-admiration, too. I think. If Laura were here, even if she wasn't actively admiring me, I could still at least hope she had a gram or two of quiet admiration.

Yet at that moment, I suspected she was admiring someone else. Who knew how actively. Or for how long. It's entirely possible there were some attributes about that guy to be admired. His wallet or physical build. Still, I doubt he could be wittier than me! That was simply out of the question.

I smirked. Had I finally gone cuckoo or just discovered a good way to ground myself in irony?

I stood by the window and stared outside into nothingness. A big BMW was creeping between the buildings. Was someone bringing you home? Or was the driver just drunk? The car came to a stop, leaving the engine running and the headlights on. Somebody must have had something going on inside.

Then, suddenly.

There you came, plodding between the buildings and wearing a white jacket. I checked the time. Two a.m. If you were wearing your old white coat, then that meant you must not have dolled yourself up much before going out. Otherwise, you'd be wearing your leather jacket with the fur collar. And you must have been coming from somewhere nearby. Had you made some friend in the area? A lover? Why else hadn't you told me?

At least you were coming home alone. No one had even cared to walk you home. Must have been a real good relationship.

I glared as you approached the building, unsure of whether it made me happy or sad. There seemed to be some sense of relief. And a fresh weight on my shoulders.

The white jacket drew closer and closer, not swaying much, then turned and disappeared between two other buildings. What the hell?! What game were you playing now? You must have had a ton of different places to go in the area, and that meant I was totally ignorant of your real life. What the fuck.

I realized I could still catch a glimpse of you from the balcony. I didn't bother putting on shoes or a jacket, afraid you'd disappear before I could.

Should I call out to you or just silently observe you walking away, carrying your phone with all my missed calls in your pocket? Would I have time to run down from the third floor and get to you before you vanished, even just wearing slippers and a t-shirt?

I hurried to the balcony. Strange—you hadn't looked up at your windows once to see if anyone was home or not. I cursed myself for not thinking of turning off the lights as soon as I spotted you.

When I got to the balcony door, I opened it as quietly as I could to prevent you from glancing up right away. What would we do if you saw me? Stare at each other in silence?

There you were, directly beneath me. You'd stopped to light a cigarette. The movements were familiar—searching for the pack in one pocket while pulling a lighter out of your other. Your head down, you lit it.

I couldn't hold back any longer.

"Well, hey there," I said, not with much volume but still clearly and distinctly so you'd certainly hear from three floors down.

You looked up.

And it wasn't you.

It was a much older woman. Now, I could also see that she had shoulder-length hair, not your buzz cut. And she was blonde, not black-haired.

The woman stared at me, and I stared back. It seemed silly to just duck quickly back inside. She seemed pensive and uninclined to react in any way. I also had no idea what to do next.

Taking another drag from her cigarette, the woman slowly walked away. I suppose she'd decided she didn't know me, or that I was simply uninteresting.

I shivered from the cold and went back into your apartment. Melissa was standing in the open doorway, looking at me quizzically.

All of a sudden, the whole situation seemed comical; or at least the fact that I was being silly and miserable. My mind was clear, the booze had evaporated from my system. I no longer felt like drinking, either. For a while, I just sat and listened to the ticking of the clock. My thoughts had quieted down a little, too. I hadn't heard the clock before; I thought the room was totally silent. Now, the ticking was distracting. Are people able to meditate to the sound of a clock? Ticking can be awful in its incessancy, but it can also offer a friendly framework to emptiness. If I were to ditch Laura's apartment now, the clock would be left ticking in an empty apartment. What poetic thoughts. Do some suicide victims smirk, too? And can death come so suddenly that the smirk remains on their face after the bullet enters their head? I doubt it.

The minutes passed with determination, but I was determined as well. Making it through the next full hours was a little bit more difficult.

I'd called quite a lot by three-thirty in the morning, but not to the police. I could just imagine their response: "So, your wife hasn't come home and isn't picking up the phone. Wait until tomorrow, I imagine she'll show up." And I knew they'd be right, too. They've got experience.

However, my own patience had run out. I did still have more drinks in the fridge, but I wanted some kind of a resolution. I wouldn't be able to sleep either way. So, I called Laura's mother in Finland. She picked up immediately and I realized I didn't really know what to say.

"I'm sorry to wake you, but I'm in a little bit of a panic here. I haven't been able to get ahold of Laura since early last evening. I don't know what's going on."

"Where are you?"

"Here. At her place."

"When did you last see her?"

I thought for a moment, but couldn't seem to remember.

"I don't know."

"Okay, I'll call her."

I continued sitting, my mind empty, and my phone rang before long. It was Laura. There was a mournful note to my voice when I answered. She immediately went on a tirade:

"What do you want? You don't go calling my mother at four o'clock at the morning, do you hear me?"

I wondered if that was all she was going to say. It was. She didn't explain where she was or with whom or why she'd been MIA. I no longer figured into the picture. She could've been a little more robust in her infidelity. Well, that was that.

"Mm-hm."

I hung up, then looked around the room. I had a lot of things in her apartment. I wouldn't be able to take all of them at once. Instead, I just went to the fridge and transferred all my drinks to a plastic bag. I'd have use for them at Koidu before the shops opened at ten a.m. I began piling food into the bag too, but realized I should be a little more selective. It would've gotten too heavy, anyway. So, I limited myself to taking the best foodstuffs, though I did leave a thing or two in the cupboard.

I felt light and empty. I genuinely had reckoned that I might feel this way when it ended. And I actually didn't care who she was with or how she would comment on it later. If she didn't want to explain anything right off the bat, then fine. I didn't need any of her excuses.

I could feel the despondency in my face while I packed the food and drinks into the bag. It was the same one I'd brought from the shop just hours earlier. The situation felt cinematic. I was the hero of a film. It made me want to laugh and cry simultaneously, though I did neither. Laura wouldn't like it. Come from wherever she may. It didn't matter when or in what condition. Everything was fine by me.

I plodded through the snow towards Koidu, filled with a pleasant emptiness. No sadness, no nothing. Had I already been expecting this liberation? For a while already? Had I wanted to be free?

Sure—I hadn't done any cheating. I'd been cheated upon. I had every right to be offended and make a scene about it, as well as every possibility to be righteously, magnanimously silent.

Shit. So, this had to happen. I suppose that for her, something'd been missing for a while already. Like the man who talked to his ex-wife's new husband, who said: "I guess there was something missing."

I guess there was. Probably. But who doesn't have something missing? Why is it women's privilege to fuck everything up if they feel that something is missing?

Right. Time to get fucked up myself to avoid feeling miserable and fall asleep. Was I out of smokes? I didn't grab any from Laura's place, did I. Shit. Once again to the gas station or a casino at this late hour. I really didn't feel like it, but I'd have insomnia otherwise. I still had a few post-divorce Dormicum sleeping pills left over from when Kusti died. That knocks you out for a good four hours. It'd be something, at least. Probably not enough to commit suicide. And I hadn't the slightest inclination to kill myself. I just wanted to sleep. Life was just getting started. How, though?

I lay in bed for a while, simply staring sleeplessly at the ceiling. I knew that if I went without rest for too long, I'd develop neurosis or some other ailment. It'd happened before. I needed sleep, so I finally took a Dormicum, though I certainly didn't want the hangover that would certainly follow. Oblivion washed over me.

I woke up.

Four hours of sleep. I gradually started to remember why I'd taken the sleeping pill. Should I have another? No! I had to manage.

Managing was rooted in the state I'd been in last night. I sat on the edge of the couch—Laura's old couch that she'd thrown out of her apartment and I had brought to Koidu; where we'd fucked back when we still fucked, had fucked quite a lot—drinking the booze I'd furiously taken from Laura's apartment and was furiously silent. Silent and ruminative. I had no idea where she'd been or who she'd been with, and I didn't want to know. I felt despondent and had no motivation to do anything. Not even take another sleeping pill.

I texted Laura: "I thought you were honest, but you're not. That came as a surprise. Huh—life still does have surprises in store. I'd never have guessed it. I'll come and pick up my things sometime in the next few days. I'll try to do it when you're not home. That probably won't be too difficult."

I spent half the day moping around. I'd promised to get my junk from Laura's apartment but wasn't in the mood to start transporting things around. I was filled with bitterness. With sadness and pain. Even so, I didn't want to just up and die right there. I sent Laura another vitriolic email.

This time she replied, asking where I'd gotten the idea she was with some guy. She claimed to have been at Piret's apartment and gotten drunk and passed out and Piret's number was blah-blah-blah if I wanted to call and confirm. I stared at the letter, not knowing how to react. I'd been in relationships before where the woman was simultaneously playing the field, and I got tired of it in the end. I suppose it just got on my nerves and made me feel crazy. And Laura had insisted before: "But I'm not *her*. I'm not *them*." But how different are people, really? Or was I wrong?

"You're right. You're not her. I don't have to compare." I'd paused for a moment before continuing: "But for some reason, all those patterns are so similar—those human patterns. It's no wonder, of course. People are identical in their primary wants and needs. But okay, you aren't her. You aren't her. I've just got to remember that, though I know how fucking much you like her. You like her more than you like me. You haven't liked me in a very long time."

I enjoyed that Laura didn't react in any way. She was mute and emotionless. I was a hopeless case.

Shit—maybe she really hadn't been with another man. More likely than not, she hadn't. Otherwise, she'd tell me. It doesn't seem like she's been lying. Fuck. But why? Why, why. It's just never happened before, and now it has. This is the way things are now, Peeter, and you'd better learn it. This is how it's going to be. BUT I DON'T WANT IT TO BE THIS WAY! We'll learn, you know? FUCK, THOSE DAYS ARE LONG GONE! I DON'T WANT TO! CAN'T I JUST BE FREE?!

Well, can't you?

What do *you* want?

What do *I* want? It took me the rest of the day to figure it out.

I'm an addict, and Laura was the drug I needed. Just being around her was enough to get all my endorphins buzzing. I was far away; I was in withdrawal. I didn't know what to do, there was nothing *to* do, all I could think about was how to get a hit of her. Having sex would be great, too, but just having her around would suffice to get out of this miserable situation.

I can't remember how it all turned around, but at some point, I started begging and pleading for Laura to let me come over, because I simply didn't know what to do with myself anymore. She wasn't particularly thrilled. No doubt she was afraid we'd start fighting.

Finally, after lots of talking, she agreed and I trotted straight to her apartment. Right into the torture chamber.

I wasn't in any kind of place to get into an argument. I just laid next to her in bed and stared at her all night long, unable to fall asleep. The next day, I continued drinking. At some point, the thought of having sex with Laura started to haunt me. I played the scene over and over in my head, my cock half-erect. I couldn't say why sex with Laura was the only conceivable situation, why no one else would do, even though I hadn't been in any mood to fuck just hours earlier. Laura's body isn't attractive to me anymore. And now, I knew that mine isn't to her, either.

So, what had happened to me? Why was I fantasizing at length about her pussy when it'd never been an enticing thought, or even a pleasant one, before? All I could think about was the way I might stroke it and touch it as gently as I could. All so she could comfortably slide into her groove. My mind was filled with her resting her slightly parted pussy on my face and coming again and again—a pussy that I used to regard as being too numb and unforgiving but now longed for.

I tried to hold back the writing thoughts and not speak them out loud, but at some point, as neutrally and indifferently as I could muster, I finally asked: "You want to fuck?"

"We can if you want," she immediately replied. I suppose my horniness had been apparent for a while. "But I don't want to. I'm not going to participate."

"I don't want it that way."

"Do it," Laura said decisively.

So, I pulled down her brown sweatpants and panties, then took off her shirt. She helped a little, raising her body slightly so I wouldn't rip the fabric.

She lay there like a mannequin, one arm covering her face. Her body was limp and her breasts drooped to the sides. I cupped my hands around them and tried to turn Laura on a little by sucking on her nipples.

"Laur, what the fuck," I sighed, seeing no effect.

"Do it."

"I can't like this." I couldn't get erect.

I went down on her and her vagina did soften and open. But Laura still had the crook of her arm over her eyes. "Laur, what the fuck."

She didn't say another word.

I was in a dilemma over whether to stop or not. Still, she herself had told me to do it and I'd been aching to for a long time. But now, I couldn't get hard.

"Hold my dick a little then, Laur. I can't do it like this."

She did, gripping it coldly and numbly until I could finally enter her, or actually until she could guide my half-erect penis into her vagina, and then I rubbed back and forth until I came. Laura's arm was still draped over her face. Later, I thought spitefully that she was like a poorly-inflated blow-up doll. But who'd inflated her so badly? I had.

I hadn't come to terms with what had happened by the following day, so I asked: "Was the last time we had sex any good for you?"

"You know I get nothing out of it that way."

The more I hang from her side, the more I distress her, the more she wants to flee somewhere else, to be with other people, and the more I in turn am alone and unable to get my hit. I'm choleric when my dealer is away and even when she comes around, she doesn't feel like handing out the drugs. That's addiction for you. I've gone through it before. A couple of times, actually. Rehabilitation took about a year because you have no inclination to wean yourself off the drug as long as there's a little to be squeezed out. I've never been tossed out, either. Laura has repeatedly, of course, but I've been able to return to her time and again for another hit. It sounds a little pathetic—a fat old geezer scratching at a young, beautiful woman's door. It's especially pathetic when you're aware of the situation but don't even care.

I hadn't phoned Piret to ask about that night. It seemed a little silly. But in the end, I did. I don't know what I was thinking. Maybe that, sometimes, you end up finding something out through a seemingly minor detail. What was I really hoping to hear? Would I have been satisfied to find something out? I doubt it. Perhaps I was seeking a possibility to cut through all the knots and ropes and send myself off to rehab on Koidu Street, given things were the way they were. But Laura's place on Vindi Street was so close and I'd most likely end up running right back to it some night. Even if I'd been cheated on, even if she'd been unfaithful, I'd plead for the chance to just sit on the floor next to Laura's bed and watch her sleep. To revel in it. Though who'd want to sleep with a maniac and a psychopath watching them all night long when they're the subject of all his delusions? Who knows what kind of thought might cross his mind. Maybe he'll just want to fuck, but maybe his mind will stray so far as to want to kill someone. Himself or his beloved. What an unimaginable bother.

"Yeah," Piret answered the phone. I didn't know her personally. I'd seen her before. And Laura had remarked: "So what if she's gay?" Could it be possible that the two of them were involved? That things had gone beyond friendship?

"Peeter here," I said, but realized that meant nothing to her. "Laura's Peeter."

"Oh, hi."

"Hey, I wanted to ask—what were you two doing that night? I can't really get Laura to say, you see, or I don't know how. She's just quiet and I can't seem to ask."

"Nothing, really. We just hung out at my place."

"And the two of you didn't go out? I don't know, dancing or anything? To some club or a bar?"

"No."

"Okay. It's just that Laura didn't answer any of my calls all night and I was wondering why she couldn't hear her phone."

"I don't know what to tell you. I guess she just didn't have it nearby. She got drunk pretty fast and fell asleep. It doesn't take much when you drink a whole bottle of gin, you know. She was out like a light by midnight, and I helped her into the twin bed."

"Okay. I just didn't know what was going on, you know? I was trying to track her down till the morning hours and she's never explained it, either. And we haven't been having sex in a long time. I don't know why that is." Why'd I have to go and say that? To justify calling?

"Um, right. Okay then."

Damn it. Still nothing, nowhere. Absolutely zero clarity. Did that contribute to my inner peace in any way? I suppose it did. I'm paranoid. True, but it sometimes used to turn out that a paranoid's paranoia wasn't that. And the paranoid was unable to see all the demons sitting outside their window. Some of them just came knocking because they wanted to be seen.

How long have I been wracking my brain over that night? Maybe I should just forget it. Good luck with that, though. Unless you go off on a trip.

DOLDRUMS

LAURA AND MY relationship was sour, tense, sullen, and silent. A couple of days later, she sent me a text: "I'm going to a birthday party. May I?"

I was bumming around my studio and immediately sent a passive aggressive reply: "Happy birthday!"

Still, my anger quickly subsided. There was no point holding a grudge now.

I made my way to the grocery store before ten and bought us some snacks and drinks, as usual. As much as my wallet would allow.

I peered up at Laura's windows from the street. Dark. She must still have been at the birthday party. Tomorrow was a day off for her, though, so let her enjoy it. Hopefully, she'd just remember what had happened and wouldn't fuck things up again by going AWOL for hours and not answering her phone. I'd wait, be patient, maybe watch some TV, and not make any big deal when she finally showed up, no matter the time. And I wouldn't start calling, either.

I made my way up the stairs and turned the key in the upper lock. Strangely, it was unlocked. I turned it back and forth several times, just in case. Did that mean she was home? Was she already in bed? I tried the door, but it wouldn't open. The lower lock was secured. She usually only uses it when she's home or leaves in the morning and I'm still sleeping. I didn't have that key.

I knocked. Nothing. I knocked again. If she was sleeping, then she probably wouldn't hear. It'd happened many a time before.

I set my heavy grocery bag down next to the wall. Well, what now? I didn't want to wake her up if she was sleeping. She was sleep-deprived most of the time already. But where was I to go and what was I to do instead?

I knocked a third time. Silence. I couldn't even hear Melissa meowing. I knocked louder. The cat had probably hidden herself in the cupboard at the noise. The neighbors could definitely hear me. Husband's knocking and wife won't open up again. I reckon they've heard plenty about our life by now. The walls are as thin as paper.

I called.

This time, Laura picked up immediately.

"What's up? Where are you?"

"I'm at the birthday party."

"I can't get in. The bottom lock is locked."

"Is it?"

"Yeah."

"Well, I don't know what to say. I'm at the birthday party."

I tried to hold back a sigh.

"Okay," I said, then hung up. I stood in the hallway for a few more minutes. The bag was a little heavy to lug all the way back to Koidu. I glanced at the balcony door. I wonder if some people die just before being executed? Such as when they've been wrongfully found guilty? I bet it's happened before.

I picked up my bag and left.

Once back in my studio, I drank to varying degrees of success.

I didn't feel like being alone, so I went down to Cabbages and continued drinking there. I wasn't the only one with booze in hand, though the others were drinking in moderation. I went back upstairs to fetch more beer. If you don't want to drink alone, then you'll always find a companion if you share, and my fridge was relatively well stocked at the moment.

However, things downstairs were starting to wrap up. I knew, of course, that they adhered to the rule where you couldn't lock the door so long as someone still wanted to hang out. I'd taken advantage of it before, but I didn't want to abuse it.

It was time to go. I noticed that Karl-Gustav seemed a little reluctant to leave, too. He's a quiet, gangly young guy who wore a keffiyeh scarf around his neck and rode his black bicycle in winter. The bike even had an alarm installed because someone had stolen his previous one.

Karl-Gustav had started living in Marten's apartment at some point. I had no idea if Marten himself still lived there, too. He'd played the double bass for poetry readings in the yard last summer. "The guy plays like a professional," Jaan told me. I made a mental note to go down and listen to him play sometime, but never made it.

"You want to hang out a little longer?"

"Your place or mine?"

"Wherever you'd like. I've got some beers in my fridge—let's go there, maybe."

"I'll be right up."

"Okay, I'll wait."

Mihkel mentioned to me a while back that Karl-Gustav suffers from depression. I had no idea. I didn't know him very well and we hadn't really clicked when he moved into the house. Still, the past has taught me that my first impressions are generally no good. When I saw Laura for the first time, for instance, I couldn't figure out why that drunk, sullen young woman was glaring at me. Maybe that's the reason I started asking around for her number the next day.

I hardly imagine that I'd like myself at first. But now, after spending years and years together, I like myself just fine. Why go looking for too much trouble with yourself? Maybe I've just gotten used to myself like you do with a dog. Though people sometimes get irritated with their dogs, too. There are always going to be little squabbles.

Karl-Gustav showed up and was rather talkative. He told me about his philosophy studies.

I tried my best to listen and not think about Laura.

Every now and then, we went to the kitchen window to smoke. Karl-Gustav rolled his own, I had the pack of cigarillos I'd bought to ward off sadness.

He kept going on about philosophical topics—the great little, the little in the greatness, the homogeneity of the world, and other such things. I could tell he was fascinated by the subject and that it wasn't at all empty talk, but gnawing at me inside was still the banal knowledge that Laura was out enjoying herself at a birthday party somewhere. All the philosophy ran off my mind like water on a duck's back. I strove to come up with some sort of honest opinion whenever Karl-Gustav asked what I thought, trying to keep me engaged in the conversation, but in reality, I had no opinion.

"I don't know," I admitted, though I suspected it might sound condescending. I don't know this, I don't know that. Are you trying to say that you don't know and genuinely don't *want* to know? To be entirely honest, I really didn't at that moment. At the same time, I was aware that I'd certainly been in Karl-Gustav's shoes at one time or another before, going on and on about some nonfiction I'd read in a magazine or a newspaper, less frequently a book, and couldn't understand why my audience, who had their own problems they probably didn't want to discuss, wasn't at all enthused.

I set some candles into empty wine bottles and lit them and talked a little about Kustas and his death. I guess I was subconsciously aware that it would at least get my mind off of Laura. However, Karl-Gustav had never known Kustas and only listened out of politeness. I knew the little black coffee table between the armchairs would soon become covered in dried candle wax, which is always a bother to scrape off, but I kept bringing more to light.

"Jaan told me you're a pretty amazing cello player," I said, trying to turn the conversation back to him.

"I play double bass," he corrected me, leaving the topic right there.

Still, neither of us wanted to sign off for the night just yet. Or we didn't want to be alone. I still had beer left in the fridge and continuously refilled our glasses.

My phone beeped. I checked it.

Laura had sent me a text: "I'm home now."

I immediately knew I wouldn't be staying the night at Koidu, even if I were to stubbornly try. My obstinacy would pass when sleep refused to come and thoughts of Laura started swirling around my head. Best to just leave immediately.

I was suddenly impatient, but Karl-Gustav had no idea yet.

"How long have you been living in our house?"

"I don't know, maybe a year. I don't live anywhere longer than one year."

"Why not?"

"I can't say. I haven't yet, at any rate."

We had another smoke at the kitchen window. Laura was the sole thing on my mind, but I tried to make it seem as if I were listening to whatever Karl-Gustav was saying. And to chip in from time to time. My challenge was to wait calmly until I could leave, all without forcing anything. Perhaps it was good not to rush straight out the door. Better if Laura was sleeping by the time I arrived—then we wouldn't fight. But I'd also be locked out again! And what would I do then? I'd just have to return to Koidu.

I eyed Karl-Gustav and tried not to look too pleading. Ah, but I did know one trick! I just had to guzzle my beer as quickly as I could, then things would wrap up. I increased the drinking tempo. One gulp, a second, a third. Karl-Gustav maintained his pace.

"I think the beer's almost run out," I noted.

He abruptly stood.

"It doesn't have to run out completely. I think it's time for me to go."

"Well . . ." I caught myself before I asked where he was running off to. "Sure, if you think so."

"It's late and everything," he drawled, appearing a little indecisive all the same.

"Sure is," I quickly replied. Should I gratefully give him a beer for the road? No, no need. "It's nice that you came. I had a good time." I genuinely had. I don't know how I would have felt being alone that night.

Karl-Gustav nodded and left.

I hastily pulled on some clothes and trotted over to Vindi Street. Laura's windows were dark.

My heart pounding in my chest, I tested the door. It was unlocked. All the lights were off and Laura was sound asleep. She'd left the door completely unlocked for me—something I, myself, never do.

I undressed and crawled into bed next to her. I couldn't see her outline in the darkness; I could only hear her soft snoring beneath the blanket.

My excitement was through the roof and I couldn't seem to fall asleep, no matter how hard I tried. I felt grateful.

It didn't cross my mind then that I'll be turning 51 soon. I thought about it just now, though. I suppose that means I'm lucky. Life hasn't been all that different at 50.

The following day, I couldn't help but bring up how terrible I felt when she was away at night and I couldn't get ahold of her and didn't know what was happening. I knew I'd already beaten that dead horse before and that it led nowhere. She would just get moody and we'd end up fighting. I forgot to explain that I wasn't saying I didn't want her to go out on her own. I simply meant, egotistically, that I didn't want to count the hours and minutes waiting for her.

Laura didn't even bother to argue back. She was simply silent, so I soon fell silent as well. We spent the rest of the day without talking, though I got the sense that things were lightening up.

Laura's party clothes, a black men's dress shirt and a yellow tie, were hanging on the living room door. Later that afternoon, I asked her if I should grab some things from the shop. No reply. Laura's eyes were closed and I reckoned she must be napping. Neither of us had made the bed that morning. I was short on cash, anyway, so I figured I wouldn't go.

Laura drowsily entered the kitchen and looked around. It's rare to see her without makeup. She's more girlish. And beautiful. A defiant little girl.

Laura grabbed her cosmetics bag and went back into the living room. I peeked in to see what was going on. She sat on the edge of the couch next to the window and started putting on makeup.

I sat down at the kitchen table, at a loss for what to do. This time, she spent what felt like forever on her face. She usually has it finished in no time. And after Laura finally put on her fancy clothes and stood in the entryway holding a gigantic handbag, her look was breathtaking. Gorgeous, in an unusual kind of way.

I was still slumped behind the kitchen table wearing a baggy t-shirt, my beer belly oozing over the waistband of my shorts, my hair messy, unshaven. And my heart was heavy.

"Laura."

"What," she curtly replied with daggers in her eyes, pupils widening and darkening. There was an electrical charge to her stance; one that warned not to come any closer.

I sighed.

"I told you, what. I spent a lot of time explaining it. I feel like shit when I've got to spend the night without you. All I can do is sit around waiting for you. All night."

Laura kept staring at me, her lips pressed tightly together and her hand resting on the doorknob. I knew there was nothing I could do. Somewhere out there was a life that made her shine. Here, there was nothing of the sort.

"I said . . ."

"That it's my own problem. Fine. But do you really feel so good that . . ."

"Yes, I do feel very good right now." There was a sparkle in her eyes and it was obvious she was telling the truth.

"Yeah, I can see that."

Laura laughed. I hadn't heard her laugh so happily in a very long time.

"Yeah."

"Go ahead, laugh away."

"I think I will."

I could tell that Laura wanted to leave, but she was seized by uncontrollable giggling and apparently didn't want to carry it out into the hallway. She had to just laugh it out. The glee spun around and around in her body, amping her laughter up to hysteria. I watched from behind my half-empty beer glass, but I didn't cry. I was simply muddled and miserable. Laura was acting like an entirely different person. Like a costumed actor from a movie or an online video. Or from the documentary about a possessed woman in Italy, who was visited by a Catholic priest every week for an exorcism. He would say a couple of prayers, then raise a Bible into the air and shout: "Hear me, evil spirit! I command you to leave this woman at once!" She would screech, bleat, and whine in alternating high and low voices, appearing to delight in the experience, then growl in a gravelly, alien voice: "I will not!" Followed by a syrupy-sweet child's voice and a cloying grin: "I will not!" At least that possessed woman enjoyed her weekly performance. Maybe the holy father was titillated by it, too.

I wondered if Laura's performance would start to repeat. Say, every other day? And would I beg like that holy father, saying: "Do not leave, Laura!" But she would only laugh and exit. That logic didn't check out. I reckoned I should flip it around. I should try to get myself to be completely uninterested in whether or where Laura was heading out to party again, or with whom. Maybe that would dampen her lust for partying. But wait—what did I want, really? For my wife not to have a good time? The kind that she hasn't enjoyed in ages and may have never even had with me?

Laura's laughter dried up as quickly as it came. Her compressed lips formed a narrow dash again, though her eyes were still sparkling like Christmas. With one controlled movement, she opened the door and left. I had no idea where she was going.

I stared at the closed door for a while. Closed. Familiar. I sipped my beer. What would I do now? The right thing was probably to go out and do something somewhere, too. But would I? My energy was trending in the opposite direction. I felt drained. No desire to party. But if I started drinking heavily and persistently, then maybe I'd be overcome by craziness and irrationality, too. I recalled a time when I was in a similar intractable state and tried to talk up a young woman to whom I had absolutely no attraction. It almost worked, too, but I dropped her right then and there before anything could happen. She threw a cup of napkins at me as I left the table. The napkins didn't fly very far, merely scattering across the floor. I saw it happen from the corner of my eye. I knew I should've gone back and apologized, but I didn't feel like it. What was the point? Did I want a repeat of that type of scene in a pub somewhere? Not really. There was nothing that I wanted besides Laura coming back home. She would, sometime, of course. All I could do was wait, regardless of whether it took hours, half the night, or lasted till morning. Though she might not come home by that time, either.

Laura went out partying six nights in a row. I didn't check the mirror to see if I'd gotten grayer. I did nothing at all. I went nowhere. I just sat on the couch and when my ass got tired, I moved to sit in the kitchen. Mechanically sipping beer was my sole activity. I paid no attention to her comings or goings, and she paid no attention to me. A new life. What do you expect when you marry a woman twenty years your junior and then totally let yourself go? I wonder what Dante's new life was like. Was he sarcastic about it as well? I bet he pursued some romance in it—what else? Though I reckon there was relatively little irony and sarcasm back in his day. Who knows, though. Maybe it helped men and women to get along better.

I finally decided to write Laura a letter. On paper:

◆

A proposal for how we can discuss the situation:

- we could both be sober when we talk
- we could think through what we want beforehand
- we could have some idea of how to continue our marriage (or not continue it)

◆

I left the letter on her kitchen table, realizing that the desire for both of us to be sober was rather far-fetched. How could I make it happen?

But that night, Laura said: "You wanted to talk. Maybe after I come home from work tomorrow. If that works for you."

"It does," I said, then opened another beer.

We didn't say another word that night. I was already excited about the next day's discussion, though. And I already knew that I certainly wouldn't manage to figure out what I wanted or how we could continue. The only things I knew how to express were what I didn't wish for and that I didn't want things to continue this way. Alas, that would lead nowhere. Only to another fight. I'd have to manage to come up with something. And to get sober by then.

After Laura left the next morning, I slept in for as long as I could, making it to around eleven. It felt like retired life.

I opened the fridge. There was still some beer left. It was hard not to open any, but I didn't. There was a weak ache near my heart. Thick blood giving my heart a hard time. I swallowed a couple of aspirin, then soaked in the tub. So, what would I say to Laura? What mattered most was that I kept my cool. Did I have any suggestions to make? Anything to which she might be favorable? Probably not. After the bath, I sat down at the kitchen table. My head was spinning. Blood sugar. My brain was trying to turn itself off. All a part of sobering up. A drink would help, but I wouldn't let myself. I rummaged through the fridge for something sugary. Cherry compote. I disliked the taste but managed to finish it off. It'd be silly to fall into a coma before Laura came home. And being in a coma was hardly likely to change our life for the better. I'd have to come up with a better trick.

I paced around the room, sitting down whenever the dizziness was too much. I was sure it'd pass before long. Pretty much routine.

Over and over, I found myself checking the time. Four-thirty was nearing at an excruciating crawl. Looking at the clock too frequently only made it worse. I flopped down on my side on the couch and closed my eyes. Immediately, I envisioned Laura naked. I played a scene of her fucking me for a while. At some point in our relationship, those fantasies had stopped doing it for me. Now, I was filled with incredible longing, but she got nothing out of sex with me anymore. Who were those characters in that old Soviet cartoon? A stork and a heron. One was infatuated with the other but not vice-versa, and then their roles switched. But they still didn't split. All they did was play that endless game. We've been playing it, too. But if we're patient, then maybe some pleasant periods will come around as well.

I called and was surprised to hear Laura pick up.

"Hey, what do you think about me coming around to meet you when you get off work? If that's okay with you, that is. Or what did you have planned?"

"Nothing. I was just going to go home. I can do it on my own, too."

"As you wish."

"But you can come to meet me if you want. Where are you at now?"

"I'm at your place. Do you get off at four-thirty or six?"

"A little earlier. I don't know when for certain yet. I can give you a call if it looks like there's not much left for me to do."

"Okay."

Being inside was oppressive. Maybe some fresh air would do me good and prevent another dizzy spell.

I pulled on my coat and started walking towards Laura's workplace. Slowly. As is appropriate for an old retired guy.

I figured I'd wander the streets in the neighborhood while waiting for her to call, and just show up by six if she didn't. It'd be lousy if we missed each other. Time would tell.

Laura called. I went and stood guard next to the door of the building like a schoolboy. All I was missing was a bouquet.

She came down and stood next to me, looking in the opposite direction. We then walked the whole way to her apartment in silence.

The kitchen. Laura sat down at the table and waited. I sat, stood, paced, sat, and stood up again, waiting for her to break the ice. She didn't.

"Maybe you want to talk about how you view our situation, Laur."

There was no need to ask twice.

"I don't know. I just go out with friends, you know? That's normal! And all you do is moan about it. You send me derisive emails . . ."

"Hold on, I don't believe I've derided you at all. I just felt like I'm having a hard time with it."

"Well, I believe you do. You said that you thought I was honest, but now you see the real me, et cetera. I haven't lied about anything."

Laura was boiling over. She felt wronged.

"Laur, wait. Let's not fight. Let's not talk about all that's happened. Let's talk about where we'd like things to go."

"I don't know. I don't see any reason for me to do anything differently. Do I have to? Why the hell should I? Because *you* want me to? You're feeling shitty? So what! How should I know the next time you're going to start having a hard time again."

"Laura, wait, stop. We're not going to get anywhere like this."

"And where do you think we should go? What's there to get to, anyway?"

"Hey, hold on, let me just tell you what's going on inside of me . . ."

I then went on at length about how I understand that she's beautiful and there's absolutely nothing wrong with her wanting to go out and have a good time partying. But at the same time, I've reached some stupid psychopathic state and am obsessed. And I could understand her feeling constricted by the way I latched on.

I went on and on about how beautiful and amazing and smart she is, and about how I've gone a little bonkers and am so infatuated with her.

Gradually and reluctantly, Laura appeared to come to terms with what I was saying. She no longer raised her voice and her cavalry didn't blow the trumpet to attack.

Ultimately, we both fell silent. But it was no longer sullen silence. More like a break. Laura stood up and stared out the window. After a little while, I slid up behind her and wrapped my arms around her. She remained motionless, but wasn't repellently rigid. All she did was rest her arm over mine to prevent me from sliding it up over her breasts. I didn't make any attempt to, either. I simply held Laura, breathing in her scent at last and kissing her tenderly on the neck. She didn't flinch from my lips, but I wasn't sure what she was feeling when it happened. How reluctant or tolerant she really was.

◆

Perhaps love needs halftimes or intermissions. Otherwise, it wears you out. It wears out the players, the spectators, and the referees. And then, you don't want anything to do with the game or the performance. Once you've smoked your cigarette or had your coffee and wine, you can go back to seeking the secret pathways between happiness and misery again.

We've all fought with our parents before and none of us wants to say we don't love them. Well, sure, there was that one woman, Dea. I was asked to relay that her father had died. For a while, I hemmed and hawed over how to tell her, but then came right out and put it plainly, albeit as casually and indifferently as I could. Dea cocked her head to the side, looked me in the eye, thought for a moment, and then burst out: "That *bastard*." I suppose it came as a relief.

After a play's intermission, most of the audience doesn't leave to watch another performance at another theater halfway through it. I suppose those switch-ups go a bit smoother in relationships. Though maybe some theater lovers do change plays at intermission. Bukowski proposed to switch women, but does it make any difference to them? Changing clothes doesn't make any difference to the garments, either, but they still get switched.

Thinking back on different women in my life, I suppose there has been some amount of change. I just can't say what it was, exactly. I suppose that's why they've all gone the way they did. And come the way they do. It's good that they do come.

RECOGNITION

I WAS ATTENDING a fancy literary awards ceremony at Gloria Restaurant. I knew they wouldn't be overly generous with the booze, so I headed to the bar right at the beginning of the night.

"Hey, Laur—I'm going to go get a drink from the bar. You want anything?"

"Gin and tonic."

"Okay."

I marched over in the middle of the speeches.

"One beer, please."

The dark-skinned barman looked this way and that, seeming to hesitate. But then, the head chef Dmitri Demyanov appeared out of nowhere in his tall white hat and gave a nod of approval.

"And a gin and tonic," I added.

The barman grabbed a bottle from the fridge. I craned my neck to see what kind they had, but there was only Saku Kuld. Boring old characterless swill, just like me. How appropriate.

He poured it into a glass and set it on the bar. I stood and stared at the drink.

"No need to pay," he commented. "It'll go on the bill."

"Gin and tonic."

He disappeared to fetch a glass and a bottle from somewhere else. It appeared he wasn't in the best mood. But maybe he'd been told to try to avoid letting people come up to order whatever they pleased from the bar, and to try to drag it out a little. Otherwise, all these writers would drink the place dry. I'd already acquired a bad reputation for ordering extra expensive drinks at public open-bar events in pricy locales. I was doing my best not to go overboard nowadays, but listening to speech after speech while sipping semi-dry wine was a bore.

I noticed the bottle he'd brought out was Bombay Sapphire. I'd never tried it before and wondered if it tasted somehow different from other gins.

Carrying both glasses, I made my way through the restaurant, then paused involuntarily to listen to the band that had taken the stage. The pretty young woman was putting on a show, and was putting it on well. She improvised as she sang, just like Jürgen Rooste often does. Jürgen had just accepted an award, his eyes glinting with intoxication, and apologized to me for not getting it myself.

I tried to comfort him as well as I could in return, though I wasn't very good at that, either.

"Here's your drink. The gin is Bombay Sapphire," I said to Laura, quickly taking a couple big gulps of my own beer. I'd genuinely thought that I would be getting the award. I dearly needed the money and had already gone so far as to make a few necessary mental purchases with it. Sorry, dude. Ah, well, at least they gave out those awards in the first place. And treated all the nominees to dinner and drinks to boot. I knew I should get back in line at the bar so I'd get more drinks while I still could. There was no need to whine when the meat ran out by the time you reached the shelves, just like back in Soviet times.

I returned to the counter persistently to refill my glass. Generally, I finished half of it by the time I was halfway back to my table, which meant I could spin right back around and finish the rest on the way to the source.

More awards were given out. Laura fell asleep. I moved to another table to chat.

At some point I noticed Jürgen poke Laura, tell her he didn't know where I'd gone off to, and invite her to Black Poodle Bar, where everybody else was going.

I called over to him. He startled, then laughed. I explained that I'd intentionally let Laura nod off there—that she never falls off her chair when she falls asleep at a pub or a concert, and she needed the sleep.

Jürgen apologized again.

"You all go ahead and we'll follow in a little bit. I'll let Laura collect herself a little."

Laura wiped the sleep out of her eyes and came with me downstairs to put on our coats. She brought two drinks along with her—half a glass of wine and the gin and tonic I'd brought her. I'd just downed what was left in Ilona's and Krista's wine glasses, perceiving that ordering new drinks could be problematic already.

I went to the toilet and let loose a gurgling stream of pee while Laura dressed to leave. Then came the diarrhea. I'd planned for it and had bought a pack of Pepto Bismol in preparation. Alas, it currently rested in my coat pocket.

As I pulled on that coat, I took a quick sip of the gin and tonic Laura had set on a table as she finished her wine. It was pretty bland. I couldn't tell any difference between it and an ordinary gin and tonic. Why should I have?

"Nasty, nasty, nasty," Laura cursed once we were outside.

"Should we go check out Poodle? Or where would you like to go? Home, maybe?"

"Let's go wherever you want."

"Well, let's go to Black Poodle, then."

I walked through the entire place, but our group wasn't there. Laura stood next to a wall the whole time, staring at the ground.

I called Jürgen.

"Hey, Peeter. We didn't go to Poodle, but to NoKu. Come here."

"Hey, Laur. They went to NoKu. Do you feel like heading over there? Or are you too tired?"

"I don't know. You do whatever you want."

"I want to be with you. Where would you like to go?"

"I don't care."

"Yeah, sure. Whatever you say. You and my friends have nothing in common. And you never need me to come along to hang out with yours. Tomorrow night, and the night after that. You'll be out the next two nights, as you said. And those'll be the eighth and ninth nights in a row that you've gone out somewhere. Where or whom you'll be with—I haven't a clue. Does everybody else always act this way? And if they do, is it even a good thing? Do they have endless money for partying? They treat their new friends to drinks every night but at home, I'm the one who has to. You've got quite the thirst. And you drink yourself to sleep at every party. I've got no idea where and how you sleep when you're out wher-ever."

I knew I was being mean, but *something* had to break out after holding my tongue for so long. Where else should I have let it loose?

"Fine, let's go home then," I sighed.

Laur took a step away from me.

I took one step closer to slide my arm beneath hers.

This time, she hopped two steps back.

"Where the fuck do you think you're going?!" she screamed.

A calm immediately came over me.

"Right, where's that. Fine. If you don't want me to come, then I guess I'll go to Koidu."

And I walked straight there on autopilot. My arms and legs moved back and forth, but my head was empty. For some reason, I was reminded of the letter Rulla once wrote to Santa: "I want a ropot. Veri mach!"

I knew there was a long stretch of emptiness ahead of me. And unknowing of what was to come. It made me simultaneously sad and cheerful.

◆

All day long, I do nothing. And I don't even do that very well. Although even if I were to do something, it might not necessarily be an act. I often accomplished a full day's worth of nothingness back when I used to go to work, but that didn't leave me in anguish. I went to work to do nothing day in, day out. Maybe that's the reason why jobs were invented. I reckon they're not all that necessary in southern lands.

And what might be the thing that could take away that anguish? I've no idea, either. Maybe when someone praises you for doing something that mattered. Mopping the floor or stuffing dirty laundry into the washer—those are nothing, really. How important is doing chores on your own, really? Or heating the stove or making soup. You've got to do all those things alongside some kind of useful activity. And what kinds of useful activities are there in life? Completed newspaper articles or advertisements? Or offices and institutions watched over as a nighttime security guard? What was the good in all that? So long as you were paid a salary, then it was seemingly praise.

However, unemployment benefits certainly aren't praise. More like scorn.

Why am I so dependent upon other people's judgement? How did that develop? From childhood? All I knew back then was whatever someone said was good or bad. I, myself, was unable to form an opinion. I still can't. But now, no one comes along to point or command or praise or find fault. Now, there is freedom. A freedom I don't know what to do with.

◆

As soon as I walked in, I could tell that something was wrong with Siskin. She was seated at my desk and didn't even turn around when I came through the door. Her gaze was simply locked on the window. My computer was open in front of her, the screen blank.

"Siska?"

"Yeah." Her voice was somehow stifled. I came closer.

"Siss, what is it?"

She spun around to face me, looking as if she'd just returned from a distant daydream.

"Honey, what's wrong?" I asked, leaning in closer. Siss flung her arms around my neck and started to cry.

"Were you crying before, too?"

"Yeah."

"Uh-huh, I can see the streaks of dried tears on your cheeks. You've got eyes like a drug addict."

"What kind of eyes are those?"

"Oh, don't pay attention to me. I'm just being silly."

"Tell me."

"Well, their pupils, the dark spots in the middle of their eyes, are either wider or teensy-tiny."

"I don't have eyes like that. I don't!"

I squatted next to her.

"Honey, what happened? What's wrong? Were you alone here for long? Did you get scared of something?"

"I wasn't alone."

I lifted Siss down into my lap. She was quite the heavy bugger already. I couldn't squat and hold her that way for long. I pushed the chair away from the table with my foot and sat down, rubbing Siskin's back and waiting for her to stop crying.

"You don't have to tell me if you don't want to," I said.

"Diana was here. And she played a Getter Jaani video on the computer."

"Getter Jaani? Your favorite?"

"Yeah. But it was totally different."

"Different how?"

"I couldn't tell if it was really her. Her eyes were way different. They were all black. It was awful!"

"What? What are you talking about? Show me. Where was it? On YouTube?"

"No. No. I don't want to see it again. I already see it in my head all the time now."

"So was it Getter Jaani or not?"

"I don't know. I think so. They'd done something to her."

"Maybe she was wearing special contact lenses. Doing a goth thing or something. You know that people can put in contact lenses that make their eyes all black, don't you? It blocks out all the white parts."

Siss sobbed.

"Maybe they were contact lenses. But why did she do that? It was so awful!"

I squeezed Siskin and stroked her head. There was nothing I could say. Her entire world had collapsed. Getter Jaani, who always exuded goodness, was suddenly made a monster. Like me finding a stranger in bed with my wife. It's happened before, and I suppose a part of my world did fall in on itself. And nothing can be done to fix it. There was no point in confusing her with some inane story. The only thing I could do was stay with her, try to get her mind onto something else after a while, and have something to eat together in the kitchen.

I made us sandwiches, we ate, and spoke about other things. She seemed to slowly recover, but nothing could bring back her former Getter. Santa Claus no longer existed, and there was no point in trying to bait her into thinking there might still be. Indrek certainly pulled off lying about God's existence in Tammsaare's *Truth and Justice*. Though I can't remember if anyone bought it. They at least respected his lie and his good intention. But I'm not even good at lying. Maybe Tammsaare just imagined it all, anyway. He *was* a writer.

Siss had stopped crying a while ago, but she sighed once more and asked: "*Why* did Diana have to show me that?"

I was wondering the same thing.

"Someone would have shown it to you sooner or later, anyway. Better to get it over with sooner and with one of your best friends, right?"

Siss took a bite of her sandwich, stared at me with a frown on her face, and seemed not to understand. I couldn't say if it meant anything either.

WORK

THE GIRL AT the unemployment office had lost hope of me ever getting my act together, even though she was the one laboring to make me look for work. I, for my own part, did my best to assert that I really was. Always and everywhere, all with a sad smile. I did attend trainings at first. Just to be polite and respond to the invitations. I spend a few hours chatting away at them, and I suppose they did put me into a good mood on several occasions. They were an opportunity for fellowship. Like visiting a pub or a church. Something to fill the day. To deceive myself and, to some extent, others. To tell myself that everything would get better soon. That's something they told us to reassure ourselves of daily. Who came up with that trick? Emilé Coué a hundred years ago? Or some American positivists and pragmatics? I bet that kind of autosuggestion works for some people. And not for others.

At first, I would show up to the unemployment office drunk and unshaven. Over time, it started to make me feel more and more guilty. Guilty for living on society's dime. So, I combed my hair, shaved, and tried not to be too intoxicated when I went. If I were to have a nice suit, carefree manners, and masterful small-talk abilities, then I could live at the taxpayer's expense for years. It would become a skill in and of itself. I'd learn how to write applications and hang out at conferences. Though I suppose the guilt would persist.

Fine, but what other choice do I have? My path leads me straight back there again and again. Back to the same questions. But if I were capable of letting those simple questions go and moving forward, then would it dispel any misery over the fundamental things in life never again coming to fruition? Infinity, immortality, and untidied home and spirit.

◆

"Ah, it's a piece of cake! You just show your face at the unemployment office once a month and they pay you benefits."

The man I was talking to had gone through that year of unemployment once before. he knew what he was talking about. He said he'd never done as many odd jobs as he had during that year. And he finished renovating his house. Like a professor on sabbatical.

"Where's the office at, anyway?"

"There's lots of them. But don't go to the one on Endla Street. It's always packed and you've got to wait in line forever. Just pick a different one."

"What's the amount you get?"

"Depends on the last salary you received. Something like half of that. And it slowly decreases over the year."

"I was only working part-time."

"Well, then I guess you'll get half of that."

Half of half, I thought. And then even less than that. But at least it would be something. Modest and penny-pinching living. Cheaper drinks in smaller quantities and less carousing. There's still a chance of me becoming a decent person yet. Sure, but what kind? And did I even want to become one? Where are those people, anyway? What type should I be? I can't seem to see or recall a single one.

I looked up the unemployment office's address. It was just around the corner, advertised with a tiny sign. I'd always imagined it to be gigantic, like the Kalev Candy Factory. The unemployed are everywhere you look. I was given a booth number at the counter. There were people sitting and waiting on small sofas.

"Who else is waiting for number twelve?"

"I am."

"Me, too."

"I am as well."

"Then I guess it's going to take a pretty long time."

"A few hours, at least."

But I didn't have to wait more than an hour.

I laid all my papers out on the counter for the young man. He read them and typed something in his computer, then shoved them back to me. They weren't enough. I needed more documents to become unemployed. Ultimately, it took me several months. Becoming and being unemployed seemed like a job in and of itself.

Back when I was employed, it never crossed my mind where all my taxes went. But here's where they were channeled, all to make sure people could sit and wait their turn on soft sofas. At least they had somewhere to go while other people were at work. They didn't have to sit at home and mope all the time.

LITERATURE

Intelligent men are said to be more monogamous, and intelligent women more polyandrous. Here, I'll cite a smart, hard-working young woman named Kadri K. And I bet I regard myself as intelligent, just like everyone else. Well, thanks. Intelligence is therefore inevitable if you're monogamous. And I should have to find a foolish woman for her to only be with me. Like how Miller found Monroe. Things didn't go well for them, though. I suppose Miller hadn't the intelligence to see that Monroe wasn't foolish enough to be faithful. Why should things go any better for me? I'm no wiser than Miller. Not enough to find myself an adequately unintelligent woman.

Kadri's arguments make sense, but I still can't completely grasp the crux of it. Consequently, I must be an idiot. But how can it be that I'm still a hardened monogamist? The exception that proves the rule? Or are intelligence and dimwittedness not necessarily positioned on the same linear scale? Can a fool be smart in another sense, and a smart person an idiot in another situation or when viewed from a different angle? Is it possible to be smart and stupid simultaneously? Can you support polygamy during one stage in your life, then switch to monogamy when you get tired of it? That's precisely what's happened to me, in any case. Nevertheless, I haven't gotten any wiser from it. And Laura has drifted from colorful relationships to simplicity. She doesn't appear to have lost any intelligence in the process.

No matter if you're smart or stupid, you still gaily play the field for half your life before wanting to peacefully settle down. But if you made a home and hung around there in the beginning, then you'll want to get your share of merrily sleeping around later, too. Oof, so many acquaintances come to mind. I'm not going to start naming names, though. Or would people like that? Quite the fascinating read, I bet. And your name figured into the list, too! No, that'd just give you a nasty start.

Madis Kõiv sometimes used initials instead of names. Vaino Vahing and Mati Unt changed the names or left them out entirely. Though I suppose you could still tell who was who. I suppose they felt that something taken from real life is more tactile than pure fantasy. Looking at it that way, you can divide literature into two groups. Is fantasy at all possible? And can one write about anything other than the contemporary world or themselves and their pretty naval, no matter what is seemingly jotted down on paper? Be it God, the Devil, humankind, truth, beer, or the future. Someone remarked that the silly redhead in that fiction is actually the author's mistress, with whom things went sour, and now he's getting his revenge. And in the very same breath, he said: "Hey, let's not write about each other, okay?"

"Fine. But what will we write about then, if not life itself? And do we know anything other than what we've seen, read, and experienced? Do we know anything that we don't know?"

Let's make things more interesting for future researchers of literature: let's rethink the entire life we've led, taking the pieces apart and stacking them again in a different way. Will it be better and more beautiful? Or more terrifying?

I suppose that what we do is describe, but we also draw conclusions and make generalizations and *that* is literature. Could we ever avoid doing all those things? Probably not.

◆

They say that sexual pleasure makes a woman more beautiful. I also remember reading somewhere about glowing cheeks and sparkling eyes. Laura certainly doesn't act that way. Laura clenches her teeth and looks as merciless as a murderer. She transforms into one. Though I don't know who she's murdering. Maybe she's simply focused on tracking down her orgasm. But is that really a good plan? If you try too hard, then the orgasm might escape you. Ah, what do I know about that. I've never seen a murderer before, either. Luckily. I suppose they just have run-of-the-mill faces. An ordinary murderer's ordinary face. Unless they're an unusual murderer.

Laura doesn't make any sounds during sex, either. It's impossible to tell if she likes it at all or finds it disagreeable. Not to mention whether she orgasms or not.

I, myself, can't hold back and whine like a pig or whimper like a dog when I'm on the verge of ejaculation. That's when I'm on the bottom and unable to really do anything. I just jerk around. I can't say if my toes curl up like Tiit mentioned. 'Toe-curling' is Tiit's code for sex.

FAMILY

S ISS SUDDENLY DECIDED to stay with me at Koidu. It was nice to have her around again; it'd been a while. And now, you're the one home alone on Vindi Street. You did come to Koidu once, but we sat down in Cabbages and in Jaan's apartment and smoked a joint and you were pretty wobbly and talked for a while about how you were going to go home because you wanted to go there and wanted to be at home and . . . and ultimately fell asleep on the couch in my studio. I heated the stove again because I knew you prefer a warm apartment, and I stayed up late and woke up early, before you woke up, to heat it again, because although it's already March, the temperature outside at night is well below zero.

You were testy again when you woke up, and I couldn't understand why.

"Did I do something wrong last night?"

"No, I just fell asleep in my clothes again."

"Yeah, I didn't want to bother you. What's wrong with that, though?"

"Nothing."

You went to the toilet and I gave up interfering. I assumed you'd leave without a word, just as you often do in the morning.

But you returned and stood in the middle of the room. I pushed myself up on an elbow in bed and stared at you drowsily.

"I'm hungry. Can I take something from the fridge and heat it up on a pan?"

"Sure. There's not much in there, to tell the truth. But Erko brought me a few slices of smoked sausage one night. You can have that. And there are fish burgers and I-can't-remember-what-else in the freezer." I then rolled over to nap a little longer.

Half-asleep, I somehow sensed that you'd finished cooking. I dragged myself into the kitchen. You'd made an omelet with pretty much everything there'd been in the fridge.

"May I eat in the other room?"

"Of course."

You filled your plate. Was it appropriate for me to take some, too? Ah, whatever. We were like two hippies who had just met. Maybe it wouldn't be a problem. Let it be. Maybe we won't lose that—being intimate, in a way. But strangers all the same. Things are good like that. Total intimacy is a false conception. But I wouldn't want to be too strange, either.

I knew that although Siskin was still asleep, I wouldn't perform too well in bed after yesterday's pot and drinking. Not that you'd feel like fucking, anyway.

So, I helped myself to a serving of omelet, then went to sit down next to you.

The days went by and Siss's stay on Koidu Street showed no signs of ending. I did my own part to make her feel comfortable and not want to leave.

And one night, you and I became officially married on Facebook. Siska and I were together at Koidu—that was why. I felt affection for the first time in I don't know how long. From you, from Siska. I heated the studio up until it was almost oppressively warm and Siss kicked the blanket off at night.

You weren't able to take the stereo system to the IT Bus for repairs, because there was no point. Fixing it would have cost the same as getting a whole new system. So, you bought a new one from the store and were even able to dispose of the old one there, and now you're listening to Spliin for the first time in forever and are calm and maybe even happy on Facebook. That makes me pretty damn content, too. I smoke an unfiltered Russian cigarette every now and then; Jürgen gave me a pack for my birthday. It was the only present I received, in addition to one of his poetry collections and a little Buddha statue. Siskin snores softly, gets up to take a quick piss, then curls up and doesn't snore again. She's nine already. Jaan was just sitting in the kitchen, having a hair of the dog and reminiscing about the first time he saw her on Hiiumaa. Siskin was about half the height she is now. She must have been four and a half at the time and decided to come care for me a little after the divorce. Her care home continues to this day. I'm glad it is.

◆

Now that your health has improved again but you still don't want to have a kid, will you stop wanting to have sex? Or if you do agree, fine, okay, then will you just lay there like a consenting corpse? You seem to have almost permanently removed the possibility of orgasming from yourself. And is that the reason why I can't seem to get a spring in my step anymore? All because you've started eating more regularly since we started living together and are fertile again?

What's better can make things suddenly worse.

But I don't want things to be worse; for there to be a trial or tribulation that makes us care more for each other and makes everything better. I really don't.

◆

Why are Märt and I so intent on drinking ourselves to death? Is sympathizing or a notion of our own deaths behind it? By delaying Märt's death, we're also delaying mine. At the same time, one of us has to follow Angelina. If it's Märt, then it's not me. And if I delay his death too long, then it could indeed be me in the end.

Märt doesn't seem to have any real qualms with being next. The faster he dies, the faster we'll have to take a number behind him. The connection to my death isn't as ambivalent as the connection to his. He's never gotten as much sympathy and attention from us as he has now, being in and out of the hospital. And drinking at home in exhaustion, causing his body to drift in and out of consciousness and lose balance. They won't admit him to the asylum anymore. They won't admit him to several hospitals where he's gotten into mischief before, squirreling away his antidepressants and smuggling in vodka and trying to hit on the nurses. We take him to hospitals and give him money for booze when he doesn't even have anything in his wallet for his kids when they need pocket change.

I reckon that Märt is enjoying it, the old trickster. The old con man. I hope he is, at least. Given his poor physical state. Then, we at least aren't duped into playing his stupid game.

Helping someone out is addicting. It's like an investment. After you've taken Märt to the hospital a couple of times and given him money for liquor, you would feel bad letting him unexpectedly kick the bucket. All your efforts would have been in vain. The last time he borrowed money off of me, he first read off how much he already owed. It created a situation where I felt like if I didn't lend him more money at that very moment, then I might lose the chance to get back what I was due. A roulette-player's logic. And that old gambler knows that there's a gambler inside of us all.

◆

I was reading about someone, or about their life, and looked them up online. From Wikipedia or Google—I can't remember. But I can't be bothered to read the information there anymore. I just look at their picture. If I were to read any deeper, I'd forget it just as quickly—their biographies, their works, their ideas. But pictures stay with me for longer.

I occasionally Google old acquaintances when they come to mind—girlfriends and the like. Or check their Facebook pictures to see what the new ones are like and what's become of them; to see what those new images say about them. (And what do new photos say about me? I really have no idea. They're all too familiar.) No one uploads pictures of the dead. Of corpses. I wonder if you could? Nice photos are always put up of dead people when they were alive, though. Search engines don't want to facilitate talk about death and actual people don't want to, either. Only distant, unfamiliar, anonymous deaths will do. They make the very best news.

Even if I were to see a picture of a familiar corpse, it wouldn't truly show my acquaintance. Let things be the way they are.

◆

I poured myself a beer in the kitchen. I didn't know what you were doing in the living room. Watching TV. Maybe already asleep.

I mused that if anything were to drive us apart, then it'd be money. You'd apparently gotten some cash from somewhere recently, though you didn't tell me how or from where. You no longer depend on me for money, though you still let me buy you groceries and booze from the store and pay your rent. All while you visit a top-notch dentist and go to a nice hair salon.

My previous life came to mind. My former wife, who, in the hopes of getting money, started going around town and sleeping with other men and ultimately divorced me.

You've told me repeatedly that you're not her. I've told you repeatedly that you're not her. Even though for a while, the two of you would go out and drink together, leaving me with no clue what to do all alone at home.

So, I simply drank beer and thought about nothing. You were probably thinking about nothing in the other room, too. I can't say which one of us is in a better position.

◆

I glanced up from behind my bottle.

"Hey. Could you please tell me that you love me?"

I was in a good mood and reckoned you might casually agree to say it.

Your nose was buried in your computer, probably playing some game. It didn't appear to be going as well as you'd have liked. After a few moments passed, I already assumed you wouldn't respond. As usual.

But then, you rapidly typed something and growled through gritted teeth: "You've asked me that so much. I don't want to anymore."

I was taken somewhat aback. I wanted to take a sip of beer, but couldn't seem to move my hand to the glass. You were right. I had asked you a lot. But so what? Couldn't you just say it again?

I sighed and managed to take another sip.

◆

Siss was coming around less frequently. I suppose her mission of helping and keeping me alive was coming to an end. I had to learn how to get by on my own. She was off doing her own thing in the city; I don't know where, exactly. Siss is getting pretty old, too. Ten, already.

But sometimes, she'd show up again out of the blue and we'd sleep in the same bed like in the olden days, hugging and telling each other silly stories. Or we'd both stay up late, each in their own corner of the room.

I was hunched over my desk, Siss was drawing across the room or just sitting quietly and doing nothing. Just like I used to do when I was young.

Suddenly, she popped up next to my desk, holding her phone and wearing a weird smile.

I waited for her to tell me what the expression meant. I'd never seen her look that way before. Siss couldn't find the words and I didn't try to prompt her.

"You know, right . . ."

"I won't until you tell me."

"I just called Diana?"

"And?"

"Look out the window. Over there, across the street. You see? She's walking her dog Pony and has that friend with her."

"So?"

"Well, I called her. I saw her outside and I called her to say I could see her . . ."

"Okay . . ."

"And it rang. And then Diana took out her phone and looked at it. And then she hung up and put it back in her pocket."

"So she hung up on you?"

"I don't know. Maybe."

"The call might have just gotten dropped. That happens sometimes. I call Laura constantly and she almost never picks up."

Siss was still wearing the odd smile.

"But Daddy, I called her *twice*. I called her *two times*."

"Maybe her battery's dead."

"Watch," Siss said, and dialed.

Diana and her friend were hanging out by a lamppost. Siss held the phone to her ear and we both watched her friend down below. Diana took out her phone, checked the screen, pressed a button, and slid it back into her pocket.

Siss's hand dropped to her side and the smile disappeared from her face.

"Are you going to cry, honey?"

"No, I'm not," she said softly.

I tried to find something to say, but couldn't think of anything. Siss went back to her corner of the room, flopping down on the couch and pretending one of her Pet Shop toys was a robot. I watched out of the corner of my eye. I'm 51,

Siss is 10, and we've got pretty similar problems and worries. And neither of us can help the other. We can be together a little, at least. At least there's that.

◆

Laura went to work in the morning and I tried to sleep a little longer, as usual. All to avoid my hangover and delay cracking open a hair of the dog. I'd have a beer later, of course, but so long as you get enough sleep, you don't have to drink so much that you get drunk again right away. And you might just manage to get something done that day aside from drinking.

Luckily, I was able to fall back asleep. The key is to simply avoid thinking. What's counting sheep or keeping track of your breath if not just avoiding thoughts? I wonder if people who meditate count sheep, too. It's just as good as saying a mantra or staring at a mandala.

Morning sleep often features plentiful dreams. I haven't had any erotic ones in a while. But I haven't had sex in a long time, either. Now, I first was trying to hit on an imaginary girl, but all I could do was stare at her like she was a work of art, unable to say or do anything more. Another girl then appeared behind a fence somewhere. The dream girls weren't drop-dead gorgeous or anything. Merely ambiguous. I pulled the second girl towards me, either over or through the fence, and stripped her breasts bare. They were tiny. She didn't protest. I licked one nipple, then the other. I pulled off her pants. The girl's genitals were strange in a dreamlike way. I was already guiding my penis into her when I remembered—hang on, I'm married! How could I do this?! But then, I realized I was dreaming and figured that dream sex wasn't all that awful, even though I have a wife.

But for some reason, I decided to end the dream and woke up. No sex for me. Neither in waking nor in dreams. Why had I stopped it from happening? Fear of guilt? Of sin? Wasn't being afraid of guilt becoming a little restraining? Who knows what might become of this great moralism? Some kind of shenanigans, for sure. All to be just; to be guiltless. To not have bad dreams. Is one notion of hell just feeling guilty and finding yourself in a nightmare that lasts and lasts and never seems to end? In life or in death.

◆

I couldn't keep my mouth shut, even though I wasn't even drunk. Not really.

"Could you please tell me you love me?"

"I've had it already! You ask that so many times."

"I know, but . . ."

"I don't want to anymore. I can't take it. I just can't take it and don't want to."

"Okay, but . . ."

"Okay *what*?!"

"Nothing. You've said before that you hate everyone and everything. And you simply want to disappear. You've said that repeatedly, too."

"Have I?"

"I think so. Maybe not so many times. But I can understand that you feel like saying it . . . and it's better to just get it out there. Then, that feeling might become less acute. That despair."

"What good does saying it do you?"

"Nothing. I'm clinging on to you, though I reckon you don't want that. The burden. Do you also hate me when you hate everyone and everything?"

"I don't know."

"There's no one else here apart from me." You didn't reply. "Maybe you're just tired. You've been going out so much lately. And sleeping so little."

"How long are you going to go on bringing all this up again?"

"What should I say, then?"

"I don't know. Nothing."

I wanted to caress you a little and calm you down, but you were stiff and bristled up. Does your being depressed make me feel better in any way? I can't remember us ever being together and depressed simultaneously. Whenever one has taken it over, the other feels light and carefree. Couples are never jealous at the same time, either.

MEMORY

I'D FINISHED TAKING a shower and was drying off. Someone's kids were running around the stairwell. They squealed and sounded young. The sounds stirred up emotions, as they do for any deadbeat dad. I wondered if I would ever have any more kids. Did I even want them? How would I know if I did? What do I know at all?

The doorknob slowly turned. The door to the sauna and shower at Koidu doesn't really lock. You can only stick the key in from inside and turn it a little to keep the door from falling open while you're showering and stay warm.

A little boy opened the door and stood there, staring at me with a pouting look and sucking on his pacifier.

"Hi," I said, still rubbing the towel over myself.

He studied me quizzically, then took the pacifier out of his mouth and announced: "You have a pee-pee."

I wasn't dry yet. I expected the boy to call to his mother or father to come see the unexpected penis, too.

"Well, I bet you don't."

"Yes I do," he said, starting to undo his pants.

Suddenly, a slightly older girl appeared next to him.

"What are you doing?" she asked.

"I have a pee-pee, too," the boy said proudly.

"You were supposed to wash your hands."

"I know, but . . ."

"Come on, let's wash them."

They walked past me to the sink. I tried to dry off a little quicker. My hair was still wet.

"You need to wash your pacifier, too."

"No, I don't. It didn't fall. It was in my hand."

"Your hands are dirty."

"No, they're not."

"Come on, wash your hands now."

The boy stuck the pacifier back into his mouth and stuck his hands under the running water.

"I have a pacifier just like yours," I continued teasing. "I'm not too old for it yet."

He didn't reply, just looking back over his shoulder as his sister helped him wash his hands. From his look, however, I could tell he was accustomed to adults lying. There was no point trusting them. All they do is taunt little kids.

I wonder which of us will remember the encounter longer or in more detail? Who knows—maybe we'll be sitting in Cabbages and drinking beer together like old men before long, and neither of us will remember a thing.

◆

I was reading, though I couldn't really say whom or what. I knew what it was, of course, but it wasn't of any consequence. The writing wasn't all that important; it simply was what it was. Brautigan said you can eat something and not really know what it is, but enjoy it all the same. I wondered—can that really be true? Maybe not quite. You may know very well what you're eating but it doesn't matter. What matters is that it tastes however it tastes at that moment and you fully give yourself over to the flavor, not wanting to think about anything else in the world.

I couldn't quite understand what I was reading, but it was nice to spend time in the text; to read slowly and allow it to flow steadily. Somewhere in the back of my mind I knew it was Kõiv, but what did that matter? I sensed that although he wrote about a particular thing, he was similarly aware that he would never truly grasp it; that it would always remain just out of reach. Still, there was a well-defined plot that could be chased like in a game of tag. Or like in a film where someone is doing their own thing in the woods, going about their business like an ant tugging around a twig. The film doesn't really start anywhere or arrive at anything, and it tells you nothing new, but still, you feel the presence of a secret. And as you watch, you don't feel the desperation you sometimes do when you don't know how to do something. Casual reading frees one of existential angst. Reading something meaningful would be a waste of time. What's the point? Where's it going to get you? Though if you know from the very start that it will ultimately lead you nowhere, that's different. Escapes like those are few and far between. Good writing is enigmatic but not complicated. Reading should be easy. And you should feel like understanding is just around the corner, right on the next page; like you're standing on the threshold of realization and discovery. At the same time, you should have the sweet awareness that true understanding will never come. Just like how there's always a little farther to go before a beautiful romance is ready and present, no matter how close you get to it.

"An eternal high," as they used to say. Dead-on.

SEXUALITY

MAYBE IT REALLY is because you eat adequately nowadays and have gotten over anorexia and could get pregnant, though you don't want to.

"I can't even handle myself. What would I do with a child?"

Unfortunately, it's killed off all your sexuality. Or at least is one of a hundred thousand reasons. Probably the latter. Western civilization won't collapse for only a single reason. Just like the rest of us.

◆

We'd fought three nights in a row, and then again the night before last, when I checked to see what Laura was up to.

I couldn't figure out how the argument began. It sprung up out of nothing. It started because it was simply time to argue. We'd drunk enough booze and had the green light to bicker. In any case, I was moaning about something as I grabbed another beer from the fridge and suddenly, Laura snapped.

"Why are you shouting stupid things at the fridge? If you've got something to say, then just say it."

"I'm not shouting things."

"Yes, you are. And at the fridge, so I can't even hear."

"*You* sure don't say stupid things. You don't say anything, for the most part, especially whenever I try to talk to you."

Et cetera. I could have started laughing, but I wasn't in the mood. Laughter wouldn't have helped anything, either. Not if I was the only one.

Another night, I made some comment and Laura answered: "Blah, blah, blah."

I snapped my mouth shut and stomped off to the toilet. When I returned, I growled: "Oh, so it's just blah, blah, blah, huh?"

"I was just about to apologize," Laura said.

I didn't speak for the rest of the night. And I was silent the following morning. Didn't I feel like I was acting petulantly? Of course I did. But I didn't know what to change. I justified myself by reasoning that if I simply slapped on a smile and pretended to be happy, it could easily be met with another "blah, blah, blah".

Nevertheless, I admitted to myself that it was just a way for me to continue sulking.

Laura was sitting in bed, staring at the sheet in front of her. The light in the room was dim, not like morning light.

"What time is it?"

"Five. I had an awful nightmare."

I rolled over. Laura went to the toilet and did something in the kitchen, then came back to bed, took my hand, and held it under her chin, a little like the way kids pose for grade school pictures. I couldn't help but touch the soft skin of her neck, then stroke it a little. She was certainly as thin as a biscuit, but not as rough as one. I told myself to stop comparing her body parts to biscuits.

Involuntarily, or perhaps not, I slid my hand down to squeeze her breast. Soon, I moved to the other. She seemed to be enjoying it. And I wasn't to blame. I wasn't sleepy anymore. I pulled up her shirt and grabbed her breast, already growing erect.

"Ow, that hurts!"

"Sorry. I didn't mean to."

I heaved my portly frame on top of Laura, knocking my knee against her spindly thigh.

"That hurts!"

"That did? I just hit your leg accidentally." I rolled off of her, then tried to caress her as tenderly as I could before going down on her.

"Could you hold my dick?"

Laura thought for a moment, then placed her hand on top of it. That helped. I'd already gotten a little limp after stroking her for so long. We always seem to go at different speeds.

"Would you get on top of me? Please?" I whispered, afraid I'd otherwise lose the erection entirely.

Laura sighed, but slid on top of me. Her eyes were closed and her head drooped. I slid her shirt upward but didn't want to take it off entirely, afraid she might get cold. We fucked for a little while, neither of us showing much emotion, and then Laur froze. She got off of me.

"It's not working for me. You can get on top."

I felt my spirits sink. I didn't want to play the role of molester I'd seemingly been offered. Or had I already taken it on myself? I went to the toilet, then had a couple sips in the kitchen before getting back into bed.

After a while, I started dreaming about women problems again. The mirage of a woman was a little like my ex-wife, but also a little like Laura, too. I realized that I was asleep and weighed whether or not it was appropriate to have dream sex when I was married in real life. I've put the kibosh on erotic dreams several times before, purely because of my marital status. This time, I even began ratio-nalizing that it wasn't good to stop in the middle of the act, either. That it was harmful to your prostate. I don't know how mine is doing in the first place. I need to take better care of myself. So, I allowed the dream to continue and pressed myself close to the woman with many forms. "Someone might come in," she said. I could also hear other people moving around the house, but I fig-ured—oh, what the hell. What did I have to fear? I was dreaming. If we get caught, we get caught. But my subconscious censor was apparently still armed. I got a little close to the woman but ejaculated before anything could really hap-pen. Oh, well. The wolf was fed and the sheep were safe, as they say. How well-fed he was, I couldn't say. As long as there was something in his belly. I felt a damp splotch spreading out beneath my thigh and tried to shift away, though there wasn't much room to maneuver.

The next day, I had a mental discussion with Laura.

"Hey, if you don't want to have sex, then that's fine. You don't have to go and pick a fight every night to zero out my sex drive."

"You think so?"

"Well, what do *you* think?"

"You know very well what I think and want. I've wanted to have sex every now and then, too. But I just fall asleep first."

"Have you, really? Why don't you say anything, then? I had no idea you did. You certainly don't let on to it in any way."

"You just haven't noticed . . ."

"Right. And a proper man would have. But not me."

"Keep it up. Who's the one picking a fight here?"

"I don't want to argue. Maybe it's a subconscious thing for you. I'm not saying that you plan to start arguments just so there's no need to mess around with sex, of course. Just . . ."

Laura was silent. In my mind. I considered why I even paint myself as a pig in my own fantasies. I could imagine myself as a noble person somehow. So why the masochism? Did I want to leave a worse impression of myself to myself when-ever I left it for others? All so I can later be surprised that I'm really not that bad? Quite the refined game, Mr. Sauter. When you beat yourself, then the other side of you still loses. Loser takes all, huh?

◆

It's a vicious circle. Or the repetition of vicious circles. I stay up and drink after you go to bed to avoid pressuring you for sex. Sure, you have to go to work in the morning, but I sleep in and when I finally do get up, I just soak in the tub and continue drinking. It's no wonder you don't pull me under the covers. And the more I drink, the worse I fuck. And the worse I fuck, the less you want to have sex with me.

Unfortunately, my libido stays strong.

Is this always the case when people marry? I suppose it didn't go this way exactly with my last marriage.

I guess we'll see how many years we stay together without sex. I don't believe we'll be able to set any kind of record. Maybe some people celebrate golden wedding anniversaries without having intercourse once over the course of their marriage. I do know of one that lasted for years without the couple sleeping together. And another that only did once every six months. And a third that was about the same. Does marriage kill eroticism? Why'd we even come up with it in the first place? Should I read Marx again? Who am I kidding—I've never read him. I only answered questions about his writing in school. About the formation of marriage, the state, and private property. I have a marriage, not too much private property, and don't really care about the state. It turns out that I only practice one of Marx's three egotistical acts of coveting. But why have marriage when I don't even have property? I could've just carried on fucking for as long as I pleased. Maybe I'd still care to in the absence of marriage.

There's another aspect, too. Laura was infertile before we married. Her physical health was just so poor from anorexia. But now, copious drinking and snacking and rest has led to her being able to have a child again. I suppose that scares her. Maybe she's afraid of dying soon, regardless, and doesn't want to abandon a possible offspring. I don't know. She's the one who said: "I can't even handle myself, much less a child."

Sure, I'd love to see who on earth is honestly all that good at handling themselves. Some might feign the ability. Maybe children are meant to mobilize their parents and get them to manage better. If only the child knew! To be fair, I never asked my parents why they had me. I suppose they didn't know, either.

A friend of mine was asked by their child: "Where was I before I was born?" I happened to be sitting next to them. And my friend replied: "Under Mommy's heart. Yeah, under Mommy's heart." *Oh, my God. Oh, my God. If I have one at all.* And what does it mean when an atheist says, "God forbid!" I guess about as much as the rest of things people say. Lots and nothing at all.

A doctor who listened to my pulse once said the heart is nothing more than a chunk of meat. She appeared to enjoy saying it—chubby, middle-aged, and slightly buzzed. I held back from replying that all the two of us really are is a couple of upright slabs of meat, ready for selling at the deli.

DEATH

"WHEN MELISSA DIES, then let's get another pet," Laura said rather enthusiastically. I think she was only on her second cider, though they were strong pints of Henry Weston's. Expensive, too. We were out at the Hell Hunt Pub.

"How old is she, anyway?"

"Nine."

"That is pretty old for a cat, I guess. What kind will you want?"

"Maybe a rat. Rats are so cute."

Laura babbled on about what kinds of amazing exotic animals people had these days. And birds. I went along with it. Laura told me once that she's semi-autistic. That she doesn't have much in the way of emotions. I certainly haven't seen her crying before. Has she ever seen me cry? Anyway, I was laughing. And she was in a good mood at that moment. Isn't that an emotion?

"Don't go for an exotic pet, though. Get some Estonian animal. A squirrel. Or a pine marten."

"Maybe a chicken."

"Sure, why not? Cluck, cluck, cluck, where's my egg, where's my egg? Who came and stole my egg?"

I was drunk, too. Several beers deep. Leffe, Hoegaarden, Hell Hunt Dark, and Hell Hunt Wheat. Who knows what else.

But whom will you take when I die? Someone exotic or Estonian? Will it break my heart if you show no emotion? Probably not.

◆

There were two big dogs roaming the neglected property in the middle of the woods. Gaunt Caucasian shepherd dogs with matted fur. They barked hoarsely and panted, their gazes somewhat crazed, watery, and unfocused. Maybe they'd drunk themselves to such a state, too. One was chained to a long overhead wire, the other was loose.

I parked the run-down old car I'd borrowed next to the house.

"I sure don't dare to get out," I said. There were two other clunkers parked out front.

"Give them some bread," Laura said, handing me a loaf we'd brought.

"I still won't."

I sat and stared out the window at the emaciated dog lunging at the car, visibly exhausted. He must have been long in the tooth. I wondered if he could bite a chunk off the car. A door handle or windshield wiper, for example. I knew a man whose dog was chewing on his wire fence, and he was worried the dog might manage to make a hole.

I checked my watch, then called Märt. He didn't answer. We sat there, unsure of what to do next. I didn't want to waste the whole day that way.

Then, I spotted a figure in a bathrobe swaying by the side of the house. Märt leaned against the wall and stared vacantly at the car. I suppose he couldn't figure out whose it was and why it was there. He didn't come any closer, probably lacking the energy. Märt waved an arm at the dog, but it moved gently and slowly in the air like a delicate angel's wing. He also opened his mouth, though I couldn't tell if any sound came out.

Laura grabbed the bread and opened her door.

"Hey, pup! Hey, pup! Come have some bread!" The dog ran around the car to Laura's side. She lifted it high into the air and commanded: "Sit!"

The dog barked furiously; I was afraid he'd jump on top of Laura and knock her flat. She ripped the loaf in two above her head and flung one chunk as far as she could towards the creek.

"Go get it!"

The dog shot after the bread. Laura then tossed the other half in the opposite direction. The dog gyrated in the air mid-leap and ran after it.

I couldn't tell if Märt was watching. He appeared so out of it that he nearly slid down to the ground, but then laboriously turned around and, supporting himself against the wall with his other arm, shuffled back towards the cellar door.

I'd spoken to Märt the previous day and just that morning, too. He usually preferred to talk at night, because he suffered from insomnia. But now, slumped on an old chair in his basement, he seemed to be observing us from somewhere far away. I thought he recognized me and at the same time also didn't, or was such a different man himself that he saw me as someone who belonged to a previous life; not this new one. Märt wore a tattered old shirt under his tattered old bathrobe and grimy sweatpants. His sparse beard was shaking, as he was shaking as well. His hands would tremble violently, then his entire body. The cigarette he held between his fingers quivered. Back in the day, our hands would tremble so violently when we were severely hung over that we'd occasionally spill soup from our spoons; now, Märt's whole frame shook that way.

"Do you have your things together?"

"Things . . . together," Märt echoed. "I'll just go . . . put."

I was losing my patience. I'd borrowed a car and we'd struck a deal to get Märt to rehab through an acquaintance. But now, he was sitting there all philosophically, relishing the final face of his downward spiral and the smell of death. Death had become a favorite topic of his recently. I didn't know how to respond. We just had to wait. Laura was silent next to me. Then, she fished through her pockets for her cigarettes and lit one, also.

"Well, go get your things together, then."

"Uh . . . they are. Somewhere . . . they are. I'll just go . . . see. My laptop . . . could you . . . buy smokes?"

"How many?"

"Don't know . . ." He paused to think for so long that I suspected nothing else would come. But then: "Ten . . . packs. For . . . starters."

"Go see where you put your things, then."

"Think she . . . packed. . . Or I . . . did . . . Could you . . . check . . . upstairs . . . A blue . . . duffel."

The few words drained Märt of his remaining energy and he started wheezing.

I went upstairs to check for his duffel bag. On the one hand, it felt like he was far gone and barely able to speak. But on the other, I got the sense that he was fully capable of coherent speech. I still felt like maybe he was just acting, speaking at a snail's pace and almost inaudibly just for show, though he, himself, didn't actually enjoy it or believe it, either. What he did enjoy—that, I couldn't say. Probably just booze and occupying a state of drunken oblivion. Who doesn't find those things dear?

I poked around. Märt's wife and his kids lived upstairs and everything was immaculately clean. Märt himself was living in the basement. It wasn't very disorderly down there, either. There wasn't much in the first place. It wasn't all that warm, either, although he had a stove. Maybe Märt spent a lot of time outside, sitting next to the creek and listening to it babble. He'd sung its praises before. And usually forgot to close the door behind him.

Being drunk out of your mind for months at a time and listening to the sound of running water? That's certainly a privilege. Though I suppose it will tire you out over time, just like any long meditation. Zen monks become exhausted by overnight meditations, but are livened right back up when a fellow man of the cloth flogs them over the back of the neck. Märt did resemble a monk in some ways. He was celibate already, living far from women and the current of life. Like a Taoist monk, to be exact. It did make me a tiny bit envious. Not that I wanted to end up like that.

I opened the fridge, not really knowing why. It was quite well-stocked. Märt's wife worked a decent job. They hadn't been an actual couple in years, though. Märt used to go to prostitutes, though I hardly imagined he was up for it anymore.

I spotted the duffel bag. There was even a clean pink towel laid on top of it, folded with love and care. The color didn't necessarily mean anything. It didn't have to be blue.

I grabbed the bag and went back downstairs.

Laura was smoking in the doorway. Märt had positioned himself to smoke at an angle allowing him to watch her from the corner of his eye. That old dog. I suppose seeing a pretty young woman like Laura breathed fresh life into him. Or did he just want to straighten up a bit around her?

"Let's go," I said, standing next to him with the bag in hand.

"Wait," he said, and reached for the bag. I handed it over to him.

Märt poked through the contents and seemed a little dissatisfied. He didn't comment, but he sighed loudly. Maybe he just had a habit of sighing occasionally. Märt appeared to be in no rush. I wanted to hurry him up a little.

"Come on, Märt . . ."

"So that's . . . your Laura . . . huh?"

"Yeah."

"And you're . . . married now . . ."

"Yeah."

"Congratulations," Märt mumbled, staring at the ground forlornly.

I felt somewhat put off by his tone, though I supposed he must have been the one feeling dejected. My stupid positive attitude probably didn't help.

All of a sudden, I realized that I couldn't remember anyone else having ever congratulated us. I suppose most people knew I didn't care for it much and refrained out of politeness. And we'd been avoiding others, too.

Several of our acquaintances believed that Laura deserved someone else. I thought their recommendations could be something that paradoxically brought us together, though it wasn't liable to last for long. Maybe such things will reach a critical mass at some point.

"Märt, let's go."

"I know," he said, sighing heavily. "But I'm not dressed. You can see that."

"They'll give you hospital gowns to wear. Everybody wears the same thing there."

"No!"

So long as you have your dignity, I suppose you still have stubbornness and personality, too. Märt didn't seem to be in a rush to die just yet. He lived in his own world, and time flowed differently there. His time was endless. And although I tried to convey the fact that I wanted to get him to rehab and myself back to the city, I just couldn't get it across to him. It may have entered his brain, but the knowledge was unimportant because nothing in the world held importance anymore. What an enviable state. Deep absence and a lack of any fucks. Also somewhat tragic and tinged in melancholy. At the same time, sincere and unfeigned. Distant existence.

Somehow, we finally managed to get Märt packed away into the car. He automatically put another cigarette to his lips.

"Hey, Märt, this isn't my car. I was asked not to smoke in it."

"So what ... really? I'll just ... crack a window."

"Hey, please. Honestly. If you want, then have a cigarette outside and we'll go when you finish."

Märt couldn't fathom my demand, but nevertheless acquiesced. Raging within him was a revolt against the world that refused to concede to his wishes. The world treated him unfairly. Märt accepted. He didn't bother to argue or struggle, but he also didn't make peace with the situation. *Some* justice had to remain, whether merely in the soul of a grizzled fighter.

"Hey, Pete—buy me a drink, okay?" he asked as he got back into the car. Just the idea of drinking injected him with a dose of energy, allowing him to ramble off an entire unbroken sentence. He had every right to make the request—he'd consented to mine and now, it was my turn.

"You know what, no. They said they wouldn't admit you if you show up drunk."

"Drunk?! I'm not going to go and drink myself drunk. I'm feeling so crummy and just one would help. My heart's a little weak and ..."

"You've told me you wanted to die so many times."

"Well, I don't know about *wanting*, but ..."

"You've told me you're dying ..."

"That's right."

I had to admit it was a great trick for asking for a little money. Like wanting a buck for your own funeral. Still, how many times can you really do that?"

◆

I descended into the dive bar Kuku in the middle of the day. I can't remember why. I had nothing else to do. I already knew the bar would be empty and I'd just have to sit there alone. But so what? I'd sit on my own with pleasure, drink a beer, and then continue my day of nothingness.

Nevertheless, I found Toomas Raudam standing next to the counter with his chin drooped to his chest, just as he usually stands. I positioned myself next to him. Raudam noticed me out of the corner of his eye and, although his expression showed no amicable change, I could tell he was still glad to see me. A tsunami of warmth seemed to emanate from his direction. I wanted to say something, but didn't know what. He was silent, too. Raudam typed his pin code into the card reader to pay for his drink. Neither of us wanted to say anything insipid or treacly to each other.

I have no idea why, but out of the blue, even though we hadn't yet said hello, I asked: "When are you going to die?"

Without skipping a beat and almost entirely bereft of intonation, he answered: "Tomorrow."

The two of us then sat and chatted about nothing for a while. I was a little bothered by having started with such an inane question, though I didn't bring it up and neither did Raudam.

◆

I went onto the balcony for another smoke at Laura's apartment. The half-liter jar of butts was filled almost to the brim. I made a mental note to empty it when I took out the trash the next day. Like that helped any—I'd completely forgotten by morning. Andres never got around to lowering the doorstep in Tammsaare's *Truth and Justice*; I failed to empty the jar of cigarette butts.

Nighttime cigarettes help to clear the mind of thoughts. I suppose it reduces blood reserves, which aren't overly plentiful to begin with, which turns off a tired brain. Why it is tired—I don't know. Doesn't dreaming drain the brain of energy? Or are those other parts of the brain that want to exercise and dream at night? Do they wait all day long for when they can get started?

◆

Heli saw us and stopped us at the Balti Jaam market, chattering ebulliently like she always has. She talked about how she was taking a Tallink cruise the next day. It didn't actually take you anywhere, but the price was next to nothing and there were clean places to sit. That was certainly true.

She eyed Laura.

"They told me your wife is half-Latvian. And an artist."

Laura was looking somewhere else; I suppose she wasn't listening. I didn't feel like correcting Heli that she was thinking of someone else. It would have entailed a longer explanation, and how could I explain something involving Laura when she was standing right next to me? But I couldn't just agree, either. Maybe Heli would think I simply didn't want to talk about it. I didn't, to be fair, but it was more like I didn't know how. My autism was coming out.

Laura told me that lately, they've been finding out that no clear autism exists. There's a spectrum that you can use to analyze everyone and find out what kind this person or that has. Being unable to cope in crowds or at school are a couple of manifestations, she said.

"I've got no problem with that," I argued. "I just get bored. Being in a crowd slows down my thoughts. Crowds don't think big—that's old news. And I suppose that's just what a lot of people need."

I wondered where Laura is on the autism spectrum. Everything has to be extremely neat and tidy. She shuts down whenever I say anything critical—no picking up the phone, no replies to emails or texts. She'll still answer other people's calls. Sometimes mine, too. But the distancing is something that's developed only recently. I suppose it's taught me not to say critical things aloud, too. If you haven't anything nice to say, then it's best to say nothing at all. Should criticism be outlawed entirely? Do I not want to hear any aimed at me, either?

KITCHEN

I SIT IN the kitchen at night, eating a slice of buttered bread with salt and pepper, just like in childhood. Sure, the kitchen is different. The bread is a little different, too—whole-wheat, not white. How different am I? I feel like I'm not a different person. Like I'm the same. But how should I know?

However, if the activity is the same and I am the same and not much has changed overall since then, couldn't you believe it's eternal? I sit in the kitchen (at night), sprinkling a little salt and a little pepper onto a slice of buttered bread, and I eat it. I can only remember the last time I did so. No doubt there were more such occasions, both before and after. They extend farther into the past than my memory can reach, and I don't know how to look into the future to see me sitting and eating this exact same way. Though perhaps I do. Perhaps I already can. And now I know what exists.

At this very moment, however, I'm frying ground beef in the kitchen and using a slice of bread to eat it. I can't remember if I ever added onion and carrots when I was a kid and made the same meal. The former, I think, but not the latter. Either way, it turns out that not just one thing, but at least two exist in the world's constancy and perpetuity and eternal existence. Both eating a salt-and-pepper sandwich in the kitchen and using a slice of bread to eat fried ground beef. The kitchens may change, but the act and the feeling remain the same. Maybe that's the trick and déjà vu and eternal repetition. One of Van Gogh's potato eaters sat in a shack somewhere and gobbled down hot potatoes with quite the same sensation. Maybe I possess a memory of him, and someone somewhere is hazily remembering me sitting in kitchens. Does it offer a secure feeling of existing in a definite cycle? Or the distress of being unable to exit it? Or is it sometimes one thing and other times another? We really have no idea what might lie outside of the cycle. Could it be something good or something bad? And what if it's nothing? Would we still want to find out? If a Buddhist wishes to not exist, then what are they? Put an end to your existence. Or are they not so sure about it? Can they also remember a situation that happened when they didn't exist? They appear to remember or imagine *something*. The great, blissful state of nonexistence. Let them have it. And I'd best stick to my buttered, salt-and-peppered bread.

Raymond Carver remarked that eating is a good thing. I suppose it can certainly provide comfort. And silence your thoughts. Pure meditation. You chew on a bite of bread, your cheeks bulging and your gaze absent. Not to even mention drinking. If beer had been available to Buddha, then would he have ever bothered to start meditating? Which is a substitute activity for which—drinking or meditation?

I checked Laura's fridge. It was empty, just as it often is when I haven't visited in a while.

"What did you eat today?" I asked casually. "You had to have had something."

I don't know if Laura had expected the question to come at some point. In any case, she'd been trying to nibble on something whenever she was alone lately.

"Um, I had . . . some bread and some sour cream."

"Sour cream on bread?"

"Yeah. I have salted bread at work sometimes, too. There's always bread left over there. Sometimes there's sour cream, too."

That's right—sour cream on bread was a childhood food, too. It doesn't matter that stores are stocked with all kinds of delicious foods. Childhood meals are nostalgic. I reckoned I should fry slices of white bread on a pan one of these days. And sprinkle sugar over them. None of these new fancy delicacies, caviar and oysters, ever put a stop to your thinking. Thoughts are halted by simple, nostalgic treats that can be chewed with stuffed cheeks and absent gazes. But why should I stop thinking in the first place? Because my thoughts have gotten somewhat lousy. I need to stop so I can start thinking again from zero.

◆

A crow and a seagull were fighting on the roof of the neighboring house. The crow was a scruffy-looking thief. The seagull was bigger and brilliantly white with gray wings and a long, hooked beak. Both rose into flight for a moment and circled each other. Neither appeared to have any buddies to gang up on their opponent. And they didn't seem to be fighting over food—neither had anything in its beak. They were fighting over which could sit on top of the chimney. (Do birds sit or stand? Do they sit while upright on both feet? When do they rest their legs?) The red tin roof actually had several white chimneys poking skyward. Nevertheless, the birds both wanted to perch on the particular one they were circling. Maybe it offered a better view of the surrounding eating grounds. Or of some other bird things. Dumpsters? The seagull was winning and sat haughtily on its throne. Neither struck any serious blow to the other. Things didn't get that hairy. They fought with measure and dignity from a distance. Or were they themselves unaware of what they were fighting over? Would the chimney have been relatively disinteresting if there hadn't been competition?

Why do Laura and I fight? Do we even know? Sometimes, it erupts with a bang. For the most part, however, we also just circle each other and screech like angry birds, but refrain from delivering serious blows. We at least hold ourselves back that much. And we never fight over food, either. Is there some kind of competition between us? Over what? Power? Determining who's superior? The possibility of being wiser and acting like the adult by giving in is never all that convincing of an idea. And if one of us were to arrogantly and condescendingly submit, saying: "Fine, you can be right, okay. Are you happy? Is this what you want?" then the other probably wouldn't accept, anyway. "Oh, so now you're talking big about giving up, huh? You think you're such hot shit, don't you?!"

The seagull wasn't eyeing up dumpsters, but arced its head back and stared at the sky. I don't know if there was some other bird circling up there, having to look down and see who the boss was. The crow certainly didn't appear to be up there. It had found something more interesting elsewhere. A new fight or a girlfriend. A tiny, lazy, lost pigeon was making its way across the roof, too. The seagull didn't even afford the pigeon a glance. Ha, as if I care—let it amble around as it pleases. Just to be certain, the pigeon didn't get too close to the base of the chimney, either.

At some point, the seagull disappeared. It had had enough of that game. And what do you know—before long, the lazy pigeon was perched upon the same chimney the seagull had abandoned. It cooed and lazed around there for a while. No other bird could be bothered to chase it away. And then, the pigeon disappeared as well.

When Laura and I split or one of us dies, then what will we miss the most? The nice times and sex we had together? Or all these fights we have? These nights where our energy boiled up and over? Are the fights a kind of high? Kaur once told me that love and violence are the same thing. It sounded like a load of bull at first. But sadomasochism? The endorphins released by sex and violence, respectively, are quite a similar cocktail. If we don't get the dose we need from sex, then I suppose we try fighting. But after a while, you can't get a high from fighting anymore, either, because you need to continually increase the doses. My biological drugs no longer have any effect. What else should I try? All we do is sit around in bitter silence.

◆

What could make me feel better? Cleaning. Obviously. But I don't. I lie on the couch in my dusty studio and wallow in how awful and depressed I feel, and in how I don't want to and can't bring myself to do anything. Such as clean. I can even manage to come up with a couple of possible activities. I know that my mood would improve if I were active. I'd put the depressing thoughts out of my mind. I should move around outside a bit.

But I don't get up. I don't go anywhere. I feel like shit and surrender to it. I won't be lazing around forever, anyway. At some point, something will force me to get up and get moving in some direction. A phone call. An invitation to visit. Not that I want to get those calls or invitations. Then, I genuinely end up doing nothing for the entire day. Time just slips away and my inner panic spreads further, even though I might put on a happy face when I'm out in someone's company.

I suppose it's all rather unoriginal. Huh—what *do* original people do? Do any even exist?

I'm hungover, too, of course. I guzzle juice and perspire, but stubbornly refuse to reach for another beer, even though it would reduce the sweating. I don't know why that is. Perspiration is a part of ending an extended bout of drinking. A beer would also tone down my depression, but I've resolved to exit this cycle. One can guess, of course, that I won't be out of it for very long. As soon as I feel like I've wormed myself out of a drinking cycle on my own, the accomplishment feels like justification for gradually getting into a new one. I've proven to myself that I can end it all on my own if I need to. Consequently, things aren't all that bad. I'm not a hopeless case and can keep on moderately tippling.

But what if I can't get myself out of the drinking cycle at some point? Will I find myself oscillating between booze and clinics like so many others I know?

◆

I heard someone cry out in a grating, unpleasant voice: "Peeter!"

I opened my eyes. I hadn't been sleeping. Where had the shout come from, though? I suppose I must have dozed off. Recently, I've been hearing my phone ring in the other room and when I go to check it, I find I have no missed calls. Nobody's looking for old Peeter. I've gotten used to it and know it's all just imagined. I'll only hear it ring once and if I pause to listen carefully, I'll realize it's stopped. Should I change my ringtone?

When I closed my eyes again, hazy gray shadows shifted and flitted back and forth behind my eyelids. Were they demons of some sort? I've only glimpsed the occasional black stripe on the edge of my vision before. Or transparent bars drifting out of focus. Akutagawa had visions of translucent gears. Can something seen become stuck and create a negative that sometimes returns? Or becomes lodged in your brain?

My memory has been escaping me, too. Names. Events. What will happen when I no longer recognize friends or can't find my way back home? I suppose there's still time before that happens. But how much? I'll sit in the hallway of an insane asylum, confused by why the restaurant has such poor service. The waiter never comes to me, no matter how long I wait. Servers are walking by constantly, or is it management? And what are those strange uniforms they're wearing? Scrubs of some sort. I've never seen a waiter wearing scrubs before. Huh. Should I call out in Russian: "*Devotchka,* come here! Serve me, too, please!" Who will I think I am, exactly? Venedikt Yerofeyev in the buffet of a Moscow train station? I suppose I'll never find myself in any of my books if I end up going crazy. I can't remember them, anyway. Instead, I'll probably be stuck in someone else's novel. I should pick out a nice one now. *War and Peace* might not be all that bad, though. It's heroic. And there are ball scenes. *Crime and Punishment* would be somewhat less pleasant. People have gotten stuck there before. Tõnu did when he was sick. As did Hasso in a dream. I've also been locked in Dostoyevsky's novel repeatedly while dreaming.

Maybe someone should hand me the book to read when I'm in a care home with Alzheimer's. It could help me to regain a smidgen of clarity. But does something lifting you momentarily out of Alzheimer's really do any good? You emerge and realize it was a brief moment of lucid thought before slipping right back in. The list of those who've hung around with the disease contains some pretty impressive names. Not bad company, at any rate.

And which is better, anyway—alcoholism or simply going insane? Memory loss, hallucinations. I wouldn't know which to choose. Gogol was terrified of being buried alive, and he was. Yes, better to be cautious. I suppose it wouldn't help much to envision yourself dying as a millionaire, surrounded in a beautiful home by a loving family. Some people wouldn't even be satisfied with that. Everything seems swell, sure, but still—death?! Does it really have to be this way?

MONOTONY

WHAT DID I do today? Anything? Why'd the question even come to mind?

I'd like to promptly answer that I've done nothing at all. It seems like more or less the truth. But what *should* I have done, anyway? What would I have been capable of accomplishing?

I don't really feel like saying that I watched the rain fall and put Siskin to bed and listened to Mihkel talk about how he's separating again. Or how Siskin and I went to renew her passport and ID card. If I hadn't done all those things, then I suppose I'd have been sitting at this desk and writing a few lines. Would that have been any better? What's the act of 'doing', anyway? What is satisfactory? Sometimes this and sometimes that, I suppose.

◆

I picked up the roll of toilet paper from the floor. A couple sheets fell back and a tiny writhing slug fell from inside the roll. I quickly squished it under my shoe before it could get far. I nearly lost my balance on the toilet seat from the shock. It left a damp stain on the floor. I didn't feel great for killing it, of course. Why didn't I take better care of my pets? Was I afraid in my delirium that it would swell and come to visit again? Didn't I have anything better to do than ponder such thoughts? What could be a better activity?

I decided to go to the store and buy slug poison. Would going out and finding a humane way to kill them make me feel any better? No. But maybe just a walk out in the fresh air would lighten my mood. At least it was an excuse to get out of the house. I'd been staring out the window for a while already, thinking about how nice the weather looked. But what was there for me to do there?

◆

When people insinuated in the early days of our relationship that it'd go sour and we'd inevitably split, it provided motivation to rebel and keep things intact. Now, I reckon our acquaintances are used to us. Or they can't be bothered to suggest it anymore. What's the point of repeating those things?

Only now have I started pondering the end of our relationship, too. How and when? And only now have I begun to wonder: what do I really want? Whenever we're together and arguing, I naturally want to be apart. And being apart quickly becomes unbearable, so I rush back and scratch at your door or your leg, begging and pleading.

Is our relationship just going to keep oscillating? Maybe. Why not, though? What could be better?

◆

You kill the feeling whenever you blab about love affairs—the emotions are chatted away and sold off. Scraps of love should be suppressed and hidden. Like Gailit wrote: if a girl brings up love, then clap your hand over her mouth. But aren't feelings smothered when they're suppressed? In the best case, they start to push back. Action creates reaction. At some point, however, you no longer feel like pushing back or simply lack the strength. It's a tale as old as time: obstructing love only makes it stronger. But who obstructs love in a marriage? No one.

◆

Lately, I've been resting a hand on Laura's shoulder at night, even though we don't have sex. Just to feel some companionship.

I watched her lying next to me, though I couldn't quite see her in the dark. I could only make out a bulge. Laura had folded every edge of the blanket beneath her, even covering her head. Maybe she was gripping the edges, too. To keep me from touching her. I suppose she has trouble sleeping when I'm touching her, even just to lay a hand upon her shoulder. It interrupts her privacy.

The bulge in the blanket didn't move or make a single sound. How was she able to breathe? Very little, I reckoned.

I turned my back to the lump and tried to fall asleep.

◆

Laur was drinking with Liis. I was hanging around my studio. I was somehow at peace. She'd been telling me in advance whenever she went out partying recently, even asking if it was okay. When someone asks like that, then of course you say: sure, sure; go ahead! And everything is fine. You're free to sit in peace and do your own thing.

So, I sat around and wasn't doing much of anything, merely enjoying time to myself. I checked the time every now and then, wondering whether Laur would be out all night. And when I'd go over to her place in that event. I suppose it didn't matter when. It could even be past midnight. Whenever I started to get drowsy and felt tired of hanging around all by myself at Koidu.

Laur called. I couldn't really tell if she was drunk or not.

"Where are you? What are you up to?"

On second thought, it was a little too talkative for her. She must have been drunk all the same.

"Nothing. Just at Koidu."

"Liis and I are at Kukeke on Telliskivi Street. I was just about to leave. Do you maybe want to come over to my place?"

"Sure thing."

"It's okay if you don't want to. Or do you?"

"No, yeah, definitely. I'll come over. When? What time will you get there?"

"I don't know. There's probably no point in taking a trolley. I'll just walk."

"You know how to get back?"

"I don't know."

"Check Google Maps. You can get from there to Madara Street, and that leads straight to Kristiine. Then, you don't have to go down the other side of the tracks."

"I know Madara Street."

We were both silent for a moment.

"Should I call you when I'm getting close to Kristiine?" Laur asked.

"Nah, no worries. I'll leave soon, too, and just meet you there."

"Okay."

I felt good. My wife had gone out to kill some time while I killed some time alone. There's nothing better in the world. I just didn't want to spend the night alone. Nights are the worst. It's good when someone's close, either Siskin or Laura. A pet would do the job, too, if I had one. But sex? We hadn't fucked in months. How did it go, anyway?

Laura approached at a quick pace, looking clear-headed and vivacious. But as soon as she was close enough to see her eyes, I couldn't look away. That would've been too telling. Having my eyes locked on hers was telling, too. She was absolutely plastered. I was a bit drunk, too, but less so. I didn't know what to do. My gaze wandered. Laura was wearing a black blouse I couldn't remember her wearing before. Was it new? It was unbuttoned halfway, though I couldn't see her breasts. Or a bra. It was certainly a sexy look.

Laur pulled her blouse closed a little. I knew I should say or do something to dispel the discomfort.

"You want to buy something to drink somewhere, too? It's ten minutes to ten."

"Something, yeah."

"Let's get the alcohol and pay for it. Then you can spend all the time you like picking out what to eat. I'll wait."

"But I don't know what to get by myself."

I was grateful for that. I wasn't hungry. Laura could probably tell. But she wanted me to come along so she wouldn't have to dump the groceries at the register and wait for me to come and pay.

After I bought the alcohol, Laura got hung up on what kind of meat to pick out. I gently pressed her to make a decision. Finally, she did.

I felt light and blissful.

"What else would you like, Laur?"

"I don't know. What do you want?"

"Cottage cheese? Bread? Some butter, maybe. I've got to pee. Let's be quick."

"Okay."

Picking out bread was a chore, as always. The aisles were long and the selection huge.

"Laur, I'll just grab this carrot bread. I need to hit the head here."

"Sure."

I paid for the groceries and legged it towards the bathrooms. I hadn't squirted any in my pants yet, but was afraid I might. At the same time, I didn't want to run far ahead of Laura with my face scrunched up. I forced myself to slow down. When we reached the bookstore, I held the bag of groceries out to her.

"I'll just be a minute."

"I've got to go, too."

Sure, she did. So, I trotted on to the toilet with the bag dangling from my grip. Where would I set it while I peed? Could I hold it in my left hand and my dick in my right? I set it down on the floor just inside the doorway. The floor itself was nice and clean. No one else was there.

The stream was long and powerful.

I heard a stall door open behind me. A guy walked out and went to the sinks. I peered back over my shoulder. A tall, heavily built Russian man. Not athletic; portly, more like. And also not as fat as me. Someone else then passed quickly behind him—a similarly tall and sturdy man. Had they been in the same stall? Apparently so. They washed their hands at the sinks while I shook the last drops off my dick and tried not to glance back at them. I hoped they wouldn't grab my bag and run. It contained a bottle of calvados and some ciders. There was nowhere else to buy booze at that hour.

Did they feel at all uncomfortable? Apparently not. Were they behaving as if I might say something? I couldn't tell. They would clearly have the physical advantage.

I fumbled with the buttons on my pants.

The guys finished washing their hands, showing no signs of self-consciousness. They didn't even look in my direction.

Laura and I stayed up late, continuing to drink. It was a quiet and amicable night.

At some point, Laur made the bed. I crawled in next to her and tried to caress her. She shoved my hand away. I rolled over and tried to fall asleep, but couldn't.

So, I got up and turned on my computer to continue reading Marten's master's thesis, but tired of it after a couple of lines. There was still some calvados left. I mixed it, then went out onto the balcony to smoke. The pack was still more than half-full, but there were only two normal matches and one spindly one left. I tried using the latter to light my cigarette. It worked. Should I smoke several in a row, using one to light the next? Otherwise, we'd run out of matches and I'd have to head over to the 24-hour casino to buy more.

What was my problem now? Being denied sex again? Laura shoving my hand away?

I pondered the question until the cigarette was almost spent, then rummaged through my pocket and pulled out the pack. I tapped ash off the first, took out another with one hand, and stuck it between my lips. The last bit of ash fell off the edge of the balcony, leaving only the glowing end of the filter.

Should I light another with the second-to-last match? No. I'd try to go to bed.

Nevertheless, I ended up sitting back down at my laptop in the kitchen. I had another smoke, successfully lighting the new one with the end of the last. I left one match in the box. I was a hero. Crawling back into bed, I turned my back to Laura.

I woke up early the next morning and lay in bed, staring at the coffee table in front of my nose. There were no drinks on it. I was pissed off at Laura. But was there any point staying angry? I'd just end up marinating in my chagrin for who-knows-how-long. Best to just forget it. To start again. I looked over at Laura. She was stretched out with her back to me. I reached out my arm and draped it over her. She didn't stir. I slid it beneath her shirt, then fondled her left breast. It seemed to stiffen a little. I tried moving to her right breast, but it was lodged halfway beneath her body. I fondled it as well as I could. My mind was empty. I wasn't expecting us to fuck. I suspected I wouldn't get hard, anyway. I just wanted to stroke her a little. My hand wandered to Laura's ass. I stroked as much of her crack as I could reach between her buttocks, which wasn't much. My hand drifted back up to her breasts.

Laura suddenly shoved it away.

I lay on my back in bed. The sky was already light. I didn't know what else to do, so I got up and went to the kitchen. I sat there in my t-shirt with my dick drooping over the edge of the chair. I turned on my laptop but didn't feel like staring at the screen, so I took a shower, got dressed, peeked back into the room (Laura was asleep), and left.

It was a Saturday. Summer already, but the mornings were still cool. I rolled down my shirt sleeves and yawned.

What next? There were pills in my pocket that I needed to take. Antibiotics for my kidney infection. I couldn't take them without drinking, but I didn't want anything to drink yet either. My kidney ached and peeing was painful. Oh, well. I went to the cheap grocery store and bought four bottles of beer, then went to Koidu. What next? Anything?

I opened my laptop and searched for the erotic picture I'd downloaded from someone's Facebook page a couple of days earlier. I've never enjoyed looking at porn. It ruins direct physical sexuality.

Even so, I stared at the picture and sipped my beer. The girl was beautiful, her vagina spread wide. Hopefully not a minor. Ilmar Kruusamäe's drawing of an old Kurt Vonnegut stared at me from the wall above the cupboard. Wide-open beavers. Uh-huh. What sentence would I be given if someone found that picture on my computer?

I flopped down on the couch, feeling sleepy and hoping for a nap. I rolled over and tried to coax sleep to me. No success.

So, I got back up and called Laura. I waited. Her phone was switched off.

Nevertheless, I tried a few minutes later and she picked up.

"Laur, I'd like to talk. What's the next step for us in life? Do you feel like talking?"

"I don't know. Go ahead and talk."

"Don't you think this is something we should discuss?"

"I don't know. We've discussed things before."

I sighed. She had a point.

"Well, maybe we could talk a little more."

"I'm near Koidu. I could come out front."

"Sure, come over."

Out front? Not inside?

For some reason, I shaved.

I then grabbed my half-finished bottle of beer and went downstairs to wait.

We discussed our situation at length, sadly and amicably, and in the end, Laura herself proposed to draw up a sex schedule if that was what I needed.

"How about twice a week?" I asked.

"Let's do one for starters."

And that's where we left the topic. Unfortunately, that's also right where it stayed. The proposal came to mind every now and then, but it seemed stupid to try to force it.

◆

I don't know what I was doing wandering around alone in Kristiine Mall. Nothing, especially. Like a teenager who hangs out at the mall just to kill time.

And then, I spotted Siska. She was standing by the entrance, eating ice cream. Waiting for somebody.

I walked up to her.

"Siss?" I asked hesitantly. She seemed bigger, older. Had I not seen her in that long?

"Daddy!" she exclaimed, wrapping an arm around me. It was all like old times again.

"How've you been doing, honey?"

"Good, I guess. I've been all over the place lately. Pärnu, and . . . At my friends' places. How are you?"

"Oh, I don't know. The usual. Are you waiting for someone?"

"No, I was just here eating ice cream."

We sat down on a bench, neither of us really knowing what to talk about. Siss shifted the ice cream cone to her other hand and grasped my left hand with her right, simply holding it.

"Are you sure everything's okay, Daddy?"

"Yeah, I'm a big boy. I've got to manage on my own."

"I'm grown up, too. I haven't been to Koidu Street in a long time. I'll come over soon."

"I don't think you've been back since that thing with Diana."

"Oh, that. I dunno. Maybe."

"I suppose you don't have any friends in the neighborhood then, huh?"

"That doesn't matter. I can just spend time with you. Are you there a lot?"

"Yes."

"What about at Laura's?"

"I'm there sometimes. Just give me a call when you're coming over."

"Okay."

Siss finished her ice cream, but we continued sitting together for a while. Although I was enjoying it, I could tell she wanted to go and didn't know how to say it.

"I'll walk you wherever you're going, honey. Where to?"

"The trolley stop. I'm going home."

I held her around the shoulders as we waited for the trolley to come. She was already tall enough to make it comfortable. I poked one of her shoulders.

"Is this a bra strap here?"

"Yeah. Mommy bought me one. Some girls in our class wear them, some don't."

I pulled her in closer and we stood that way until the trolly pulled up. Siss went up on her tiptoes to kiss me and climbed in. Looking out the window, she made the same face she did when we had her passport picture taken in the booth. She held the grin for several drawn-out seconds until the trolley pulled away from the stop, waving slowly. I felt unable to muster up an equal smile but tried to look casual. It took everything I had to hold back a tear.

PEACE

THINGS WERE PEACEFUL. Nothing was good, but there was peace, and that was good enough. I suppose we weren't drinking very much at the time.

"Hey. Piret's going to be staying at that boy's place for a week, taking care of him while his parents are away. Her laptop's not working, so she can't play the games she usually plays. I'd like to go and see her."

"Sure."

Laura left. It felt great to be alone at her apartment for the first time in forever. The TV was silent, for a change. I didn't turn on the radio, either. "Silence drives me crazy," Laur said one day when I turned the volume on the TV all the way down. My mind was short-circuiting with the sounds of music and some show playing all at once. Not that I've never short-circuited before.

Later that evening, she sent me a text saying she was staying the night there. I slept alone on her couch, taking up all the space I wanted.

She was back for a night, but then gone the next and I didn't know if she'd be returning or not. Only later did I notice she'd taken along her toothbrush and toothpaste.

I was aware that Piret would be taking care of the boy for a week. *Honeymoon*, I reassured myself. *Honeymoon*. However, it sparked no real emotion in me. I considered going back to Koidu, as I suspected I'd probably start complaining if I were to spend a few more nights alone at Laura's apartment. Mulling bitter thoughts back at my studio wasn't a great option, either.

But soon, there was a small gathering in the yard at Koidu and Laur bought two kilos of shish kebabs and grilled it all herself. There weren't very many takers, but she gave it her all regardless. I'd brought four bottles of wine; Laur paid for one of them. The guests had brought their own beverages as well. Later, after everyone had left, there was still a lot left to drink. So, we went up to sit in my kitchen, where we continued drinking steadily and were generally quiet. Laura made some remark, but I didn't really feel like answering. I suspected that an argument could arise out of pretty much anything with both of us in that state. Best to just stay silent. I marveled at how magnanimous I was by agreeing with everything and not saying a word. In reality, I suppose much of the situation was already disagreeable to me. Things were shit, but I didn't want to discuss it.

"Our relationship is fucked," Laura suddenly said.

This time, I couldn't hold back.

"Maybe," I mumbled. Even if that was true, what could we really do about it?

"We should think about how to end this thing nicely." That took the wind out of me. I was afraid of making any comment that would take responsibility.

Just before dawn, we climbed onto Laura's old couch in my studio, each resentfully retreating to their own corner. I tried programming my mind not to snore.

In the morning, we finished off the rest of the wine in the kitchen. There wasn't much left.

"Did you say there was some of our wine left down in Cabbages?"

"I saw half a bottle of white in the fridge. And another half a bottle on a bookshelf."

I went down to peek into the basement fridge. The Cabbages guys themselves were away on one of the islands. Huh, nope—some bottle of "Missionaries-brand wine. I couldn't remember buying it myself.

I shuffled back upstairs, wondering if Laura remembered what she'd said the previous night.

"Do you know what you said last night? You said we're fucked and should think about how to end this nicely."

"Yeah. I felt like that's what you want, actually. That's why I said it."

What a joke. You didn't bother to ask what I feel or want. You don't even express your own desires or opinions but try to pick mine out of thin air and voice them instead. I reckoned it was best to put a stop to the subject right then and there.

There was nothing new about it, either. I pondered whether it was my turn now or not. Or would we just delay things again and again and again? Endlessly? Nothing new would ever arise that way. Not that I really know anything new I could possibly want, either.

◆

Whenever I take advantage of someone, they start getting on my nerves sooner or later. Why is that? Simply because they're the kind of idiot who lets someone else take advantage of them. Even worse, they pretend like they have no idea it's happening even though I reckon they're fully conscious of the situation. And yet, they're benevolently silent. They're above it all. They're better than me. They're a jerk and seeing them reminds me that *I'm* the jerk who takes advantage of others. Well, fuck. It's nice to be a walking and talking reproach, isn't it? What other choice do I have? Apologizing and trying to return everything I've taken from them? That's ridiculous. I'm not going to turn myself into such a fool, either.

◆

Chanterelle mushrooms fried in butter. With onion. The aroma never crossed my mind once all year. And sour cream on top. I never even recalled the taste. Pretty damn good. And now, I suppose I'll forget about it for yet another year. I must not miss it all that much. What other wonderful and beautiful things have I experienced and no longer even remember? Maybe I've even done something good that I never noticed, though I can't say what that might be. You certainly recall the awful things you've done, and the shame. Fears enter your dreams. They repeat over and over again. Would a long nightmare be a manifestation of hell? What'd Dostoyevsky mean when he wrote that being unable to love is hell? It must have just been bullshit. Do I love, though? Whom? What? Am I living in Thornton Wilder's hell? What did he love, anyway? A food or drink? Or people? Why did he love them? Were they all that pleasant? Or should one simply love for love's sake? Why? Because it's ordained? Just to not be a jerk and not occupy a hell? It still seems rather self-serving.

◆

I occasionally told her I love her. Just because. A little jokingly. Maybe I was attempting to reassure myself more than her, albeit not too seriously. It seemed strange or inappropriate to stubbornly refuse to say such things at all. But was I at all in love with her? Perhaps not. At least not like I used to be.

Still, I felt a little down in the dumps. Serotonin deficiency. Everything just feels hazy, in love or not. It'll just take time. Time and more time. How much on this occasion? Do they make a Nicorette for divorcees? Antidepressants, sure. Laur took them anyway, way back when. I wonder if she still does it out of habit. Or did she feel pressured by the situation forever already and only broke free just now? No matter. I need the masochistic bitterness of reckoning she's probably better off this way. One could guess. Maybe I'll even spot her with somebody else. I bet I will at some point, sooner or later. Probably better later, though.

It's a good thing we never moved in together. Laura doesn't have any crap at my place, either. I've still got a ton of stuff at hers, though.

◆

It was afternoon. I'd been bumming around my studio for most of the day and went down to hang out in Cabbages. It was cold and empty. I grabbed an old newspaper from the table and sat down in the armchair. However, I didn't open it. I just stared at the wall of the dim basement-level room. How can I get back to where I used to be? Back to when nothing was fine but every trivial little thing that passed was still somehow nice? Back to experiencing, watching, observing that? I didn't really need all that much. A little chat with someone, a little busy work, not making any big plans. It was simple. How did I lose that ability? Oh, right. The trick to it was probably something else in life going well and being right where it should be—a relationship or whatnot. Even if it wasn't quite where it should have been, it still existed, at any rate. Right now, there's nothing.

What happened to Kerouac that one time? He rid himself of every possible relationship because the writer needed to write; to fill all those notebooks and then rewrite whatever he'd written. But when the writing was finished, no matter whether temporarily or for good, there was no one left who'd want to come back and say: "Oh, Jack—*now* you've got time for me! Let's do something. What would you like?" No one was left. Only Jack, all alone. *All work and no play makes Jack a dull boy.*

But I'm not there, of course. Where I am, I do not know. In order to see wherever I'm positioned, I should stand at a distance and watch everything as a bystander. Then, I might be able to give myself advice. Alas, it's impossible.

I checked the date on the paper. Last week's. I opened it to see what was news back then.

◆

So what that we have misunderstandings? So long as you have the fortitude to stand by and remain stupid and inept, everything will gradually shift back into place. You must be foolish so life can teach you, and unwise so it can hit and hurt you to show you just how smart you really are. It's difficult to believe in and tolerate the rules of chaos. But I suppose you have no other choice. Things might get a little better if you could ever take away the words "rules" and "chaos." But can space and quantum mechanics be discussed without them? I suppose you'd run out of things to say. Or must every discussion get tangled and hit a dead end when it's meaningful? All possible talk about relationships, too. And then, there's silence. Nice, empty silence; sometimes with a tinge of sadness. All until the next discussion arises.

OMELET

W E'D BEEN APART, each doing our own thing, for several weeks. Almost zero contact aside of the occasional toxic text or email. Breakups take much more time and energy than moving in together. Those *give* you energy. I wonder if that energy is just lent at first and in the end, you're forced to pay it all back with interest. I sat around doing nothing. Every now and then, I'd leap to my feet to attempt to do something, anything, but since every possible activity seemed pointless, I found myself sitting back down before long and just wasting time again. My mind was empty, too. I felt nothing. Tragedy was the past—it had transformed into a depression that dribbled like snot and slobber.

One Saturday evening, I'd already drunk myself to a stupor but found it impossible to fall asleep. Simply tossing and turning finally tired me out, and my sides were already tender. I sat up on the edge of the couch and turned on the tiny light fixture on the wall. It was almost midnight. I pulled on a t-shirt to do something, whether it was merely to make myself something to eat. I got one pant leg on before giving up and opening a magazine to continue reading Krugman's economic ramblings where I'd left off earlier. I'd hoped it would put me to sleep because I couldn't understand much of it and didn't actually want to understand. It was exasperatingly repetitive and read like religious propaganda, in my opinion. Over and over about how countries should push more and more into circulation during economic crises, no matter how cheap things became. Krugman could have summed it up in a couple of sentences, I thought, but he's a professor and a Nobel Prize winner and couldn't be bothered to write any less. Who's going to give you a Nobel Prize for aphorisms? Krugman could've sent me a little cash instead of blabbering on. I'd manage to send it straight into circulation and maybe save Estonia's economy.

I thought I heard someone fumbling at the door, but every wall in the house is paper-thin and you can never tell if your place is haunted or Jaan Pehk is just doing something in the bathroom next-door or Marten coming back from a party or cooking up some science downstairs. I cocked my ear to listen. The sound was slow and steady. Someone drunk, probably. Who was trying to get into my place at such an hour? Margus, confused? I hadn't seen him that muddled in ages, however. Talking someone out of committing suicide would certainly be a fine way to pass the time. Especially if he had a bottle with him, just like the last time.

I pulled up my other pant leg.

It was Laura, swaying and gripping an open bottle of sparkling wine. She didn't even glance in my direction; her gaze was locked on the kitchen door.

"Can I smoke a cigarette by your kitchen window?" she asked with exceptionally clear diction, just as any drunk does when feeling the need to maintain complete control over themselves.

"Sure," I replied, waiting to feel an emotion. None came.

I followed her to the kitchen out of politeness, sitting down on a stool. Laur smoked her cigarette and drank with a focused look. Both of us were silent.

"Could I maybe lie down somewhere?" she asked, her eyes on the ground.

"Of course you can."

I went and pulled her pillow and blanket out of the drawer beneath the futon and laid them next to the wall, just like old times. But now, I didn't feel like lying down next to her right away. I sat down at my desk with the magazine and strained to read through to the end of Krugman's article. Finally, I finished, then tackled the next economics expert. Märt had filled the whole issue with them. Old Keynes claimed that work would run out before long and then, we wouldn't know what to do with ourselves. I suppose he was already doing well in life and could make out the end of his career—the man knew what he was talking about.

Laura also appeared reluctant to crawl into bed. She'd dozed off in her old armchair, her mouth hanging drunkenly open and her chin resting against her chest. I wasn't about to poke her.

A couple of times, I realized I had no idea what I'd read in the last half-page. Success. I soon felt sleep creeping up and went to bed.

At one point in the night, I realized, half-asleep, that Laur had curled up on her side of the bed, though we both went to painstaking lengths to ensure we would not touch.

Even so, Laur draped her arm over me, above the blanket, sometime before dawn. It immediately dispelled sleep from my senses. I lay there motionless with my back to her and my eyes wide open, feeling the weight of her arm upon me. I didn't push it away or make any favoring motion in return. Then, she took her arm back and I was able to sleep a little longer.

When I felt I'd had enough shut-eye, I went to check if the shower in the basement had been fixed. It hadn't. I returned to my kitchen and whipped up an omelet with chanterelles, parsley, onion, some sausage, dill and sour cream.

Laur appeared and brushed her teeth, both the false ones and her own.

"I made an omelet. You want some?"

"Yeah."

We tried to be polite without trying too hard. Neutral. No eye-contact. That lasted until neither of us knew what else to do and Laur left.

And all of a sudden, everything was light and uplifting.

I felt that we might even be able to continue getting along under such circumstances. Wishing for nothing aside from sitting together for a bit in peace. I felt that I'd lost a wife but gained a friend, and that that is something much more genuine.

A tiny secret door leading out of depression had been opened for me. It was incredibly easy to find and had been there all along. How hadn't I noticed it before?

Mundane everyday tasks were suddenly enjoyable and made me happy again. And there were no greater things. I didn't need them. Every object and event was rather equal. There was no rush to go anywhere, nothing that had to be done. A blissful state had been returned to me.

I wondered—has any other relationship ever ended and immediately transformed into a friendship? Not especially. There were a couple such cases, though, and those friendships are for life. Friendships where all has been forgiven, no demands are made, and a smidgen of sweetly aching nostalgia remains. Such friends are incredibly rare, of course. Still, things with them are more than easy. Even if you don't speak for years, the relationship stays the same until you find yourselves chatting again.

I felt that I hadn't been so happy in ages. I felt that I hadn't been so sad in forever. A great event seemed to be ongoing or only beginning. There was nowhere farther or ahead to go—just allowing life to unfold until I hadn't the strength anymore. Until reaching a state of exhaustion from living the good life. What was to come? Who knows. It didn't matter, just so long as what was happening at that moment continued to happen. Something great. Nothing had to be done about that great thing; there was truly nothing to undertake. And no one else would ever know or see. It would merely transpire, quietly, for me. All on its own.

GLOSSARY OF ESTONIAN CULTURAL FIGURES

AHI, EDA (1990)
a poet and translator.

BASKIN, EINO (1929–2015)
a theater actor and director. He founded two theaters of his own, one of which still operates.

BAUMAN, RUTS (BORN RUDOLF BAUMAN, 1892–1960)
a theater and television actor.

GAILIT, AUGUST (1891–1960)
a writer of novels, short stories, and *feuilletons*.

HALLAS, JAAKKO(1948)
a translator and columnist.

HIRV, INDREK (1956)
a poet, translator, and artist.

HVOSTOV, ANDREI (1963)
a journalist and author.

JAANI, GETTER (1993)
a pop singer.

JOALA, JAAK (1950–2014)
a musician and producer active mostly during the Soviet period. He was renowned across the entire USSR.

JÄRVI, NEEME (1937)
a conductor.

KAEVATS, MIHKEL (1983)
a poet, translator, and essayist.

KALJUSTE, TÕNU (1953)
a Grammy Award-winning conductor and founder of the Estonian Philharmonic Chamber Choir.

KALLAS, TEET (1943)
a writer and former politician.

KEKISHEV, MARKO (1963)
an artist and graphic designer.

KIIK, HEINO (1927–2013)
a writer.

KOORT, ANDRES (1969)
an artist, designer, and curator.

KROSS, JAAN (1920–2007)
a literary classic who wrote the epic tetralogy *Between Three Plagues*.

KRULL, HASSO (1964)
a writer, translator, and essayist.

KRUUSAMÄE, ILMAR (1957)
a painter.

KURVITZ, RAOUL (1961)
an artist.

KÕIV, MADIS (1929–2014)
a writer, physician, and philosopher.

LANGEMETS, ANDRES (1948)
a poet, literary critic, editor, and essayist.

LAPIN, LEONHARD (1947)
a prolific architect, artist, and poet writing under the pseudonym Albert Trapeež.

LIIV, JUHAN (1864–1913)
one of Estonia's most outstanding and highly celebrated early prose and poetry writers.

LINNUSTE, VAHUR (1925)
an academic, cultural journalist, and translator who lived in exile during the Soviet occupation.

LUIK, VIIVI (1946)
a writer of poetry, prose, and essays.

MALIN, JAAN (1960)
a poet and sound artist.

MASING, UKU (1909–1985)
a poet and philosopher who received the Righteous Among the Nations Award for safely harboring a Jew until the end of the Holocaust in Estonia.

NIIT, ELLEN (1928–2016)
a poet and translator

NUTER, EGON (1955)
a theatrical director and actor.

OJA, ARNO (1950)
a journalist and cultural critic.

OJAVER, JÜRI (1955)
an artist and sculptor.

PÄRN, PRIIT (1946)
a graphic artist and animated film director.

RAMMO, HELJU (1926–1998)
a children's author and playwright.

RAUD, MIHKEL (1969)
a musician, TV celebrity, and writer.

RAUDAM, TOOMAS (1947)
an author.

REPNAU, LILLI-KRÕÕT (1982)
an artist and art instructor.

SAAR, MART (1882–1963)
a composer for piano and choir.

SINIJÄRV, KARL-MARTIN (1971)
a poet, journalist, and former head of the Estonian Writers' Union.

TAMMSAARE, A. H. (1878–1940)
a literary classic and author of the monumental *Truth and Justice* trilogy.

TEDER, TARMO (1958)
a writer and literary critic.

TOOMIK, JAAN (1961)
a painter, filmmaker, and video artist.

TRUBETSKY, TÕNU (1963)
a musician and author. He was a leader of Estonia's punk movement during the 1980s.

TUGLAS, FRIEDEBERT (1886–1971)
a writer, critic, translator, editor, and journalist. Elo Tuglas (1896–1970, née Emma Elisabet Oinas) was his wife.

UNT, MATI (1944–2005)
a prolific author, playwright, and theater producer.

UUSPÕLD, JAN (1973)
a theater, television, and film actor, primarily known for comedic roles.

VAHING, VAINO (1940–2008)
a writer, playwright, and psychologist.

VALLISOO, MARI (1950–2013)
a poet.

VIHMA, PEETER (1980)
a sociologist and documentary filmmaker.

VIIDING, JUHAN (1948–1995)
an actor, playwright, theatrical producer, and poet.

VOLKONSKI, PEETER (1954)
an actor, musician, and theater director. Among other artistic projects, his band ROSTA Aknad founded the satirical "Estonian Slave Party" at a performance in 1987.

VSEVIOV, DAVID (1949)
a Jewish-Estonian historian, journalist, and writer.

NOTES

1. A small rectangular ventilation window common in Russia and former Soviet republics.
2. In the Soviet Union, "Stakhanovite" was a term used for someone who dedicated themselves to working ever harder and more efficiently.
3. hello (Russian)
4. man, fellow (Russian)
5. "My address isn't a house or street." Russian lyrics from a once-popular Soviet song that continues: "My address is the Soviet Union."
6. An Estonian cultural weekly published since 1940.
7. A senior military officer (Russian)
8. A lieutenant colonel in Slavic countries.
9. Anna Petrovna Kern (1800–1879) was a Russian socialite and the subject of a famous love poem by Alexander Pushkin.
10. Mikhail Artsybashev (1878–1927) was a Russian writer and anti-Bolshevik. "Nina" is a character from one of his stories.